D1548547

# I, II, & III JOHN

Judith M. Lieu

# I, II, & III John

## A Commentary

Westminster John Knox Press
LOUISVILLE • LONDON

© 2008 Judith M. Lieu

*All rights reserved.* No part of this book may be reproduced or transmitted in any form or by any means, electronic or mechanical, including photocopying, recording, or by any information storage or retrieval system, without permission in writing from the publisher. For information, address Westminster John Knox Press, 100 Witherspoon Street, Louisville, Kentucky 40202-1396.

*Book design by Jennifer K. Cox*

*First edition*
Published by Westminster John Knox Press
Louisville, Kentucky

This book is printed on acid-free paper that meets the American National Standards Institute Z39.48 standard. ∞

PRINTED IN THE UNITED STATES OF AMERICA

08  09  10  11  12  13  14  15  16  17—10 9 8 7 6 5 4 3 2 1

**Library of Congress Cataloging-in-Publication Data**

Lieu, Judith.
    I, II, & III John : a commentary / Judith M. Lieu. — 1st ed.
        p. cm. — (The New Testament library)
    Includes bibliographical references and indexes.
    ISBN 978-0-664-22098-3 (alk. paper)
    1. Bible. N.T. Epistles of John—Commentaries.   I. Title.   II. Title: First, Second, and Third John.
    BS2805.53.L534 2008
    227'.9407—dc22
                                   2008001277

# CONTENTS

| | | |
|---|---|---:|
| **Preface** | | **ix** |
| **Abbreviations** | | **xi** |
| **Bibliography** | | **xiii** |
| **Introduction** | | **1** |
| 1 | The First, Second, and Third Letters of John? | 1 |
| | 1.1 John | 2 |
| | 1.2 Letters | 4 |
| 2 | The Setting of the Letters | 6 |
| | 2.1 Author and Audience | 6 |
| | 2.2 Situation | 9 |
| 3 | The Structure, Background, and Thought of the Letters | 14 |
| | 3.1 Argument and Style | 14 |
| | 3.2 Johannine Tradition | 17 |
| | 3.3 The Thought of the Letters | 18 |
| | 3.4 Background | 23 |
| 4 | The Reception of the Letters and Their Importance in Recent Study | 25 |
| | 4.1 Reception and Text | 25 |
| | 4.2 The Importance of the Letters | 28 |
| 5 | Translation and Language | 30 |

**COMMENTARY**

| | | |
|---|---|---:|
| **1 JOHN** | | **35** |
| 1 John 1:1–4 | The Prologue | 35 |
| 1:1–3 | The Opening | 37 |

| | | |
|---|---|---|
| 1:4 | The Purpose in Writing | 46 |
| 1 John 1:5–2:2 | Living in the Light of God | 48 |
| 1:5 | God Is Light | 49 |
| 1:6–10 | Saying and Doing | 52 |
| 2:1–2 | The Assurance of Forgiveness | 60 |
| 1 John 2:3–11 | From Knowledge of God to Love of a Fellow Believer | 67 |
| 2:3–6 | Knowledge and Obedience | 68 |
| 2:7–11 | Hearing the Command and Loving a Fellow Believer | 75 |
| 1 John 2:12–17 | Encouragement to Persevere | 84 |
| 2:12–14 | Children, Fathers, and Youths | 85 |
| 2:15–17 | Do Not Love the World | 91 |
| 1 John 2:18–28 | Standing Firm against Deceit | 97 |
| 2:18–23 | The Appearance of the Antichrists | 97 |
| 2:24–28 | The Call to Remain Faithful | 108 |
| 1 John 2:29–3:12 | The Identity of Those Who Are (or Are Not) Children of God | 116 |
| 2:29–3:3 | The Confidence of the Children of God | 118 |
| 3:4–10a | The Two Ways | 126 |
| 3:10b–12 | Justice and Love as the Marks of the Children of God | 141 |
| 1 John 3:13–24 | Love within the Community and Confidence before God | 145 |
| 3:13–18 | The Bonds of Love | 146 |
| 3:19–24 | Confidence before God | 153 |
| 1 John 4:1–6 | Testing the Spirits | 161 |
| 1 John 4:7–5:4 | The Love That Is God's | 175 |
| 4:7–10 | In Celebration of God's Love | 176 |
| 4:11–16 | God's Love as the Source of Our Love | 184 |
| 4:17–19 | Confidence in Love | 193 |
| 4:20–5:4 | Obedience to God and Love for Others | 196 |

| | | | |
|---|---|---|---|
| 1 John | 5:4–13 | Belief in the Son of God | 205 |
| | 5:4–8 | Jesus, the Son of God | 205 |
| | 5:9–12 | God's Own Testimony to the Son of God | 216 |
| | 5:13 | "This Is Why I Have Written" | 220 |
| 1 John | 5:14–21 | Exercising the Privileges of Life | 222 |
| | 5:14–17 | Seeking Life | 222 |
| | 5:18–21 | The Ultimate Confidence | 229 |
| **2 JOHN** | | | **239** |
| | 1–3 | The Greeting | 240 |
| | 4–8 | Encouragement to Steadfastness | 248 |
| | 9–13 | Holding on to the Teaching | 257 |
| **3 JOHN** | | | **265** |
| | 1–4 | Opening Pleasantries | 266 |
| | 5–12 | The Test of Loyalty | 270 |
| | 13–15 | Closing Formalities | 281 |
| **Index of Ancient Sources** | | | **285** |
| **Index of Subjects** | | | **297** |

# PREFACE

The Johannine Epistles have often been treated as footnotes to the Gospel, supplying supplementary resources for expositions of the latter's theology. Where attention has focused on them, as it has in the last thirty years, this has often been because of the glimpses they are believed to offer into the history of the tradition and community of which the Gospel is the most creative expression. Yet in the history of reception 1 John has provided a number of memorable affirmations: God is love; if we say we have no sin we deceive ourselves; the one who does not love the brother (or sister) whom s/he has seen cannot love God whom s/he has not seen. Curiously, these familiar affirmations sit uneasily with the picture often drawn of the ethos of the Epistles, and even of the Gospel, as profoundly sectarian, more ready to exclude than to include. In this way they exemplify a focal problem in the hermeneutical significance of the historical approach to the New Testament writings, which gives pride of place to the discovery of the original setting and function. This is a particular challenge in writings that take the form of letters: how are such specifically located writings, which may even emerge as parochial in concerns and outlook, to be understood two millennia later, not least by those who accord them particular value and authority? While in this commentary I will not claim to solve such conundra, I have written in the conviction that the Letters can and should be understood free from the shadow of the Fourth Gospel, to which they are undoubtedly related. First John in particular is an exercise in urgent and sustained persuasion crafted with great skill; while we cannot be certain whether it succeeded in persuading all its readers, as modern readers we can enter into its world and come to our own judgment as to how at home we may feel there. On the other hand, 2 and 3 John are striking if only for the surprise of their preservation when many have found little memorable within them. This too should excite not only historical imagination but also theological reflection.

It was the challenge proffered by the two smaller letters that first drew me to the Johannine Epistles in my doctoral work. Writing this commentary after many years of further exploration has brought together a number of threads that I first began to identify and weave then. The challenge of close and consistent attention to the details of the text and to the overall pattern of argument has also stimulated new questions and new perspectives. Since I began my study of the Epistles, interest in them has blossomed, and a number of major commentaries and other studies have been dedicated to them as well as to the broader Johannine tradition. Interest in the background of the tradition has flourished, particularly in the light of new perceptions of Judaism and of the discovery of the Dead Sea Scrolls; its location within the development of early Christian thought and structures has been recognized as a valuable companion to new understandings of Paul.

My own research is deeply indebted to this rich seam of study, to publications in many different settings, but also to seminars, papers, and discussions with other enthusiasts. However, I have made the decision that detailed engagement with other interpreters, whether in agreement or debate, does not belong in a commentary of this kind; instead the task is to offer a coherent and sustained reading of the Letters, indicating how they are shaped both by events and ideas from outside, and by the purpose they are designed to fulfill. Hence reference to other secondary literature has been kept to a minimum, and that to other commentaries almost entirely excluded. Where interpretation is uncertain or the decision is finely balanced, I have indicated the options and the arguments on each side, while those who are familiar with the field may recognize where I agree or disagree with others. In addition, the bibliography is intended only to direct readers to other key studies, and in no way reflects the wealth of work from which I have learned so much. Although the constraints of space and, as already explained, my understanding of the task of the commentary prevent me listing them by name, I gladly acknowledge my many debts.

I am grateful to the publisher and editors of the New Testament Library for the invitation to contribute this volume to the series, and for their patience and encouragement as the task accompanied me across two moves of continent and three of institution. I was privileged in my colleagues at King's College London, where most of the work was done, and I am particularly grateful to Wesley College, Cambridge, which offered me a home on my move to Cambridge, where I was able to complete the manuscript. As ever, the support of Sam and of Esther is my chief delight.

# ABBREVIATIONS

| | |
|---|---|
| AB | Anchor Bible |
| *AUSS* | *Andrews University Seminary Studies* |
| BETL | Bibliotheca ephemeridum theologicarum lovaniensium |
| BGU | *Äegyptische Urkunden aus den Königlichen Staatlichen Museen zu Berlin, Griechische Urkunden.* 15 vols. Berlin, 1892–1983 |
| *Bib* | *Biblica* |
| BIS | Biblical Interpretation Series |
| *BJRL* | *Bulletin of the John Rylands University Library of Manchester* |
| BWANT | Beiträge zur Wissenschaft vom Alten und Neuen Testament |
| *BZ* | *Biblische Zeitschrift* |
| BZNW | Beihefte zur Zeitschrift für die neutestamentliche Wissenschaft |
| *CBQ* | *Catholic Biblical Quarterly* |
| *CP* | *Classical Philology* |
| *EA* | *Epigraphica anatolica* |
| EKK | Evangelisch-katholischer Kommentar |
| *ETL* | *Ephemerides theologicae Lovanienses* |
| fem. | feminine |
| FRLANT | Forschungen zur Religion und Literatur des Alten und Neuen Testaments |
| ICC | International Critical Commentary |
| *IG* | *Inscriptiones Graecae.* Berlin, 1873– |
| *JBL* | *Journal of Biblical Literature* |
| JSJSup | Supplements to the Journal for the Study of Judaism |
| *JSNT* | *Journal for the Study of the New Testament* |
| JSNTSup | Journal for the Study of the New Testament Supplements |
| *JTS* | *Journal of Theological Studies* |
| KJV | King James Version |
| LCL | Loeb Classical Library |
| lit. | literally |
| LSJ | H. G. Liddell, R. Scott, H. S. Jones, and R. McKenzie, *A Greek-English Lexicon.* 9th ed. Oxford, 1996 |

| | |
|---|---|
| LXX | Septuagint |
| *MAMA* | *Monumenta Asiae Minoris Antiqua*. Manchester and London, 1928–1993 |
| masc. | masculine |
| NA[27] | *Novum Testamentum Graece*, Nestle-Aland, 27th edition |
| NCB | New Century Bible |
| n.f. | neue folge |
| NHC | Nag Hammadi Codex |
| NIV | New International Version |
| *NovT* | *Novum Testamentum* |
| NRSV | New Revised Standard Version |
| NT | New Testament |
| NTA | Neutestamentliche Abhandlungen |
| NTL | New Testament Library |
| *NTS* | *New Testament Studies* |
| NTTS | New Testament Tools and Studies |
| OT | Old Testament |
| P.Fay. | *Fayum Towns and Their Papyri*, ed. B. P. Grenfell, A. S. Hunt, and D. G. Hogarth. London, 1900 |
| P.Oxy. | *The Oxyrhynchus Papyri*. London, 1898– |
| PG | Patrologia graeca, ed. J.-P. Migne. 162 vols. Paris, 1857–1891 |
| RV | Revised Version |
| SBLSymS | Society of Biblical Literature Symposium Series |
| *SJT* | *Scottish Journal of Theology* |
| SNTW | Studies in the New Testament and Its World |
| *TDNT* | *Theological Dictionary of the New Testament*, ed. G. Kittel and G. Friedrich, trans. G. W. Bromiley. 10 vols. Grand Rapids: Eerdmans, 1964–1976 |
| *TZ* | *Theologische Zeitschrift* |
| WBC | Word Biblical Commentary |
| WUNT | Wissenschaftliche Untersuchungen zum Neuen Testament |
| *ZNW* | *Zeitschrift für die neutestamentamentliche Wissenschaft und die Kunde der älteren Kirche* |
| *ZTK* | *Zeitschrift für Theologie und Kirche* |

# BIBLIOGRAPHY

*Commentaries*

Beutler, Johannes. *Die Johannesbriefe*. Regensburger Neues Testament. Regensburg: Friedrich Pustet, 2000.

Brooke, A. E. *A Critical and Exegetical Commentary on the Johannine Epistles*. ICC. Edinburgh: T. & T. Clark, 1912.

Brown, Raymond E. *The Epistles of John: A New Translation with Introduction and Commentary*. AB 30. Garden City, N.Y.: Doubleday, 1982.

Bultmann, Rudolf. *The Johannine Epistles*. Translated by R. P. O'Hara with Lane McGaughy and Robert Funk. Hermeneia. Philadelphia: Fortress, 1973.

Dodd, C. H. *The Johannine Epistles*. Moffatt New Testament Commentaries. London: Hodder & Stoughton, 1947.

Gaugler, Ernst. *Die Johannesbriefe*. Auslegung neutestamentlicher Schriften. Zurich: EVZ, 1964.

Gore, Charles. *The Epistles of St. John*. London: John Murray, 1920.

Grayston, Kenneth. *The Johannine Epistles*. NCB. Grand Rapids: Eerdmans, 1984.

Houlden, J. L. *The Johannine Epistles*. Black's New Testament Commentaries. 2nd ed. London: A & C Black, 1994.

Klauck, Hans-Josef. *Der erste Johannesbrief*. EKK 23/1. Zurich and Braunschweig: Benziger; Neukirchen-Vluyn: Neukirchener Verlag, 1991.

———. *Der Zweite und Dritte Johannesbrief*. EKK 23/2. Zurich and Braunschweig: Benziger; Neukirchen-Vluyn: Neukirchener Verlag, 1992.

Loader, William. *The Johannine Epistles*. Epworth Commentaries. London: Epworth, 1992.

Morgen, Michèle. *Les épîtres de Jean*. Commentaire biblique: Nouveau Testament. Paris: Cerf, 2005.

Painter, John. *1, 2, and 3 John*. Sacra Pagina 18. Collegeville, Minn.: Liturgical Press, 2002.

Perkins, Pheme. *The Johannine Epistles*. New Testament Message 21. Wilmington, Del.: Glazier, 1979.

Rensberger, David. *1 John, 2 John, 3 John*. Abingdon New Testament Commentaries. Nashville: Abingdon, 1997.

Schnackenburg, Rudolf. *The Johannine Epistles: Introduction and Commentary.* Translated by R. and I. Fuller. New York: Crossroad, 1992.

Schunack, Gerd. *Die Briefe des Johannes.* Zürcher Bibelkommentare NT 17. Zurich: Theologischer Verlag, 1982.

Smalley, Stephen S. *1, 2, 3 John.* WBC 51. Waco: Word, 1984.

Strecker, Georg. *Die Johannesbriefe.* Meyers Kommentar. Göttingen: Vandenhoeck & Ruprecht, 1989 (= *The Johannine Letters. A Commentary on 1, 2, and 3 John.* Translated by Linda M. Maloney. Hermeneia. Minneapolis: Fortress, 1996).

Vouga, François. *Die Johannesbriefe.* Handbuch zum Neuen Testament 15/3. Tübingen: Mohr, 1990.

Westcott, B. F. *The Epistles of St. John.* London: MacMillan, 1883.

*Monographs and Important Articles*

Ayres, Lewis. "Augustine, Christology, and God as Love: An Introduction to the Homilies on 1 John." Pages 67–93 in *Nothing Greater, Nothing Better: Theological Essays on the Love of God.* Edited by Kevin J. Vanhoozer. Grand Rapids: Eerdmans, 2001.

Balz, Horst. "Johanneische Theologie und Ethik im Licht der 'letzten Stunde.'" Pages 53–56 in *Studien zum Text und Ethik des Neuen Testaments: Festschrift zum 80. Geburtstag von Heinrich Greeven.* Edited by W. Schrage. BZNW 47. Berlin: de Gruyter, 1986.

Bergmeier, R. *Glaube als Gabe.* BWANT 112. Stuttgart: Kohlhammer, 1980.

———. "Zum Verfasserproblem des II und III Johannesbriefes." *ZNW* 57 (1966): 93–100.

Black, C. Clifton, II. "The Johannine Epistles and the Question of Early Catholicism." *NovT* 28 (1986): 131–58.

Black, David. "An Overlooked Stylistic Argument in Favor of πάντα in 1 John 2:20." *Filologia neotestamentaria* 10 (1992): 205–8.

Boer, Martinus de. "The Death of Jesus and His Coming in the Flesh." *NovT* 33 (1991): 326–46.

———. *Johannine Perspectives on the Death of Jesus.* Kampen: Kok Pharos, 1996.

Boismard, P. "La première épître de Jean est-elle johannique?" Pages 301–5 in *L'Évangile de Jean.* Edited by M. de Jonge. Louvain: Peeters, 1977.

Bonsack, Bernhard. "Der Presbyter des dritten Briefes und der geliebte Jünger des Evangeliums nach Johannes." *ZNW* 79 (1988): 45–62.

Braun, F.-M. "La réduction du pluriel au singulier dans l'évangile et la première lettre de Jean." *NTS* 24 (1977/78): 40–67.

Brown, R. E. *The Community of the Beloved Disciple.* New York: Paulist Press, 1979.

————. "The Relationship to the Fourth Gospel Shared by the Author of 1 John and by His Opponents." Pages 57–68 in *Text and Interpretation: Studies in the New Testament Presented to Matthew Black*. Edited by E. Best and R. Mcl. Wilson. Cambridge: Cambridge University Press, 1979.

Bultmann, Rudolf. "Analyse des ersten Johannesbriefs." Pages 138–58 in *Festgabe für Adolf Jülicher zum 70. Geburtstag*. Edited by R. Bultmann and H. von Soden. Tübingen: Mohr, 1927.

Cassem, N. H. "A Grammatical and Contextual Inventory of the Use of κόσμος in the Johannine Corpus with Some Implications for a Johannine Cosmic Theology." *NTS* 19 (1972/73): 81–91.

Conzelmann, H. "Was von Anfang war." Pages 194–201 in *Neutestamentliche Studien für Rudolf Bultmann zu seinem siebzigsten Geburtstag am 20. August 1954*. Edited by W. Eltester. Berlin: Töpelmann, 1954.

Culpepper, R. Alan, and C. Clifton Black, eds. *Exploring the Gospel of John: In Honor of D. Moody Smith*. Louisville: Westminster John Knox, 1996.

DeConick, April D., ed. *Paradise Now: Essays on Early Jewish and Christian Mysticism*. SBLSymS 11. Atlanta: Society of Biblical Literature, 2006.

De Waal Dryden, J. "The Sense of σπέρμα in 1 John 3:9 in Light of Lexical Evidence." *Filología neotestamentaria* 11 (1998): 85–100.

Dobschütz, E. von. "Johanneische Studien." *ZNW* 8 (1907): 1–8.

Dodd, C. H. "The First Epistle of John and the Fourth Gospel." *BJRL* 21 (1937): 129–56.

Donfried, Karl P. "Ecclesiastical Authority in 2-3 John." Pages 325–33 in *L'Évangile de Jean: Sources, rédaction, théologie*. Edited by M. de Jonge. BETL 44. Gembloux: Duculot, 1977.

du Rand, Jan A. *Johannine Perspectives: Introduction to the Johannine Writings—Part 1*. New York: Orion, 1991.

Ehrman, Bart D. "1 John 4:3 and the Orthodox Corruption of Scripture." Pages 221–46 in *Studies in the Textual Criticism of the New Testament*. NTTS 33. Leiden: Brill, 2006. Repr. from *ZNW* 79 (1988): 221–43.

Edwards, M. J. "Martyrdom and the First Epistle of John." *NovT* 31 (1989): 164–71.

Feuillet, A. "Étude structurale de la première épître de saint Jean." Pages 307–27 in *Neues Testament im Geschichte: Historisches Geschehen und Deutung im Neuen Testament, Oscar Cullmann zum 70. Geburtstag*. Edited by H. Baltensweiser and B. Reicke. Tübingen: Mohr, 1972.

Griffith, Terry. *Keep Yourselves from Idols: A New Look at 1 John*. JSNTSup 233. Sheffield: Sheffield Academic Press, 2002.

Haas, C., M. de Jonge, and J. L. Swellengrebel. *A Translator's Handbook on the Letters of John*. Helps for Translators 13. London: United Bible Societies, 1972.

Harnack, Adolf von. "Über den dritten Johannesbrief." *Texte und Untersuchungen* 15.3 Leipzig: Hinrichs'sche, 1897.

Heise, Jürgen. *Bleiben: Menein in den Johanneischen Schriften.* Hermeneutische Untersuchungen zur Theologie 8. Tübingen: Mohr, 1967.

Hengel, Martin, *Die johanneische Frage: Ein Lösungsversuch.* With "Beitrag zur Apokalypse" by Jörg Frey. WUNT 67. Tübingen: Mohr, 1993.

———. *The Johannine Question.* Translated by J. Bowden. London: SCM, 1989.

Hill, Charles E. *The Johannine Corpus in the Early Church.* Oxford: Oxford University Press, 2004.

Hills, Julian. "A Genre for 1 John." Pages 367–77 in *The Future of Early Christianity: Essays in Honor of Helmut Koester.* Edited by Birger Pearson. Minneapolis: Fortress, 1991.

———. "'Little children, keep yourselves from idols': 1 John 5:21 Reconsidered." *CBQ* 51 (1989): 285–310.

———. "'Sin is Lawlessness' (1 John 3:4): Social Definition in the Johannine Community." Pages 286–99 in *Common Life in the Early Church: Essays Honoring Graydon F. Snyder.* Edited by Julian V. Hills. Harrisburg: Trinity Press International, 1998.

Howard, W. F. "The Common Authorship of the Johannine Gospel and Epistles." *JTS* 48 (1947): 12–25.

Johnson, Sherman. "Parallels between the Letters of Ignatius and the Johannine Epistles." Pages 327–38 in *Perspectives on Language and Text: Essays and Poems in Honor of Francis I. Andersen's Sixtieth Birthday, July 28, 1985.* Edited by Edgar W. Conrad and Edward G. Newing. Winona Lake, Ind.: Eisenbrauns, 1987.

Jonge, M. de. "To Love as God Loves (1 John 4:7)." Pages 110–27 in *Jesus: Inspiring and Disturbing Presence.* Nashville: Abingdon, 1976.

Käsemann, E. "Ketzer und Zeuge." *ZTK* 48 (1951): 292–311.

Klauck, Hans-Josef. "Brudermord und Bruderliebe: Ethische Paradigmen in 1 Joh 3,11–17." Pages 151–71 in *Neues Testament und Ethik: Für Rudolf Schnackenburg.* Edited by Helmut Merklein. Freiburg: Herder, 1989.

———. "Gemeinde ohne Amt? Erfahrungen mit der Kirche in den johanneischen Schriften." *BZ* 29 (1985): 193–220.

———. *Die Johannesbriefe.* Erträge der Forschung 276. Darmstadt: Wissenschaftliche Buchgesellschaft, 1991.

———. "κυρία ἐκκλησία in Bauers Wörterbuch und die Exegese des zweiten Johannesbriefes." *ZNW* 81 (1990): 135–38.

———. "Der 'Rückgriff' auf Jesus im Prolog des ersten Johannesbriefes (1 Joh 1,1–4)." Pages 433–51 in *Vom Urchristentum zu Jesus für Joachim Gnilka.* Edited by Hubert Frankenmölle and Karl Kertelge. Freiburg: Herder, 1989.

———. "Zur rhetorischen Analyse der Johannesbriefe." *ZNW* 81 (1990): 205–24.

Kruijf, Th. C. de. "Nicht wie Kain (der) vom Bösen war . . .' 1 Joh. 3,12." *Bijdragen* 41 (1980): 47–63.

Lazure, Noël. "La convoitise de la chair en 1 Jean II, 16." *Revue biblique* 76 (1969): 161–205.

———. *Les valeurs morales de la théologie johannique.* Études bibliques. Paris: Gabalda, 1965.

Lieu, Judith. "Blindness in the Johannine Tradition." *NTS* 34 (1988): 83–95.

———. *The Second and Third Epistles of John.* SNTW. Edinburgh: T. & T. Clark, 1986.

———. *The Theology of the Johannine Epistles.* New Testament Theology. Cambridge: Cambridge University Press, 1991.

———. "Us or You? Persuasion and Identity in 1 John." *JBL* forthcoming.

———. "What Was from the Beginning: Scripture and Tradition in the Johannine Epistles." *NTS* 39 (1993): 458–77.

Longacre, Robert. "Towards an Exegesis of 1 John Based on the Discourse Analysis of the Greek Text." Pages 271–86 in *Linguistics and New Testament Interpretation: Essays on Discourse Analysis.* Edited by David A. Black. Nashville: Broadman, 1992.

Malatesta, Edward. "τὴν ἀγάπην ἣν ἔχει ὁ θεὸς ἐν ἡμῖν: A Note on 1 John 4:16a." Pages 301–11 in vol. 2 of *The New Testament Age: Essays in Honor of Bo Reicke.* Edited by William C. Weinrich. 2 vols. Macon, GA: Mercer University Press, 1984.

Malherbe, A. J. "The Inhospitality of Diotrephes." Pages 222–32 in *God's Christ and His People: Studies in Honour of Nils Alstrup Dahl.* Edited by Jacob Jervell and Wayne A. Meeks. Oslo: Universitetsforlaget, 1977.

Malina, B. J. "The Received View and What It Cannot Do: III John and Hospitality." Pages 171–89 in *Social-Scientific Criticism of the New Testament and Its Social World.* Edited by John H. Elliott. Semeia 35. Decatur, GA: Scholars Press, 1986.

Minear, Paul. "The Idea of Incarnation in First John." *Interpretation* 24 (1970): 291–302.

Nauck, Wolfgang. *Die Tradition und Charakter des ersten Johannesbriefes.* WUNT 3. Tübingen: Mohr, 1957.

Neufeld, Dietmar. *Reconceiving Texts as Speech Acts: An Analysis of 1 John.* BIS 7. Leiden: Brill, 1994.

O'Neill, John. *The Puzzle of 1 John: A New Examination of Origins.* London: SPCK, 1966.

Piper, Otto A. "1 John and the Didache of the Primitive Church." *JBL* 66 (1947): 437–51.

Potterie, Ignace de la. "La notion de 'commencement' dans les écrits johanniques." Pages 379–403 in *Die Kirche des Anfangs: Für Heinz Schürmann*. Edited by Rudolf Schnackenburg, Josef Ernst, and Joachim Wanke. Freiburg: Herder, 1978.

Quispel, G. "Qumran, John and Jewish Christianity." Pages 137–55 in *John and Qumran*. Edited by J. H. Charlesworth. London: Geoffrey Chapman, 1972.

Rese, M. "Das Gebot der Bruderliebe in den Johannesbriefen." *TZ* 41 (1985): 44–58.

Richards, W. Larry. "An Analysis of Aland's *Textstellen* in 1 John." *NTS* 44 (1998): 26–44.

———. *The Classification of the Greek Manuscripts of the Johannine Epistles*. Society of Biblical Literature Dissertation Series 35. Missoula, Mont.: Scholars Press, 1977.

Riesenfeld, Harald. "Zur den johanneischen ἵνα-Sätzen." *Studia theologica* 19 (1965): 213–20.

Rusam, Dietrich. *Die Gemeinschaft der Kinder Gottes: Das Motiv der Gotteskindschaft und die Gemeinden der johanneischen Briefe*. BWANT 133. Stuttgart: Kohlhammer, 1993.

Schenke, H.-M. "Determination und Ethik im ersten Johannesbrief." *ZTK* 60 (1963): 203–16.

Schenke, Ludger. "Das johanneische Schisma und die 'zwolf' (1 Johannes 6.60–71)." *NTS* 38 (1992): 105–21.

Schmid, Hansjörg. *Gegner im 1. Johannesbrief? Zu Konstruktion und Selbstreferenz im johanneischen Sinnsystem*. BWANT 8.19. Stuttgart: Kohlhammer, 2002.

Schmidt, Andreas. "Erwägungen zur Eschatologie des 2 Thessalonicher und des 2 Johannes." *NTS* 38 (1992): 477–80.

Schmithals, Walter. *Johannesevangelium und Johannesbriefe: Forschungsgeschichte und Analyse*. BZNW 64. Berlin: de Gruyter, 1992.

Schnackenburg, Rudolf. "Die johanneische Gemeinde und ihre Geisterfahrung." Pages 277–306 in *Die Kirche des Anfangs: Für Heinz Schürmann*. Edited by Rudolf Schnackenburg, Josef Ernst, and Joachim Wanke. Freiburg: Herder, 1978.

Schnelle, Ulrich. *Antidoketische Christologie im Johannesevangelium*. FRLANT 144. Göttingen: Vandenhoeck & Ruprecht, 1987. (= *Antidocetic Christology in the Gospel of John*. Translated by L. Maloney. Minneapolis: Fortress, 1992).

Scholtissek, Klaus. *In ihm sein und bleiben: Die Sprache der Immanenz in den Johanneischen Schriften*. Herders biblische Studien 21. Freiburg: Herder, 2000.

Söding, Thomas. "'Gott ist Liebe': 1 Joh 4,8–16 als Spitzensatz biblischer Theologie." Pages 306–57 in *Der lebendige Gott: Studien zur Theologie des*

*Neuen Testaments. Festschrift für Wilhelm Thüsing zum 75. Geburtstag.* Edited by Thomas Söding. NTA n.f. 31. Münster: Aschendorff, 1996.

Stegemann, E. "Kindlein, hütet euch vor den Götterbildern." *TZ* 41 (1985): 284–94.

Suggit, J. N. "1 John 5:21: ΤΕΚΝΙΑ, ΦΥΛΑΞΑΤΕ ΕΑΥΤΑ ΑΠΟ ΤΩΝ ΕΙΔΩ-ΛΩΝ." *JTS* 36 (1985): 386–90.

Swadling, Henry. "Sin and Sinlessness in 1 John." *SJT* 35 (1982): 205–11.

Taeger, Jens-Werner. "Der konservative Rebell: Zum Widerstand des Diotrephes gegen des Presbyter." *ZNW* 78 (1987): 267–87.

Theobald, Michael. *Die Fleischwerdung des Logos: Studien zum Verhältnis des Johannesprologs zum Corpus des Evangeliums und zu 1 Joh.* NTA n.f. 20. Münster: Aschendorff, 1988.

Thiele, W. "Beobachtungen zum Comma Iohanneum (1 Joh 5 7f)." *ZNW* 50 (1959): 61–73.

———. *Wortschatzuntersuchungen zu den lateinischen Texten der Johannesbriefe.* Vetus Latina: Aus der Geschichte der lateinischen Bibel 2. Freiburg: Herder, 1958.

Thomas, John Christopher. "The Literary Structure of 1 John." *NovT* 40 (1998): 369–81.

———. "The Order of the Composition of the Johannine Epistles." *NovT* 37 (1995): 68–75.

Thompson, Marianne Meye. "Intercession in the Johannine Community: 1 John 5:16 in the Context of the Gospel and Epistles of John." Pages 225–45 in *Worship, Theology and Ministry in the Early Church: Essays in Honor of Ralph P. Martin.* Edited by Michael J. Wilkins and Terence Paige. JSNTSup 87. Sheffield: Sheffield Academic Press, 1992.

Thüsing, Wilhelm. "Glaube an die Liebe: Die Johannesbriefe." Pages 216–32 in *Studien zur neutestamentlichen Theologie.* Edited by Thomas Söding. WUNT 82. Tübingen: Mohr, 1995.

Thyen, H. "'. . . den wir lieben dir Brüder' (1 Joh 3,14)." Pages 527–42 in *Rechtfertigung: Festschrift für Ernst Käsemann zum 70. Geburtstag.* Edited by Johannes Friedrich, Wolfgang Pohlmann, and Peter Stuhlmacher. Tübingen: Mohr, 1976.

Trudinger, Paul. "Concerning Sins, Mortal and Otherwise." *Bib* 52 (1971): 541–42.

Uebele, Wolfram. *"Viele Verführer sind in die Welt ausgegangen": Die Gegner in den Briefen des Ignatius von Antiochen und in den Johannesbriefen.* BWANT 151. Stuttgart: Kohlhammer, 2001.

Venetz, Hermann-Josef. "'Durch Wasser und Blut gekommen': Exegetische Überlegungen zu 1 Joh 5,6." Pages 345–61 in *Die Mitte des Neuen Testaments: Festschrift für Eduard Schweizer.* Edited by Ulrich Luz and Hans Weder. Göttingen: Vandenhoeck & Ruprecht, 1983.

Vouga, François. "The Johannine School: A Gnostic Tradition in Primitive Christianity." *Bib* 69 (1988): 371–85.

Vitrano, Steven. "The Doctrine of Sin in 1 John." *AUSS* 25 (1987): 123–31.

Watson, Duane F. "Amplification Techniques in 1 John: The Interaction of Rhetorical Style and Invention." *JSNT* 51 (1993): 99–123.

———. "1 John 2.12–14 as *Distributio, Conduplicatio,* and *Expolitio*: A Rhetorical Understanding." *JSNT* 35 (1989): 97–110.

———. "A Rhetorical Analysis of 2 John according to Greco-Roman Convention." *NTS* 35 (1989): 104–30.

Wengst, K. *Häresie und Orthodoxie im Spiegel des ersten Johannesbriefes.* Gütersloh: Mohn, 1976.

Witherington, Ben. "The Waters of Birth: John 3.5 and 1 John 5.6–8." *NTS* 35 (1989): 155–60.

Zumstein, Jean. "Der Prozess der Relecture in der johanneischen Literatur." *NTS* 42 (1996): 394–411.

# INTRODUCTION

The three Letters of John represent a distinctive voice among the epistolary literature of the New Testament; together with the Gospel of John, forming the "Johannine corpus," they also contribute to a major thread within New Testament and early Christian thought, one that is to be set alongside and balances the Pauline tradition in influence and importance. Central to this contribution is the understanding of God, of the place of Jesus within any experience and articulation of God's acting, and of the transformation that becomes a lived reality for those who share that understanding and experience. Alongside the general impact of these theological achievements, 1 John is the source of a number of formulations that have become familiar in subsequent Christian liturgy and language, for example, the exhortation to confession and the assurance of forgiveness (1 John 1:8–9) or the lapidary, "God is love" (1 John 4:8, 16). Despite this, the conventional label "the Johannine Epistles" or "the Letters of John," although justified by some of the earliest references to these three texts and by the manuscript evidence for them, already points to a number of the uncertainties that surround them. In what sense do they belong together? Are they all rightly described as "letters" (or in older terminology "epistles")? What is implied by calling them "Johannine" or "of John"? These questions are not new, although in the early centuries they focused primarily on the two shorter letters, and only in more recent scholarship have they also included 1 John. Such questions are not only matters of resolving historical uncertainties, for answers to them have a decisive effect on how one interprets the texts.

## 1. The First, Second, and Third Letters of John?

The manuscript evidence is almost unanimous in identifying the three writings by these labels and in their present canonical order (allowing for the fact that the three letters are not all extant or complete in the same manuscripts, and that the label, at beginning or end, may sometimes be missing). Yet what is striking about them is the explicit anonymity of the first, and the effective anonymity of the two smaller letters, inasmuch as "the Elder" could be applied to a number of figures and is given no means of further identification. The dramatic opening of 1 John and the self-conscious use of the first person plural "we" in a text that thereafter is explicitly the work of a single author (2:1; 5:13) show that this anonymity is deliberate, as in another sense must be the absence of any personal name in 2 and 3 John. In the case of 1 John, this is matched by the anonymity of the recipients, who, in contrast to most New Testament letters, are not identified by their location, or even by the general language of a shared calling (cf. Jude 1; 2 Pet 1:1). In interpreting the letters it will be important to take this anonymity seriously and to examine how it contributes to the way in which the letters seek to achieve their purpose; for the interpreter to supply specific details of authorship or of audience would be to ignore the conscious strategy implicit in these writings themselves.

### *1.1 John*

Despite these cautions, the traditional labels are already attached to the writings in the earliest references to them in the early church. For 1 John this is Eusebius's statement that Papias, probably near the beginning of the second century, made use of testimonies from "the former letter of John and likewise that of Peter" (Eusebius, *Ecclesiastical History* 3.39.17). If this was Papias's own description, the identification of the letter as "of John" would be earlier than any explicit attribution of the Fourth Gospel also to a "John"; moreover, "former" might also indicate that Papias knew at least one other letter. However, it is more likely that it was Eusebius or an intermediate source who identified the origins of the "testimonies" or allusions and used these labels. If this is so, a key figure in the labeling of the letters must be Irenaeus, who cites words from both the first and the second letters as spoken by "John, the disciple of the Lord," whom he identifies with the author of the Fourth Gospel and as the son of Zebedee.[1] He does not, however, number these letters, and he appears to treat the quotations as coming from the same writing, while he betrays no knowledge of 3 John (*Against Heresies* 3.16.8 [see commentary on 2 John 7]; cf. 1.16.3). For that we have to wait for Origen in the first half of the third century who, according to Eusebius again, reported that, along with the Gospel *and* Revelation, John also left a letter; "there may also be a second and third, but not all say these are genuine" (Eusebius, *Ecclesiastical History* 6.25.9–10). Whether Origen himself had seen these last two is uncertain—he appears not to have quoted them in his surviving writings. It is striking that the first explicit testimony to 3 John already doubts its "authenticity," but in so doing presupposes an attribution to "John" that is not drawn from the text itself.

So firm was this association with "John" that subsequent writers who questioned whether the two minor letters carried the authority of the first and of the

---

1. See commentary on 1 John 4:2 and below, §4.1, for the possibility that Polycarp, *Phil.* 7.1, quotes or alludes to that verse; if this is a quotation it is not so identified.

Gospel were constrained to hypothesize the existence of some other "of the same name." In this they were helped by traditions, going back to Papias, of another John, fortuitously labeled "the Elder," and also by accounts of two memorials "of John" in Ephesus (see commentary on 2 John 1 and below). Both of these traditions will be shown to be irrelevant for the two letters. Evidently, in whatever way and at whatever point the association of any of the "Johannine" writings with "John" began, there was never any alternative tradition of authorship, despite the anonymity of all four texts—Revelation, which is explicitly attributed to "John" (Rev 1:1, 9), has a separate though eventually overlapping history. Although the history of the reception and of the place within the canon of the three letters as well as of the Fourth Gospel is yet more complex and follows a different pattern in different geographical areas (see §4.1 below), somewhere there must have been a firm tradition of grouping them together, perhaps reinforced by the form in which the texts were copied. One persuasive suggestion would be that before the rise of the "four Gospel canon" and of the developing collection of non-Pauline Catholic Epistles, "a Johannine canon," consisting of Gospel and Letters, perhaps accompanied by Revelation, was held in special respect in some areas.[2] Indeed, it is remarkable that the closing affidavit of the Gospel, "we know his testimony is true" (John 21:24), is echoed by and even reinforced by that which closes 3 John, and hence that which also closes both the letter corpus and the "Johannine canon": "you know that our testimony is true" (3 John 12). The subsequent reconfigurations that separated texts of different genres, Gospel from Letters, would have undermined the cohesion of this group, something that would have left 2 and 3 John without any substantial rationale.

The hypothesis of a Johannine canon does not settle questions of authorship and purpose, nor indeed the attribution to "John." John 21:24 already demonstrates that more than one person claimed some responsibility for the publication of the Gospel, and it also reinforces the habit of anonymity that is equally characteristic of the Letters. In contrast to the writings associated with Paul, the Johannine tradition was not one that drew its authority from a single named individual. Instead, the closing affidavits appeal to the giving, the acceptance, and the passing on of testimony, a strategy that will emerge as central to the task of 1 John. It is difficult to determine whether the association of this testimony with "John" arose from the same types of deduction as exercised by more recent readers—for example, the absence of John the son of Zebedee, a key player in the Synoptic accounts, from the narrative action of the Gospel—or

---

2. This would parallel the "Pauline canon" of Luke's Gospel and the Pauline Letters promoted but not necessarily conceived by Marcion; in the Cheltenham List the three letters of John follow the Apocalypse and so, unusually, precede the Petrine Epistles (see below), and perhaps this is what Tertullian means by his phrase "the Johannine record" ("Instrumentum Iohannis," *On Resurrection* 38).

from independent tradition. The question is probably of less significance than it is often accorded: the writings ask to be read with an ear to the testimony they give, not to the person who originated it. For the same reason, the failure of any of these writings, other than 2 and 3 John, to claim to be written by the same author as any other must be taken seriously; the question of authorship has to start as an open one, although still one that merits consideration (see below).

What, of course, is presupposed throughout this discussion is that these writings belong together not just by tradition but because they share a family likeness; this family likeness can, for convenience, be called "Johannine." It is constituted by a shared worldview, which is sharply dualist (light versus darkness, truth versus falsehood), by a common vocabulary that articulates that worldview, and even by fixed phrases and habits of speech. To that extent it forms what sociolinguistics would call an idiolect, the dialect of an in-group, a form of subdialect not only of Koine Greek but even of early Christian discourse, although it shares some features with other near-contemporary Jewish writings. I shall argue that this distinctive "habit" extends beyond linguistic choices to patterns of argument and to the development of ideas. The consequence is that superficially similar language and ideas are not necessarily evidence of common authorship or of literary dependency: the Johannine style is not difficult to imitate. A more difficult question will be whether they are evidence of defined circles not only of those who wrote but also of those who received and read (or heard) these writings.

## 1.2 Letters

Before these issues can be explored further there is one more question provoked by the familiar title, "the Johannine Letters." Of them, and indeed of all the so-called New Testament letters, 3 John comes closest to what ancient readers would have expected of a letter. In the commentary I will demonstrate just how close 3 John is to some of the thousands of letters that have survived from antiquity in the rubbish heaps of ancient Egypt. Second John shares a number of these features, although it conveys a somewhat less natural air; this in itself would not disqualify it as a "letter" since the letter format was widely used both in fictional contexts, for example to carry a novelistic plot, and to convey philosophical teaching, whether in pithy or more argumentative form. This wide use of the letter format in antiquity has provoked attempts to distinguish different categories, for example, between "real" letters and those that self-consciously use the format for other literary purposes.[3] Such attempts ultimately fail for the same reason: some writers penned "real" letters to actual recipients even while intending to publish them, while official rescripts addressed to cities might

---

3. Older scholarship sometimes used "epistles" of the more artificial category.

adopt many of the conventions of a personal letter. Indeed, it is this flexibility that explains why the first readers had no problem in identifying the long and complex Pauline letters as such, even if more recent interpreters have sought to refine or modify that description.

First John is much more difficult to classify, although that the epithet "letter" is given it in the early church without quibble again shows that readers accepted that general categorization. First John lacks any of the conventional components of a letter such as even shape the framework of the Pauline letters, a salutation, expressions of concern or delight concerning the well-being of the recipients, the sharing of greetings from or to common acquaintances. Neither author nor recipients are identified, by name or by location. Within the New Testament, Hebrews is closest to this in resisting easy classification, although it does exchange closing greetings while describing itself as a "word of exhortation" (Heb 13:22–25). First John might invite a similar epithet, and it has sometimes been described as a homily or a sermon, which has been written down in order for it to be circulated among a wider audience. However, the author's repeated references to his reasons for *writing* to them, and the absence of any other first person verbs, for example of exhortation, show that the written form is not a second level of the text's production (1 John 2:1, 12–14, 21, 26; 5:13).[4] Given that the majority of an ancient audience would hear rather than read a text, it may be difficult to identify techniques specifically designed to draw the attention of or to persuade *readers* (see below), but there is a sense in which many of 1 John's persuasive strategies are literary in that they appeal to textual echoes both within and external to this writing.

For convenience I will refer to 1 John, as also 2 and 3 John, as letters—certainly no other more useful descriptor has been found. To do so does not prejudice any conclusion about why and to whom each was written. The early Christians evidently found the epistolary format one that they could exploit and modify just as they did other literary genres; the production of pseudonymous letters, which if not written by the supposed *author* perhaps were not received by the supposed *audience* either, underlines the conscious exploitation of the genre; they have to be read both with respect to their epistolary format as part of a consciously chosen strategy, but without being constrained by a known context. Such a framework may be particularly suitable for 2 John.

The label "catholic letter" seems first to have been used of 1 John by Origen, who also applied it to 1 Peter and to the *Letter of Barnabas*, probably in the sense of each being a "general" letter not intended for a single community or individual—in contrast to the letters of Paul.[5] Only later did the label come

---

4. The only other first person verb, in 5:16, is best understood as "I mean"; see commentary.

5. Earlier the anti-Montanist writer had condemned a certain Themiso for composing a "catholic letter" in imitation of the apostle, possibly but not necessarily John (Eusebius, *Ecclesiastical History* 5.18.5).

to be affixed to the "seven catholic letters," despite the supposedly specific address of 2 and of 3 John (see Eusebius, *Ecclesiastical History* 2.23.25, who qualifies the designation by "so-called"). The uneven reception history of each of the seven renders it difficult to determine quite how, when, and where this sense of their being a group arose, and studies of the development of the text have done little to settle this.

## 2. The Setting of the Letters

### 2.1 Author and Audience

Only 3 John identifies its recipient by name, Gaius; the "elect lady" to whom 2 John is written has no name and, I will argue, is a semifictional cover. The author of both shorter letters identifies himself as "the elder," an epithet that reveals little of his role or of his status. Third John also mentions other individuals and implies a specific context of dispute, while the situation behind 2 John is much more elusive; in addition, shared greetings with friends suggest a wider network within which these individuals are placed (3 John 15; cf. 2 John 13). However, none of these details can certainly be confidently related to any specific individuals, places, or situations in the early church known from other sources (see below and commentary on 2 John 1; 3 John 1). Yet any attempt to comment on and to explain the letters is bound to make some judgment about the possible circumstances surrounding them; although this is the task of the detailed commentary, the letters have sometimes been interpreted as providing valuable glimpses on key moments in the early church's history, and these will be discussed later.

All this is even more pertinent to 1 John, which is marked by a thoroughgoing anonymity—of author, of recipients, and of their context. Even characterizing them from within the text is difficult. The opening of the letter could suggest that the recipients are only now hearing the proclamation regarding eternal life (1 John 1:2, 3, 5), yet subsequently the author is emphatic that they can put their confidence in the assurance that they already possess, and he repeatedly appeals to the message they have heard and held "from the beginning" (2:7, 20–21, 24; 3:11). He addresses them as "my children" (2:1, 18, etc.), and yet he never indicates that they have any past relationship with him or would recognize their dependency on him or their obligation to him. The author also betrays nothing about himself or his own status; the singular "I" only appears as the subject of writing, "I write" (other than the explanatory 5:16). Apparently undermining this reticence is the dramatic affirmation that opens the letter, voiced in a repeated first person plural, "*we* have heard, *we* have seen, *we* have observed, *our* hands have touched, *we* bear witness, and *we* proclaim *to you*." Evidently the author must be related to this "we," not least because "*we* also write these things" (1:4), and yet this relationship is never made explicit;

indeed, at times the author distances his own role ("I have written") from that which "we" have done and experienced (2:19, 21).[6] It is as if the author observes and writes about "us," just as he observes and writes about, as well as to, "you" (see 4:4–6 and commentary). Finally, there is nothing that would indicate the location or the situation of either party other than the reference to those who "went out from us" (2:19).

All this means that 1 John cannot be treated in the same way as 1 Corinthians or Galatians might be, with careful reference to the context of the community, to the challenges they faced in society, or to Paul's endeavors to integrate their personal and communal lives with his interpretation of the Christian message. Yet there is a degree of specificity about 1 John: the argument is designed not to provide a generally relevant encouragement but to create a relationship; it is not a "general" letter addressed to anyone who might encounter it, nor even, probably, to a range of scattered communities over a broad area (cf. 1 Pet 1:1, and contrast the assumptions in the label "catholic"; see above). It presupposes a particular experience of Christian teaching and familiarity with specific ("Johannine") traditions. Just as its overt purpose is to enable "fellowship" (1 John 1:3), it will become evident that the whole strategy of the letter is to foster a tight communal identity, to create an imagined community whose distance from "the world" and whose adherence to all that the author represents is beyond question (5:19; see below). Yet it is impossible to determine whether this "imagined community" took shape in one actual congregation or in a number of them, perhaps closely connected to one another.

These uncertainties would not be solved were the relationship among the three letters known, but some of the unknowns might acquire possible identities—for example, if the elder of 2 and 3 John were to be identified with and so to provide a profile for the "I" of 1 John. From the beginning the early church was undecided on this issue, Irenaeus assuming the common authorship of 1 and 2 John, Origen reporting doubts (see above). While their eventual inclusion in the canon reinforced the former position, the latter has never totally disappeared, although probably from the start this was because of the apparently limited value of 2 and 3 John rather than because of any alternative tradition as to their origin. The letters are too short to make stylistic arguments for or against common authorship decisive, although in the commentary I will suggest reasons for supposing that 2 John is derivative from 1 John. Early attestation may indicate that there were times or places when 2 John was separated from 3 John, but the exegesis will show that it is 3 John that is more securely a genuine letter. Although this curious pattern of relationships among the three letters provokes unresolved questions, the claim of the two smaller ones alone to be the work of the self-styled "elder" must initially be respected.

6. See commentary.

Although in parts of the church 1 John was not given canonical authority as quickly as was the Gospel (see below), this does not seem to have been because of uncertainties about its authorship by the apostle, and only since the twentieth century has the common authorship of the Gospel of John and 1 John been seriously questioned. Since there are no explicit claims to authorship, issues of style and of language, as well as of theology, have played a major role here; for example, terms important in the Gospel, such as "glory" (*doxa*), are absent from the letter, while the latter lacks the understanding of the spirit and the richness of Christology and realized eschatology characteristic of the former.[7] A growing weight of scholarship has moved toward favoring the separate authorship of the two writings but there is no consensus, and a number of general assumptions about early Christian writings are also at play in any conclusion. The debate has been made more complicated by theories that the Gospel itself may be the result of layers of editing so that identifying *the* (or a single) author becomes impossible. Thus some would argue that 1 John may be the work of or be linked to a particular redactor or stage in the production of the Gospel. For example, many of the parallels between the First Epistle and the Gospel are found in the Farewell Discourses (John 14–17), especially in the second half (John 15–16, 17), which is sometimes seen as redactionally independent.[8] This is a topic that is often extensively discussed and illustrated in introductions to commentaries on the Letters.[9] I will not explore it further here: I argue in the commentary and below that 1 John nowhere appeals to or assumes knowledge of the Gospel, and indeed that the latter seems unlikely; rather each writing is, largely independently, reworking common or shared traditions. The task is to interpret 1 John in its own terms, respecting the chosen anonymity of its author; inevitably in so doing it will be necessary to refer to the Gospel's treatment of some of the same themes, not as if that were the source of the letter's own interpretation, but because it represents another exploration of the same underlying tradition.

This decision—to respect the self-presentation of the author of each letter—is in part a consequence of seeing the task of a commentary as to explore and unfold a text as far as possible first of all within its own terms. In this case it is strengthened by the inconclusive nature of the evidence and of the arguments regarding each aspect of the authorship debate. It will be obvious that a specific identification of the author(s) is even more decisively excluded. The traditional association with John the son of Zebedee, usually seen as represented by the

7. Classic articles are C. H. Dodd, "The First Epistle of John and the Fourth Gospel," *BJRL* 21 (1937): 129–56; countered by W. F. Howard, "The Common Authorship of the Johannine Gospel and Epistles," *JTS* 48 (1947): 12–25. On 1 John's understanding of the spirit see commentary on 3:24.

8. For example, the importance of indwelling (*menō*; see commentary on 1 John 2:6), and of the love command is characteristic of the Farewell Discourses and 1 John.

9. See Lieu, *The Second and Third Epistles of John* (SNTW; Edinburgh: T. & T. Clark, 1986), 210–13.

Beloved Disciple (John 13:23; 19:26; etc.), belongs to a study of the Gospel. Nothing in the letters would independently point to such an association, and there is much that points away from it. Suggestions that some other John was responsible are attempts to preserve the traditional association while acknowledging the many objections to it, and are equally without any support in the text.[10]

This determination to respect the chosen anonymity of the letters is not purely negative. Such anonymity is, it has already been suggested, a deliberate technique in the Johannine literature; as such it is not a blanket anonymity but a coded one, in the sense that it is an integral element in these writings' repeated appeal to the ability to offer and to authenticate testimony. Authority lies not in individual status or calling but in the shared giving and receiving of witness. Contrary to those interpretations that assumed that such witness always means eyewitness—and that from this sought to preserve an apostolic ("Johannine") connection—the source of witness and its authentication are explored in a number of different ways within the Johannine literature (see 3 John 12; 1 John 4:14, 16; 5:9–11; and commentary). Although to the outside observer or reader these appeals may sometimes seem self-fulfilling, for the insider testimony is and can only be self-authenticating, while it is by accepting testimony that one becomes and is reinforced as an insider.

### 2.2 Situation

Each of the letters seeks to win its reader(s) in the face of a threat that challenges the author's own standing. In 3 John this situation is most explicit: the elder feels himself to have been rebuffed and even slandered by a certain Diotrephes, and he energetically seeks to win Gaius to his cause and to action that Diotrephes would prohibit. In 2 John the elder warns "the elect lady" against showing any form of hospitality to a visitor who does not offer the correct form of teaching; if they falter it is not only they who will suffer but "what we have worked for" will come to nothing. The author of 1 John does not prescribe any response to the threat he envisages other than continuing fidelity, but this threat is one that has its origins in a recent schism that potentially undermined the assurance that characterized those who declared themselves part of that "we" (2:19). There is no reason why these situations should be related to each other.

Although 1 John argues allusively and refracts the whole situation through a lens of the expected troubles of the eschatological countdown (2:18; 4:1; see commentary), the author apparently understands the problem to be centered on the proper acknowledgment of Jesus, in his relationship to God as Father and in his mission. Whether Christology was the overt cause of conflict and would have been identified as such by the other side is less certain since the letter never

10. See commentary on 2 John 1 and below.

reveals what they did claim, although it is widely supposed that it was so. Second John's repeated emphasis suggests that whether "the teaching" was properly recognized and authorized is as much at issue as its precise content; the opponents again may be characterized by christological failure (2 John 7), but here this serves more to exclude them (in terms familiar from 1 John) than to identify precisely the point at dispute. Yet in 3 John the elder neither defends his own doctrinal purity nor impugns that of Diotrephes; for all that, the strategies of retaliation—rigorous exclusion—are remarkably similar in the two shorter letters, although undertaken by opposite sides (2 John 10–11; 3 John 10). Once again 2 John serves as a bridge, with points of contact to both 1 and 3 John.

It is not surprising that interpreters of the letters have often started by attempting to identify "the opponents." In the case of 1 John this usually involves five elements:

1. Which passages in the letter are directed against the opponents and therefore indirectly portray their ethos have to be identified. For example, while few would doubt a christological dispute (1 John 2:18; 4:2), it is more contentious whether the author's rejection of anyone claiming "not to have sin," or to know or love God while failing in obedience to the command of fraternal[11] love (1:8, 10; 2:4; 4:20), equally presupposes those who did just that—that there is also a moral dimension to the dispute.

2. Since 1 John emphasizes confession of Jesus as *the Christ* (2:22), one has to decide whether this is a "Jewish" denial of Jesus' messiahship or is something more complex, namely that "Christ" has mutated from its original meaning to carry a distinctive Christian or even "Johannine" sense, however this may then be understood.

3. In the latter case, similar profiles may be sought elsewhere in the early church. Older commentators focused on named individuals, most notably Cerinthus, whose encounter with the apostle John Irenaeus recounts, and who, according to Irenaeus, taught that the divine Christ descended upon the human Jesus at baptism and departed before his suffering and death (*Against Heresies* 1.26.1; 3.3.4).[12] For others, Ignatius's tirades against his anonymous opponents who doubt that Jesus was *truly* born, died, or risen, apparently a form of Docetism—that Jesus' humanity was in appearance only—better coheres with 1 John's emphasis on "having come in flesh" (1 John 4:2).[13]

---

11. See below §5 on language and 2:9.

12. Other sources give a different focus to Cerinthus's teaching, which further complicates this line of argument; see Charles E. Hill, "Cerinthus, Gnostic or Chiliast? A New Solution to an Old Problem," *Journal of Early Christian Studies* 8 (2000): 135–72.

13. Ignatius, *Trall.* 9–10, "Jesus Christ . . . who was truly born, ate and drank, persecuted under Pontius Pilate, crucified and died . . . truly raised from the dead. . . . If then, as some, godless, that is unbelieving, say that his having suffered was an appearance . . ."; cf. *Smyrn.* 2–3. See commentary on 1 John 4:2.

4. Since the schism was internal ("they went out from us," 2:19), there may be other evidence within the Johannine tradition, namely from the Gospel, that might reflect or explain the origins of such a profile. For example, John 1:14, "the Word became flesh," has often also been seen as refuting a docetic position, as too has the insistence on "eating my flesh and drinking my blood" (6:53–56), whether these passages are considered original to the Gospel or subsequent redactional additions. On the other hand, the Gospel's own high Christology (10:30) and its arguable lack of interest in Jesus' human experience might have led some to disregard his "flesh" as significant.[14]

5. Most would then reconstruct a broader scenario within which these elements might come together, whether in relation to contemporary Jewish communities, to incipient "Gnosticism" (see below), or (less commonly) to the pressures of Roman persecution.

As even this outline demonstrates, at each stage of the analysis there is considerable uncertainty, and the argument necessarily depends more on interpreters' decisions about other texts and contexts than on the Epistles themselves. While this should undermine confidence in the whole approach there are also further fundamental weaknesses. The wording of the key passages of 1 John (see 1 above) lacks the specificity of the sources often used to interpret the letter (3), with the result that many recent interpreters have been much more reticent in drawing direct links with other known polemics and situations from the early church. More importantly, the author's concern consistently is *not* with what is going on outside but with the internal commitment and adherence of those to whom the letter is written. He does not engage in attacking positions held by others but focuses on exploring the implications of those already held by himself and by his readers. It is they who can indeed say they have known God and love God (1 John 2:3, 13–14; 5:2); it is they who in some circumstances may be able to say they do not sin—although this is something that the author never totally resolves (see 3:4–10; 5:16–18; and commentary). His questioning, hypothesizing style (1:6, "If we say"; 2:9, "The one who says"; see below) is designed to engage his readers and to draw them inevitably toward the position that he holds. Even his christological assertions are concerned with what must be said, not with any alternative view held by others, and they can be seen to hold firm to a point—that the Son of God really did fulfill his mission in human form in the person of Jesus— in which for long passages he himself expresses little interest. The comfortable assurance of the group of believers he represents has undoubtedly been shaken, but not necessarily that of his readers—it was *us* from whom they departed, not

---

14. For example, the absence of an agony in Gethsemane and Jesus' unflinching control in his trial and crucifixion; independent of this is the debate whether such a reading of the Gospel would be appropriate or would be a misreading. This, on the assumption of the primacy of the Gospel, would explain how the opponents could have been "among us" (1 John 2:19).

from *you* (2:19); certainly this could present a danger, perhaps that his readers would be persuaded by *them* and not by *us* (4:4–6). To address this the author draws on an evocative verbal arsenal of images taken from traditional eschatological warning (2:18; 4:1; see commentary), and it may be that right confession of Christ belonged as much to this arsenal as it did to contemporary dispute. The author builds a universe of meaning shaped by his understanding of what God has done and of how those who have responded to this action find and keep their place within it; those who belong outside this, whether labeled "the world," the antichrists, or merely "them" (4:3, 5), are of no real interest to him. Readers, both the first intended readers and subsequent ones, are invited to enter into this universe and to find themselves constituted as an (imagined) community.

If the "opponents" of 1 John are thus to be relegated to the shadows, this is even more the case for 2 John, which adds nothing to their depiction.[15] Despite this, 2 John *is* concerned with how to treat such outsiders, but only if they attempt to become insiders, to visit. In the commentary on the letter that concern will be related to widespread evidence in the early church of the important role played by traveling teachers, and of the need to test their credentials (2 John 9–11). The prevalence of such issues does nothing to determine their particular form in this instance, although 2 John's rigorous attitude does fit the other evidence in the Johannine tradition of a strong sense of boundaries and of their control (see below). Remarkably, 3 John makes no use in its defense against Diotrephes of the arsenal developed by 1 John; indeed, Christology plays no obvious role, and neither does any of the other yardsticks, knowledge of God, obedience to the commands, love of the brother or sister. Diotrephes refuses to offer support to "brothers" commended by the elder, and supposedly slanders the latter, actions that could have been inspired by doctrinal differences, but the elder appears unaware of this, or unwilling to acknowledge it. From his perspective the problem is one of personal ambition (3 John 9–10), suggesting that it was a matter of structural or/and of political differences.

Once again, interpretation has attempted to relate this to known situations in the early church and to the tendencies within Johannine thought. Diotrephes' actions appear to be focused on the local community, refusing hospitality and ejecting those who wish to offer it. Adopting the elder's perspective, he may be a local upstart, overly ambitious, perhaps even assuming that as head of a household and in control of its visitors he can extend that authority to the community within his home. Yet other sources indicate that local communities did begin to express autonomous leadership; Ignatius already demands almost unquestioning submission to the bishop "as the representation of the father" (*Trallians* 2–3). Whether the position that Diotrephes apparently exercises is

---

15. See commentary on 2 John 7 for the argument that the different wording of the failed confession does not represent a different situation.

credited with formal or with usurped status depends on the alternative position occupied by the elder. The letters imply that the influence he held (or claimed) extended beyond the local community; he was part of a network, perhaps even its focus, of traveling "brothers" and of greetings among "friends" (3 John 3, 6, 15). He thinks of Gaius as among his "children" (3 John 4), but how many there were and what gave them this status is never explained; for example, was he responsible for their conversion (cf. Gal 4:19) or did he act as their mentor (cf. 1 Tim 1:2, 18)? From this some have supposed that the elder held regional authority, although there is little early evidence for such a pattern and in practice the elder's network may have been limited to a few communities, perhaps in a city and its surroundings. Others have suggested that he represents a form of authority outside the local community, perhaps more in sympathy with that of the traveling teachers but also founded on some personal status or qualities. In either case, the clash is between conflicting styles of leadership and patterns of legitimation. Neither the Gospel nor 1 John gives obvious support to any particular model of church structure; although it is often argued that both express a sense of a closed tight-knit group aware of a sharp distinction from those outside, there seems little overt concern as to how that group should be ordered. This itself might be significant, especially if combined with an emphasis on the guidance of the spirit (John 14:26–27; 16:12–14) and on the confidence that all have equal access to knowledge (1 John 2:20). At the same time, such an ethos might be open to abuse and might readily invite insistence on more formal and accountable strategies of control.

All this is highly suggestive and has been used creatively to reconstruct a context for 3 John, whether it be the elder or Diotrephes who represents the "charismatic" voice on the one hand or the advocate of greater control on the other. Yet the letter supplies too little hard evidence to settle decisively on one or other reconstruction. Certainly it testifies to the tensions that surrounded the emergence of early Christian communities, and suggests that there was no single pattern of development and no obvious model to follow.

Such tensions could arise entirely independently of any disagreements about doctrinal positions, although particular doctrinal positions might favor particular styles of leadership. Third John betrays no clear awareness of theological conflict between the elder and Diotrephes, although the parallel between Diotrephes' harsh response to the brethren and that counseled by the elder in 2 John (see above) could suggest that there was one, at least in Diotrephes' eyes. Attempts by interpreters to label either Diotrephes or the elder as the heretic have stumbled over the silence, but also wrongly presuppose that the lines of division would have been agreed in principle by both sides. Yet the vigorous efforts of most of the New Testament and contemporary early Christian writings to exclude false teachers often do more to suggest that the process was contested and only sometimes effective; indeed, "false teaching" is always a matter of definition by one particular perspective in relation to another. Once again, 3 John may testify to the struggles inherent in this situation, and may show how theological differences can appear to be matters of structure and personal ambition, just as 2 or 1 John could show how structural or political differences can be expressed as matters of fundamental theological principle.

There is nothing in these uncertainties that could either help determine or be resolved by knowing the location from or to which the letters were written. The Johannine tradition was early associated with Ephesus; a setting in Asia Minor might be supported by the parallel to 1 John 4:2 in Polycarp's *Letter to the Philippians*, by Papias's apparent knowledge at least of 1 John, and perhaps by supposed similarities of situation behind Ignatius's letters (although this could also point to his home city of Antioch). Irenaeus's particular sources regarding the disciple Jesus loved may also be traced to Asia Minor. None of this is decisive, and the absence of any explicit appeal to "John" by either Polycarp or by Ignatius writing to Ephesus might seem to point in the opposite direction. In any case, the question is not fundamental for the interpretation of the letters.

## 3. The Structure, Background, and Thought of the Letters

### 3.1 Argument and Style

Despite the occasional allusive "we" (3 John 8, 9–10), the Elder of 3 John is not afraid of asserting his own position, his pleasure and his hopes in his dealings with Gaius, and his frustration regarding Diotrephes' behavior. By contrast, the author of 1 John is remarkably reticent and sparing in the use of "I."[16] Yet 1 John does represent a sustained effort to win readers over to the author's position; he does this not by personal exhortation and argument but through a range of persuasive strategies. These may be dubbed a rhetoric of persuasion; this does not mean that they show knowledge of formal rhetorical techniques discussed by Greek and Roman authors, although there are occasional parallels. Their effectiveness is enriched by the way that they are combined and by the sudden switches between different styles and patterns of appeal.

It is much easier to trace these patterns in the subunits of 1 John than it is to detect its overall structure. Various attempts have been made to identify major breaks in the letter: 2:18 introduces the "antichrists" and a concern for Christology for the first time; in 3:11 "this is the message" repeats (with minor changes) the wording of 1:5 and introduces a heightened (but not a new) emphasis on love; 5:13 can be read as summarizing the purpose of the letter so that the following verses may be viewed as an appendix. Yet none of these marks a

---

16. In 3 John there are 11 first person singular verbs from 10 different verbs; in 1 John there are 12 of which 11 are from "write." In 2 John first person singular verbs (6 times) belong mainly to the epistolary framework and conventions shared with 3 John.

major change of style or of focus, and in the commentary I will argue that the last two fall toward the end of and not at the beginning of subunits. Even the subunits are not sharply delimited, and there are occasions where the same verse may complete one section and introduce another (e.g., 5:4), acting as a bridge in what may otherwise seem a disjointed "stream of consciousness." This lack of clear argumentative structure is exacerbated by formulae such as "and this is" (1:5; 2:25, etc.) or "in this way" (2:3; 3:19, etc.), which either may pick up a previous statement or may anticipate one to come. Thus, although the outline of the commentary provided by the Contents (pp. v–vii) offers a general guide to the structure, it does not represent a précis of a single argument through the letter. On the other hand, in some themes there is a development of thought, and it would not be possible to reorder the sections without damage to the argument. In particular this is true of the treatment of sin, of the acknowledgment of the Son of God, and of the relationship between "we" and "you."

The third of these is a key strategy in the letter. In contrast to the careful anonymity discussed earlier, the dominant use in the letter of first and second person plural verbs and pronouns ("we" and "you") is particularly striking. Yet whereas the identity of "you," those receiving the letter, is constant even if the way they are viewed is not, that of "we" is more open to change. The letter opens with a fanfare of claims that "we" can make in order to be able to proclaim "to you also," but this "you" are given no identity, no qualifications, even no explicit responsibility for response. This imbalance in relationship is not sustained: on the one hand it becomes evident that "you" are rooted in that "from the beginning" quality that first characterized "us" (1:1; 2:7, 13–14, 21, 27, etc.); on the other, it is "we" from whom the antichrists have departed with potentially destabilizing consequences (2:19). More important, as the letter progresses "we" comes to be inclusive, and most decisively in 4:4–6 "you" and "we" are united in common cause against the "they" of the world; thereafter the author speaks consistently of "we" so that those who received the letter are able to join in the affirmation "we have seen and give testimony" (4:14; see commentary). In this way the letter brings "you" into that fellowship with "us" that was its initial avowed intent (1:3); to read the letter is to accept this process, particularly since there are no points at which it is suggested that "you" might have taken or might be planning to take some other course of action.

The author also adopts a different use of the first person plural, here without the emphatic pronoun "we." This is to explore different possibilities, some of which it will become self-evident are to be excluded, others to be affirmed: "if we say we have no sin we deceive ourselves . . . if we acknowledge our sins he [will] . . . forgive" (1:8–9). A similar pattern of argument is expressed by a more impersonal third person singular: "the one who says . . . [but] . . ." (2:4, 9), "if anyone says . . . [but] . . ." (4:20), "the one who loves/hates" (2:10, 11). Whereas the last of these may be self-explanatory, the first two express real dilemmas: it is not the saying—"I have known him" (2:4)—that is a problem, for such claims are affirmed elsewhere (2:13), but the mismatch between claim and subsequent behavior—not keeping his commands (2:4). This process of deliberation invites readers to reach the conclusion that the author wishes them to without his simply laying it down as instruction or as prohibition. At times it tackles the dangers inherent in his own pattern of thought with its strong emphasis on the assurance that those who believe should experience, and it does so in a way that does not overtly undermine that assurance but that equally allows of no other conclusion. This confirms that there is no need to suppose that there were others who were making such claims but failing in the appropriate behavior: the argument is not directed outside (to supposed opponents) but within.

At other times the author appeals to what they ("you" or "we") already know (2:29; 3:2, 5, 14, 15; 5:18–20). Such appeals may be self-fulfilling, so that it would be hard for someone to respond, "No, we don't," but it appears more probable that they refer to ideas already established earlier in the letter or familiar to the first readers—in the latter case they sometimes occur in a different form in the Gospel (see below and commentary on 2:29). Similar internal or external (within the "Johannine tradition") cross-referencing sometimes occurs without explicit marking, although readers who recognized it would have appreciated the way that the author modified such sentiments or drew new conclusions from them (e.g., 1:1–3; 2:11; see commentary).

Although it is not possible to identify specific literary sources underlying 1 John, there are passages where the author is either switching to a rhythmic style or may be taking over earlier units. First John 2:12–14 probably belongs to the former category, whereas 4:7–10 is often set out in verse form in translations and has sometimes been supposed to be a "hymn to love" known to the readers, although in the commentary I will argue that it belongs firmly within the more extensive passage, 4:7–5:4. The section 2:29–3:10a appears to be structured around a series of antithetical couplets, "everyone who does [present participle] . . . has been born [of God]" or "is . . ." (cf. 5:1); these have been broken up to provide a framework for further reflection on the stark alternatives they project, centered around God or the devil. The prologue (1:1–4) with its repetitions and sudden breaks may also be an expansion of a simpler core. If some of this earlier material were known to the readers the author would be demonstrating both the new perspectives it could generate and how his own conclusions were not novelties but built on that which they had heard (cf. 2:7; 3:11).

Less obvious, perhaps even to the initial audience, are the echoes of Scripture. Although 1 John makes only one explicit reference, and it is to a familiar story and not to scriptural authority (3:12, "Cain . . . murdered his brother"), other allusions can be detected. In the commentary I will argue that the Cain narrative in practice has left its mark throughout 3:8 to 3:21, that Isa 6:10 is the ultimate source of 1 John 2:11, and that Exod 34:6–7 has contributed to 1 John 1:9;

2:1. Second Isaiah lies behind some of the language associated with witnessing and perhaps the final warning against idols, and Deuteronomy influences 1 John 4:20–5:3. In some, if not all, cases the author and even the readers may have been more familiar with a tradition of the interpretation of these passages than with them within a scriptural context, and this means that they are not being used within a theory of prophetic fulfillment or of the place of the Law. Rather, they are another element among the resources on which the author draws to establish the integrity of his own position; familiarity encourages assent.

### 3.2 Johannine Tradition

All this indicates that 1 John is not intended for outsiders or even for new converts but for those already familiar, and that they are assumed to be familiar not just with the Christian message in general but with a particular form of its expression, namely that which is also represented by the Fourth Gospel. The close parallels between the Gospel and 1 John have frequently been set out, especially in discussions of authorship (see above); they extend beyond a favored vocabulary and worldview to particular turns of phrase (e.g., "have passed from death to life," 1 John 3:14; John 5:24).[17] The extent of these has often led to the assumption that the relationship between the two writings is one of literary dependence, even (or especially) if it is not one of common authorship. Some have even found a common structure between the two writings, a prologue (1 John 1:1–4; John 1:1–18) and a closing followed by an epilogue (1 John 5:13, 14–21; John 20:30–31; 21:1–25), although reasons for such a slavish imitation between two different genres are hard to understand. Although some have argued that 1 John is the earlier, the more common position has been to place the Gospel first even if not in its final form (see above). The debate does not only turn on the literary parallels; there are nuanced differences, for example, the newness of the command in John (13:34) contrasted with it being "not new . . . yet new" in 1 John (2:7–8); it is also argued that the eschatology of 1 John retains a stronger future dimension (2:28; 4:17) and that the letter does not reflect the developed high Christology of the Gospel (e.g., John 1:1; 10:30); further, that its enemies are not external ("the Jews") but internal may explain some differences but also invites explanation.

The position taken here is that there is no compelling evidence of a direct literary relationship between 1 John and the Gospel in anything like the latter's current form; on the contrary, the consistent subtle differences of wording, inference, context, and combination even where parallels appear close suggest that both writings draw independently on earlier formulations. Good examples are the way that 1 John 2:11 draws on a similar exegesis of Isa 6:10 to that

---

17. On what follows see the commentary to the passages referenced.

found, more extensively, in John 12:40, or the different settings in which the formula "because his/their/its deeds were evil" appears (1 John 3:12; John 3:19; 7:7; cf. 2 John 11; 3 John 10). Such earlier materials would have included scriptural exegesis, such as the story of Cain (see above, 1 John 3:12, and John 8:44, where it is only implicit). It has also been suggested that sermonic material may lie behind some of the Gospel's discourses, sometimes interpreting earlier formulations from the traditions about Jesus and his teaching, and this too would offer a setting in which linguistic patterns and theological formulations could achieve some regularity. Whether such resources were available to the authors of the Gospel or Epistles in oral or written form cannot be determined; here I will refer to them as "Johannine tradition," and where a Gospel reference is given this indicates a parallel expression and not the literary source.

Second and Third John undoubtedly belong to the same tradition, although it is much more evident in the second letter. Here, however, a literary relationship between 1 and 2 John, the latter dependent on the former, will appear most probable (see especially 2 John 5–6, 7). Although it would not be surprising if the same author used similar conventions in two separate letters, in the commentary I will suggest that 2 John may draw on 3 John, which represents more authentically the form of a genuine letter. To fix 3 (and perhaps 2) John any more firmly at a specific point in the Johannine tradition largely depends on general assumptions about their historical setting. They have frequently been seen as coming last in order, particularly when they alone were not attributed to the apostle. Certainly at times they may seem to use "Johannine" language in a more formulaic way, such as the repeated "in truth" (see 2 John 1, 3; and commentary), and yet the mere fact of 3 John's survival may favor it having a more pivotal position (see below, §4.1).

### 3.3 The Thought of the Letters

The "Johannine tradition" does not just refer to a way of speaking or writing but to a way of thinking; the distinctive Johannine vocabulary and formulations reflect a distinctive worldview and understanding of the significance of the coming of Jesus Christ.[18] Here only the broad pattern can be sketched with detailed discussion belonging in the commentary. Most fundamentally this worldview is characterized by a dualism between light and darkness, truth and falsehood, life and death, love and hatred; in the Gospel, but not in 1 John, there is a vertical dimension, above and below, and both writings set the (or this) world against that which is "not of the world." As is frequently the case, such dualism leaves little room for a mediating position; people belong to one or the

---

18. See further Judith M. Lieu, *The Theology of the Johannine Epistles* (New Testament Theology; Cambridge: Cambridge University Press, 1991).

other side, and there can be no easy or repeated movement between the two. This means that decision is demanded and cannot be postponed, although there is also a strong tendency to see the ultimate decider not as the individual but as God: those who respond do so by God's prior choice.

In 1 John this is expressed by the startling image of "having been born" or "begotten from God" (cf. 2:29), a process that might suggest passivity as well as irreversibility. Yet other expressions are more ambiguous, such as being "from" or "of God" (cf. 2:16; 3:9), or else they focus not on the initiating event but on the continuing relationship, "being" or "remaining" or "indwelling in God" (cf. 2:5–6) or "possessing the Father" (cf. 2:23; 2 John 9). These allow for more conditionality than does birth—"remaining" might suggest the possibility of failing to do so. Part of the letter's purpose is to set out the conditions for such remaining or indwelling, or at least the certifiable marks of so doing. Yet it often feels as if the author is walking a tightrope, unwilling to suggest that it is possible for God's transforming act to be undone, even by human failure. Hence he explains "those who went out" not as apostates or as having lost the faith they once held but as never having actually been "of us," despite all appearances to the contrary (2:19). Similarly, although obedience to God's commands and love toward a fellow member are for the most part the unmistakable and necessary characteristics of anyone who truly belongs to God or who can validly claim to "have known him" (2:4; 4:20), at one point the author reverses the logic so that the less tangible love toward God becomes the test of authentic love of the other (5:2).

Both the dualism and this assurance suggest a degree of realized eschatology: the experiences usually associated with the age to come are already a present reality, eternal life and having "passed from death to life" (3:14). From another perspective, those to whom the author writes already know the truth or even are taught about everything not by some external authority but by "the anointing" they already possess (2:20–21, 27). In contrast to the opening fanfare, as has been seen, the readers already possess all the resources that they need, and are not expected to view themselves as anticipating further growth or as needing to rely on the author's continued guidance. This does not seem to be just part of the writer's rhetorical strategy but is integral to the thought of the letter. It is, however, qualified at points: a day of judgment still appears to be in the future even if it should inspire no fear (4:17); moreover, future transformation is expected when "he is revealed" and "we shall see him as he is," whether the one appearing is God or Jesus (2:28–3:2). Yet this produces no hiatus between present and future, nor does it diminish the confidence that the present already ensures.

A more substantial tension emerges over the question of sin.[19] The logic of 1 John's position could be that just as believers no longer belong to the sphere

---

19. On what follows see commentary on 3:6–10; 5:16–17.

of death (3:14), so also they no longer belong to the sphere of sin. There is a self-evident logic about the assertion that the one who has been born of God does not sin (3:9), for the inability to sin (and not just the ability not to sin) must surely be an inalienable part of God's being and of God's genetic donation to divine offspring. Yet without so modifying the meaning of sin or the completeness of birth from God as to empty them of serious value, the logic neither matches actual experience nor provides a means of addressing such experience. It seems likely that the acknowledgment of sin was part of the (liturgical) practice of those to whom the letter is written (1:9–10), so that the denial of sin would also undermine a key element of their common life and of the exercise of their relationship with God. This is one of the points where the sequence of the letter is important; the author opens by reaffirming the reality of the experience of sin, but not as something merely to be accepted, with regret, as part of life. Sin is to be acknowledged, for to acknowledge it is once again to acknowledge the primacy of God's action. Yet this does not lead him subsequently to waver in the assertion that those who do sin show their origin to be not God but, the only alternative in his dualist worldview, the devil (3:8). The contradiction is not to be resolved by suggesting that believers inconsistently or incompletely belong to the sphere of God, for birth cannot be incomplete; the contradiction is certainly there but it cannot be due to any inadequacy in God's transforming act or in the certain opposition between light and darkness so much as in the actualities of human, even believers', existence. The author does not explain this dilemma, and his subsequent distinction between sin that is irrevocably death-bound and sin that is not (5:16–17) does nothing to resolve it. From his understanding of God and of what God has done it must be equally true that "if anyone does sin, we have an advocate before the Father, Jesus Christ, the just one" (2:1), and that "everyone born from God does not sin, but the one who was born" or "begotten from God [i.e., God's Son] protects them" (5:18; see commentary). Any incompatibility between these truths points to the perplexities of the present that he is not concerned to, and perhaps would have found it difficult to, explain.

Of itself a dualist scheme could be timeless, fixed in the nature of God and in the belief in a system of opposition to God; this is hinted at by the assertion that "the devil sinned from the beginning" (3:8). If this dualism were not to so continue its resolution would have to depend on the ultimate victory of one or the other side, usually postponed to the future.[20] For 1 John the decisive moment of resolution has taken place already even if there is a future revelation yet to come. The author describes this resolution in what might be called mythic terms, the defeat of the devil's achievements by the Son of God (3:8).

---

20. Thus the Dead Sea Scrolls reserve the resolution for the future, "for the sons of light will be brilliant and all the sons of darkness will be dark . . . the sons of light will go to the light . . . and all the sons of darkness will go to the shades, to death" (4Q548 *Visions of Amram* 1, 9–13).

How and where this defeat took place is not described, and it is only implicit that birth from God could only really be a possibility after it. However, this defeat is not just a story, nor is it restricted to a spiritual world, but it was achieved in the sphere of human experience in the person of Jesus Christ. Hence, while the author wants his believers to experience life through the Son of God (5:12–13), he is even more insistent that Jesus must be acknowledged as this Son (5:5) and, apparently, that as such he entered the sphere of human existence ("flesh") that believers share (4:2). It is possible that "Son of God" was originally the title of a figure, perhaps a messianic figure, who would win victory over the forces opposed to God, and was drawn from earlier patterns of Jewish belief, as is suggested by a text among the Dead Sea Scrolls (4Q246). However, there is no appeal to the fulfillment of expected models here, and the story of God, the devil, and the victorious Son of God was more probably a self-contained one, already shaped by interpretations of Jesus' achievement. Therefore the call to acknowledge Jesus as the Christ or the Son of God does not mean to identify him with a figure from a more widespread expectation; both "Christ" and "Son of God" have already been transformed from any earlier meaning to carry resonances distinctive to this specific understanding of Jesus' advent.

So also, again contrary to what might be deduced from a simple dualist pattern, any relationship with God demands acknowledgment of the Son; there is no relationship with God apart from and independent of the Son. It is on this basis that God is called Father: father implies son, and son father (2:23). Yet while 1 John is clear that some roles are distinctive to God, such as the begetting both of believers and of the "one begotten," and others are distinctive to Jesus, frequently the distinction between them is of no interest; repeatedly an ambiguous "he" or "him" will fail to specify whether God or the Son is in view (see 2:4, 27–28). This need not reflect a high Christology whereby the Son is being identified with God, although at one point 1 John comes close to suggesting this (5:20); elsewhere there is a clear distinction in place and role between them (2:1). Rather, a relationship with God is necessarily a relationship with the Son, and vice versa; one cannot be understood apart from the other. However, 1 John understands "Son of God" only in relationship to the specific story of Jesus, and not as part of the eternal being of God.

Beyond this, and the determination to identify Jesus with the Son, the author has little interest in Jesus; although Jesus is seen as the means of dealing with sin, there is no consistent way of expressing this, nor is there any certain emphasis on the death of Jesus, still less any reference to his resurrection. Jesus' human experience as something shared with believers does appear to be important (2:6; 4:2), but it is not possible to determine what further knowledge of Jesus traditions the author presupposes.

Alongside the proper acknowledgment of Jesus as Son of God or as Christ, a second key theme is the relationship of those who share this belief with one another. Belonging to the light binds one to those who belong to the same sphere; yet also being the recipients of God's free act commits one to imitation toward those who are equally dependent on it. For 1 John this can be articulated through loving: love is at once God's action toward believers, and their response to God as well as to those who are also the objects of God's love. 1 John draws on two earlier traditions to explore this: one is also found in the Fourth Gospel as Jesus' (new) command to "love one another" (3:11; cf. John 13:34; 15:12); the other, not found in the Fourth Gospel, is the identification of the one who loves a brother (or sister, 2:10; see below).[21] The logic of his position demands that the other or brother loved is a fellow believer, not anyone outside; because the author does little to specify what such love might mean in practice (but see 3:17–18), it would be easy to conclude that by love he means the maintenance of the bonds of unity within and around the community, perhaps in contrast to those who had split it. In practice this may be the effect, but love for him is more dynamic than this, because it is rooted in his understanding of the priority of God's act in sending the Son, which has so dramatically reshaped the dualist world. Love is, therefore, the mark of those who have been born into this new sphere of existence; 1 John would not be able to suppose that the schismatics loved one another, still less that "the world" did.

Although 1 John moves within a dualist worldview, it is a profoundly Jewish one; in many ways, like other early Christian literature, this is an apocalyptic interpretation of history and experience. The denigration of "the (or this) world" owes something to the contrast in apocalyptic thought with "the world (or age) to come," although that concept is not used in the Johannine literature (see commentary on 2:15–17); the world, like the darkness, is passing away, to be overtaken by the light (2:8, 17). This is not a process of natural transition: 1 John's favorite term for the eruption into the world of the Son of God is the verb *phaneroō*, to "reveal" or "manifest"; it refers to the past but also to the anticipated future revelation (2:28; 3:2, 5, 8). The emergence of the antichrists is a spurious imitative manifestation (2:19), and, although probably experienced in terms of human schism and conflict, they are described in all the language of the eschatological dénouement (2:18–21; 4:1–3; cf. 2 John 8). Such ideas give urgency to the author's message; here victory over the world is not a private or spiritual conquest but participates in the once-for-all moment that will allow for no latecomers. Human effort will not secure this victory, and, typically, there is little if any concern for the rest of society; inasmuch as they belong to the world they are congenitally deaf to any alternative (4:5). Those who believe are in a sense out of place and out of time, already belonging to the sphere of life and bound to exhibit its characteristics; it is this disjunction in their location that, as has been seen, gives rise to the perplexities over sin.

21. See further commentary on 3:11.

Like the apocalyptic worldview, the stage is peopled not only by its human actors; the archopponent is not only the antichrist but also the devil, less easily reduced to a human manifestation. Beyond this, however, the author shows little interest in any heavenly sphere. His expectation of future transformation, to be "like him because we shall see him as he is" (3:2), betrays some echoes of Jewish mystical texts, which were themselves fully compatible with a heightened apocalyptic expectation, as witnessed by the *Songs of the Sabbath Sacrifice* among the Dead Sea Scrolls.[22] Yet this is not developed, and it is not even certain whether it is God or Jesus who will be manifested, still less where that will take place and what else will accompany or follow it.

The two smaller letters do not substantially challenge this outlook, but neither do they add much to it. Although the failed confession of 2 John 7 can and has been taken as referring to Jesus' future coming "in flesh," this is unlikely. Third John suggests a more positive approach to missionary activity among "the Gentiles" (3 John 7), but there is no indication whether this resulted in or from a changed perception of the latter's role in the order of things. Second and 3 John are more concerned with practical responses to actual or anticipated events, and to the extent that they draw from theological positions they do so to achieve a desired end. Since this is in part a function of their brevity it cannot be used to detect a loss of theological creativity within the tradition as a whole.

### 3.4 Background

In the past the Johannine Letters were sometimes judged to be more Hellenistic than the Gospel. This was partly because of the absence of explicit scriptural quotations other than the reference to Cain and Abel, and because of the absence of "the Jews" as opponents, as they are in the Fourth Gospel. Concepts such as "the anointing" (2:20, 27) and perhaps "seed" (3:9) could also be seen as more "Greek," and where the schismatics were identified with the position of Cerinthus as portrayed by Irenaeus or with that of Ignatius's Docetists (see above, §2.2), it was supposed that the problem was generated by a "Greek" antipathy to the body especially as the medium of divine revelation. More generally, 1 John has in the past been taken as evidence of the church's battle against Gnosticism, itself understood as a Hellenistic or Greek phenomenon. Almost every element in such a position has been effectively challenged. Even if Gnosticism were in view, it has been shown to be as much a Jewish phenomenon as it is Greek; however, this is probably irrelevant since there is nothing to align any supposed opponents of 1 John with a given "gnostic" position.

---

22. See P. Alexander, *The Mystical Texts: Songs of the Sabbath Sacrifice and Related Manuscripts* (Companion to the Qumran Scrolls 7; Library of Second Temple Studies 61; London: T & T Clark, 2006), and n. 64 below on 1 John 3:2–3.

Conversely, 1 John itself certainly values knowledge of God, and its dualist determinism, by which some are "of God," can be compared with texts from a more certainly "gnostic" environment (see commentary on 2:3), but these values are equally characteristic of other Jewish texts of the period and reflect something of the general zeitgeist. Moreover, scriptural allusions are far from absent (see above), although 1 John's engagement with Scripture may be more with traditions of its interpretation and reworking than directly with the text.

Two bodies of texts provide particularly close parallels to the thought of 1 John (other than the broader Johannine tradition). The first of these is the Dead Sea Scrolls, including but not restricted to the *Rule of the Community* (1QS).[23] One passage, which describes the two spirits that govern human behavior, has even sometimes been cited as a literary source for 1 John and as evidence for the author's original environment (1QS III, 13–IV, 7; see commentary on 1 John 1:5; 4:6). This is both unlikely and unnecessary, but it is noteworthy that both writings may well stem from relatively closed communities with a strong sense of their calling by God and of living in the final times, and (less certainly in the case of 1 John) with well-defined procedures for membership and also for exclusion. Thus the Scrolls have provided a useful model for examining the sociological function as well as the theological shape of the language of the Johannine tradition, including 1 John. In the commentary I will also trace numerous parallels between 1 John and *The Testaments of the Twelve Patriarchs*. The choice between two ways, the call to love a brother/sister or one another and to observe God's commands, the power of the prince of darkness to make eyes blind, and even the warning against idols are common to both writings. While the *Community Rule* parallels the probable communal destination of 1 John, the format of the *Testaments*, a (deathbed) exhortation by the aged patriarch to his children, shares some of its style and ethos.

Interpreting these parallels is made difficult by uncertainty regarding the origins of the *Testaments*: although often classified as evidence of Hellenistic Judaism, they survive only through Christian transmission. Whereas some would argue for the possibility of removing the obvious layers of Christian redaction in order to expose the "Jewish" core, others would conclude that to attempt this presupposes a clear distinction between "Christian" and "Jewish" that is both anachronistic and inappropriate for these writings.[24] Dependent on this debate is any decision as to the date of the supposed earliest form of the *Testaments*; in their present form they certainly postdate 1 John, but it is not unreasonable to suggest that they contain traditions that are at least contemporary with it.

---

23. Cf. also the dualist language cited in n. 20 above.

24. On this general problem see James R. Davila, *The Provenance of the Pseudepigrapha: Jewish, Christian, or Other?* (JSJSup 105; Leiden: Brill, 2005).

In fact, 1 John presents a problem that is not so different from that of the *Testaments*. Certainly 1 John is a "Christian" text in the sense that the place of Jesus Christ is central in its argument; yet the explicit references to Jesus are unevenly scattered through the letter and in places do not systematically affect its thought. It is not difficult to extract from the letter passages that are coherent in their own right without explicit reference to the role of Jesus (2:3–5; 3:9–10), and also passages where a christological reference may read like an uncomfortable expansion (e.g., 1:7). Indeed, one proposal has been to reconstruct a core "Jewish" substratum separate from supposedly subsequent "Christian" editing; according to this theory the debate is over Jesus as Messiah, and the "schism" of 2:18–19 is between those who have maintained and those who have reneged on that confession.[25] This, so I will argue, does not provide a persuasive reading of the letter as a whole, but it does demonstrate that the relationship between "Jewish" and "Christian" should not be seen as antithetical and mutually exclusive; the integration of Jesus into the understanding of God and God's activity did not always have the transformative effect that it does in Paul. This does not mean that 1 John should be labeled "Jewish Christian," a label whose imprecision renders it of little use; neither is it certain whether the readers were Jewish-born or Gentile, or a mix of both.[26] None of the dilemmas that mark the relationship between Gentile and Jewish believers, and their relationship with God's past promises, in the Pauline letters is evident in 1 John. First John can be said to reflect a pattern of thought that is Jewish in ethos even if it does not address the issues that were to fracture relations between those Jews who believed in Jesus and those who did not, yet our knowledge of early Christian groups is too limited to determine how to interpret this.

### 4. The Reception of the Letters and Their Importance in Recent Study

*4.1 Reception and Text*

As already explained, the earliest publication and circulation of the Johannine Letters is hidden from us, although it would seem likely that among the circles most closely associated with them they were linked together from an early date, perhaps together with the Gospel and even the Apocalypse. For these circles 3 John, and possibly also 2 John, may have had a particular place in recalling their origins. As significant texts were shared more widely among Christian groups, such private associations were less important; the identity of the authors, never exploited within the Johannine circles, was forgotten, and other factors determined their usefulness and hence their copying and further circulation. The

---

25. So J. C. O'Neill, *The Puzzle of 1 John: A New Examination of Origins* (London: SPCK, 1966).
26. This is equally difficult in the case of the Fourth Gospel.

result was that there is no single pattern of the reception of the Johannine Letters, although, because of the brevity of 2 and 3 John, any account is bound to be tentative.[27]

As already noted, the earliest explicit reference to any of the Johannine letters is made by Irenaeus, who quotes both 1 and 2 John, although as if both were from the same letter, and who unhesitatingly attributes them to the author of the Fourth Gospel, whom he identifies with the Beloved Disciple and with John the son of Zebedee. That Papias explicitly quoted the letter is doubtful; further, Polycarp's warning, "Everyone who does not acknowledge that Jesus Christ has come in flesh is an antichrist and whoever does not acknowledge the testimony of the cross is of the devil," certainly sounds Johannine; but whether it is a direct allusion to 1 John 4:2 or stems from a shared tradition may be debated (*Phil.* 7.1).[28] From this point, however, three major different patterns in the knowledge of and authority attributed to the Johannine Epistles may be traced.

1. Like Irenaeus some authors cite both 1 and 2 John but betray no knowledge of a third letter. Particularly striking is the commentary of Clement of Alexandria surviving only in Latin on 1 Peter, Jude, 1 and 2 John (the *Hypotypōseis* [Latin: *Adumbrationes*]). Clement's description of 2 John as written "to the virgins" must be related to the curious tradition in Augustine and later writers that 1 John was "to the Parthians," and this also suggests that the two letters were transmitted in close association.[29] Here the apparent absence of any trace of a commentary by Clement on 3 John is telling, while in other cases silence as to 3 John's existence can only be ambiguous. However, knowledge of 2 John is supplied by the citation of verse 10 at the Council of Carthage in 256 C.E. in support of demanding the rebaptism of heretics, even though Cyprian, writing at the same time, displays knowledge only of 1 Peter and 1 John among the Catholic Epistles. Possibly reflecting the same position is the Muratorian Canon, which, after rejecting the fictional letters of Paul to the Laodiceans and to the Alexandrians, continues, "the letter of Jude and two with the title 'of John' [*or* two of the John mentioned above] are held in the catholic [? church]" (11a, 6–7). Only surviving in Latin, this text conventionally has been traced to a Greek original of the second century, more or less contempo-

---

27. On what follows see Lieu, *Second and Third Epistles*, 5–36.

28. Polycarp uses the perfect infinitive, appropriately translated "that . . ."; see commentary on 1 John 4:2.

29. The Latin *virgines* implies a Greek *parthenous*; the pseudo-Augustinian *Speculum* describes 2 John as "To the *partos*" or "*partes* (parts)" or "*pastores* (shepherds)," the variants indicating that the sense had been lost. Cassiodorus (early sixth century), the Latin translator of Clement's expositions, reports them as covering 1 Peter, 1 and 2 John, and (mistakenly) James; although Eusebius describes Clement as including "the disputed writings, namely Jude and the other Catholic Epistles, Barnabas and the Apocalypse of Peter" (*Ecclesiastical History* 6.14.1), there is no trace of his knowledge of 3 John.

rary with Irenaeus and Clement. A good case can, however, be made for its origin in the fourth century, a period when such listing seems to have become popular; in this setting an original wording and intention, "two . . . are held with the catholic one," a reference back to a citation from 1 John in an earlier comment on the Gospel (10a, 26–30), cannot be excluded.[30] Even so, the isolation of 3 John from 1 and 2 John does appear to be confirmed by the textual history of the Latin translation and by commentators dependent on it: to the extent that it is possible to trace a development in the choice of translation equivalents, 3 John lags behind 2 John.[31] It would seem that there were circles and settings where 1 and 2 John might be copied and expounded without reference to a third letter by the "same" author.

2. At the same time a number of authors are familiar with 1 John, often alongside 1 Peter and sometimes James as well,[32] but appear unaware of either of the two smaller letters, a position represented by Cyprian (see above) and before him by Tertullian. This became the normative pattern among Syriac churches; 2 Peter, 2 and 3 John, and Jude were translated into Syriac only in the sixth-century Philoxenian version used among non-Chalcedonians, and rarely attracted attention. In fact, the earliest form of the Syriac canon did not include any of the Catholic Epistles, and there continued to be authors who avoided citing them or who judged even 1 Peter and 1 John, translated with James in the third-century Peshitto, to be inferior.

3. As 2 and 3 John were circulated with the First Epistle, many continued to question both their authorship and whether they should be "received"—a fate they shared with 2 Peter, to a lesser extent with Jude despite its early attestation, and even with James. Indeed, it is in this context that the first explicit reference to 3 John appears, when Origen, according to Eusebius, followed a reference to John, the author of Gospel, Apocalypse, and Letter, with: "there may also be a second and third but not all say they are genuine" (*Ecclesiastical History* 6.25.9–10; see above, §1.1). Eusebius continues this position by including 1 John among the recognized books and 2 and 3 John among those that have been disputed but are "known to most" (*Ecclesiastical History* 3.24.17–25.7). The tradition, going back to Papias, of "another John" identified as "the Elder" (see commentary on 2 John 1) proved useful in providing another candidate for the authorship of these two disputed letters (e.g., Jerome, *On Illustrious Men* 18). This, however, is clearly a second-level explanation seeking to harmonize the doubts held by some with the alternative association with the apostle: the first person to exploit the Papias tradition, Dionysius of Alexandria

---

30. Emendation to "among the catholic ones" is less persuasive.

31. For details see Lieu, *Second and Third Epistles*, 23–27.

32. The varying attestation and fortunes of James cannot be discussed here; while both Cyprian and Tertullian are silent about James the latter does know Jude.

in the mid-third-century, did so to justify distinguishing the author of the Apocalypse from the apostle who wrote the Gospel and Letter, and even the "second and third letters that are in circulation," and it was he who also first appealed to a tradition of two memorials "of John" in Ephesus (Eusebius, *Ecclesiastical History* 7.25.7–27). This hesitation and the proposed solution continue to be repeated even by those who accept the "general consensus of the church that the apostle John also wrote these letters" (Bede, *On 1, 2, 3 John*);[33] it was revived again at the time of the Reformation and again in recent times, but without any additional evidence.

Exactly how these different patterns were expressed in material form—in copies, reading, argument, and familiarity—is impossible to determine. The formal setting out of a canon and of whole Bibles in a single collection was a largely post-fourth-century phenomenon, and the collection of the seven Catholic Epistles was part of this process. Presumably it involved a degree of sharing of resources, and demanded some retrospective justification to explain the varying positions inherited from the past. Actual memory of the origins of any of these writings had been lost probably from the moment they began to circulate beyond their point of first production and reception. The complex history of the Johannine Epistles is not surprising, and the survival of the two shorter ones in the face of their limited utility may be the strongest argument for their significance at that earliest point; perhaps 3 John, most readily ignored, preserves most succinctly a pivotal moment for the tradition as a whole.

### 4.2 The Importance of the Letters

In the early period 1 John's style and memorable phrasing made it valuable in commentary and theological reflection, while 2 John is cited mainly for its rejection of hospitality, readily reapplied to a variety of schismatics and heretics.[34] In recent scholarship the letters have been studied chiefly as providing a window onto a specific corner of early Christianity. What earlier in this introduction has been identified as "Johannine tradition" is often understood as maintained, developed, and handed on within a "Johannine school," whether represented by the characteristic "we" of John 21:24 and similar passages or

---

33. For example, in the fourth-century Cheltenham List (Canon Mommseniensis), three epistles of John and two of Peter are listed, in each case followed by the word "one only," perhaps the protest of a scribe; alternatively the reference may be to James and to Jude, not otherwise listed, although this does not explain the "only." Similarly the Decree of Damasus (or Gelasius) (382 C.E.) lists "Of John the apostle one letter, of another John the elder two letters."

34. See Lieu, *Second and Third Epistles*, 32–34; Optatus refutes the Donatists' use of it against catholic Christians (*Against the Donatists* 4.5); Augustine rejected its earlier use to forbid rebaptism of schismatics (*On Baptism* 7.89); it is cited against the Arians by Alexander of Alexandria, *Letter* 2.6; Ambrose, *Letter* 11.4; cf. also Amrosiaster, *Comm. on Rom.* 169C.

belonging to a wider group. While "school" puts the emphasis on the initiators of the tradition and literature, "the Johannine community" is used to encompass the audience who presumably were equally at home with its distinctive language and thought. Second and 3 John give some support to such an idea with their assumption of different communities in close contact with each other and arguably seeing themselves as part of a larger unit. Against this background the schism implied by 1 John 2:18–19 has been understood as an event within the recent history of this community, while other stages have been detected in the Gospel—for example, in the desertion of some of the disciples in John 6:60, 66, or in the experiences of the man born blind in John 9, both being interpreted as mirroring events familiar to readers of the text.[35] A consequence of this narrower focus on a particular community or network of communities is that the doctrinal disputes implied by the texts have been interpreted in local terms and not in relation to more widespread or well-known conflicts from the early church (see above). In addition, as already discussed, 3 John has been used to cast light on the evolution of patterns of ministry in early Christianity, and the polarized positions evidenced by it and by 2 John have offered food for reflection in relation both to the theological and the ecclesiological tendencies of Johannine thought, and to contemporary church patterns.

However, such an exercise of reconstructing a situation for the letters and then interpreting them in its light involves a degree of circularity that may prove sterile. In the commentary I argue that the letters are best understood as far as possible in their own terms with minimal reference to any proposed setting. First John offers a fascinating insight into the shaping of a self-consciously distinctive interpretation of life. While acknowledging that readers will find themselves in a minority, powerless in the face of the forces and attitudes subsumed under "the world," the letter weaves into a coherent whole a transformed worldview, shaped by a conviction of the victory won by God through God's Son in a battle that is to be recognized as waged against even the devil. As explored above, readers are invited to discover themselves as members of an "imagined community," the beneficiaries of this victory that has yet to be acknowledged by those outside; yet they are also shown how easy it would be to stray outside, misjudging the inescapable expectations demanded of members. Hints of opposition and of alternative stances serve more to reinforce allegiance than to allude to identifiable opponents or situations. While it is likely that there was a specific setting out of which 1 John was written, the absence of any particular identification means that 1 John does not have first to be precisely contextualized

---

35. See R. E. Brown, *The Community of the Beloved Disciple* (New York: Paulist Press, 1979); a different "history" is proposed by M. Hengel, *Die johanneische Frage: Ein Lösungsversuch* with "Beitrag zur Apokalypse" by Jörg Frey (WUNT 67, Tübingen: Mohr, 1993); see also idem, *The Johannine Question* (trans. John Bowden; London: SCM, 1989).

in order to be decontextualized for subsequent readers as would be the case with most of the Pauline letters, which were explicitly sent to specific situations. Further, it is characteristic of 1 John that it is developed in such a way that readers have no real option to dissent; unlike the Pauline letters, which are open about Paul's struggles to persuade, there is never any suggestion that 1 John's audience might come to some other conclusion or behave in some other way—on the contrary, they are repeatedly confirmed in a sense of security. Contemporary readers may not feel so constrained, and are able to reflect on the strengths but also on the weaknesses of 1 John's sharply dualistic worldview. The challenges this offers are not unique to 1 John: the conviction that God has acted decisively within a world in which the opposition to God extends from the human into the suprahuman sphere, and the confidence that those who respond already share the benefits of God's victory, are integral to Christian thought and have provoked different theological responses over the centuries.

Just as since their earliest circulation, the place of 2 and 3 John within the canon of the New Testament may continue to perplex readers. Some have seen in them a salutary reminder of the infighting and retreat into slogans that have so frequently afflicted Christian communities. Perhaps more positively, 2 John's exclusionary tactics invite, if not imitation, then reasoned reflection as to whether, where, and why they may have ever been justified. Although the letter does not articulate a theology of the church, it may, within a Johannine trajectory, presuppose one—namely one that is more ready to preserve controlled boundaries than to risk the hazards of openness to new challenges. If 3 John belongs either at the start or at a pivotal point in the evolution of the Johannine tradition, then it serves to underline in a very particular, if opaque, setting an enigma that lies at the heart of the theology of the Fourth Gospel, a Gospel that demands that its testimony to the truth of Jesus Christ has to be accepted on its own terms and not because of any external source of authority.

## 5. Translation and Language

The "family likeness" of the Johannine literature extends to its vocabulary, its style, and its distinctive figures of speech. This poses particular challenges for the translator: are the striking images to be rendered literally or in a form more immediately meaningful? For example, 1 John 1:5–7 sets out the possibility of people "walking in the light" or "in the darkness." Such language has biblical precedent but is also immediately evocative, particularly in a world without artificial light sources (see commentary); at the same time, the verb "to walk" was used in Jewish as well as Greek thought of "living." So would it be better to translate "live in the light" (so J. B. Phillips), expressing the sense but losing one aspect of the metaphor while retaining another—since evidently literal light or darkness is not in mind? Yet this may lose some of the effect of the picture in 2:11 of the one who walks in darkness not knowing where he (or she) is going, and of the possibility of stumbling in the previous verse. It is notable that in John 11:9 Phillips feels bound to retain "*walking* in the day" or "night" since here "living" would undermine the vivid image. Second and 3 John, however, offer a variant figure, "walking in (the) truth" (see commentary on 2 John 4); the effect is different, since while it is possible literally to walk where there is light or darkness, "truth" is an abstract noun. Phillips here renders "living the life of truth," a fair translation but one that may lose the subtle contrast with the person who "goes ahead and does not remain in the teaching" in 2 John 9.

A more difficult problem is posed by the term used for fellow believers or members of the community, *adelphos*, in the masculine form, "brother" (1 John 2:10; 3:13; etc.). This is a common term in the New Testament, and in recognition that early Christian communities had both female and male members it is often now translated "brothers and sisters" (see NRSV in 1 Cor 4:6) but sometimes as "believers" (NRSV in 1 Cor 6:5–6, 8; 8:11).[36] While this may make the text more accessible to contemporary readers, it may also obscure the mindset of the earliest authors, who probably took for granted that priority of the masculine address. This is a particular problem in 1 John, which models the pattern of *brotherly* love or hatred against the behavior of Cain, who slew his *brother* Abel (3:12)—murder of a sister might not have carried quite the same feel in the ancient world.[37] When the author addresses his readers under three categories in 2:12–14, the NRSV is surely right to retain "fathers" but is probably misjudged in following with "young people," which in a contemporary situation may provoke images of enthusiastic nights out. The associated image of strength and of victory over the evil one is apposite for the young male (*neaniskos*) but not for his coeval "sister." Although it is unlikely that 1 John is addressed to an all-male community, such a reading would not be impossible.[38]

The translation offered in this commentary is deliberately conservative. The singular (and plural in 3:14, 16; 3 John 3, 5) "brother" is retained because this does seem to reflect the author's frame of reference, while acknowledging that

36. In Greek "sister" uses the same root with a feminine ending; the English term "sibling" does not have the sort of currency that would make it usable in translation. The NRSV footnotes "Gk *brother*" in each case.

37. The NRSV consistently translates "brother(s) or sister(s)" except at 2:11, "another believer"; surprisingly at 3:14 "love the *brothers*" is translated "love one another," perhaps an oversight. Another consequence is that the plural is introduced where the Greek uses the singular, e.g., 3:13. At 3 John 3, 5 the NRSV translates "friends" and so does not mark the difference from the term used in v. 15 (and obscures the relationship with John 21:23, where it translates "the community").

38. The parallels with the *Testaments of the Twelve Patriarchs* might also encourage the model of a senior male figure addressing his male successors or protégés. An all-male audience is suggested by J. C. O'Neill, "New Testament Monasteries," in *Common Life in the Early Church: Essays Honoring Graydon F. Snyder* (ed. Julian V. Hills; Harrisburg: Trinity Press International, 1998), 118–32.

this may be more suitable to a commentary than it would be for public reading, and that it does pose very sharply the question of just how inclusive the mind-set of the letters is. The same question is raised by 1 John's characteristic "the one who" (e.g., 2:4–6, 9–11) and "if anyone" (e.g., 4:20); although not gender-specific in principle, in grammatical form such sentences are exclusively masculine. To translate with a gender-neutral plural "they" would obscure the deliberate focus on the individual's response; to translate with an alternative "she" may credit the author with a more inclusive vision than he had. Hence, while acknowledging the difficulty posed for many readers, the masculine has been retained where unavoidable.[39] Similarly, the figures of speech have been translated relatively literally in order to be able to capture some of the associations they would carry. Again this may be more readily justified for a commentary.

A further characteristic of 1 John is its use of the pronoun "he" (*autos*) where the reference may be to God or to Jesus/the Son (e.g., 1 John 2:3); whether this has conscious theological implications is debatable and will be discussed in the commentary, but it would be a misrepresentation to obscure it, for example by identifying the referent and so avoiding the masculine.

Finally, the anonymity of 1 John demands a decision as to how its author or its intentions as well as its recipients are to be described. In the commentary I will use the term "the author" and occasionally "1 John," and also "the readers," without prejudice as to the identity of any of these or whether many initially heard rather than read the text for themselves.

---

39. An indefinite "the one," "whoever" followed by "they," "their," "them" representing an inclusive third person singular is now being adopted in some translations.

# COMMENTARY

# 1 JOHN

## 1 John 1:1–4—The Prologue

Beginnings of documents are important, for they alert the reader to what to expect from all that follows. In some types of texts the author(s) and/or the intended reader(s) are hidden, giving subsequent readers the feeling of unmediated access to their meaning.[1] In others the author(s) and/or reader(s) take center stage, and where both are present the relationship between them shapes all that follows; in such cases subsequent readers may feel themselves to be observers of how this relationship is played out, or they may find themselves invited into it. The opening of 1 John emphatically belongs to the second of these main types: "we" address "you," explicitly seeking to enrich the relationship thus established. In that sense 1 John is evidently not an essay or a narrative, but closer to a letter. Yet ancient letters for over a millennium followed a remarkably stable pattern, opening with a formal salutation in the third person, often followed by a word of greeting: "X to Y (greeting)." Other New Testament letters follow a pattern apparently established by Paul with a distinctive offer of the divinely given grace and peace (e.g., 1 Cor 1:3).[2] First John does not do either of these, and, in contrast to what might be expected in a letter, neither the author(s) nor the readers are further identified, for example by their names or location. Moreover, although from 1:4 onward there is a repeated emphasis on this as a written document (cf. 2:1, 7–8, 12–14, 21, 26; 5:13), these initial verses use the language of proclamation, which, while not inappropriate for a written communication, retains a sense of direct oral address. First John may for convenience be called a letter, but its opening alerts us to its distinctive strategy.

The opening of a letter usually not only identifies the author and addressees but also establishes the relationship between them, for example, whether there is a disparity in status. This can be done explicitly, such as in the way that Paul emphasizes his apostolic status (Gal 1:1), or implicitly in the language, for example in the way that different forms of the standard opening greeting were used in different social contexts. Although using neither of these techniques, these verses establish a clear distinction between "we" who initiate the relationship and "you" who receive. The vigor with which that is done in this opening salvo sets a tone that is not fully maintained in what follows, although it is

---

1. An example might be a novel. In the earliest period "hearers" might be substituted for "readers"; see above p. 5.

2. See further commentary on 2 John 1–3 and on 3 John 1 and the example cited there.

recalled at the end of the letter (5:13). Not only does the author after these verses write only in his own person, the first person singular, but he also repeatedly expresses confidence in the faith of those whom he addresses (see 2:20, 27). By contrast, here at the start they are invited to recognize themselves as those who have much to discover, dependent on those with the authority to guide them, but as the letter proceeds this opposition between "we" and "you" is progressively challenged.

The confident assertion of an incontrovertible authority to proclaim and persuade those addressed could suggest that these verses serve the function of the exordium or proemium in the construction of a spoken or written discourse, according to the rules of classical rhetoric: in this the subject of the discourse was set out and the credibility of the speaker established for the audience. Such rhetorical analysis has proved useful in the understanding of the argumentative structure of other New Testament writings. However, although 1 John does at times appear to use rhetorically effective strategies, the letter as a whole is not easily analyzed in these terms.

More generally, these opening verses are sometimes described as a prologue because they introduce what follows but are not themselves part of the argument. Calling them a prologue has sometimes invited a comparison with the prologue of the Fourth Gospel (John 1:1–18), which shares some of the same language with these verses and which is in some ways also disconnected from what follows. These commonalities of language are due to the fact that both the Gospel and 1 John draw on earlier ideas and formulations that had already begun to take a characteristic form within what can be called "the Johannine tradition," but they are applied in different ways.[3] This pattern of evoking and reworking familiar material will prove to be one of the notable characteristics of 1 John, and essential to its persuasive effectiveness. Moreover, the two "prologues" also have very different emphases and functions. One of these differences is precisely this focus here on the "we" whose experience gives them the authority to proclaim to "you," who, it is implied, have not had the same direct experience. What that experience is shall be discussed in detail in the commentary; although the language of seeing and hearing evokes the idea of immediate eye- or ear-witness, the object is not a person but an object ("that which . . . ," v. 1), or, more abstractly, "eternal life" (v. 2). The goal of this proclamation is fellowship between those who make it and the audience, a fellowship that is not merely a social community because it is also a fellowship with God and with God's Son, Jesus Christ. It is only with the last verse, verse 4, that what could have been understood as oral proclamation is identified as what is now being written; this verse may be treated as the conclusion of this prologue because by introducing the "writing" it prepares for the chapters to follow.

---

3. See Introduction §3.2.

## 1 John 1:1–3—Opening

Although the general theme of the first three verses can be easily described, their structure is difficult. Verse 2 does not seem to be tightly connected to verse 1 or to verse 3, which itself repeats some of the words of verse 1 as if resuming following a parenthesis. On a more detailed level, the final words of verse 1 are in their present context imprecise, while it is not clear whether the opening words, "That which was from the beginning," stand apart as a sort of heading. One reason for this lack of coherence appears to be that the author is alluding to and reworking earlier ideas and formulations; some of these were perhaps familiar to the first readers, while they may be equally familiar to later readers because they were also used in the prologue and elsewhere in the Gospel of John.

1:1 That which[a] was from the beginning, which we have heard, which we have seen with our eyes, which we beheld and our hands felt, concerning the word of life—2 and the life was revealed, and we have seen and we bear testimony and proclaim to you the eternal life, which was in the presence of the Father and was revealed to us—;[b] 3 that which we have seen and heard we proclaim to you also so that you too may have fellowship with us.[c] Indeed, our fellowship is with the Father and with his Son Jesus Christ.

a. One problem, discussed in the commentary, is the relationship of the four relative clauses in v. 1 to one another: although all begin with the relative pronoun "[that] which" (*ho*), the last three in v. 1 could either be parallel to the first or dependent on it.

b. Although the earliest Greek manuscripts did not have any such punctuation, the dashes around v. 2 (following NA[27] and most translations) indicate that this appears to be a self-contained sentence without any close link to its context other than the introductory "and." These problems of translation are inseparable from those of interpretation discussed below.

c. The structure of these opening verses is difficult to trace; although grammatically the sentence begun at v. 1 continues to the middle of v. 3, the semicolon in the translation at the end of v. 2 indicates that only at the beginning of v. 3 does the language begin to flow more naturally. This means that the opening clauses are left without a main verb, which is perhaps what it would feel like for those listening to it being read out loud.

[1] The opening words of the letter sound two notes that will echo on through the argument: the appeal to "the beginning" and more generally to that which is already assured, and the further appeal to "we" and to our experience, although the identity of that "we" will change as the letter progresses. While at this point the ability to relate to "the beginning" apparently characterizes the "we" whose voice is here heard, later the author will recall the readers to the "command *you* have had from the beginning" (2:7), and he will urge them to

let "what you have heard from the beginning" remain in them (2:24; cf. 3:11). In those passages it would seem that "the beginning" takes them back to the origins of their faith experience (see commentary), and in the present context the following "we have heard" and the identification of "the word" of life at the end of this verse similarly suggest something proclaimed. However, in 2:13–14 the author reassures those whom he calls "fathers" that they have known "the one from the beginning," while in 3:8 he describes the devil as sinning "from the beginning"; this might suggest an earlier, even a primordial, beginning. It is not surprising that some subsequent interpreters have seen a connection with the opening words of the prologue of the Fourth Gospel, "In the beginning was the word," and have concluded that here also the reference is to the time before creation. Yet the sustained use of the neuter "that which," repeated before each of the following verbs and resumed at the beginning of verse 3, creates an emphatic difference from the masculine both of 2:13–14 and of "the word" of John 1:1. This difference from the Gospel is highlighted by the curiously loose connection ("concerning") with "the word of life" at the end of the verse. For 1 John the opening appeal is not to a (preexistent) person but to some *thing* whose identity and significance is defined by its relationship with the beginning, i.e. its "ab-origin-ality."

Just how important this is for 1 John is indicated by its position as the opening words of the letter. Grammatically this takes the form of a relative clause ("That which . . ."), and within the structure of the opening sentence as a whole it must be the object of the main verb, which is postponed until verse 3 ("we proclaim to you"). Some English versions address this by repeating that verb at the beginning of verse 1 (cf. NRSV), but although this results in a more fluent translation, it loses the intended rhetorical focus on the continuity from the beginning. There is a further grammatical obscurity in this opening volley, namely the relationship of the four relative clauses ("that which"/"which") to one another. It would be possible to translate them in parallel with one another, "that which was from the beginning, that which we heard," and so forth, hence as a series of descriptors, all of equal significance; the whole sequence would then serve as the object of the main verb, "we proclaim" (postponed until v. 3), where the object is resumed by the middle two of the relative clauses, in reverse order, "what we have seen and heard." Translations that move the verb "we proclaim" to the front necessarily adopt this interpretation (see NRSV). In the translation given here, however, the opening clause takes a lead position, "That which [or "what"] was from the beginning"; it is then further qualified by three subordinate relative clauses as something "which" we have heard (and so forth). It is true that this makes the link with verse 3 less smooth—it would be expected that what we proclaimed there would be "that which was from the beginning"— but it seems to represent better the dramatic opening and its pervasive presence as a theme in the letter.

Although this repeated concern may be driven in part by disquiet about novelty (see 2:7–8), it particularly expresses a strong sense of the continuity that binds the readers of this letter to the tradition into which they have been brought, a sense that is not merely defensive. It is within this framework that the use of the first person plural "we" in these verses should be understood. Elsewhere the author represents himself—a masculine author is being assumed here—in the singular ("I"; cf. 2:1), and, as we shall see, the plural "we" more commonly binds author and readers together (e.g., 1:6). At this point, however, the "we" who have heard, seen, and proclaim (v. 3) are different from "you." Although much effort has sometimes gone into an attempt to identify the "we" as if the reference were to a specific group, this misunderstands the force of the opening verses. The intentional effect is to deflect attention away from the author as if he were speaking only on his own authority or of something that ultimately depends only on his experience and on his interpretation of it. Instead it creates a sense of corporate unity and of continuity reaching beyond the present situation and players; as the readers acknowledge the claims that "we" make they will also find themselves invited to make common cause and identify themselves with that "we" (see 4:4–6, 14; and commentary). Perhaps in the face of other challenges to their loyalty or of uncertainty about where they belong, readers who find themselves addressed embark on a reading journey that will disclose the way forward.

The language of sensory experience appears to have been readily used in Johannine circles to express believers' appropriation of the faith tradition, almost invariably in association with others, as members of those who claim "we. . . ." Thus the author will include the readers with him when he says, "We have seen and bear witness that the Father has sent the Son as savior of the world" (4:14), while the author of the Gospel probably reflects a similar convention in John 1:14 (see also John 3:11). Here giving first place to hearing before seeing effectively provides the framework within which all claims to see are to be placed, that of the obedient reception of the message and its further transmission; hence subsequently it is with having *heard* that "from the beginning" is associated (2:24; 3:11). Even so, the language remains surprisingly realistic, particularly the assertion that "we have seen with our eyes" and, even more so, "our hands felt," where the simple past tense (the aorist) could be taken to refer to a particular past event. If in such terminology the author is drawing on earlier traditions and language, two possible sources for his thought may be traced.

The first of these is suggested from later in the letter: 2:11 will speak of the darkness as having blinded the eyes of the one who hates a brother. That verse itself echoes a number of scriptural passages, including Isa 59:9–10 where the people complain that, although they wait for light, there is darkness and they walk in the gloom, and then continue, "We grope like the blind along a wall, groping like those who have no eyes" (see commentary on 2:11). The verb translated here as "grope," which is also used of the blind Isaac gropingly touching and "recognizing" Jacob-in-disguise as Esau (Gen 27:21–22), is the verb translated "felt" in 1 John 1:1 (*psēlaphaō*). This results in the irony that just as the language appears to become more assertively physical, so it becomes more insecure, open to misapprehension. First John contains repeated echoes of Second Isaiah, although because these are not explicit quotations it is rarely possible to determine how far they contribute to the author's argument or how far he was conscious of them. Second Isaiah, where the appeal to hearing and sight is frequently made, certainly helped shape the language and the imagery of the Johannine tradition, and is even more clearly influential in the Fourth Gospel. Another possible intertext might be Psalm 115 (= LXX 113:9–26) with its vivid mockery of the idols of the nations, who "have eyes and will not see, have ears and will not hear, have noses and will not smell, have hands and will not touch (*psēlaphaō*)"; those alert to this echo would find a satisfying *inclusio* with the intriguing closing exhortation of the letter, "Keep yourselves from idols" (5:21; see commentary). To turn to whatever might be represented by the idols would be to reject those who *have* seen, heard, and touched.

For modern readers, although not necessarily for the earliest ones, a more familiar echo would be the narratives of encounters with the risen Jesus. Luke describes how Jesus invited those who could not believe that it was he whom they saw, "Touch (*psēlaphaō*) me and see" (Luke 24:39). John's account is even more vivid, although the implication is probably that Thomas does not after all need to confirm the wounds in Jesus' hands and side before he believes (John 20:25–29), and John does not use the key verb of touch here. In the Fourth Gospel that incident is the culmination of a sustained attempt to wrestle with the significance of the actual direct experience of Jesus and of the inability of later generations literally to share it. The Gospel, which is presenting an account of Jesus, as it were making him visible, and is relying on traditions of his life, both affirms the testimony of having seen (John 20:18, 25) and relativizes it, knowing that sight alone does not create faith (20:29; cf. 2:23–25), and that there is a form of seeing that transcends mere physical sight (9:39–41). First John does not struggle with this dilemma, perhaps precisely because it does not intend to describe or even to appeal to specific traditions of Jesus' life and teaching (although see commentary on 2:6). If it is drawing on resurrection traditions—and the absence of any interest in resurrection elsewhere makes this entirely hypothetical—it takes the language of sensory experience, on which the proclamation of the message rests, and makes it its own, inviting readers to do likewise.

All this indicates that the assertion that "we have heard . . . we have seen" is not a claim to an eyewitness experience of the historical ministry of Jesus made by a group of the original disciples. It is not surprising that the words were subsequently read as such when the author was assumed to be John the apostle, also identified as the author of the Fourth Gospel, but this is an assumption that is neither required by the letter nor makes good sense of it. Nor are the words a claim to be embedded within a line of tradition that ultimately reaches back to the earliest witnesses, as some who surrender apostolic authorship have suggested.[4] In this last view the plural "we" is taken to acknowledge that membership of that tradition is intrinsically corporate and not individual. First John does not, however, base its argument on appeals to the precise detail and character of verifiable events; although the letter does evoke a sense of solidarity, its chief effort is to invite its readers to be attuned to the echoes and associations of the unequivocal authority of sensory experience, to test it, and to determine whether they will affirm it and, by affirming it, whether they will shape their own lives by the pattern of consequences that the rest of the letter will trace.

The final words of the verse reinforce this indeterminacy, and also the priority of hearing; it would make good sense to have heard, or even, anticipating verse 3, to proclaim, "concerning the word of life," but the prepositional phrase follows less naturally after the verbs of seeing or touching. Even so, the preposition "concerning" (*peri*) distances "the word" from any direct identification as that which has been heard, or even as that which was from the beginning. Later in the letter the actual relationship is made more precise, and "the word that you heard" is identified with "the command that you had from the beginning" (2:7). It is unlikely, however, that the "word" should be restricted to the "command"; elsewhere 1 John speaks of the indwelling word that is the word of God (1:10; 2:14). Here it is "the word *of* life," perhaps that which gives life, or contains life, or is about life: eternal life is the content of the promise and is the ultimate goal of this letter (2:25; 5:13). In practice "the word" (*ho logos*) may particularly denote or be embodied in the proclamation on which faith and obedience are founded, but as such it is not to be reduced to a matter of words: while 1 John does switch between the singular and plural of "command(s)," "word" is always found in the singular. The word carries the power and authenticity of the aboriginal proclamation and of what it makes known about God. Such an objectification, and even personification, of the word of God is widespread in the New Testament, and has roots in the prophetic and creative power of God's word in the Scriptures (Isa 55:11; Acts 6:7; 1 Cor 1:18; 14:36); it is, however, particularly characteristic of Johannine thought, reaching an apogee in the prologue of the Fourth Gospel, "In the beginning was the word . . . in him [or it] was life" (John 1:4). Once again, a shared tradition has been developed in strikingly different ways by Gospel and by Letter.

**[2]** The mention of "life" prompts a new thought, although one that grammatically is unrelated to verse 1, which will be resumed in verse 3; as in NA[27]

---

4. On the association with the apostle, see Introduction §§1.1 and 2.1; on the interpretation of "the elder" as a member of a tradition-bearing group see commentary on 2 John 1.

and many translations of the New Testament, verse 2 is best treated as a separate comment. It is not, however, entirely independent, for it also repeats the verb "we have seen" from verse 1, and anticipates both its repetition and the continuation "we proclaim" in verse 3. That which has been seen is "life"; this life in one sense is rooted in the past, for it "was revealed," the aorist tense of the verb suggesting a specific moment, not a general truth. At the same time this life belongs to the present, for the "we" who speak can give testimony to it and proclaim it to those they address. Indeed, because this life can be qualified as "eternal" it stands outside the restrictions of any temporal scheme. The juxtaposition of these different temporal perspectives is a startling one. For 1 John the verb "reveal" (*phaneroō*) signifies a decisive moment in the story of the Son of God or of God both in the past (using the same tense as here, 3:5, 8; 4:9), and in the future (2:28; 3:2), as well as in that of the community (2:19).[5] What is eternal, however, belongs specifically to God, untrammeled by the uncertainties of time and change (Isa 26:4; 55:3). "Eternal life" signifies the life that is in the presence of God; within Jewish future expectation, adopted by the early believers in Jesus, it belongs specifically to the age to come (Dan 12:2; 4 Macc 15:3; Luke 10:25; Gal 6:8), but in the Johannine tradition in particular it is already given in the present in response to believing, although it does not lose its essential reference to the future (John 3:15; 5:40; 17:2–3).

This juxtaposition of perspectives is reinforced as this eternal life is described as having been "in the presence (*pros*) of the Father"; elsewhere in 1 John God is "Father" specifically in relation to "his Son" (see 1:3 and commentary and the introduction §3.2). Yet, it is repeated, this same life was nonetheless revealed, this time with an emphatic "to us"—to those who not only saw but who now testify and proclaim. It would seem that the author wants both to appeal to the decisive intervention in human history in the coming of the Son of God and to interpret this not as the story of a person but as the opening up of a new form of existence that will transform those who accept the proclamation and who identify with what has been revealed, a new form of existence that will become the primary theme of the letter (5:13, 20). The inescapable resonances with the prologue of the Gospel of John give some indication of the sources of 1 John's thought. There it is the word (*logos*) that was "in the presence of *God*" (John 1:1). That image belongs to the tradition of the Wisdom of God (see Prov 8:22–31), where Wisdom comes close to being personified as God's agent in creation, redemption, and revelation; such ideas about Wisdom provided the author of the Fourth Gospel, or the traditions on which he drew, with a framework for understanding the word who was made flesh. The comparison serves to highlight 1 John's very different emphasis, and confirms that he is not simply appealing to the eyewitness experience of the historical Jesus.

---

5. See commentary on each of these passages for the nuances of reference.

The certainty of the past moment is a disclosure ("revealed") only as its true significance is acknowledged and becomes that to which testimony can be given and offered to others in the gift of life.

Although "proclaim" (*apangellō*) might suggest an oral proclamation, slightly at odds with the deliberately written text it introduces here, the emphasis of the verb gains more from its scriptural use for both the psalmist's and the prophets' declaration of what God has done or will do (e.g., Ps 71 [LXX 70]:17–18; Mic 3:8; Isa 57:12 [LXX]). Outside the Johannine tradition the root is less common in the New Testament than one might expect, but in the Fourth Gospel it expresses the task both of Jesus and of the spirit (John 16:25; cf. 4:25; 16:13–15 [*anangellō*]; also 20:18 [*angellō*]), and it is particularly indebted to the language of Second Isaiah.[6] That influence is even stronger in the combination of testifying and proclaiming: "Do not hide yourselves; have you not heard from the beginning and I have proclaimed to you? You are my witnesses whether there is any God but me" (Isa 44:8 LXX). The theme of testimony will be taken up again at the end of the letter (1 John 4:14; 5:6–11), no longer as the possession of a few but as available to all who believe. The authority of the letter is embedded not in the status of its author but in the fulfillment of the task to bear witness.

[3] It is this that determines the purpose of the prologue and, perhaps, of the letter: the movement from those who can claim the right to give testimony ("we") to those who will now hear it for themselves ("you"); the emphasis falls on the repeated verbs, not on the still imprecise "that which." As recipients of the proclamation, they ("you") *also* (twice emphasized) can be brought into that fellowship that the author, effacing himself, has so far signaled by "we." "Fellowship," *koinōnia*, will provide a lead into the first main section of the letter, where the author is quick to guard against abuses of its privileges (1:6, 7). This term does not have the scriptural resonances of the author's other language so far, but it is rich in associations in a broader early Christian and Jewish context. *Koinōnia* generally implies the equality of partners in some common enterprise or entity; it is a familiar term in political and commercial contexts (cf. Luke 5:10, where the personal noun is used). In Paul's Letters it and related words can express the new experiences of shared calling and vocation, for example between the Gentiles and the community of Jewish believers in Jerusalem, or between Paul and his congregations (Rom 12:12; 15:26–27; Phil 1:5; 4:15); but Paul also speaks of the "fellowship of the (Holy) Spirit" (2 Cor 13:13; Phil 2:1), where the thought may be either the common participation in God's gift of the Spirit, or that oneness which can only be created by the Spirit. For Paul there are very specific outworkings of *koinōnia*, although he did not always find them

---

6. More common in the LXX of Isaiah is the form *anangellō* (e.g., Isa. 41:22–28; cf. 1 John 1:5), but both this and *apangellō* represent the Hebrew root *ngd* (in the causative Hiphil).

exemplified in the churches to which he wrote, and it is this that has prompted the enthusiasm with which the concept has been taken up in contemporary ecumenical discussion. The exhortation of the *Didache*, "You shall not reject the needy, but you shall share in common everything with your brother [or sister], and you shall not say they are your own; for if you are common partners in what is immortal how much more so in mortal things?" (*Did.* 4.8), forms a bridge to the traditions of material communalism in the early church according to Acts (Acts 2:42–47 [note *koinōnia* in v. 42]; 4:32–35). Behind this may lie a more widespread practice in Jewish groups of the period: both Josephus and Philo describe how the Essenes hold their material possessions in common as a demonstration of their deeper commitment to one another (Josephus, *War* 2.122; Philo, *Hypothetica* 11.10–13), and the Dead Sea Scrolls detail the practicalities involved (1QS V, 1–5; VI, 17–23).

First John does not, however, share in this exploration of the idea of *koinōnia* or of its practical expression beyond the limited concerns in 1:6, 7, after which the term is not used again: he does not appeal to it in 3:17–18 when urging compassion to a fellow believer in need. Nonetheless, in this verse it is evident that it has both a horizontal ("with us") and a vertical ("with the Father") dimension; indeed, the main burden of what follows is that these two dimensions cannot be separated from each other. In the rest of the letter this will be demonstrated in terms of love and of "indwelling" or "abiding," ideas that the author develops much more richly.

The idea of fellowship between God and humans is not unknown in the ancient nonbiblical world: the philosopher Epictetus, at the end of the first century C.E., projects the ideal philosopher as someone who "in this poor dead body [would] think of his fellowship with Zeus" (*Diss.* 2.19.27), although he does not expect to be able to find such a person. However, many would have agreed with Josephus that "fellowship with what is mortal is unfitting for the divine" (*War* 7.344). Although written by a Jew, Josephus, and put in the mouth of the defender of Masada against the Romans, Eleazar, that sentiment reflects Greco-Roman ideas of the incompatibility between human corporeality and the nature of God. The biblical tradition does, of course, know of the deeply intimate relationship between God and God's people or particular individuals—for example, Hosea's use of marriage imagery, Psalm 139's confidence in God's continual presence, or the description in Exod 33:11 of God's converse with Moses "as a man speaks with a friend." These too are surely models of "fellowship," although 1 John's language will go beyond them and prompt the need to clarify how it, and especially that of mutual indwelling (e.g., 3:23), still maintains both the priority of God's action and the limitations inherent in being human.

At this point fellowship with God remains only implicitly on offer for the readers, potentially mediated through "us," whose experience it emphatically is. Although there is no verb in the final sentence of verse 3, it seems best to translate it as a statement, "our fellowship *is*," rather than as a wish, "may it be" (as in the Latin tradition).[7] A wish would have brought 1 John closer to other New Testament letter greetings: "may grace be with you and peace from God the Father and the Lord Jesus Christ" (1 Cor 1:3; although the verb is also not expressed here it is certainly to be understood, while in 1 Pet 1:2 it is explicit). However, the rest of the letter seeks to persuade the readers to make common allegiance with those whom the author represents as "us," and in the shadows lurks the possibility of alternative allegiances to be avoided; that call to association may be underlined by the unusual and repeated "fellowship *with* (*meta*)."[8] The emphasis here is to remind the readers that only by choosing the former can they have access to the life that has been revealed.

Just as that life was "in the presence of the Father," so is fellowship with "the Father" but also equally (marked by the repeated "with") with his Son Jesus Christ. There is no hint of polemic against alternative views here, but it will be an important theme in the latter part of this letter that God can be known as Father only in virtue of the confession of Jesus as God's Son (2:22–23); the term "son" is not used again between this verse and that passage, but from then on it will dominate the letter. God is Father specifically in relation to Jesus Christ as his Son, and only then perhaps potentially in relation to those who rightly believe (see 2:1, 14; 3:1); certainly 1 John does not think of God as father of all people in virtue of having created them. Taking this sentence as a statement, Jesus Christ, the Son, like the Father, belongs firmly to the sphere of present experience; the author gives no hint that he is to be identified with what was seen or heard from the beginning.

Although the task must be to interpret the text in its current form, the repetitions and breaks in coherence may suggest that the opening prologue of the letter has been expanded from an original core, possibly of traditional material. For example, the opening clauses of verses 1 and 3 would together give a neatly balanced affirmation: "That which was from the beginning, which we have heard, which we have seen—that which we have seen and heard we proclaim to you also"; this traces the movement from the origins of the proclamation, through the experience of the "we" who now speak, to its reception among this particular group. This core has then been developed at two significant points, but still using language that is recognizably "Johannine":

1. The initial affirmations of verse 1 have been expanded, by the qualification "with our eyes," by the redundant "we have beheld" (the verb also used at 4:14; cf. 2 below), and by the curious appeal to "our hands have touched," as well as by the awkward "concerning the word of life." It is the first three of these additions that both permit the detection of an allusion to a simple bald

---

7. Parts of the Old Latin tradition read, "may *your* fellowship be with the father. . . ."
8. More commonly the preposition "in" is used.

appeal to the physical life and death (and/or resurrection) of Jesus, and at the same time create a distance between what is being claimed and such an appeal. However, whether the addition of "concerning the word of life" in verse 1 prompted the further expansion in verse 2, or was itself prompted by that verse, is uncertain.

2. Verse 2 has been added, adopting language drawn from its context. It develops from the "we have seen" of verse 1 a new phrase, "we have seen and bear testimony." John 3:11 and 19:35 have similar wording, in both cases as if spoken by a voice that stands back from the narrative context. First John will not return to the language of testimony until 4:14, "We have beheld [cf. 1 above] and bear testimony," although in that context the "we" encompasses all believers. Similarly the two phrases "we proclaim to you" and "the Father" have been adopted from verse 3, even though their anticipation somewhat spoils their impact there, particularly as "the Father" now first appears independently of "the Son" who defines him as such. What verse 2 then does is, despite the past tenses, to point its readers to the real meaning not of a past event but of eternal life as a present and future assurance for all who believe; this too will form the closing affirmation of the letter (5:11, 13, 20).

It is only through this cumulative process toward the current form of 1:1–3 that what are often seen as echoes of the prologue of the Fourth Gospel emerge—the explicit use of "word" and "life" (John 1:1, 4); the phrase "in the presence of the [Father]" (also in 1 John 2:1; John 1:2); the verb "we beheld" (John 1:14); perhaps the dative "to us" (cf. "tabernacled among us" in John 1:14), and also the introduction of "the Father" (cf. John 1:14, but note that the word for "son" is not used there). These do not indicate literary dependence so much as the varying reuse of a distinctive set of "Johannine" language. Similarly, the cross-references with subsequent passages in 1 John indicate that this process is not a case of editorial work alien to and subsequent to the writing of the letter. Evidently this is an author who works by allusion to shared tradition, by reworking and modifying it, by presenting what seems familiar and then challenging readers to rethink as the familiar slips away again. This pattern is one that will emerge repeatedly through the letter and undoubtedly undergirds its persuasive effectiveness.

### *1 John 1:4—The Purpose in Writing*

1:4 And these things we ourselves are writing so that our[a] joy may be made complete.

a. There is considerable textual support for "we are writing *to you*," and for "your" joy. Variations like these are common throughout 1 John, partly because there was little difference in the pronunciation of the Greek words for "we" and "you," which differ only in their initial, similar sounding letters (*hēmeis/hymeis*), and partly because scribes would often write what they expected to hear, and they may have expected further references to the audience in this verse. The double first person plural is well attested and is the more difficult reading, but entirely within the style of the prologue.

[4] As the author moves into the letter proper he effects a transition by maintaining the first person plural of the preceding verses, here made yet more emphatic, "we ourselves," and yet replacing the language of proclamation that belonged to the traditions he was using with that which properly indicates a document evidently devised as a *written* one. Hereafter he consistently uses the singular, "I am writing" (2:1, 7, 8, 12, 13; cf. 2:14, 21, 26; 5:13).[9] This does not mean that between verses 4 and 5 a group of authors handed over the pen to one representative; verse 5 will cement the transition by a backward-looking "we declare also to you." The author's writing remains an exercise in mediation between the recipients and the anonymous "we" of the prologue.

A further expression of purpose, separate from although not contradictory to the hope for fellowship in verse 3, reinforces the primacy of "our" position: "that our joy may be made complete." The standard prescript and other opening conventions of a letter normally served to reinforce the relationship between writer and those written to (see commentary on 3 John 1–4). Here, by contrast, there is no reference to the audience, no hope for their well-being, an omission sufficiently surprising to prompt later scribes to introduce one by changing the pronoun to "you"/"your" (see note a on text). The goal of the letter appears to serve only "our" interest. In practice, what follows much of the time suggests otherwise, and the explicit statement of purpose at the end of the letter (5:13) has the readers' own situation entirely in mind. However, by then it will be evident that the readers' assurance necessarily entails their identification with "us": in the language of the present context, if "you" do have fellowship with "us," then "our" complete joy will embrace "you."

Although the language of "joy" (*chara*) permits some echo of conventional epistolary expressions of pleasure (*echarēn*, 3 John 3–4), and even of the standard "greeting" (*chairein*), its real origin is again the familiar language of the Johannine tradition. Perhaps in imitation of this verse, the elder will close 2 John with the same hope (2 John 12). In the Fourth Gospel, however, the same aspiration, although a formula, is far from formulaic: Jesus invites his disciples to ask of God in prayer that they might receive "and your joy may be made complete," while he offers his own final prayer "so that they might have my joy complete in themselves" (John 16:24; 17:13, both using the perfect passive as in 1 and 2 John; cf. John 15:11). John the Baptist has already used the same words of his own experience at recognizing in Jesus the goal to which his task

---

9. Subsequent references supply "to you," absent here according to the text accepted above.

was directed (John 3:29)—evidence of how different voices within the Johannine tradition, in narrative and in redaction, speak in one voice. Each of these occurrences carries an unmistakable eschatological note: the verb "to be complete" (*pleroō*) points to the fulfillment of Jesus' hour (John 7:8), and also both of Scripture and of Jesus' own word (12:38; 18:9); "joy" is promised to the disciples as an unalienable certainty beyond the coming distress (16:20–22). Such a note is far less evident in 1 John, which does not otherwise use the verb "complete" or the noun "joy," although if pressed the author might have protested that his letter was not ephemeral or transitory but makes a demand no less decisive.

These opening verses do not encourage attempts to identify either the author or the readers, nor their setting, although that has not deterred interpreters from endeavoring to do so. Although the careful anonymity may conceal an intimate relationship and a shared concern about an all too familiar situation, it seems rather to be designed to invite readers to enter into the reflections and debates that will follow. With most private letters their specificity is a problem once they become public and circulate beyond their original audience; readers may then choose to view from outside a glimpse into "somewhere else," or they may ask whether they can imaginatively picture themselves within the interaction that is taking place. By contrast, the vigorously affirmed authority and yet deliberate anonymity of the prologue of 1 John directly invites readers, both those originally included and those who subsequently find themselves included among those addressed as "you," to acknowledge the claims with which the letter comes, and also to hear what is proclaimed and so to be brought into that *koinōnia* that will allow them to make the claims "our" own. This explains the abrupt change that follows: despite the apparent promises of the prologue, no further appeal is made to the experience of others; instead readers are brought into a process of shared reflection on the faith and experience they already acknowledge.

### 1 John 1:5–2:2—Living in the Light of God

First John cannot easily be divided into separate sections. Rather than follow a carefully argued logical structure, the train of thought consists of a number of overlapping reflections or exhortations, which, some feel, could have been put in some other sequence without much damage to the overall argument; words or ideas are taken up in a new direction, or their consequences are explored in ways that may even sometimes seem to challenge what has already been said. This opening section of the letter is linked to the preceding prologue by an appeal to what "we have heard," but the certainty of fellowship as discovered through hearing the message is now put under the spotlight. Although the message may be about God, this section establishes from the start that simple theological assertions are never independent of consequences for how people live. First John does not separate theological reflection from paraenesis or encouragement, in contrast, for example, to the way in which only in Romans 12 does Paul turn to exhort his readers to appropriate behavior after long chapters of wrestling with the nature of God's action toward humankind. On the other hand, unlike those following chapters of Romans, 1 John does not spell out in any significant detail what his understanding of right living means in specific ethical contexts.

One could argue that the section that begins with 1:5 continues until 2:11; thus it begins with God as the light in whom there is no darkness and it ends with the power of darkness to cause blindness—after this the language of light and dark disappears from the letter. Between these two points those who are invited to hear the message struggle to shape their lives. However, this shaping takes different forms or can be approached in different ways; this will suggest marking a division between 2:2 and 2:3, although, as so often in 1 John, there are several links between these sections. The main concern of the first section will crystallize around the nature of sin among those who confess belief in God: can there be in the lives of those who claim fellowship with God that which fails to reflect God's nature? This is a recurring theme in the letter and it will be treated in a very different way in chapters 3 and 5 (3:4–10; 5:16–19); those later passages will raise acutely the question of how consistent 1 John is in the way it deals with the subject (see commentary).

### 1 John 1:5—God Is Light

1:5 And this is[a] the message[b] that we have heard from him and announce to you, that God is light and in him there is no darkness at all.

a. Some manuscripts reorder "And this is" to conform to 2:25; 3:11; 5:11, where the phrase is also used.
b. Influence from 2:25 has led some manuscripts to read "promise (*epangelia*)" instead of "message (*angelia*)" here.

[5] The unspecified "we have heard" of the prologue now takes shape as a message to be announced, using words related to the proclamation declared in verses 2 and 3: "message," *angelia*, represents the root from which both "announce," *anangellō*,[10] and "proclaim," *apangellō* (vv. 2–3), are formed. However, this verse is not intended to sum up the prologue, in contrast to 2:25 (and possibly 5:11), where the phrase "and this is" (in a slightly different word order from that here) does come toward the end of the section. The grandiose building up of ideas has culminated in the climactic declaration of writing in verse 4. As frequently in 1 John, shared vocabulary provides a transition from what precedes, but this is unmistakably a new unit of thought.

10. See n. 6 above.

Not only is "message" somewhat more limited in scope than the sensory verbs of the prologue, but it has been heard "from him." First John frequently uses "he/him" in an indeterminate way, where the reference arguably could be either to God or to Jesus. This does not mean that the author does not distinguish them, or that he identifies Jesus as God, so much as that he appears unconcerned to specify one or the other where it would have little significant effect. Here the most natural reference is to Jesus since the content of the message is about God. Does this mean that the author has among his resources traditions about the teaching of Jesus? In 2:25 the author appeals to "the promise he promised us," and in 4:21 to "the command we have from him" (cf. 3:23), while Jesus' own pattern of life may be recalled in 2:6 (see commentary). In each of these, and similar, cases Jesus is not named, and in a different context the reference could be to any preacher or teacher to whose authority appeal was to be made. Although the wording of proclamation might suggest that those who have no prior knowledge of this are being told something new, this cannot be the case; they must be able to identify the source of the message, the "him," as Jesus. Once again, it looks as if familiar material is being reworked here for a new purpose.

The content of the message, that "God is light," may appear somewhat restricted after the dramatic buildup of the prologue. Yet the expression is a striking and somewhat unexpected one. The sentiment is not part of the tradition of Jesus' words as subsequently handed down, although the image of light is common in the Fourth Gospel; in John Jesus declares himself to be the light of the world and he urges his followers to take advantage of what will prove to be an all too brief period of light (John 8:12; 12:35–36); earlier the prologue had portrayed Jesus' coming as that of true light in the midst of darkness (John 1:4–9). Elsewhere in the New Testament it is believers who are the light of the world or who are children of the light (Matt 5:14; Luke 16:8; Eph 5:8; 1 Thess 5:5). Certainly, the psalmist may say, "God is my light and my salvation," and Isaiah anticipates the day when rather than the sun or moon, whose light is dimmed at the end of the day or night, God will be their "eternal light" (Ps 27:1; Isa 60:19–20); but this is the language of metaphor and of relationship, not of God's own being. None of this imagery is surprising: for obvious reasons, particularly in a world without multiple possibilities of artificial light, in a range of religious and cultural conditions light represents life, hope, blessing, and also that which is not ashamed to be seen.

One might also argue that biblical thought generally does not identify God by abstracts but by what God does. First John's second "God is" affirmation will in this context be less troubling, for that "God is love" becomes evident through the love that God displayed in the sending of the Son (4:8–16). By contrast, the closest parallels to 1 John's assertion here draw on the creation narratives and present God as the primordial light: Philo quotes Ps 27:1 to assert that "God is light," only to differentiate "the archetype of every other light" from the sun and all created lights (*On Dreams* 1.75); God has no need of any light to see, for God sees by the light of God's self (*On the Unchangeableness of God* 58; *On Flight* 235). Similarly, Jas 1:17 identifies God, "the father of lights in whom there is no variation or shadow of changing," as the source of all good gifts. Unlike Philo, however, 1 John is not drawing on philosophical ideas of the pure intellectual realm, nor is he concerned to emphasize the otherness of God or the means by which God can be apprehended, but rather the consequences in living of making such a claim.

It is also hardly surprising that negative associations should cluster around darkness, and the balancing very strong negative affirmation, that in God "there is no darkness," might seem only to strengthen the positive claim already made. However, counterposing the two, light and darkness, introduces a dualist pattern that provides a major structuring framework throughout 1 John, and that has sometimes been seen as alien to the biblical worldview. In Genesis 1 darkness may already be there prior to God's first act, and it does remain when God has created light, but by naming it "night" God declares sovereignty over it (Gen 1:1–5). Isaiah 45:7 celebrates God as the one who creates both light and darkness, wholeness and distress. None of this implies that there is darkness in God, but it does set God above a dualism that could conceive of darkness as a power opposed to God, and to that extent independent of God; this remains the case even if it might be debated in these passages whether darkness is merely the absence of light or has an independent existence in its own right.

However, a more dualistic worldview did become part of some Jewish thought during the late Second Temple period. A passage in the *Community Rule* provides here, and elsewhere, a number of striking parallels with the thought of 1 John:

> 15 From the God of knowledge stems all that there is and all there shall be. Before they existed he established their entire design. . . . 17 He created man to rule 18 the world and placed within him two spirits so that he would walk in them until the moment of his visitation: they are the spirits 19 of truth and of deceit. From the spring of light stem the generations of truth, and from the source of darkness the generations of deceit. 20 And in the hand of the Prince of Lights is dominion over all the sons of justice; they walk on paths of light. And in the hand of the Angel 21 of Darkness is total dominion over the sons of deceit; they walk on paths of darkness. (1QS III, 15–21)[11]

Passages such as this have dispelled earlier suggestions that 1 John is here operating within a more Hellenistic framework. What is still notable in this passage is the firm statement that God is the source of all: it is sometimes difficult to press dualistic texts to a strictly logical conclusion as to whether God did

---

11. See below for further parallels with this passage, pp. 134, 161, 174.

create darkness, or whether darkness stands to some extent independent of God, even though a biblically rooted monotheism was bound to affirm God's ultimate control over, and defeat of, the opposing powers of darkness. In some ways 1 John does less to address this dilemma, as will become explicit in the assertion that the darkness has blinded the eyes of the one who hates a brother or sister (2:11; see commentary). If the author is taking an affirmation that was familiar to readers from a different context, some of these questions may have been answered: in the present context the letter is not concerned with abstract definitions of the Divine, or even with the problem of the sources of the powers of evil and darkness or of their final destiny. What matters is that the nature of God is foundational for the behavior of those who claim a relationship with God.

### *1 John 1:6–10—Saying and Doing*

1:6 If we say that we do have fellowship with him while we walk in the dark, we are lying and are not acting upon the truth; 7 if we walk in the light, as he is in the light, we do have fellowship with one another, and the blood of Jesus, his Son,[a] purifies us from every sin. 8 If we say that we do not have sin, we are deceiving ourselves, and the truth is not in us. 9 If we acknowledge our sins, he is faithful and just so as to forgive us[b] sins and to purify us from all injustice. 10 If we say that we have not committed sin, we treat him as a liar, and his word is not in us.

a. Perhaps in imitation of v. 3, some manuscripts read, "Jesus Christ, his Son," others "Jesus Christ."
b. Some manuscripts read, "to forgive (us) our sins."

The argument moves into a style of debate and reflection. The author does not make his point by demonstration, "If God is light then to [do] . . . would be self-evidently wrong." Instead, he spells out the various possibilities and invites his readers to enter into the process of drawing the appropriate conclusions. At first sight the author may seem to be saying the same thing first in one way, then by inverting it; yet the initial appearance of a common pattern is misleading. There are numerous interconnections and shifts in nuance as each possibility is explored. Thus, although verses 6, 8, and 10 all begin with the hypothetical "if we say that," in the first, verse 6, it is the relationship between saying and doing that is examined, in the second two it is the claims themselves that are challenged. Verses 8 and 10 may appear to say the same thing, but, as will be seen, the emphasis is different, while the relationship between "the truth" and "his word," which in each case may not be "in us," is left open to reflection.

[6–7] The argument builds on the preceding affirmation about God, but the claim to "have fellowship with him" is one that has already been authorized by the prologue's affirmation, "our fellowship is with the Father" (v. 3). From now on, however, it appears that the "we" who speak are no longer those of the prologue who were contrasted with the readers, "you"; instead the readers are invited to consider this possibility and its consequences for themselves. In 4:20 the author will present the same exercise in reflection by suggesting, "if anyone says. . . ." In both cases the things that might be said are in themselves not merely valid but positively desirable claims, to have fellowship with God, to love God; what falsifies such assertions is behavior that is incompatible with them, not because of any logical incoherence but because it fails to recognize the moral implications of the nature of the God with whom a relationship is claimed.

Here such inappropriate behavior is described literally as "walking in the dark"; darkness, it has just been said, is what is utterly absent from God. The different term here for "dark" (*skotos*) from that in verse 5 (*skotia*; also in 2:8, 11) may betray the author's hand in bringing together traditions from different contexts, but the sense is the same. *Skotos* is the more common of the two words in the Septuagint, and it is used in Isa 59:9, quoted earlier in the discussion of 1 John 1:1, and also in the opening verses of Genesis 1. "Walking" in the biblical tradition (Hebrew *hālak*—the LXX generally translates with the Greek verb *poreuesthai*, "to go") can simply mean "living"; hence those who "walk (go) in darkness" in Isa 9:2 (LXX 1; cf. also Job 29:3) are living in the absence of God and of hope rather than doing anything wrong; indeed, they are experiencing the distress into which the coming of God's saving light is promised. Within this framework, 1 John 1:6 is affirming that there are two realms or two sources of being or power, light and darkness. Since they are antithetical and reciprocally exclusive, dual location or allegiance is not possible, at least for those for whom God's presence is a reality. Thus far, what "walking in darkness" might entail in practice remains open-ended.

Elsewhere in the New Testament, however, "walking"—more frequently *peripateō*, as here, than the Septuagint's preferred *poreuomai* ("proceeding")—regularly expresses moral behavior, whether used on its own (1 Cor 7:17; 1 Thess 4:1) or qualified in a variety of ways—"in newness of life"; "according to the flesh"; "in wisdom" (Rom 6:4; 8:4; Col 4:5). This, too, has biblical roots in the use of *hālak* (see Ps 1:1, LXX *poreuomai*), and rules concerning behavior in later Jewish thought came under the heading of *halakah*, "walking." More specifically, in Jewish literature of the period the idea emerges that human beings must choose between two ways in which to walk, the way of light or life and the way of darkness or death: "God gave humankind two ways and two dispositions and two types of action and two manners and two goals . . . two ways, of good and evil" (*T. Ash.* 1.3–5). The passage concerning the two spirits in the *Community Rule* cited earlier describes the paths belonging to the spirits of light and of darkness with their different characteristics. Perhaps drawing from such traditions, early Christian sources describe the two ways, of light and of darkness, that stretch out before people (*Barn.* 18–20; *Did.* 1–5); the characteristics of the two ways are spelled out there in detailed moral exhortation drawn from Jewish and from specific Jesus traditions. In *Barnabas* the two ways have a cosmic dimension, being under the governorship of the "light-giving angels of God and the angels of Satan; and one is the Lord from eternity through eternity, and the other the ruler of the present age of iniquity" (*Barn.* 18.1–2). Again, there are echoes of such thinking elsewhere in 1 John, which also knows of two spirits, the spirit of truth and the spirit of error (4:6). Yet 1 John does not relate these two spirits to the two contexts of walking: the spirit is first mentioned in 3:24, while the image of walking and the language of light and darkness disappear after 2:10, and 1 John nowhere speaks of "ways." In its dualistic outlook 1 John shares roots with these other traditions, but the differences are more striking than the similarities. Most of all, for 1 John light and darkness do not represent fixed intrinsic patterns of behavior but are determined by their reference to God.

It follows that claiming fellowship with God while living within the realm of darkness is incoherent; it is a lie (*pseudo-*). For 1 John such falsehood is not merely a mark of moral weakness (cf. 2:4); in 1:10 the author will raise the charge of treating God as a liar (cf. 5:10), while in 2:22 he will describe the one who denies that Jesus is the Christ as the liar, and sharply distance the teaching available to true believers from any lie (2:27). On the horizon loom those whom in 4:1 he will call "false" or "lying prophets" (*pseudoprophētai*). Lying belongs to darkness as truth belongs to light. In accordance with this it would be possible to translate the last line as "and we do not act truth*fully*." Yet more than this seems to be in mind: verse 8 (cf. 2:4) speaks of "the truth [being] in us," apparently in parallel to "his word [being] in us" (1:10), and truth will continue to play a key role as that whose possession is both urged upon and assured for believers (cf. 2:21). Those who do not act upon the truth will be those who are failing to express in what they do the salient characteristic of what fellowship with God and possession of God's truth must entail.

The other side of the coin, then, is not about making other, more honest, claims, but about actually belonging to the realm of light, not now because God is light but inasmuch as this is also the sphere to which "he" belongs. In the context of what follows "he" must here still refer to God because of the phrase "his Son" later in the verse, although if that phrase were omitted (see below), the reference could be to Jesus. However, the consequence of sharing ("walking in") this location is not, as the logic would suggest, the assurance of fellowship with God, although that can hardly be denied, but of fellowship with one another, with those who also belong to the same sphere. This shift of perspective from the vertical, Godward, to the horizontal, one another, was there in reverse in the initial offer of fellowship in verse 3, and it will be a repeated theme throughout the letter: the relationship with God cannot be spoken of or experienced independently of the network of relationships between those who would so speak or experience; there is here no room for the solitary communion with the divine, nor for an ascent to the realm of light. The first person plural, "we," is never a cover for "I," "me." On the other hand, at this stage the author gives no indication of how that fellowship is to be expressed, nor even whether it must inevitably take a particular social form: there is here no covert ecclesiology.

At this point the picture appears to be complete, the negative (v. 6) and positive (v. 7a) rounding out the circle. Instead, a final affirmation disrupts the harmony. So far there has been no reference to sin, nor any obvious need for one. What place can there be for sin in the simple dichotomy between living in the realm of darkness and living in the realm of light? How can those who belong to the realm of light, which is the realm of God, be in a position where purifying from sin is required as is here declared? This imbalance has led some interpreters to suggest that the final clause, "and the blood of Jesus, his Son, purifies us from every sin," is an editorial or redactional addition to an earlier balanced and coherent pattern. It was added, according to this view, precisely because that pattern left no obvious role for Jesus and his death, and because it failed to address the experience of sin among those who belonged to the light. In support of this view one can argue that the sacrificial imagery of the purifying effect of blood is alien to the general thought of the letter, while "blood" is referred to again only in an obscure passage in 5:6, 8 (see commentary); such imagery might be seen as more redolent of the sacrificial and priestly thought-world developed particularly in the letter to the Hebrews (e.g., Heb 9:12–14). On this account, the addition of this clause reflects an attempt to align 1 John with ideas of atonement developing elsewhere in the Christian tradition.

Certainly 1 John does not offer a consistent, or a fully articulated, understanding of the role of Jesus in relation to forgiveness, as shall be evident in the discussion of 2:1–2 (cf. 4:10). "Sin," however, does provide a major theme in the letter, although complicating any discussion of its meaning in this passage are the apparent contradictions in what is said, particularly between the assumptions here and in verses 8–10, and those in 3:4–9 that exclude the possibility of sin (see commentary on these passages). In part the unevenness and even inconsistencies arise because 1 John is working with earlier traditions and formulations; his technique is not to rewrite or correct, but to modify by organization, by addition, or by qualification, even when such supplementary material also bears the marks of being sourced from earlier traditions. Here is one of those occasions where a close reading suggests an addition has been poorly integrated into the context of a different perspective; on the other hand, subsequent liturgical usage of verse 7 has sensed no disharmony at all, finding in the verse a promise that the securing of forgiveness is not the prior condition of a relationship with God and of the building of community, but becomes possible as the consequence of them.

First John does not at this point define sin, and it would be wrong to read into the letter ideas taken from elsewhere in the New Testament of inherent human sinfulness, or of sin as a pervasive power or as a state of being. Within a biblical context the language of purification (*katharizō*) used here and in verse 9 suggests the removal of that which leads to separation from the presence or the purposes of God. Although such imagery originally belongs within the cultic sphere, in Judaism at the time the search for purity was no longer limited to the possibility of access to the Temple, but was seen as itself desirable for all God's people. Even within the cult it is not only contact with a corpse, semen, or menstrual blood, for example, that is a source of pollution; the Day of Atonement provides an occasion when the people can be purified from all their sins so as to be pure before God (Lev 16:30). This is not to be understood as a metaphorical application of the language of pollution so much as a recognition of the effect of rejecting God's will in whatever form. So, perhaps in a noncultic or nonsacrificial context, the psalmist can pray to God: "Wash me thoroughly from my iniquity and purify me from my sin" (Ps 51:2); similarly, the *Psalms of Solomon* praise God, who "will purify from sin the soul in its confession" (*Pss. Sol.* 9.6; cf. 10.1), while the *Hymn Scroll* looks forward to the time when God will purify his remnant from guilt (1QH XIV, 8). Yet always the goal of such purification is to be fit for fellowship with God; frequently associated with such language is that of holiness as an expression of God's own character and of that which can be in God's presence (cf. Eph 5:26–27).

Here in verse 7, however, it is not God but blood that purifies. Within the sacrificial system the manipulation of blood played a central role (e.g., Lev 16:15–19). Whatever the origins of this, there is rarely any attempt in the biblical texts themselves to interpret how or why the blood "works"; instead it is seen as part of the mechanisms that God has provided for the proper response to God, and especially for the restoration of right relations with God. It is within this framework that Lev 17:11 says that blood is the life of all flesh and that God has given it on the altar as a means of forgiveness (or atonement; see commentary on 2:2). So understood, it is not the blood that has been shed itself, nor the death of the animal that it represents, that effects forgiveness, but God through divine grace, and this means that there can be no automatic equation between the sacrificial shedding of blood and the granting of forgiveness. The words of Heb 9:22, "Indeed, almost everything is purified with blood according to the Law, and without the shedding of blood there is no forgiveness," should be seen as an exaggeration that suits that author's argument, not as a statement of first-century experience. Despite this background, to translate "blood" in 1 John 1:7 by "sacrificial death," as do some (similarly Rom 3:25; 5:9), may obscure the origins of the image and may also imply particular interpretations of the efficacy of Jesus' death that, however valid in themselves, are not here in mind. First John does not look back to a single past act of purification but sees this as available in the present ("purifies"); the emphasis is not on the past moment of death but on the ever-present gift of forgiveness and life.

**[8–9]** Now that verse 7 has introduced the idea of sin, verse 8 takes it up. There is a logic here; as already seen, a simple opposition between either walking in darkness or walking in light on the face of it leaves little place for sin: for those who belong to the light sin might seem to be excluded by definition; conversely, if darkness is the sphere opposed to God, sin—defined not as a moral category but as that which disrupts the fellowship with God that is otherwise possible—also does not properly belong there. An opposition between light and darkness and the language of sin apparently belong to two different ways of thinking about the relationship with God. It is easy, then, to see how the questions might arise: cannot, then, those in the light claim to be without sin? Or, alternatively, are those who have been purified of "every sin" now free from sin?

This time it is not a mismatch between valid claim and invalid behavior that is at issue; any assertion "that we do not have sin" is simply excluded. Moreover, the author declares it to be not a lie but self-deception: whereas earlier he appeals to God as light or as in the light as providing the grounds for how "we" should walk, here the author does not argue the case but simply states it. Either this was self-evident to the community, rooted in the traditions of the request for forgiveness and of the assurance of it that he will go on to affirm, or it could easily be made so. This will be made clearer in verse 10, where it is God's fidelity that is at stake: claiming not to have sin is not a matter of arrogant self-righteousness but of misrepresenting the very nature of God. The same is also implied by verse 9, which presents the appropriate alternative as "acknowledging" or "confessing sins"; this suggests that it is not simply the theoretical denial of sin that the author challenges but the refusal to share in an act of confession. While it may be human sin that calls forth God's forgiveness, it is the reality of God's forgiveness that ultimately exposes human sin for what it is: "whose sins will you forgive except those who have sinned?" (*Pss. Sol.* 9.7). Hence, that "the truth is not in us" is not another way of saying "we are wrong": "the truth" represents the bedrock of understanding and sharing in all that belongs to God's side of the divide already traced between light and darkness (1 John 2:21; 3:19).

The verb "to acknowledge" (*homologeō*) is not commonly used of sin, and elsewhere in 1 John it refers to the acknowledgment of Jesus, particularly as the Christ or as Son of God (2:23; 4:2; etc.);[12] what is in mind here is not just the acknowledgment of the fact of sin but the declaration of them before God.

---

12. The NT does not use the term most commonly used in the LXX for the confession of sin, *exagoreuō* (Lev 5:5; 16:21, etc.). Matthew 3:6; Jas 5:16; *Pss. Sol.* 9.6 use *exhomologein*; *T. Gad* 2.1 and 6.3 also use *homologeō* of sin, as does Philo, *On Rewards* 163; see p. 62.

The plural "we" belongs to the debating style of the letter, but may also indicate a public, corporate context for such confession; the formulaic phrasing that follows in the assurance of forgiveness also suggests this.

This time the repeated promise of "purifying" is supplemented by the more general "forgive" (*aphiēmi*); these are achieved not through a sacrificial means but because of the very nature of the one who is "faithful and just." Although in 2:1 it is Jesus who is described as "just" (or "righteous": *dikaios*), here God is almost certainly identified as the one who therefore forgives. In describing God's readiness to forgive in terms of God's own nature the author draws on earlier traditions that were probably familiar also to the readers, but that are not developed elsewhere in the Johannine literature. Such earlier traditions have their roots in Scripture, although 1 John does not quote any particular passage directly; Scripture is not for him an authority to be quoted but part of a shared heritage of resources, here offering a vocabulary for celebrating the experience of forgiveness. Thus it is intrinsic to God's self-revelation to Moses in Exod 34:6–7 that forgiveness is rooted in the very character of God: "The LORD, the LORD, a God merciful and gracious, slow to anger and abounding in steadfast love and truth, keeping steadfast love for the thousandth generation, forgiving iniquity and wickedness (LXX *adikia*) and sin (LXX *hamartia*), but he will not purify (LXX *katharizō*) the guilty." Echoes of this formulaic tradition reemerge in different forms and contexts, prophetic and liturgical, throughout the biblical tradition and beyond, providing a framework for understanding God's judgment as well as God's forbearance, and for the appeal to God's mercy (Num 14:18–19; Nah 1:3; Joel 2:13; Jonah 4:2; Neh 9:17; Pss 86:15; 103:8; 145:8; 1QH XIV, 8–9; *Jos. Asen.* 11.10). Sirach appeals to the same tradition—"For the Lord is merciful and gracious and forgives sins and saves in a time of distress" (Sir 2:11)—but also knows how it might be abused: "Do not say, 'I sinned and what happened to me?' for the Lord is slow to anger. Do not be so unconcerned about pardon as to add sin upon sins. Do not say, 'His mercifulness is abundant, he will forgive the multitude of my sins'" (6:4–6). Where Sirach warned against arrogantly taking advantage of the assurance of divine forgiveness in heedless wrongdoing, 1 John here affirms that God's faithfulness in granting forgiveness demands the acknowledgment of sins that need to be forgiven.

Although the Septuagint does translate "keeping steadfast love" (Exod 34:7) by "keeping justice" (*dikaiosynē*), these passages do not explain the specific appeal in 1 John to God as "faithful and just." Again, there are scriptural echoes, notably Deut 7:9, which also invokes the character of God as "faithful [*pistos*] and keeping covenant and steadfast love," and Deut 32:4, which praises God as "faithful [*pistos*], and without injustice, a *just* [*dikaios*] LORD," although neither context applies this to God's forgiveness of sin. More importantly, although God is not described as "faithful" elsewhere in the Johannine literature, that God is "just" suits 1 John's particular understanding of sin: "justice" or "what is right" is the opposite of sin (3:7–8), which, as it is here, can also be called "in-justice" (*adikia*, "wickedness"; cf. 5:17); as the letter progresses the author will repeatedly invoke God and/or Jesus as "just" as he tackles the problem of the behavior of believers (2:1, 29; 3:7).

The description of God as "faithful and just" may also have carried more specific resonances for the audience. In the Greco-Roman world deities were regularly acknowledged as "just," but surviving dedicatory inscriptions from Asia Minor show that in the second and third centuries C.E. people gave thanks or made vows to a god addressed simply as "holy and just" (*hosios kai dikaios*).[13] This was a local cult centered in Phrygia, and the god has no other name—indeed, one of the inscriptions refers to a priest "of the one and only god"; it reflects the piety of the area as one within which Jewish and Christian ideas may not have seemed so alien. Since there is no certain evidence for locating 1 John—and its traditional home in Ephesus would be too far west to directly echo these particular dedications—the letter cannot be immediately related to such a piety; however, were the letter to find readers from such a background, they would be challenged to wrestle, as does 1 John, with the experience of forgiveness amid the certainty of transformed lives.

It is this interweaving of traditions that has prompted the change from the singular "sin" in verses 7 and 8 to the plural in verse 9 (and 2:2), and not any subtle difference in meaning; there are no grounds, for example, for referring the plural to the multiple sins that people commit and the singular to sin as a power or state, or for distinguishing between "sin" and "wickedness."

[10] The author underlines the conclusion he has reached, once again taking it a step further. What is now excluded is not merely the claim not to possess sin, but any assertion not to have sinned. The perfect tense, "we have [not] sinned" (*hēmartēkamen*) draws attention both to the past wrong acts and to their continuing effect. Since, as has just been shown, the very fact of divine forgiveness demonstrates the reality of sin, and since God's character both defines sin and inspires the forgiveness that God offers, then any denial of sin calls into question God's fidelity and truthfulness, treats God as a liar. What was earlier labeled "truth" can now be labeled God's "word," since for 1 John that word represents the understanding of God and of God's action now experienced by those who believe. What those who respond to God's word discover is not that their true origin is as a child of the light or of God; rather, they experience that sin has been and can be dealt with. At the same time this further denial of mistaken conclusions will form a bridge to what the author goes on to say; verse 10 both looks back to what precedes and prepares for what is to follow as the

---

13. See M. Ricl, "Hosios kai Dikaios. Première partie: Catalogue des inscriptions," *EA* 18 (1991): 1–49; idem, "Seconde partie: Analyse," *EA* 19 (1992): 71–102; idem, "Hosios kai Dikaios: Nouveaux Documents," *EA* 20 (1992): 95–100.

author turns from shared reflection to a more authoritative word of direction and assurance.

Throughout this section the author has been inviting his readers to reflect on what "we may say." The tradition from which he and his readers came looked to God as the source of forgiveness and interpreted Jesus' shed blood as dealing with sin. The repeated "we/us," therefore, is not a cover for each individual but looks to the corporate life of believers. The liturgical and experiential resources of their community life provided a protective framework within which he could explore the assurances of transformation. Some of the things that the author will subsequently assert might seem to suggest that those who believe are free from sin (3:8); his dualistic understanding of light against darkness, God against the world or the devil, does not easily accommodate the ambiguities of sinful behavior. In the overall logic of the letter he has already anticipated the potential consequences of his own theology, and excluded the claims they might give rise to. This means that he does not have in view others who really did claim to have no sin or never to have sinned. Despite his subsequent warning against those who are trying to deceive them (cf. 3:7), it would be wrong to find in verse 6 and in every other claim that the author voices only to dismiss (1:10; 2:4, 9, etc.) a shadowy opposition whom he is challenging as he seeks to protect the readers from their seduction (see further, Introduction §2.2). The letter is an invitation to look not outside but inside, and to embark on a journey that in the end will demand a decision as to where indeed the truth is to be found.

## 1 John 2:1–2—The Assurance of Forgiveness

2:1 My children, I am writing this to you with the intention that you do not sin. Yet if anyone does sin, we have an advocate before the Father, Jesus Christ, the just one. 2 He indeed is forgiveness for our sins, and not only for ours but also for the whole world.

[2:1–2] The direct address does not mark a new section so much as call his audience's attention to his purpose in all this for them (so also 2:28; 3:7, 18; 5:21). From the reflective logic of the previous verses, "If *we* say . . . ," the author now assumes the first person authority of the letter writer whose main concern is those whom he is addressing. However, the form of address gives little indication of precisely the sort of authority he held. Although grammatically a diminutive, "little children" (*teknia*), there is neither patronage nor particular affection here, and the author may be avoiding the normal term that he reserves for "children" of God or of the devil (*tekna*, 3:1–2, 10; 5:2). Since *teknion* otherwise appears in the New Testament only in Jesus' address to his disciples in John 13:33, it may have been conventional in the Johannine tradition;[14] this should not be overemphasized, for the author also addresses his readers not only as *paidia*, another diminutive also translated as "children" (1 John 2:14, 18; cf. John 21:5), but also as *agapētoi*, "beloved" (1 John 2:7; 3:2, 21; 4:1, 7, 11), and as *adelphoi*, "brothers [and sisters]" (3:13), both of which are common in other New Testament letters. "My child" is a common form of address in Wisdom literature (Sir 2:1; 3:1, 17, etc.), and reveals nothing about the relative age and experience of the author and those to whom he writes, but his use of other epithets indicates that even if this is one voice he adopts, his authority is not ultimately that of a teacher of wisdom. The effect at this point is, however, to return the readers to a position of dependency on the experience of the author.

It may be impossible to claim not to have committed sin, but that is hardly grounds for treating lightly any failure to live according to God's requirements. The purpose of God's forgiveness is to prompt those who experience it not to repeat the wrongs of the past. Did the author seriously expect that his stated intention, that they not sin, could be fulfilled? In theory probably he did, for in chapter 3 he will draw on traditions that distanced the world of sin from that of the children of God. Yet what he presents as a concession, "if anyone does sin," in practice is the norm. His audience would have recognized this, for, as we shall see, he once again draws from earlier tradition to explore how sin could still be dealt with.

The verbs "sin" in 2:1 are in the aorist tense, which could be understood as individual acts of wrongdoing in contrast to the present tense of 1:8 ("we have sin") and the perfect of 1:10, both of which put some emphasis on persistence. Some interpreters have tried to explain the apparent contradiction with the flat denial of sin among believers in 1 John 3:4–10 by appealing to these different tenses; as will become evident, however, it is difficult to detect a consistent and nuanced pattern in the tenses used and in the ways of expressing sin in 1 John, and this does not provide an adequate explanation of any inherent tensions in the author's thought (see commentary on 3:6).

As the author appeals again to the remedy for sins "someone" might commit, he returns to the first person plural, "we," not only because he himself is no less dependent on that remedy but also because he is invoking the liturgical experience that they all share. As in 1:7 it is Jesus who offers the solution, but the present tense "we have" points even more clearly not back to any past stage in Jesus' life or death but to the role that he now fulfills. This will again be the case, for example, in 3:3, 7: although 1 John may be aware of traditions about Jesus' life (see commentary on 2:6), they do not play any significant role for the author's thought; it is who Jesus now is in relation to their needs that matters.

---

14. It is a variant reading at Gal 4:19.

The author does not offer any sustained explanation of how Jesus offers an answer to the fact of sin; instead he evokes a number of different images without weaving these threads into a single picture.

First, Jesus is an "advocate" (*paraklētos*); this translation is suggested by the normal usage of the Greek root, which means calling on someone for help, and which can have a specifically legal context. If this context were stressed the picture would be of a heavenly law court in which God sits as judge, hence the "before [*pros*] the Father" that follows. A similar picture is implied in 1 John's repeated assurance of the boldness (*parrēsia*) that believers have "before" God, both in the present and in the future (2:28; 3:21; 4:17), although only in the last of these passages does Jesus play any role. With less emphasis on the legal framework, "intercessor" is another possible translation. In either case it is remarkable that the term is otherwise used in the New Testament only in the Gospel of John, but is there taken in a very different direction (John 14:16, 26; 15:26; 16:7). There it is applied to the Spirit of truth or Holy Spirit, whose coming is dependent on Jesus' departure, and who is presented as *another* "paraclete"; while in principle this does not rule out, and might even support, Jesus as also being a paraclete, the point in the Gospel seems to be that if Jesus were a paraclete, something that is never stated, he was so during his ministry and he can no longer so act thereafter. Moreover, in the Gospel the task of the Spirit as paraclete is to be a presence with the disciples in the absence of Jesus, and to prompt them into holding on to the traditions about Jesus, and bearing witness to them, probably through creative reinterpretation. Dealing with sin is not the task of the paraclete of the Gospel, and legal advocacy in the presence of God is not in view—although John 16:8–11 could imply a court context with "the world" in the dock. It is part of the fertility of the Johannine tradition that concepts and ideas are reworked and reapplied, although it is not possible to trace the process involved or the direction in which the tradition has been developed.

Also difficult to trace are the origins of this use of the term; the noun *paraklētos* appears nowhere in the Septuagint, although related terms suggest encouragement (Job 16:2; Zech 1:13), and the cognate verb (*parakaleō*) refers to God's encouragement and consolation of the people (Isa 40:1–2; 49:10; 66:13; Ps 22:4). While this might offer some explanation of the concept in the Gospel, it does not suit 1 John's association with sin. Yet 1 John is not totally isolated: when Philo anticipates the possible conversion of those who have apostasized from Jewish belief and practice, and their physical return to the land, he states that they will have "three advocates (*paraklētoi*) for their reconciliation with the Father,"[15] the clemency and kindness of the one to whom they appeal, the holiness of the founders of the nation, and the reformation of those who are being led to the solemn treaties (*On Rewards* 165–67).

---

15. *Pros ton patera* as in 1 John 2:1.

Contemporary Jewish thought also provides a setting for the idea of such a representative or advocate, although not this particular term. In this period there developed the role of heavenly beings who represent and defend those who are faithful to God through the difficult times of eschatological conflict. For example, a fragmentary text among the Dead Sea Scrolls identifies the one who will proclaim peace according to Isa 61:1 as "Melchizedek," and appears to picture this Melchizedek as God's coming agent in executing judgment and bringing freedom for those who have suffered through their faithfulness to God (11Q13 *Melchizedek*). In other texts one or more of God's chief angels act in a mediating role between human wrongdoing and need and God's intervention (*1 En.* 8.2–10.12).

Jesus is able to fulfill this role because he is "just" (*dikaios*); the same adjective was applied to God two verses earlier, where it described God in contradistinction to the sin that God nonetheless forgives (1:9). Here the word carries a different set of overtones, reflecting the author's turn to another pattern of traditions. There may be an anticipation of the story of Cain and Abel (Gen 4:1–16), which offers an important interpretive model for 1 John, for Abel was "just" (3:12 [see commentary]; cf. Matt 23:35). The death of Abel, favored by God for his offering, could be seen as paradigmatic of the true martyr, and in Jewish thought the term "the just" comes to be used of those who are faithful to God, especially in time of persecution. In Wis 2:10–24 the fate of "the just one" at the hands of those who think they can act with impunity is vividly described: "If the just one is a son of God, he will help him and rescue him from the hands of his opponents" (Wis 2:18). Some interpreters have argued that Paul's appeal to Hab 2:11 ("the just one shall live by his faith[fulness]") in Rom 1:17 has been refracted through the lens of this passage from the Wisdom of Solomon, itself interpreted as a reference to the Messiah or Christ. Certainly by the second century C.E. Wis 2:12, "Let us persecute the just one because he is displeasing to us," had become a popular proof text in Christian thought of Jesus' death (for example, in Justin Martyr, *Dialogue with Trypho* 136.2). When Peter is represented as charging his Jewish audience, "You denied the holy and just one" (Acts 3:14; cf. 7:52), he may be echoing the same tradition, evidence of its early roots. Against this background 1 John suggests that Jesus' ability to act as intercessor depends not on his divine status as Son of God, but on his role as the one who has remained faithful to God, even to death. Contemporary Jewish sources show how an intercessory role was being ascribed to those martyred for their faith: the seven brothers who die for God's law in the persecution of Antiochus Epiphanes pray to God to show mercy to the beleaguered nation (2 Macc 7:37–38), while in 4 Maccabees it is because of these martyrs that "the homeland is purified, for they became, as it were, a ransom (*antipsychon*) for the sin of the nation, and through the blood of those devout ones and through the atoning sacrifice (*hilastērion*) of their death, the divine Providence saved the oppressed nation" (4 Macc 17:21–22).

In such responses to the undeserved death of those who were faithful to God in the midst of national distress, the traditional language of sacrifice was being recast without any detailed reflection on why or how their deaths might be efficacious. Something similar lies behind the description here of Jesus as "forgiveness." The Greek word *hilasmos* appears only here and at 1 John 4:10 in the New Testament; its form as a noun emphasizes action more than agent or means, hence the slightly clumsy translation "he indeed is forgiveness." Although the term could reflect a cultic context—in Lev 25:9 it is used of the Day of Atonement—there is nothing essentially cultic in the word itself. In some Greek versions of Neh 9:17 and Dan 9:9 it is simply used of God's forgiveness, translating the Hebrew *sĕlîḥâ*, which is increasingly used of the divine forgiveness in texts associated with the Exodus 34 tradition already noted above (see commentary on 1:8–9); similarly, Ps 130 (LXX 129):4 appeals to God with the words, "For with you is forgiveness (*hilasmos*)." The context here in 1 John supports a neutral translation rather than a cultic one; there is no reference here to Jesus' blood or death and no hint of a sacrificial framework. It is true that some have suggested that the phrase "concerning (our) sins" (*peri tōn hamartiōn*) does carry sacrificial associations; however, in Leviticus where a sacrifice is for sin the phrase is routinely in the singular, "concerning sin" (*peri tēs hamartias*); the plural is much less common and is not restricted to a sacrificial context (e.g., Tob 3:5).[16] As in Ps 130:4, the idea surely points to the activity of God through Jesus, not to Jesus in some way changing God's intention.

Another passage that has often been explored as part of the background to 1 John's thought here is Isa 52:13–53:11, the so-called Suffering Servant passage. In particular, the servant is described as "a just one" (53:11), his death is "concerning sin [singular]" (*peri hamartias*, 53:10), and, at least in the Masoretic (Hebrew) text, he "bore the sins of many and intercedes for transgressors" (53:12; LXX, "he bore the sins of many and was handed over on account of their sins"). Indeed, 1 John 3:5, "there is no sin in him," may echo Isa 53:9, "he did not do any iniquity, neither was any guile found in his mouth" (see commentary). Certainly later interpreters found Jesus clearly anticipated by the passage from Isaiah (1 Pet 2:21–25), but it is generally far less visible throughout the New Testament than might be expected in retrospect, providing little evidence for the view that the early believers in Jesus, and perhaps Jesus himself, immediately made the connection. Verbal links between Isa 52:13–53:12 and 1 John are very limited beyond the epithet "just," for which other parallels can be suggested (see above). This does not mean that the Isaiah passage has not colored 1 John's understanding of Jesus or the communal traditions he echoes,

---

16. The old-fashioned but familiar English term "propitiation" (KJV) is particularly misleading, for it suggests that God is the object of the activity involved, that God is to be appeased; this is not in mind in the term nor in the OT background, neither is it suggested by the context in 1 John.

for indirect allusions to Scripture seem to be more characteristic of this author than indisputable citations; however, 1 John can be understood, and arguably was understood by its first readers, without relying on any such allusions.

Moreover, once again early readers of the passage may have heard echoes from closer to their own experience. A series of "pagan"[17] inscriptions from western Asia Minor spread over two hundred years from the middle of the first to the middle of the third century C.E. acknowledges sins committed and the experience of divine punishment, and seeks or welcomes divine forgiveness. Although the dedications are to the gods, including Zeus, they share some of the vocabulary of 1 John, including "sin" (*hamartia*), "punishment" (*kolasis*, as in 1 John 4:18), and the verb "to forgive" (*hilaskomai*), which is the root of 1 John's *hilasmos*. In one of these the suppliant records how, in the form of a court scene, he had experienced "Zeus as an advocate (*paraklēton*)"; the formula used for forgiveness is "to take away sin" (*apairō hamartian*; 1 John 3:5 uses the related *airō hamartian*); and the punishment that the man had experienced as divinely sent was in his eyes (blindness), which invites comparison with 1 John 2:11, although a literal affliction may have been intended. This particular inscription is late, from 235/236 C.E., but it shows no evidence of having been influenced by Jewish or Christian language or thought.[18] Whether it is a chance survival of familiar language can hardly be decided; the remarkable parallels with 1 John serve as a reminder that early readers would have come to the text from a variety of backgrounds, and may not have read it with "biblical" images only in mind.

That Jesus *is* (present, not past) the means of dealing with the sins of those who rightly confess them has by now been well established, but the author goes on beyond this: Jesus is also forgiveness for "the whole world"—presumably an abbreviation for "the sins of the whole world." This is the first occurrence of the word "world" (*kosmos*), although hereafter it will come repeatedly, regularly as that which is totally opposed to God and to all that belongs to God (2:15–17; see commentary). For 1 John "the world" is not simply a location, although 4:9 does say that God sent the Son into the world; while it undoubtedly encompasses the world of men and women, of humankind in its rejection of God, at times *kosmos* appears to be more than the sum of the people who inhabit it, but becomes a sphere characterized as irrevocably antithetical to God (4:5; 5:19).

First John 2:2 is one of two exceptions to this negative picture, the other being 4:14, where Jesus is sent as "savior of the world." The latter makes little

---

17. Although an unsatisfactory term it is used here to signal that they are neither Jewish nor Christian.

18. See G. Petzl, *Die Beichtinschriften Westkleinasiens = EA* 22 (1994); idem, "Sünde, Strafe, Widergutmachung," *EA* 12 (1988): 155–66, commenting on the inscription published by H. Malay, "New Confession-Inscriptions in the Manisa and Bergama Museums," *EA* 12 (1988): 147–54, no. 5 (p. 151); l.18 reads, "I had Zeus as paraclete" (Greek: *escha paraklēton ton Deian*).

impact on the immediate context or on the overall thought of the letter, and conceivably it is a traditional phrase (see commentary and John 4:42). In contrast, the lack of obvious parallels makes it more difficult to dismiss 1 John 2:2 as a relic of earlier tradition with no serious contribution to the thought.[19] On the other hand, the verse leaves open whether Jesus is only *potentially* an offer of forgiveness for the world: to be effective does this have to be taken up through belief and confession of sin, even though in this verse there has been no mention of "our" confession either? One might also ask whether a world that believed and confessed would still be, in 1 John's terms, *world*. The intention may be to emphasize that, although the "world" does constitute a sphere that is indelibly and constitutionally opposed to God, it is not so by the will of God, or by some act of exclusion or omission on God's part. It would be easy to conclude elsewhere from 1 John's language of God versus the world, and of light versus darkness, that these oppositions are embedded in the very being of things, and therefore presumably by the intent of their creator, God; this could readily be inferred from 4:6, "We belong to God; the one who knows God listens to us, while the one who does not belong to God does not listen to us" (and similarly in the Gospel, "For this reason you do not hear, because you do not belong to God," John 8:47). 1 John 2:2 may, then, offer some hope to those yet to become members of the community of believers, and provide a counterbalance to the negativity of the only other occurrence of "the whole world" in the letter, "We know that we are from God and that the whole world lies in the power of the evil one" (5:19). It is but a slender thread, however, and does little to change the overall pattern of the letter; it is not followed by exhortations to share the message of forgiveness or by any further promise of hope. Indeed, the phrase may do more to establish Jesus' significance—he is not just for us—than to offer hope for anyone else.

First John shares this overall pattern of thought with the Fourth Gospel, in which both the disciples and Jesus are "in" but not "of" the world, and which takes for granted the hatred of the world for them equally (John 15:18–19; 17:13–16). Yet the Gospel does acknowledge that "the world came about through" the Logos while also affirming that it did not know him (John 1:10); it also describes God's love for the world, the purpose of which is that *all* who believe might experience life; and it represents Jesus as the "light of the world" and as the source of life for the world (3:16; 6:51; 8:12). In 1 John such positive notes are rare, and it is striking that 1 John 4:9, which in many ways echoes John 3:16, makes clear that it is "we" who are the objects of God's love and

---

19. Although John 11:50–52 has a similar structure—Jesus' death is "not on behalf of the nation alone but in order to gather into one the scattered children of God"—it is not at all surprising that the "scattered children of God" should be the object of the extension of salvation.

offer of life, and that the world is only the place into which the Son is sent (see commentary).

The author of 1 John lives in a thought-world of confident assertions and clear certainties. At the heart of that confidence lies a certainty about God, that there can be no confusion between that which belongs to God, bathed in light, and that which does not. This will shape all that follows in the letter even when its source, that God is light, is not articulated. It would be easy to move directly from this clarity of distinction in relation to God to a mirroring clarity of distinction in the human sphere, so that those who belonged to God would be unsullied by and totally separate from anything that did not belong to God. At times the author appears to go down this route, but in this opening passage he is very careful to avoid it. Human experience does not fit into a neat either/or; it does not belong either to one or to the other side of a great divide. That this is so is fundamental to the Jewish and to the Christian—a later differentiation our author does not know—belief in God; fundamental to the Jewish and the Christian experience of God is that it is God who offers the means for overcoming the mismatch between humanity and God, and who makes fellowship between them possible. This is where Jesus belongs; not to the past, enabling a transfer from one sphere to the other, but as the continuing means of maintaining and restoring fellowship, if only those who would claim it also acknowledge their need. Ironically, but on reflection not surprisingly, only those who have experienced belonging to the light and who see that as their proper sphere can claim what God in Jesus offers. Indeed, the mark of the integrity of their absorption of what it is to be in relation to God as the source of light is their acknowledgment of need. This emphasis on God as the starting point warns against any interpretation of Jesus as winning forgiveness by somehow changing God's mind, or making God act contrary to what might otherwise be the case. It also, although the letter makes little of this, forbids any view that too arrogantly assumes that we alone are the objects of God's concern.

### 1 John 2:3–11—From Knowledge of God to Love of a Fellow Believer

This new section does not exhibit a clear structural unity, although it does appear to be distinct both from what precedes and from what follows. However, just as in the previous section the deliberative "if we say" provided a recurring theme, so here the repeated "the one who says" (*ho legōn*: vv. 4, 6, 9) provokes reflection and drives the thought forward. Once again, there is no suggestion that there were those who did make these statements, and whom the author is concerned to expose and refute. In each case the things that might be said are things that the author would encourage his readers to say; what matters is that they work through the consequences. These are spelled out, both in failures for word to be matched by act, but also by the intervening positive and negative examples, "the one who . . ." (2:5, 10, 11). Through these steps the thought moves from the vertical Godward relationship, which itself moves from knowledge to obedience, to the horizontal relationship with fellow believers. However, typically of this author, other themes are also interwoven, and it will become evident that again the author is not composing from scratch but is weaving in ideas and formulations that he has drawn from earlier traditions, and that may have been familiar to his readers. In so doing he introduces concepts that will be picked up and developed further as the letter progresses.

## *1 John 2:3–6—Knowledge and Obedience*

2:3 In this way, then, we know that we have known him, if we observe his commands. 4 The one who says, "I have known him," while not observing his commands, is a liar and the truth in not in such.[a] 5 As for whoever keeps his word, the love of God is truly made complete in them;[b] in this way we know that we are in him. 6 The one who says that he indwells in him, ought himself to walk in the very way[c] that that man walked.

a. There is considerable manuscript variation in the order of words here as scribes tried to make the author consistent with his use of similar phrases elsewhere.

b. As in v. 4, the manuscripts vary in word order. In the commentary I will discuss whether there should be a semicolon (as translated) or a full stop here: in the latter case v. 5 would end with a colon rather than a full stop. Because of this ambiguity a few manuscripts, mainly in the Latin tradition, add at the end of v. 5, "if we are perfected in him."

c. Many manuscripts omit *houtōs*, "in the very way."

[3] "In this way . . ." is another of 1 John's favored means of developing an argument (cf. 2:5; 3:10, 19, etc.); as here, he uses it to show how something that might seem to be beyond demonstration can be tested and demonstrated. In this case the phrase looks forward, to the obedience to commands that is the sure evidence of a knowledge of God or of Jesus that cannot otherwise be proven. In other cases (see v. 5) the argument, although designed to clarify, is less easy to trace. As a technique it underlines that faith claims have little coherence unless they can be demonstrated in the way people live. Yet the focus is not outward, not to how other people can be persuaded of "our" integrity; it is "we" ourselves who need constantly to validate the religious certainties we think we hold.

Here that certainty is expressed in terms of knowledge, that "we have known him." The perfect tense points to the continuing relationship founded on past experience. Clearly knowledge here cannot refer to acquaintance with Jesus during his ministry; that could hardly be something that one could be unsure about. Indeed, it is not clear whether the "he" ("him") of the masculine pronoun throughout this section, as frequently elsewhere in 1 John, refers to God or to Jesus (see 1:5 and commentary). Although in some contexts the author is concerned to name Father and Son, separately and in relation to each other (2:22–23), in others this is not an issue. A reference to Jesus would be supported by the specific identification of the love as "of God" (v. 5), arguably indicating that God has not previously been mentioned, and by the natural expectation that "his commands" (vv. 3, 4, 5 ["word"]) would refer to Jesus' command to love one another (see 3:11). However, a reference to God is not excluded since the commands can be God's in 1 John (3:23), and the phrase "the love of God" might be conventional (5:3; 4:12, 17). First John 4:6–8 explicitly refers to knowledge of God (cf. 2:13), while 3:1 and 6 again speak of knowing "him," and 5:20 is particularly ambiguous (see commentary).

Knowledge, always expressed through the verb "to know" (*ginōskō*)[20] rather than through the noun "knowledge" (*gnōsis*), belongs to the distinctive vocabulary of religious experience in the Johannine tradition. As in 1 John, in the Gospel knowledge of God is the goal, there of Jesus' mission, although it is possible only through knowledge first of Jesus (John 14:7; 17:3); similarly, as in 1 John 3:1, failure to know God is not just the consequence of unbelief, it is its cause (John 8:55). Such ideas are not foreign to the biblical tradition: Jer 31:31–34 looks forward to the day when all shall know God, something that is contingent on God's forgiveness of their sins and that is not purely intellectual or abstract, but is relational; the similar promise in Hos 2:20, "I shall take you for my wife in faithfulness, and you shall know the LORD," draws on the use of "to know" for sexual intercourse. However, a search for insight and understanding does seem to have been a significant aspect of the religious mood of the turn of the eras. For example, among the Dead Sea Scrolls, the hymnist praises God "because you have given your servant the insight of knowledge to understand your wonders" (1QH XIX, 28). Although 1 John, like the Fourth Gospel, at times could be interpreted as understanding "knowing God" as the bestowal of special knowledge or as an exclusive relationship from which the hapless are forever excluded (4:6), both remain within this development of the scriptural tradition.

This scriptural shaping is reinforced by the test of knowledge offered here, keeping his commands. These have yet to be identified, but in 3:23 God's command is belief in the Son and love of one another, and it is the latter that dominates the thought of the letter. By not spelling them out at this point 1 John indicates that it is not a particular set of instructions about behavior that proves knowledge of God; what comes first is an acceptance that to be brought into and to remain in a relationship with God is to recognize and to respond to whatever God requires, simply because it is what God requires. It is not that knowledge must be followed by obedience but that the latter is constitutive of the former.

This emphasis marks 1 John's position in relation to the broader trends of the period often labeled as "gnostic"; these defined salvation in terms of illumination

---

20. 1 John 25 times; John 56 times.

and of the acquisition of knowledge (*gnōsis*) about oneself, one's origins, and one's destiny, and about the true nature of the world and of the means of liberation. It is now widely accepted that there was not a single movement, "Gnosticism," and the texts that have been recovered over the last century that reflect this sort of worldview reveal something much more varied and even more comprehensible than might be pictured from the hostile accounts of the early church writers against those they portrayed as heretics.[21] In turn, this means that older debates as to whether 1 John and, perhaps even more, the Gospel of John are either (incipiently) gnostic or are using the same tools but in an antignostic direction appear too simple. Both writings share some of the formulations of some of these other texts, and perhaps aspects of their worldview and aspirations, but they also differ from them in significant ways. Thus 1 John's emphasis on practical consequences may be set alongside the *Gospel of Truth*, a second-century gnostic writing, where the primary theme is that the rescue of those who experience redemption is out of oblivion, ignorance, or error: "He who is to have knowledge in this manner knows where he comes from and where he is going. He knows as one who having become drunk has turned away from his drunkenness" (*Gospel of Truth* [NHC I.3] 22, 14–18). Although the preceding lines have declared, "Having knowledge, he does the will of the one who called him, he wishes to be pleasing to him, he receives rest" (22, 9–12), there is nothing in the *Gospel of Truth* to give this any active practical content.

[4–5] The principle in verse 3 is reinforced by a negative and then by a positive demonstration of the point. In each case "the one who says" or "whoever" remains a hypothetical or rhetorical possibility, not among those now outside the circle of readers but firmly within it; the former possibility perhaps is to be excluded before ever taking form, the second to be affirmed, before the author finally (v. 6) introduces a model that he urges upon his readers. This author thinks in terms of opposites, and the language of lying and falsehood (cf. 1:6, 10) highlights its obverse, truth; this represents the integrity and authenticity of the message that ultimately comes from God. If in 1:8 (see commentary) the claim not to have sin demonstrated the absence of any genuine possession of the reality of God's revelation, here so too does the claim to have known God where it is not accompanied by the behavior to match.

It is the positive message that is the author's primary concern, and the introductory "whoever" invites the possibility of response. He does not simply repeat the preceding verse, only reversing the negatives, but makes two modifications to bring his readers forward. First, observing "his commands" is replaced by observing "his word." In 1:8 and 10 "truth" and "word" appeared

21. See M. A. Williams, *Rethinking "Gnosticism": An Argument for Dismantling a Dubious Category* (Princeton: Princeton University Press, 1996); C. Markschies, *Gnosis: An Introduction* (trans. J. Bowden; London: T.&T. Clark, 2003).

to be equivalents; here it is "word" and "command" that are used in parallel, a parallel that will be reinforced in verse 7. The effect is not to reduce the scope of "word" to only the command to love one another (3:11), but to elevate the idea of the command so that it is intrinsic to the message about Jesus, and about God's activity in Jesus (see 1:2). Second, the conclusion is not, as might have been expected, that "such a person has indeed known God"; that theme is now dropped, although it will be picked up again shortly (2:13–14). Instead, what was denied in verse 4, that "truth is not in such," is recalled, but the positive exceeds the mere reverse of the negative; "truth," still echoed by the adverb "truly," is replaced by—or perhaps, given the importance of the theme in the letter, transcended by—"love," while the simple "is" becomes the much more weighty "made complete."

On one level this prepares for, and would be unexceptional to those familiar with, the tradition of the specific command to love one another, which will begin to be more clearly echoed in the next section (2:7–11). Yet here love is explicitly love *of God*, and is significantly identified as such at the first mention of love in the letter—thereafter the noun occurs 17 further times and the verb 21 times. This phrase could be understood as "love for God" (an objective genitive; so 5:3), as "love from God" (a subjective genitive; so 4:9 and probably 4:12, where the same verb of completion as here is used), or, more generally, as "the sort of love that has to do with God" (a genitive of quality), which would anticipate the declaration of 4:8 that God is love; 2:15 ("love of the Father") and 3:17 are similarly ambiguous. Although the context is concerned with what believers do, it seems best to understand the reference here as to the love that comes from God. First John is confident that God's love for those who believe is a given, made evident in the sending of Jesus, a past act on which all else can be predicated and which is not dependent on any prior action or belief (4:9–10). Yet here he seems to imply that there is a conditionality about the *fullness* of God's love realized in someone: it is contingent upon obedience to God's commands, and in 4:12 upon mutual love. First John uses this verb of completing or making full (*teleioō*) only with reference to love, and does so four times, in each case both in the passive voice and in the perfect tense, which itself emphasizes the continuing effect of that action (2:5; 4:12, 17, 18; cf. 4:18, "complete love" and see commentary on 4:17–18). The effect is to preserve the priority of God's love: God's love is in no way diminished by the failures or inadequacies of human response, and yet, at the same time, a responsive obedience to God's commands is not an optional or a negotiable extra. First John would not have been able to conceive of God's love as partly or incompletely realized in anyone, not just because the author instinctively thinks in terms of all or nothing, but because that would be incompatible with the very nature of God's love itself. The author does not spell this out specifically, but presumably although God has demonstrated God's love for those who respond, that love becomes realized and embedded within anyone only in so far as they actively express that response, and this can only be by obedience; yet it is of the nature of *God's* love that once realized in any-one God's love inevitably will be *fully* realized, "made complete." As the per-fect tense also demonstrates, the completion of God's love is not dependent on obedience; rather, when someone expresses obedience, then, and only then, is it possible to speak of the fullness of God's love in them and for them.

The author repeats the formula that began this train of thought in order to bring it to a conclusion, "in this way we know" (see 2:3). This time "this way" refers back, to the "test" of keeping God's word (or commands), while the switch from the third person "whoever (keeps)" to the first plural "we (know)" forces home the point of the general hypothetical case, giving the readers no room for dissent. Characteristically, however, the language describing the rela-tionship with God has changed again: whereas the preceding affirmation had spoken of the love of God being within the one who obeys God's command, here the indwelling is reversed and it is "we" who are in "him." Such language of indwelling will become an important ingredient in 1 John's understanding of the relationship of believers with God, although it will be more commonly expressed, not with the simple verb "to be" as here (cf. 5:20), but with the verb "to indwell," as in verse 6: the implications and the background of the idea will be discussed in greater detail in the commentary at that point.

This interpretation assumes that a full stop is to be placed at the end of verse 5 (so also NA$^{27}$ and RV). It would be possible, however, to make the break fol-lowing "love of God is truly made complete in them," so that "in this way" starts a new sentence, pointing forward and picked up by the explanation given in verse 6, which continues the theme of indwelling ("By this we may be sure that we are in him: whoever says . . .": NRSV; cf. NIV). On the surface this would give two examples (vv. 3–5a and 5b–6), each introduced by "in this way we know," with what we know—that "we have known him" and that "we are in him"—each then being explored. However, the apparent parallelism is deceptive, and the con-structions used are different (see below); further, on this reading there is no clear connection between the two examples and between the images they employ. Hence the punctuation adopted above is to be preferred. That some readers have found the second reading persuasive, however, suggests that this last clause can also act as a bridge, concluding what precedes but providing the link that intro-duces the following verse. Such bridges are part of this author's style, but they have also been prompted by his use of what was probably traditional phrasing; through a form of association of ideas—what would now be labeled "stream of consciousness"—this has then provoked what follows.

**[6]** A new introduction makes a strongly worded call to appropriate behav-ior; the style has switched from reasoning and reflection to prescription. Although verse 6 starts in the same way as verse 4, "The one who says," the construction that follows is different (an infinitive representing indirect speech rather than a "that" clause introducing direct speech) and leads not into the disconfirming behavior of the person who wrongly makes such a claim but into an unequivocal obligation.

The language of "being in" (*einai en*) in the previous verse prepares for that of "indwelling" (*menōein en*) in this verse. The latter verb is particularly frequent in 1 John (23 times) and encompasses a range of relationships. Here it is a matter of "indwelling in him," characteristically imprecise but probably a reference to God, given the differentiating "that man" (= Jesus) that follows. First John can equally speak of "God indwelling in you" (4:12), and of the indwelling being fully reciprocal (2:24; 3:24; 4:15); other things also indwell believers, including "what you have heard from the beginning" (2:24), "the anointing" (2:27), or "eternal life" (3:15), while believers also indwell, for example, in love (4:16). Naturally, it will prove difficult to find a single explanation of the background or of the meaning of this variety.

Again, the metaphor of indwelling is a distinctively Johannine one and is equally important in the Fourth Gospel (27 times, in addition to 13 in the normal locative sense "to stay"). In the Gospel "being in" is almost as important as "indwelling in," and the thought is also both more structured and more restrained: there is a mutual "in-being" of Father and Son, and on that depends the being-in of believers in the Son, and only through the Son in the Father (John 14:10–11, 20; 17:21); similarly, in John, believers' reciprocal indwelling is with Jesus, the Son (6:56; 15:1–10), whose indwelling is, in turn, with the Father (14:10). This indwelling between Son and Father is not found in 1 John, and the letter also does not share the Gospel's theological reflection concerning that divine relationship and concerning the foundation that it offers for believers. Moreover, the ambiguous "in him" in 1 John (cf. 2:27, 28; 3:6, 24; 4:13) leaves unclear whether the believer dwells in the Son, as in the Gospel, or only in God (4:12, 15). For whatever reason, the thought of the First Epistle does not exhibit the discipline of the Gospel.

Close parallels in Greek thought to Johannine divine indwelling are few, and the most probable roots are to be found in earlier Jewish thought. As with the language of "knowing," the basic pattern of thought is not alien, but there are no simple lines of continuity: Wisdom finds a home or resting place in Israel and Jerusalem (Sir 24:8–12), but also, while "remaining in herself," moves into the lives of the holy (Wis 7:27); contrary to the inconstancy of people, God's word, like God, remains forever (Isa 40:6–8; Pss 9:7; 102:12, 26–27); the faithful are urged to wait in or upon God (*emmenō*, Isa 30:18), or they long to live in God's tent or presence (Ps 61:4, 7);[22] Israel is urged to keep God's commands within their innermost being (Deut 6:6), and the book of Jeremiah looked forward to

---

22. Although references follow the English versions of the Bible, in some cases the Greek translation uses "remain" where the Hebrew and English speak of enthronement.

the day when God would inscribe "my laws in their understanding and write them on their hearts," a day when there would be no need for one to say to another, "Know the LORD," for all would know God (Jer 31:31–34). Closer to the time as well as to the thought of 1 John, the *Testaments of the Twelve Patri- archs* promise that God will dwell among those who are faithful: "Observe the commands of the Lord, my children, and keep his law; stay away from wrath and hate falsehood, so that the Lord may dwell among you and Beliar flee from you" (*T. Dan* 5.1; cf. *T. Benj.* 6.4).[23]

Three things stand out from this survey. First, there is a variety of images of dwelling in earlier sources, several of which echo one aspect of Johannine thought but none of which quite explains the metaphor; indeed, the particular verb "indwell" (*menō*) is rare in this sense in earlier Jewish writing. The Johan- nine tradition is a richly creative one; part of that creativity is the ability to use a single term to explore the interrelationships of different experiences and atti- tudes, and it would be mistaken to enforce on all the patterns of "indwelling in" a single meaning. Second, the picture is not of an inner personal or mystical experience, but is often corporate, involving the community of the faithful. This is even true of Jeremiah's "law written on the heart" or of Ezekiel's new heart and new spirit (Ezek 11:19–20; 36:26–27). Although 1 John 2:6 does use the singular, "the one . . . in him," elsewhere in 1 John the plural is used, both "you [plural] dwell in him," and "he dwells in us" (2:28; 3:24). Third, there is a strong sense of continuing and of constancy, which can be lost in translations that put the emphasis on interiority or on union with the Divine. The translation given, "indwell," is intended to capture this richness of association.

That 1 John does not permit any escape into introspection or spiritual self- examination is made absolutely clear by the implied command that follows. There is no qualification about this "ought"—as if one ought to but might not. In 3:16 and 4:11 obligation is rooted in God's prior act: the consequence is inescapable. Here it is a matter of imitation: "just as" (*kathōs*) regularly intro- duces appeals to "his" (Jesus' or God's) instruction and example (2:6, 27; 3:2, 3, 7, 23; 4:17; cf. 3:12, "not like Cain"). The same pattern is found in the Fourth Gospel (John 13:14–15, "If, then, I . . . you also *ought* . . . I have given a model to you so that *just as* I have done for you, you too might do"; cf. John 13:34; 15:10, 12), and more widely (Rom 15:7; Col 3:13). What God has done in Christ is not only a source of hope and forgiveness; it is the lodestone for the behav- ior of those who claim that forgiveness.

Here the appeal is not just to the basic fact of God's love. On a number of occasions 1 John uses "that man," the demonstrative pronoun (*ekeinos*), to appeal to Jesus as a model or basis for the behavior of believers, several intro-

---

23. There are many parallels between 1 John and the *Testaments*, and yet they are difficult to interpret because of debates about the latter's date and origin; see Introduction, p. 24.

duced by *kathōs*, "in the very way," "just as" (2:6; 3:3, 7; 4:17; also 3:5, 16). Here the past tense, "walked," points to Jesus' earthly life (contrast the present tense in 3:3, 7; 4:17, and see commentary on these); the verb (*peripateō*) has its familiar meaning of living and of behavior without the qualifying metaphorical "in the light/darkness" (see commentary on 1:6–7). It is possible that this appeal recalls specific traditions of Jesus' life known to the audience of the letter, which they are being called to imitate—a reminder that the letter draws on knowledge that those who receive it already have (cf. 2:18). Yet particular traditions about the life of Jesus are relatively rare in the New Testament letters, and more often Jesus' death and its effect for believers is the primary ethical model (so Rom 15:7; Col 3:13); as in 1 John 3:16 and 4:11, it may be this that is in mind here.

This does not allow for any deception of self or of others. Despite the seemingly inward language of knowing, being in, and indwelling, the verse and the section end with the unequivocal "ought themselves to walk in the very way"; spiritual feeling and assurance are not matters only for the individual. Just as the language of lying recalled its earlier occurrences and prepares for subsequent ones (2:22; 4:20), by resuming the term "walk" the author recalls the section that began with 1:6. This demonstrates the extent to which 1 John resists being divided into discrete units and achieves its rhetorical effect by internal echoes as well as external ones: the reference is not to outsiders who made these claims but to the ever present threat of deception within. Finally, the author would see no inconsistency in having moved from "he"/God being in the light to how "he"/Jesus walked; instead, that earlier image is given specificity by the example of Jesus, while the instruction so to walk is set within the two mutually exclusive possibilities of walking in the darkness or walking in the light, a distinction that will also form the climax of the next section.

### 1 John 2:7–11—Hearing the Command and Loving a Fellow Believer

2:7 Beloved, I am writing to you not a new command but an old command, which you have had from the beginning. The old command is the word that you heard. 8 Yet I am writing to you a new command, something that is true in him and in you, inasmuch as the darkness is passing away and the true light is already shining. 9 The one who says that he is in the light and hates his brother or sister[a] is in the darkness even now. 10 The one who loves his brother dwells in the light and there is no source of stumbling in him.[b] 11 The one who hates his brother is in the darkness and walks in the darkness, and does not know where he is going, because the darkness has blinded his eyes.

a. The Greek has one word in the masculine (*adelphos*); the author presumably would not have excluded female members of the community from this, but at times his argument presupposes the masculine only (see commentary on 3:12), and *adelphos* will be translated "brother" hereafter; similarly, the masculine ("he is . . . ," "his") has been retained; on the problem see Introduction §5.

b. "In him" (masc.) or "in it" (neuter); see commentary.

[7] Addressing his readers as "Beloved" (also 3:2, 21; 4:1, 7, 11) does not mark any significant change of tone from the earlier "My children" (2:1); this is a common form of address in New Testament letters (2 Cor 7:1; 1 Pet 4:12; Jude 3; etc.), and although appropriate to the network of love that follows it is probably not stimulated by it. Hence it is not possible to determine whether the emphasis is on the writer's love for them (as in Phil 2:12) or on their status as loved by God (cf. Eph 5:1). The address serves only to mark a new section, although, as always, there are numerous connections with what has preceded.

Even though the keeping of "his" commands had earlier been a test of authentic knowledge of God (1 John 2:4), there has been little preparation for the introduction now of a single command or for the almost apologetic defense of its age. Although possible in context, it is unlikely that the author is identifying as the not-new command the implied injunction of the previous verse to walk as "he" did. More probably, the concern in what follows here with love for a fellow believer anticipates the subsequent explicit definition of "the command" as belief in Jesus and as love for one another (3:23; cf. 3:11). The author's surprising failure to elucidate its content is compounded by his anxious determination to start by denying its novelty.

An obvious reason for this could be that the addressees already know its content: as he says, it is one they have had "from the beginning." The opening of the letter already signaled the importance of this theme, but here it clearly points back to the beginning of their experience, most probably of their experience as a community formed by belief in Jesus. It would be possible that "the beginning" refers even further back; if this community had come to belief in Jesus out of a Jewish context then it could refer back to a Mosaic commandment that was part of their original tradition, and most naturally in context this would be Lev 19:17–18, "you shall not hate your brother (LXX *adelphos*) . . . you shall love your neighbor (LXX *plēsion*) as yourself," where "brother" and "neighbor" are probably to be taken as equivalents (see further commentary on 3:11). In this case, the author would be emphasizing the continuity in God's purposes and will, an emphasis that would be effective against anyone offering an alternative, new message, but equally against anyone who rejected the "new" faith as being a denial of the past. Just as in the previous larger section, the conviction that God is light, familiar in principle from the Scriptures, moved seamlessly to an exhortation to imitate Jesus, so here the same seamless continuity with past certainties would be affirmed.

However, that this is not the main thrust of the author's argument is shown when he identifies the command as "the word that you heard." In 3:11 the command to love one another is "the message that you heard from the beginning" (cf. 2:24). More than the somewhat neutral "you have had," the appeal to what they have heard is an appeal to their own reception of the message and not just to something inherited from the past (cf. 2:18; 4:3). Moreover, "hearing" is not passive listening but implies active response (cf. 4:5–6). At the beginning of the letter the authority lay with what "we" have heard and so could pass on to others; now the author acknowledges that those whom he addresses are not novices. They can test what is being offered by their own grasp of what they had not merely listened to but had accepted. As in 2:4–6, the switch between "command" and "word" confirms that the former is not an optional extra to the central message proclaimed, but is integral to it.

Both verbs, "had" and "heard," are in the simple past tense, the aorist (in contrast to the perfect "have heard" in 1:1, 3, 5): the emphasis is not on their continuing retention but on that moment of hearing and reception. It is very unlikely that the reference is, as some have suggested, to a significant point of instruction and acceptance such as baptism; there are no explicit references to baptism in 1 John, and supposedly implicit ones in 2:20 and 27—the context for the similar reference to "what you have heard from the beginning" in 2:24— are improbable (see commentary). Those who are convinced that baptism was the normative and decisive experience of all believers may explain the comparative rarity of direct references in the New Testament as because it was taken for granted, and find numerous indirect allusions. Even so, "you heard" would not be the most obvious way of referring to baptism or to its accompanying catechetical instruction. The reference is more likely to their adoption of the proclamation that was their foundation as a community—hence the plural "you" even if different members had joined at different times.

The contrast between "old" and "new" is a common one; often it leads to the detriment of the old, for example in Paul's contrast between the oldness of the letter and newness of the spirit (Rom 7:6). This sense of newness will be developed in the next verse; in the world of the first century, however, antiquity was valued more than novelty, as is captured by the slightly derogatory remarks about the Athenians' delight in novelty in Acts 17:19–21. Even in a parable that seems to accept and celebrate the radical newness of Jesus' teaching, Luke 5:37–39 perceptively adds the comment, "No one who has drunk the old wants new wine; for they will say, 'The old is better.'" In this period those who wanted to win respect for their teaching would endeavor to demonstrate not that it had just been discovered or invented but that it was older than their competitors. Jewish apologists delighted in declaring that Abraham or Moses predated by far the revered figures of Greek wisdom such as Plato, and even tried to demonstrate that the latter had learned from the former two. The antiquity that the author claims for the command is indeed not of that order, but it is its equal, for it goes back to "the beginning," even if that is a beginning valued only by members of the community, the only beginning that matters to them.

For those familiar with the broader Johannine tradition such a reference would be beyond question. In the Fourth Gospel Jesus gives to his disciples a "new command," namely that they should love one another as he, Jesus, has loved them (John 13:34; cf. 15:12, 17, where the command is not described as "new").[24] More dogmatic than this author, but perhaps dependent on him, the elder of 2 John exhorts his readers, "not as if writing a new command for you but one that we have held from the beginning, that we should love one another" (see commentary on 2 John 5). This reinforces the sense of this author's caution, and he does not identify the command until much later in his letter (see 3:11 and the commentary there for the history of the "Johannine love command").

**[8]** Drawing on this tradition of Johannine language, however, the author simultaneously affirms the newness of the command. The claim to newness is pervasive in the New Testament. As in the image adopted from Jer 31:31 of the "new covenant" (Luke 22:20; 1 Cor 11:25; 2 Cor 3:6; Heb 8:8; 9:15), "newness" is seen not as a fresh version of the old, but as something transformed and transformative; when Paul speaks of a "new creation" or Revelation of a "new Jerusalem" (2 Cor 5:17; Rev 3:12; cf. 21:5), they are drawing on Jewish eschatological hopes of the transformation of God's final age, the promise of "new heavens and a new earth" (Isa 65:17; 66:22).

This also seems to be how our author understands the newness of the command. "Which" (*ho*) in Greek is neuter, and not feminine, as would be needed if it referred directly to the command, a feminine noun in Greek. Such unexpected uses of the neuter are a feature of Johannine style (see 5:4 and commentary), but the effect here may be to look beyond the mere content of the command to its context and significance. So it is not the command that is "true in him and in you" but its newness and its authority. In the opening main section of the letter light and darkness could have been taken as fixed, timeless categories or spheres (1:5–7); yet they are more than this, for within the biblical and subsequent tradition darkness represents the sphere opposed to God, and light is that which represents God's will and purpose. To that extent, light belongs to God's future, and darkness is ultimately certain to be overcome; but the future that belongs to God is also in a sense present. In part this is because God's sovereignty means that darkness never has total control, but more specifically it is a consequence of the conviction that God has already acted decisively to bring about the final victory. This is why it can be said that "the true light,"

---

24. The address *teknia* and the formula "in this way" appear only in 13:33–35 in the Gospel, making it unlikely that 1 John, where both are found more widely, is dependent on the Gospel.

that which represents God's presence and power, "is *already* shining," and this is also the source of the confidence that, however things may appear, "the darkness is passing [present tense] away." This may not always be evident: the author and readers of 1 John felt that they lived in a world where the forces hostile to God appeared to be in total control; they do not seem to have felt that they could see glimpses of God's truth and presence in other places and people. For them, the truth of the newness that belongs to the command and the reality of the shining of the light were to be found embodied only in "him," presumably in Jesus, and in the corporate life of the community, in "you."

**[9–10]** The description of the light in verse 8 as "true" or "authentic" may have been a traditional phrase (cf. John 1:9 and below), but it immediately triggers the next step, not that there may be false lights but that there might be false claims to participating in the light. A confidence of belonging to God's new age might lead to complacency, to an assumption that, come what may, the sphere of darkness has been abandoned once and for all. Again the author drives home that his real point is not assurance alone, but the testing of that assurance by the lived experience.

Earlier (1:6–7) "walking in the light" described a way or sphere of being that was self-evident and needed no further description or testing; here "being in the light" is, like "being" or "dwelling in him" (2:5–6), something that someone might assert for oneself but that requires demonstration or falsification by what one does. The thought is the same as that of 2:4, but the behavior that demonstrates the falsity of any claim is not simply a failure to keep his commands, but is hatred of a brother (or sister). This author deals in antitheses, light against darkness, love against hatred: he knows of no middle or neutral ground. At this point, neither hatred nor love (in the next verse) has any specific content; the former may be only the absence of the latter rather than active emotion or behavior, but the active content of love will as yet be left unexplored (see 3:13–18).

A brother is one from whom one might expect love, and whom one might expect to love, although there are enough stories in Scripture, and outside, to demonstrate that the bitterest hostility may also arise between siblings. The archetypal story is that of Cain and Abel in Genesis 4, which the author will recall in 1 John 3:12 (see commentary), although that does not mean that violence and murder are already in mind in the hatred here rejected. Another familiar example would have been that of Joseph and his brothers; the *Testaments of the Twelve Patriarchs* use the device of the brothers' reminiscences to portray the consequences of hatred of a brother, and to exhort readers "each to love his brother(s)" (*T. Gad* 6.1; *T. Sim.* 4.7). First John shares this pattern of ethical exhortation (in contrast to the Gospel, where "brother" is not used in this context).[25] As will

---

25. "Brother" appears in John 2:12; 7:3, 5 of Jesus' actual brothers, in 20:17 ("my brothers") of the disciples, and in 21:23 presumably of other "Johannine believers," but these do not sufficiently explain the usage in 1 John.

become explicit as the letter progresses, a "brother" is a fellow member of the community or a fellow believer, a potential part of the plural "you" (cf. 5:16). This is common in the New Testament (Gal 1:2; Jas 2:15); although it could belong to the picture of a new family, its use of fellow members of a group or association is not peculiar to early Christianity in the ancient world and may have been more casually employed. Hence the translation given above has used in verse 9 "a brother or sister" to indicate that it is unlikely that the writer was addressing an all-male community, nor would he, if asked, have excluded women from his concern for loving and being loved—although in his own time it is equally unlikely that he would have been asked or would have asked himself. However, behind the exhortation lies the image of familial solidarity, so easily disrupted by jealousy and competition, which most ancient readers would have envisaged as a male exercise; for this reason, and in anticipation of the appeal to Cain and Abel (3:12), the translation hereafter will use the exclusive "brother(s)."

Again, it is a misunderstanding to suppose that the author is attacking opponents who did claim "to be in the light," but whose behavior the author identifies as "hatred" and so as excluding them from genuine membership. On that reading, since hatred appears to mean little more than the absence of love, which itself might be reduced to faithful adherence to the community, the author would be berating others for the same pattern of behavior as he is practicing, the rejection of others as fellow members of the community of faith. This is certainly not an impossible reconstruction; there have been many such examples of reciprocal name-calling and denunciation, and a dualistic or antithetical worldview where people are either "in" or "out" perhaps encourages such polarization. However, this is to diminish the thought of the letter by introducing unnecessary players. Rather, the author is working through what the formulations of faith and exhortation that are part of his and of their heritage mean, how they fit together. What are the consequences of believing that the light that belongs to God and God's truth are already active; that, although things may not seem to have changed, the age of darkness is in its terminal stages of decay? How can one live in the light of that certainty? What guidelines are there, what resources for encouragement and warning? There are no real opponents, just alternative ways forward, among which the authentic have to be isolated. The author's earlier attempts to wrestle with this have focused on the individual ("the one who"), while assuming their participation in a community, but now it is their life together that he addresses. This need not mean that he was aware of failings in their corporate life—unlike Paul, our author does not address such concerns directly, rendering their presence hidden. Rather, the antitheses of light and darkness are being transformed within the community into an antithesis of love and hatred; those who heard these words would find themselves being shaped and reinforced as a tight-knit group whose priority was to avoid anything that might splinter it. Such threats might come from outside or from within.

The Dead Sea Scrolls again offer a point of comparison: there those who come together to form a community commit themselves to "love all the sons of light . . . and to detest all the sons of darkness" (1QS I, 9–10). First John does not counsel hatred, although 2:15 may come close to it, because for the author hatred and its exercise belong only to the sphere of darkness and the outside (3:13). Rather than attempting to identify those inside over against those outside, he looks only within. Only those who sustain the common life of the community truly belong to the sphere of the light.

For such there is no likelihood of stumbling, because there is sufficient light around them. This, at any rate, seems to be the meaning of the final phrase of verse 10, literally "there is no stumbling" or "cause of stumbling in him/it." In the background is the idea, forbidden by Lev 19:14, of something left in the way of a blind person that s/he might stumble over, but the metaphor is a natural one: without the imagery of light, Ps 119 (LXX 118):165 declares, "there is abundant peace for those who love your law and there is no stumbling for them." However, "in him" should not be pushed to suggest that such a source of error might otherwise arise from within; to do so would put too much weight on a preposition, "in," that the letter uses with great frequency and imprecision. An alternative but much less satisfactory explanation would be the interpretation that there will be no cause of difficulty or error *for others* in the one who loves, much as Jesus accuses Peter of being a source of stumbling for him in Matt 16:23, or as Paul describes the crucifixion of Jesus as a source of difficulty for Jews (1 Cor 1:23); however, there seems no need to introduce other people into the argument at this point. A further possible alternative translation, "there is no cause of stumbling in it [the light]," echoing the sense of 1:5, would merely reinforce the positive message and seems somewhat redundant.

[11] The contrasting picture is developed more elaborately. One who hates one's brother (or sister) is thoroughly enmeshed in darkness, and is either lost or totally unable to proceed. First John's style of arguing through balanced opposites means that he does not ask whether those who do not love and those who are not loved are still brothers (or sisters). Their failure to love—which is enough to qualify as hatred—establishes their real identity and location, belonging not to the new inbreaking of light, but to the already dissipating world of darkness. To be in total darkness, rare in the modern world with its ever present artificial light, is to experience blindness, to be disoriented without any sense of direction; to "walk in darkness (*skotia*)" might just be a natural image of bewilderment and of the loss of any understanding (see commentary on 1:6 for the ambiguity). The final clause goes further than this: darkness does not just belong to the metaphor of confusion but indicates its source as well as its consequence. The darkness that creates blindness is more than the effect of being in black night, and is more than the absence of light; instead, darkness appears almost as an active force for evil, willfully opposing

God's work of bringing light, and ensuring the lasting incapacity of those who are in its thrall.

This picture invites the question, which comes first? Does the refusal to love set people in the sphere of darkness, with such inescapable results, or does it make evident something that was already true; does their failure to love reveal that, and is it a consequence of the fact that, darkness had already overwhelmed them? The same question is provoked by 1 John's account of the children of God and the children of the devil (3:8–10): is paternity chosen or is it assigned; does it determine or is it determined by behavior? A sharply dualistic, either-or, outlook, with little capacity for any middle ground, could easily support the view that people have been assigned to one category or the other; in answer to the question, Why do some fail to love? would come the answer, Because darkness has destroyed their capacity to see and to respond to the light. For those who read or heard this letter the message is clear: to love or not to love is not a second-level option, subordinate to the confidence of sharing in God's light, nor is it a matter for discussion; it is not something one would then do with a greater or lesser degree of success. To fail to see the inevitability of love within the community is to acknowledge that one has no place there.

As so often 1 John reaches this point not by logic and demonstration but by exploring the consequences of different positions. Yet the persuasiveness of the argument for his first audience also lies in the way that he weaves together earlier traditions. That he is doing so can be recognized by a comparison with the Fourth Gospel, which exhibits a pattern of thought that is similar and yet subtly different. There, Jesus is the light, and belief in him brings one out of walking in darkness (*skotia*: John 8:12; 12:46). Yet there is a note of anxiety, for Jesus' presence among them is not permanent; Jesus' words in 12:35, "The light is among you for a little longer; walk while you have the light, lest the darkness overcome you, since the one who walks in darkness *does not know where he is going*" (the same phrase as in 1 John 2:11), warn against any assumption that once the light of faith has been experienced it cannot be lost, and they recognize the continuing threat of the power of darkness. For would-be disciples beyond the time of Jesus' ministry, these words are a continued call to faith in him. There is a similar idea in John 11:9–10, "if anyone walks in the night, they stumble"; the verb here, *proskoptō*, suggests a similar idea to the interpretation accepted for *skandalon* in 1 John 2:10, and both can represent the same Hebrew root in the Septuagint. Finally, John 12:39–40 sums up the lack of response Jesus encountered by quoting Isa 6:10: "Therefore they were unable to believe, because Isaiah again said, 'He has *blinded* their eyes and he hardened their heart.'" This Isaianic passage is a familiar one in the New Testament, used to reflect on unbelief (Mark 4:11–12; Matt 13:13–15; Acts 28:25–28), but John is distinctive both in reordering the images so that blinding comes first and in using the common verb "to blind" (*typhloō*), rather than the verb "to shut" used by the Septuagint and other New Testament quotations. Despite the different tense (aorist instead of perfect) and person ("his" instead of "their"), 1 John uses the same vocabulary, suggesting a common source with the quotation in John. These shared echoes but different formulations and applications suggest that both writings are drawing on the same tradition, a tradition of language and imagery, and also of biblical exegesis. No doubt this would resonate with 1 John's first audience in ways it can no longer for a contemporary one. Particularly striking is that whereas John 12:40 leaves it open as to who "blinded"—most naturally it is God, as in Isaiah—1 John specifies that it is "the darkness."[26]

Rooted in earlier biblical tradition, such ways of thinking are not peculiar to the Johannine writings. Paul speaks of the "god of this age" as having blinded the minds of unbelievers to make them impervious to the illumination of the gospel (2 Cor 4:4). "Blindness of eyes" is one of the attributes of the spirit of deceit in a passage from the *Community Rule* that offers a number of parallels to 1 John (1QS IV, 11): "To the spirit of injustice belong greed . . . lying and deceit . . . a blaspheming tongue, blind eyes, a deaf ear, a stiff neck, a stubborn heart causing a man to walk in all the ways of darkness."[27] Similarly, Judah attributes his errors to the fact that "the ruler of error" had blinded him (*T. Jud.* 19.4). In these examples, as in 1 John, the source of failure is not God but a power that opposes God. The earlier biblical tradition saw no problem in making God responsible for disobedience, and knew of no other figure to blame, even if this left an element of mystery about the ways of a God who would so act. Within a more dualistic framework it became possible, and perhaps theologically more attractive, to shift the blame to alternative hostile powers. Nonetheless, the terms used, "error," "deceit," "this age," and, in 1 John, "darkness," at the same time indicate the shallowness and ultimate insubstantiality of the opposition. The difficulty that results from this pattern of thought is that when God is held responsible, God may also reverse that act and bring sight and illumination (Isa 29:18; 42:7); when the forces opposed to God are responsible, the hope of reversal may disappear, leaving an explanation of a situation that cannot be altered.

The author of 1 John, however, is not describing particular individuals and then metaphorically washing his hands of them. His goal is exhortation, to use the rhetorical possibility of the alternative to reinforce his own urgent purposes. A passage in the *Testament of Gad*, in terms not unlike 1 John, warns,

> Listen now, my children, to the words of truth, so that you do justice and the whole law of the Most High, and are not led astray by the spirit of hatred, because it is evil for all human deeds. For everything that the one who hates does is defiled; if someone does the law of the Lord, he does not praise them; if someone fears the

26. See further J. M. Lieu, "Blindness in the Johannine Tradition," *NTS* 34 (1988): 83–95.
27. See above on 1 John 1:5 and n. 9.

Lord and desires what is just, he does not love them. He disparages the truth, he is envious of the one who behaves honestly, he welcomes gossip, he loves pride. Because hatred has blinded his soul, just as I perceived in the case of Joseph. Guard against hatred, then, my children, because it works iniquity against the Lord himself. For he does not want to listen to the words of his commands concerning love of neighbor, and he sins against God. (*T. Gad* 3.1–4.1)

The dramatic image of darkness destroying sight brings this section of 1 John to a close. If this was an allusion to a familiar biblical passage, it may also have provided a sense of satisfied closure—the reverse of the modern sermon that starts from a biblical passage and then travels in unexpected directions. The central theme, however, has not been to explain hostility or conflict, nor to challenge those who engaged in it, but repeatedly to bring those who hear or read into commitment to one another. That which binds them together is not the merits of solidarity, nor is it, as in Paul, their mutual interdependence in Christ, but their existence in a world where the only options are light or darkness, truth or falsehood. They have been brought into that world through their past reception of teaching, whose contours are shadowy, but to which the author constantly recalls them. It may appear that he darts about, approaching his focal concern, now from here, now from there, each time assuring them, often by allusions, that they are starting from familiar ground. Yet the process is not haphazard, even while precise vocabulary changes; this major section started from the opposition of light and darkness, and it finishes there; it started with God, in whom there is no darkness, it finishes with the destructive activity of darkness; it starts with "us," and it finishes with the individual and her/his love for another individual, in implied community. Perhaps this is why, although commentators sometimes struggle to do more than paraphrase these verses, they have become so familiar, easily memorized and easily summoned in liturgy.

## 1 John 2:12–17—Encouragement to Persevere

In the first part of the letter the author has addressed his readers only indirectly; although he acknowledges their presence (1:5; 2:1, 7–8, "you"), he has sought their acquiescence in an argument that is overtly directed elsewhere—"if we . . . ," "the one who. . . ." Now he turns to them to assure them that nothing he has said need undermine the confidence they have. The mood and style change dramatically: a number of the themes from the beginning of the letter are recalled, but alongside them are new ones, and together these take the section in a new direction. Some of the new ideas will be picked up later in the letter, and there are also clear links with the broader range of Johannine thought. Again, the author has taken existing formulae or units of tradition whose familiarity will perhaps make them more persuasive, in order to ensure that he keeps his audience with him. This author does not harangue or express his disappointment at their failures, but by encouragement, by an invitation into a debate where the outcome is known, and by the occasional exhortation, he works to ensure that his readers will see things as he does, and in that so doing their community will be strengthened against danger.

That danger will be described for the first time in 2:18, so introducing a new stage in the letter; hence, despite its independent feel, the present section acts as a conclusion to the first major division of the letter or as an interlude between the first and second parts. The first half of this section, verses 12–14, has a formal stylized character, and expresses the assurance; the second half, verses 15–17, turns to urgent exhortation. Together they create a picture that has already become familiar from the earlier imagery of light and darkness; that on the one side there is God and all that belongs to God's sphere, on the other all that opposes God, here labeled "the world." There is no common ground between them, no room for negotiation or compromise, and no possibility of a halfhearted commitment to each. This is a way of understanding commitment that does not think in terms of growth, or of the painful experiences of failure and struggle by which growth is often achieved. The confident affirmation that those who hear this letter have made their choice is at the same time an encouragement to stand firm by it. Although the author means by "the world" much more than the pressures of daily life, the introduction of this term in place of "darkness" prepares the way for relating the oppositional understanding of the existence of the believers to the real situations in which they find themselves.

### *1 John 2:12–14—Children, Fathers, and Youths*

**2:12** I am writing to you, children, because your sins have been forgiven on account of his name; **13** I am writing to you, fathers, because you have known the one from the beginning; I am writing to you, young men, because you have won the victory over the evil one.[a] **14** I wrote[b] to you, children,[c] because you have known the Father; I wrote to you, fathers, because you have known the one[d] from the beginning; I wrote to you, young men, because you are strong and the word of God dwells in you and you have won the victory over the evil one.

a. Codex Sinaiticus reads the neuter, but 1 John's usage elsewhere means this is unlikely to be correct.

b. So the best manuscripts against the Majority text, which continues the present tense, "I am writing," from vv. 12–13.

c. This is a different word from that used in v. 12, but English does not have an alternative; see commentary.

d. Codex Vaticanus reads the neuter, but given the limited manuscript support for this it is unlikely to be original.

A sudden change of style together with the repeated self-reference of this written missive draws the attention. The repetition and balanced phrases appear formulaic, and, although the lines are not poetic, many translations do set them out as if in verse. The first striking division is that between verses 12–13 and verse 14, marked by the change in tense of the main verb from present to past. It is unlikely that this refers to two different occasions and that verse 14 refers to an earlier letter. It is standard in Greek letters to use both the present, "I am writing," reflecting the author's standpoint, and the past "I have written," reflecting the readers' standpoint (cf. 2:1 and 5:13). The author once again takes the opportunity to bind his own experience with that of his readers, while using repetition lightened by variation to drive the point home.

These two divisions are each subdivided into a threefold address, which combines the author's habitual mode of apostrophe, "children" (cf. 2:1), with two further appropriate designations of age, "fathers," "young men." The resultant pattern is open to being understood in two ways, either as a tripartite division (1 + 2 + 3), or as a binary subdivision of those all of whom here as elsewhere can be addressed as children (1 – [a + b]). The ambiguity is probably deliberate; the binary pattern carries associations familiar from other early Christian writings, but when it is combined with the author's own "children" it allows him to exploit both the rhetorical effect of a threefold structure and the expectations of each age group.

That the second pattern, a twofold subdivision, age and youth, is primary is suggested by the unexpected order, "fathers" preceding "young men" and following the initial "children." Binary divisions within the community are found elsewhere in the New Testament, especially in the so-called household codes, which regulate the relationships between wives and husbands, children and parents, slaves and masters (Col 3:18–4:1; Eph 5:25–6:9).[28] Closer to this passage are 1 Peter's exhortation to "elders" followed by that to "younger men, be subject to the elders" (1 Pet 5:1–5), or the Pastor's encouragement to Timothy, "Do not rebuke an elder but exhort him as a father, and younger men as brothers" (1 Tim 5:1; cf. also *1 Clem.* 21.6); in contrast to the normal pattern of the household codes, the senior figure is in these examples placed first, as it is in 1 John. In these passages it is unclear whether the "elders" (*presbyteroi*) hold some office or are merely older in age or experience, and likewise, whether the "younger men" (*neōteroi*) represent a distinct group with particular functions and expectations or are merely the rest, so defined by contrast. The issue is made more complicated in 1 Timothy in that although elsewhere the Pastor treats "elders" as a quasi-official group (1 Tim 5:17), 5:1–2 continues, "exhort . . . older women as mothers, younger women as sisters," where a reference to female elders is widely rejected.[29]

---

28. Col 3:21, "Fathers, do not provoke your children" (cf. Eph 6:4).
29. See Raymond F. Collins, *I and II Timothy and Titus: A Commentary* (NTL; Louisville: Westminster John Knox, 2002), 132–34.

It is true that, unlike these passages, 1 John 2:12–14 is not concerned with reciprocal relationships; nonetheless, they do indicate that this was a familiar technique of dividing up the wider community in order to reinforce its cohesion, regardless of whether such divisions had any further role in the life of the community. In 1 John it seems unlikely that they did: the letter implies that there were no gradations of seniority and experience (2:20, 27), and, generally, the Johannine literature gives little indication of the structures of the community it represents.[30] These are not offices or fixed roles but serve to invite the community to look at itself as combining complementary strengths and insights.

The resultant threefold pattern echoes the standard categories of age and of participation in civic life in the ancient world. These varied in detail: Philo, for example, lists seven stages, each of multiples of seven years: the little child (*paidion*: to age 7), the child (*pais*: to 14), the youth (*meirakion*: to 21), the young man (*neaniskos*: to 28), the man (*anēr*: to 49), the elder (*presbytēs*: to 56), and the old man (*gerōn*) (*On the Creation of the World* 103–5). The three categories of 1 John 2:12–14 would be a natural simplification of this scheme, and in identifying the characteristics of each group the author exploits the conventional expectations associated with them. Like this passage, Greek divisions of the "ages of man" were not interested in women since they would not grow up to play their part in the life of the city.

A further question is whether different groups within the community are being addressed, or whether the community as a whole is being viewed from different perspectives, with the achievements of each stage of life being highlighted. The difference between the two may not be so great, particularly given the replacement of "elders" by "fathers." The characteristics ascribed to each are elsewhere applied to the whole community, and the author would probably not have been too anxious with which any of his readers identified themselves. The masculine form, which I have deliberately retained in the translation, underlines that this is an artificial device dependent on fixed models. It does not mean that there were no women members, and, since the categories are not official, it has nothing to contribute to discussions of women's leadership, or of its absence, in the early church—although the author evidently had no qualms about his silence, which he maintains throughout the letter. This means that little can be concluded about the understanding of the community's constitution; the unexpected "fathers," which belongs to the household codes (Col 3:21), might suggest a family model of the church rather than one based on a civic community, but the absence of women subverts this.

[12–13] The first word of assurance echoes the theme of the first part of the body of the letter (1:7–2:2), and the address to them as "children" (*teknia*) echoes the similar address to all in 2:1. But while all believers are undoubtedly

---

30. See, however, 3 John 9–10 and the commentary there.

dependent on forgiveness, within the threefold pattern only this group are the passive recipients of what has been done for them, a condition appropriate for children. Whereas in the earlier treatment of sin and forgiveness the emphasis was on the reality of the former and on their continuing dependence on the latter, here the emphasis is that forgiveness *has been* granted and *is* now a secure possession. This is not something they need telling—although "because" could be translated "[I am writing . . .] that," this would make the whole section banal; rather, it is the firm foundation on which everything that follows rests, both assurance and warning. As indicated by the perfect tense, forgiveness is a completed past act, a state in which they now live. Its source or basis is "his name"; as elsewhere in the New Testament "the name" (*to onoma*) represents the person and their authority, and the nonspecific "his" presumably indicates Jesus, although subsequent references to "the name" specify this (3:23; 5:13). The phrase "on account of (*dia*) his name" is more frequently used for the grounds of persecution (John 15:21; cf. Matt 10:22; 24:9; Rev 2:3), and here it sounds more formulaic than precise: the author is not concerned to specify how the person of Jesus effects or is a cause of forgiveness or how this relates to the models used earlier in the letter (1 John 1:7–2:2); he has no single story or theology of salvation.[31]

The address to the fathers takes up the theme of "knowing him," which also followed the initial concern with forgiveness (2:3–4). In the commentary at those verses I traced the religious background to the idea of knowing the Divine, but here it is not a matter of testing and demonstrating a claim but of establishing a secure basis for what will follow. Again, the perfect tense emphasizes that such knowledge is a confident possession, a relationship rooted in the past, something perhaps appropriate for those addressed as "fathers," even though this assurance also could be claimed for all the faithful. The one whom they know is "the one from the beginning"; in contrast to the neuter pronoun of 1:1, the masculine article is personal but would equally suit a reference to God or to Jesus. As elsewhere in 1 John, a firm conclusion is not possible: the regular indeterminacy of references to God and/or Jesus as "him," together with the probability that these verses draw on familiar phrases from the community's worship or teaching, exclude certainty. The specific "you have known *the Father*" in verse 14 might suggest by contrast that "the one" here refers to Jesus. The epithet would be appropriate to Jesus inasmuch as he belongs to the proclamation "from the beginning" to which the author repeatedly appeals (2:7, 24; 3:11; cf. commentary on 1:1). However, equally if not more probably here "the beginning" is the beginning of all things, as it is in 3:8, where the devil sins "from the beginning." Since 1 John otherwise shows no interest in the preexistence of the Son or Word,

---

31. This is a different formula from Acts 10:43, where forgiveness is "*through* his name," using the same preposition (*dia*) but followed by the genitive case.

any such reference here would probably indicate that the author is citing a familiar creedal formula (cf. John 1:1, "In the beginning was the word"), something the style of these verses would support. Yet a creedal or formulaic reference to God, whom according to 1 John 2:3–4 "we" may claim to "have known" (see commentary), would also fit the style and rhythm well.

In the passage quoted earlier from Philo the "young men" (*neaniskoi*) were those in their twenties, so it is appropriate that their achievement here carries a military note, although later (4:4) everyone addressed shares in the victory won. Again, the perfect tense emphasizes not the struggle but the victory achieved as one that cannot be reversed. As the context shows "the evil one" (*ho ponēros*) is not anyone who is wicked (as in Matt 5:39; 12:34–35), but, as frequently elsewhere in the New Testament, the archopponent of God, who might also be labeled "the devil" or "Satan" (cf. Matt 13:19 with the parallels in Mark 4:15; Luke 8:12). The idea of such a figure has its roots in the biblical period, when Satan, initially a sort of public prosecutor in the service of God (Job 1–2), becomes one who is determined to incite men and women into disobedience toward God (1 Chronicles 21). In the subsequent "intertestamental" literature this figure, his story and activities, and his names develop quickly, but no single label or account predominates, and this is also the case in the New Testament. The term "the evil one" is particularly favored by 1 John (2:13–14; 3:12; 5:18–19), and, unlike the possible ambiguity elsewhere in the New Testament (cf. John 17:15), the form is clearly masculine, not neuter. The choice of epithet takes the focus away from a strange figure, neither human nor divine, who inhabits the world of story and vision, and fixes it instead on the moral dimension. Later an integral connection will be made between Cain's evil deeds and his origin from the evil one (1 John 3:12). This does not mean that the power of evil is seen only in human terms; 1 John will place its power in sharp antithesis to the power and protection of God (5:18–19). That later passage will suggest that such protection is still needed, but here the emphasis lies on the celebration of defeat, not for all people and for all time, but by these members of the community, who therefore have no more to fear. Distinctively, the victory is theirs, a perspective 1 John maintains, reaffirming later that it is the faithful members of the community who have won a victory both over the world and over its more mundane representatives (4:4; 5:4–5); in contrast, in John 16:33 Jesus says, "Do not be afraid, *I* have conquered the world."

The language of total victory draws on the imagery of a final battle between God and all that opposes God's kingdom. A vivid account of such a conviction is given in the *War Scroll* (1QM), which describes in great detail the coming conflict between "the sons of light" and "the sons of darkness [and] the company of Belial" (1QM I, 1); this itself draws on the older traditions of Israel's capture of the land of Canaan understood as a "holy war," on the mythologization of these and similar traditions in the Psalms, and on their subsequent transformation in the prophetic and apocalyptic hopes for the future (Deuteronomy 20; Psalms 83; 98; Zechariah 14). Within the New Testament these traditions are most distinctively taken up in Revelation, where the faithful who win their victory are constantly in view (Rev 2:7, 11, 17; 12:11, etc.). It is easy to see how such expectations, with their graphic imagery, could give hope and meaning to groups who felt themselves alienated and powerless in society, and whose conviction of the supreme power of God and of their place in God's purposes seemed to have little realization in the present. They are also open to abuse, especially when taken up by those who hold real power and particularly when they are used to justify aggression or domination in the present. In 1 John, as in the Gospel, the victory lies not in the future but in the past, but it has no visible effects and brings no visible benefits; it is experienced only by faith.

[14] The second stanza reiterates the first, with sufficient changes to avoid tedium. A more familiar word for "children" (*paidia*) is used; this would give a closer echo of the Greek categories of age, but since Jesus uses the same address to his disciples in John 21:5, it may belong to the Johannine vocabulary of community, and the author uses it again for all his readers to introduce the next section (2:18). Like the fathers, they "have known"—the perfect tense again—but the one whom they have known is "the Father" (see above)—perhaps an appropriate variation for those described as "children." It has already been said that fellowship is with the Father and that forgiveness is assured through the paraclete before the Father, and the next section will speak of those who deny the Father as well as the Son (1:3; 2:1, 22); the next two verses will contrast the world and the Father (2:15–16). God is Father because God is the Father of the Son, Jesus Christ (see also 2:23–24; 4:14), just as in the Gospel Jesus speaks of God as "the Father" and not as "my" or "your Father" until 20:17, "I am going to my Father and your Father, my God and your God." First John does not exploit the potential of "father" to evoke relationship and intimacy; it is more of a designation of who God is: 3:1 will celebrate the fact not that we can call God "Father," but that we are called "children of God." Nonetheless 1 John does not understand Father and Son in terms of the inner being of God as in later trinitarian doctrine.

Although the fathers are addressed in the same terms as in the first stanza, the account of the young men is expanded, producing something of a rhetorical climax. Thus, appropriately to their age and military victory, they are "strong," but the term (*ischyros*), which is not used elsewhere in the Epistles or in the Gospel, does not appear to carry any deeper associations. Just as these verses opened with an echo of the earlier section of the letter, so they now close with one: 1:10 had already declared that "his word is not in" those who claim not to have sinned, but here the emphasis is again on the positive—the word of God does dwell in them. For the first time, "the word," which in 1:10 and 2:5 was the indeterminate "his," is identified as "of God," but the earlier uses (cf.

also 2:7) show that secure possession and internalization of the message that comes from God, the message on which preaching and reflection depend, is intended, and not any christological reference. This is in contrast to Rev 19:13, where "the Word of God" is the name given to the rider of the white horse, but it is closer to other New Testament practice where the phrase indicates the proclamation of the gospel message (Acts 4:31; 6:2; 13:5; 1 Cor 14:36). In John's Gospel Jesus declared that those who refused to accept that he acted as sent by God did not "have the word of God dwelling" in them (John 5:38), and there that word was expressed in the Scriptures on which they relied but was not limited by them (see also 10:35); Jesus also offered his own word as that on which faith depended (8:31, 51; 12:48; 15:7), although its origin was in God (14:24; 17:14, 17). Although 1 John's exploration of the theme has a narrower focus, it moves within the same atmosphere.

This is the last reference to "word" in the letter (other than the adverbial use in 3:18), and this means that it effectively rounds off the pattern that began with the first reference in 1:1. In the prologue "the word" belonged to the experience that "we" proclaimed to "you"; here it belongs firmly and without mediation or dependence to "you," the young men but also the whole community addressed. The author maintains a careful balance between assurance and guidance, as also between assurance and exhortation.

### *1 John 2:15–17—Do Not Love the World*

> 2:15 Do not love the world, or the things that are in the world. If anyone does love the world, the love of the Father[a] is not in them; 16 for everything that is in the world, the desire that pertains to the flesh, and the desire that pertains to the eyes, and the arrogance that pertains to life, belongs not to the Father but to the world. 17 The world is passing away as is the desire that pertains to it, but the one who does the will of God continues forever.[b]

> a. Several manuscripts, including Alexandrinus, substitute the more familiar "love of God," and there is considerable variation in the word order.
> b. Some Latin and Coptic (Sahidic) manuscripts add, "as that one also continues forever."

[15] The previous verses have rhetorically set the readers on a firm platform; they have achieved a certainty of faith and show no signs of instability. For the author, however, this offers no grounds for complacency. It has served to present a worldview where there is no room for negotiation between the sphere that belongs to God and to possession of God's word, and the sphere that belongs to the evil one. The exhortation that follows presupposes the same

uncompromising division. Here, for the first time, the negative side of that division is labeled "world." On three occasions 1 John uses "world" (*kosmos*) for the whole totality that is the setting for and the object of the salvation and forgiveness brought by Jesus (2:2; 4:9, 14; see commentary), but these phrases sound formulaic, and do not represent the main thrust of his thought. More frequently in 1 John "world" denotes a reality that is fundamentally negative: believers necessarily engage with the world, but it is intrinsically hostile to them and to the ways of God: they are to expect to experience its hatred (3:13). Insofar as the world is capable of response (4:5), it is personalized if not embodied in actual men and women; but it is more than the sum total of people, or even of those people who reject the message. In its totality it represents that sphere which is under the sway of the evil one (5:19), and it has its own inherent character and power, which come close to setting it in antithesis to God (4:4–5).

This means that the *kosmos* to a large degree constitutes the negative pole in 1 John's dualistic framework, as it does also in the Fourth Gospel. Although positive formulations are more focal there (John 4:42; 8:12), Jesus describes his disciples as hated by the world because they do not belong to the world, just as he does not belong to the world; and he announces that he does not pray for the world (17:9, 14–16). The formulation "this world" (11:9; 13:1; cf. 1 John 4:17) betrays that the origins of this pattern of thinking belong in a Jewish apocalyptic perspective that contrasted this present age with the age to come (cf. Matt 12:32; Mark 10:30). Inevitably, the present age is characterized by opposition to God, just as the age to come will witness the fulfillment of God's purposes and sovereignty. In the Pauline literature the normal Greek (and LXX) term for "age" (= period of time), *aiōn*, is used alongside *kosmos* (1 Cor 1:20–21; 3:18–19; Eph 2:2) with this meaning; Paul also uses *kosmos* on its own in this sense, particularly in 1 Corinthians (1 Cor 2:12; 5:10). Although there are parallels to a disparagement of social ties and material life, there does not seem to be any precedent in Greek or Hellenistic Jewish thought for *kosmos* being so used; with its root meaning of order and arrangement, *kosmos* usually carried positive overtones about the coherence, and even beauty, of the universe and the proper ordering of society. Some have argued that in 1 Corinthians Paul was deliberately redefining a familiar concept in a distinctive way in order to resocialize his readers into a new understanding of contemporary society as something alien to them and as under God's judgment (1 Cor 1:27–28).[32] However, although this distinctive use of *kosmos* is part of Paul's broader cosmology, as it is for the Gospel and First Letter of John, there are no obvious connections between the two sets of writings. Neither the Gospel nor 1 John uses the more familiar "age," *aiōn*, in this way, and, unlike 1 Corinthians, the Johannine *kosmos* is not expressed within

---

32. See E. Adams, *Constructing the World: A Study in Paul's Cosmological Language* (SNTW; Edinburgh: T. & T. Clark, 2000).

patterns of social experience—such as the concerns of the married (1 Cor 7:33–34); instead it appears to constitute a force and a character of its own. The possibility cannot be excluded that there was some precedent perhaps in Hellenistic Jewish thought now lost to us. However, a simultaneous, parallel development in Paul and in the Johannine tradition is not impossible, and would suggest that both arose from a similar experience of fundamental alienation from contemporary assumptions about the virtues of organized society.

Therefore, when the author forbids any love of the world, this is not in itself a rejection of the accoutrements of a comfortable life, or of social success and its benefits; neither is it a repudiation of anything associated with human bodily existence as if this was by definition something to be escaped from—although conceivably these might follow. There is not here an idealization of a spiritual life that advocates contemplation against action, neither is there a denial of the Matthean exhortation to "love your enemies" (Matt 5:44). Both love and the world have to be understood within the framework of 1 John's thought; as already in 1 John 2:10, and as will be developed in the second half of the letter, love is that which binds the believers together because it constitutes and confirms their participation in a network of love that has its origins in God (4:7–12). If "the world" represents the forces antithetical to God, then it is self-evident that it is not possible to be part of a network of love both with the world and with God. These are two mutually exclusive patterns of loyalty, and those who have been addressed in the previous verses are already identified as excluded from the former.

The last clause of the verse reinforces this: love for the world is incompatible with "the love of the Father"—the one whom the "children" have known (2:14). The translation deliberately reflects the ambiguity of the Greek (i.e., love from or for God; cf. 2:5, "love of God," and see commentary). If precision is demanded, "love for the Father," an objective genitive, is most likely to be intended in parallel to loving the world: this anticipates the opposition in the next verse between what belongs to the Father and what belongs to the world, and is itself partly anticipated by verse 14 where the Father is the one known by the "children." Thus no one who loves the world can claim to harbor love for the Father;[33] 4:20–5:1 will complete the circle with the assertion that no one can claim to love God and fail to love his or her fellow believer. The alternative, a subjective genitive as in 2:5, the love that comes from the Father, also makes good sense: someone who loves the world cannot be the place wherein the Father's love is secured. Given 1 John's many ambiguities of expression, however, it may be mistaken to ask of his thought a precision that it did not have.

If the first phrase and the last clause repeat the impossibility of love for the *kosmos* by those who know and love God, the expansion, "(do not love) the things that are in the world," apparently gives more content to what such love

33. For the idea cf. Jas 4:4.

might mean beyond commitment and loyalty alone. Whereas the Gospel of John acknowledges that disciples are necessarily "in the world" (John 16:33; 17:11–13), 1 John is somewhat more ambivalent about this (see commentary on 4:4, 17). Here what is in the world is excluded from being the object of love simply in virtue of its being there.

[16] Given this framework, the "world" needs no further definition. On this basis an encouragement to avoid it could only mean an encouragement to stick closely together with fellow believers. However, 1 John is not satisfied with this, but goes on to define "everything" that is in the world, and that cannot be the object of the attention and the intention of believers; to do so he uses language that is rare in or otherwise absent from the Gospel and Letters, but which reflects ethical traditions widespread elsewhere. Although "desire" (*epithymia*) can be used of appropriate longing, its negative potential is explored extensively in both Greek and Jewish thought. Thucydides already contrasts acting from desire with doing so by foresight, while it was a commonplace in philosophy that desire always threatens to overturn the rational mind, and needs to be controlled with regular practice (Thucydides, *Hist.* 6.13; Epictetus, *Diss.* 2.18). Psalm 106 (LXX 105):14 describes the Israelites' testing of God in the wilderness as because of their "desire," while the Wisdom of Solomon assumes that "roving desire" is as damaging as a "fascination with wickedness" (Wis 4:12). Some scholars have also pointed to the rabbinic concept of the "evil inclination," the built-in human propensity to choose evil; but the basic idea, and the use of the Greek term, are already sufficiently widespread not to require direct dependence on that.

Close to 1 John's language is the warning in Gal 5:16 that they not fulfill "the desire of the flesh"; or Eph 2:3, which describes its readers as having formerly lived "in the desires of your flesh"; or the description in 2 Pet 2:10 of those who "indulge their flesh in depraved desire." In such formulations "flesh," *sarx*, is entirely negative, representing the human capacity for self-indulgence and self-preoccupation that ignores the requirements and purposes of God. This type of polemic was encouraged by Greek thought, in which greed, uncontrolled emotions, and particularly sexual passion were associated with the body, but it also went beyond that in constructing "flesh" (and not "body") in opposition to God and to God's creative power (or spirit). First John has brought together the Johannine cosmological dualism and mythologization of "the world," with this separate ethical tradition that also works with a form of dualism, but with one that is more moral and anthropological. However, he does so only here, and it has no further effect on the rest of the letter: there are limited connections with the other uses of "flesh," "eyes," and "life" (*bios*) elsewhere in 1 John (4:2; 1:1; 3:17 [see commentary]; "desire" is found only here).

This background suggests that it would be looking for too much precision to ask whether the flesh and the eyes are the sources of desire, or its location, or whether they are its objects (i.e., what the eyes see, the external); similarly, there is no need to determine quite how arrogance and life relate to each other, although it is probably significant that the word used (*bios*) is a different one from the divinely revealed life (*zōē*) of 1 John 1:1–2. For the same reason it is probably unnecessary to identify separate activities among the three phrases—for example, that the desire of the flesh is sexual, the desire of the eyes is covetousness, and the arrogance of life is wealth—or to relate them to the attractions of the forbidden tree in Gen 3:6, "good for food . . . a delight to the eyes . . . to be desired to make one wise." A threefold formula is, as already demonstrated by verses 12–14, a familiar and effective rhetorical device, and verse 17 will show that there is but one desire. Again, the *Testament of Judah* invites comparison, where Judah exhorts his sons, "Now, children, listen to your father, as to whatever I command you, and observe all my words, so you do the just requirements of the Lord and obey the command of the Lord God. And do not live in pursuit of your desires, in the longings of your thoughts, or in the arrogance of your heart" (*T. Jud.* 13.1–2). First John is not advocating an ascetic rejection of any physical pleasures. Rather the author is drawing on what were probably conventional formulations in order to infuse the rather abstract concept of "the world" with the immediacy of potential threat—something that, in the Greek as well as in other New Testament traditions, required continuous vigilance.

These seductive possibilities to be avoided are not just "in the world," they belong to the world and not to the Father: with this the author returns to the contrast between loving the world and love of the Father in the previous verse.[34] "Belongs to" represents the Greek preposition *ek*, usually translated "from." The same preposition is used in 4:4–5, "You are *ek* God . . . they are *ek* the world (*kosmos*)"; and in John 17:14, where Jesus speaks of his disciples, like he himself, as not being "*ek* the world." This is an unusual use of the preposition and it seems to have been a Johannine formulation: 1 John 3:19 affirms that "we are *ek* the truth," and the Gospel also speaks of being *ek* below or above, *ek* the earth or heaven (John 3:31; 8:23). The phrase could be translated as "come from" God (or the world), or, even more strongly, as "have as [their/your] origin" in God or the world. This last possibility would emphasize much more strongly that there is something intrinsic and potentially irreversible about one or other possibility. Certainly this is implied by the image of "birth *ek*" in 1 John 5:1 (see commentary). In the present verse, however, the difference would be slight; at stake is the utter incompatibility of anything that might be identified with "world" and anything to be identified with the "Father," and the consequent need for readers to be single-minded about their loyalties. How this is to be expressed is yet to be made clear.

---

34. The phrase "of the father" and the word "desire" also appear together in John 8:44 and not otherwise in the Gospel or Letters, but in the Gospel "the father" is the devil; however, there may be an echo here of related traditions developed in very different directions.

[17] Although the language of "the world" against "the Father" repeats the sharp dualism that shapes the thought of 1 John, this is not a fixed, unchanging opposition. Earlier in this chapter, in 2:8, the author described the darkness as "on the way out" (*paragetai*); now he uses the same verb of the world and of its desire. The use of the singular here, rather than the plural "desires," shows it to be more than a number of inappropriate human longings, namely the negative aspiration and mind-set that the author has identified as alien to God; it is indelibly marked by its association with "the world." In affirming the passing of the world the author probably did not have in mind any cosmological eschatological catastrophe; this is not the disappearance of the first heaven and earth of Rev 21:1, where a transformed new heaven and earth will replace the old. In 1 John's thought such vivid eschatological imagery has been transformed to become a way of expressing the utter incompatibility between the sphere that represents God's will and intention, and all that opposes it, as well as the complete certainty that, regardless of whatever might have been happening in society and to this community of believers, the opposition to God was irreversibly doomed. Moreover, the community of believers should think of themselves as living already in the shadow, or rather in the light, of this final confirmation of God's will and purposes. But the contrast is not really between present and future but between transience and permanence, between the already-disappearing world and the immovability of the one who does the will of God. It would be mistaken to press this last phrase to ask whether 1 John is now concerned with specific ethical patterns: the phrase "to do the will of God" is a traditional one in the Gospel (John 6:38–40; 7:17) but also elsewhere (Matt 7:21; 12:50; Rom 12:2), and it requires no elaboration.

This section has served as something of an interlude, bridging the transition between the more internal conversation of the first part of the letter and the sense of threat to the well-being of the community that will shape what follows. It expresses a tension that lies at the heart of 1 John between the certain assurance that is promised to those who have experienced the knowledge and forgiveness of God, and the devastating consequences of compromising their total commitment to God. From the subsequent verses the test of such commitment appears to be focused in allegiance to the community or to the fellowship fostered by the author, but he does not, at this point or later, use the language of structural membership. It seems likely that a particular, limited, group is being addressed, although again, despite the parallels found for verses 12–14, its shape and structures are of little interest to the author; rather, he sets them on a stage where the opposing forces are "the world," and time is not a matter of today or tomorrow but of the passing of an age. The author shows no awareness that some may struggle with the clear alternatives he lays before them, but equally he offers few guidelines as to how to apply them to the dilemmas of a daily life where presumably members of his audience lived alongside many who did not share their convictions. The section that follows may explain his attitude, but for an analysis of the ambiguities even of faith and Christian living one would have to look outside this letter.

## 1 John 2:18–28—Standing Firm against Deceit

Up to this point the letter has directed its readers' attention to the authenticity of their own lives and convictions. There have been glimpses of the possibility of misjudged or misdirected assumptions of faithfulness, and the readers have been left in no doubt that there is no room for wavering or for compromise. Only now does what drives the sense of urgency and threat that shapes the author's understanding of the present context become explicit. The situation he describes is veiled by the allusive and evocative language that he uses: he implies a recent decisive and disturbing division, but he explains it in terms drawn from expectations of a final conflict between the forces of God and those that oppose God; at the same time, he fails to give any clear account of what has generated the crisis, taking refuge in formulae that he feels to be threatened. This allusiveness has not prevented subsequent readers from attempting to reconstruct and explain the situation; however, any such attempt may distract attention from the main thrust of the author's own argument, which is both to reassure his readers and at the same time to warn them against deviating from the tradition of faith that has held them together so far. Indeed, this emphasis may even suggest that his avoidance of detail, evidence, or argument is deliberate, designed to reinforce the mutual commitment and loyalty of those whom he addresses.

### *1 John 2:18–23—The Appearance of the Antichrists*

**2:18** Children, it is the last hour; indeed, just as you heard that an antichrist[a] is to come, so even now many antichrists have made their appearance. It is from this that we know that it is the last hour. **19** They did go out from among us, but they did not belong[b] to us; indeed, if they had belonged to us, they would have remained with us. Instead, the purpose was that they might be revealed, all of them, as not belonging to us.[c] **20** But you, however, possess an anointing from the holy one, and you all know.[d] **21** I have not written to you because you do not know the truth but because you know it, and know[e] that no lie belongs to the truth. **22** Who is the liar other than the one who denies that Jesus is the Christ?[f] Such a one is the antichrist, the one who denies the Father and the Son. **23** Everyone who denies the Son does not possess the Father either; the one who acknowledges the Son also possesses the Father.[g]

a. Some manuscripts make this specific, "the antichrist," and the English "an" may be more indefinite than the Greek implies; see commentary.

b. In English translation it is difficult to show that "belong[ed]" is the same Greek word as "from among" (*ek*); see commentary on 2:16 and on this verse.

c. Some manuscripts and versions read, "the purpose was that it might be shown that they [or "all"] do [or "did"] not belong to us"; this is an attempt to simplify the difficult Greek; see commentary.

d. Some manuscripts read "you know all things"; see commentary.

e. The verb "know" is not repeated here in the Greek.

f. Because there is an article with "Christ" but not with "Jesus," this could be translated "that the Christ is Jesus." The absence of the article with a proper name is not unusual and the translation given will be defended in the commentary.

g. This last clause is omitted in the later Majority text and put in italics by the KJV, but the omission is probably due to it and the previous clause ending with the same five words, making it easy for a scribe to skip a line.

**[18]** The address marks a new section (see 2:1), although the use of the same term for "children" as in verse 14 also provides some continuity; this section also will confirm the knowledge they hold, and their relationship with the Father. The author has already expressed his conviction that they were living at the turn of the ages, when the era of darkness and of the world was fading (2:8, 17); but there that certainty sounded a note of reassurance that the choices they had made would be vindicated. Here urgency and potential danger dominate. However, by starting with something they share before reinterpreting it he cleverly keeps his readers with him in this new territory.

In the Hebrew Bible the phrase "the latter days" or "the following days" is used not just generally of the future (as in Num 24:14) but of a time when God's purposes will become manifest (Isa 2:2); the Septuagint translation, "the last days," sharpened the sense of finality that could be heard in such passages, particularly as the idea developed of a climactic final stage in God's dealings with God's people and the world (e.g., Dan 11:40–12:13, especially 12:13, "the end of the days," where, however, a different term is used for "the end"). While some New Testament writers saw themselves as already living in that period since the coming of Christ (Acts 2:17; Heb 1:2), others retained it for a future that still loomed (2 Tim 3:1; 2 Pet 3:3). In passages such as the latter, the last days would be marked by an intensification of opposition to God and of danger to God's people. This is also a widespread theme: 1 Thessalonians 5 assumes that readers will be anticipating the sudden arrival of "the day of the Lord" bringing destruction for the unprepared, while in Mark 13 Jesus addresses the question of the signs of the end with warnings of persecution, betrayal, and great suffering even before days that will be marked by cosmic upheaval preceding the "day or hour no one knows." Here too such beliefs are to be set within a wider pattern of Jewish expectations about the end. A common theme in such expectations is that opposition to God will be focused in a single figure, mirroring and challenging God's claim to sovereignty, perhaps also with an accompanying court; 2 Thess 2:1–12 warns against overenthusiastic or overanxious expectation, setting out a timetable in which the appearance of "the lawless one" who "opposes and sets himself above every so-called god" provokes the final appearance of Jesus. Perhaps slightly more mundanely, Mark 13 anticipated "false messiahs and false prophets" who might even, were it possible, lead astray the elect (Mark 13:21–22; cf. vv. 5–6). An extensive history-of-religions background has been traced for such beliefs,[35] but since they probably took many different forms, their precise shape among 1 John's readers can only be determined from what the letter implies.

First John uses, but only here, the distinctive phrase "the last hour"; "hour" can indicate not a specific measure of time but a significant moment, as it does in Mark 13:32 (cf. Rev 3:3), where it also has an eschatological reference. The Fourth Gospel also uses the term, but with reference to Jesus' hour, implicitly culminating in his death, which was also his return to his Father (John 2:4; 7:30; 12:23; 13:1; etc.); although Jesus' hour is an eschatological event, the moment of judgment (12:31), when referring to a future judgment and resurrection the Johannine Jesus by contrast speaks of "the last day" (6:39–44; 12:48).[36] Hence Gospel and Letter share the term "hour," but the frameworks within which they use it are very different, with no obvious connection. First John is closer to the eschatological pattern of other contemporary writings.

The expectation of the arrival of an "antichrist" fits this pattern, although the specific term is distinctive, coming only in 1 John (2:18, 22; 4:3) and 2 John (7) in the New Testament and subsequently in writers dependent on these traditions (Polycarp, *Phil.* 7.1). It is therefore difficult to know whether readers would have recognized the term itself as a quasi-technical term, or whether the author has coined it to give a precise identity to a more indeterminate figure; the use of the unusual *chrisma* ("anointing") in this passage (1 John 2:20, 27), which shares the *chris-* root, suggests that it was either his coinage or part of a set of terms current in the group. Although in form ("anti-") the term could mean one who claims the place of (the) Christ or Messiah (cf. Mark 13:21, "pseudochrists"), the concern about correct belief in the Christ that follows (1 John 2:22) suggests that it means one who opposes (the) Christ (or Messiah) (cf. 2 Thess 2:4). However, the author is less concerned with details and more to use that shared expectation to interpret recent events. Other New Testament authors probably identified the semimythological figure of eschatological expectation with real or

---

35. See already W. Bousset, *The Antichrist Legend: A Chapter in Christian and Jewish Folklore* (trans. A. H. Keane; London: Hutchinson, 1896); more recently, L. J. Lietaert Peerbolte, *The Antecedents of Antichrist: A Traditio-Historical Study of the Earliest Christian Views on Eschatological Opponents* (JSJSup 49; Leiden: Brill, 1996).

36. Some would see in the different terminology and focus the sign of a later editorial hand.

anticipated historical figures (so also Rev 13:11–18), but 1 John looks not to the
world stage but to something much more immediate to their experience; so *an*
antichrist becomes "many antichrists."

It would be logical to suppose that it was an existing eschatological expectation that looked for the imminent coming of an antichrist which prompted the
identification of the many as antichrists, and in practice this may be how the
author's argument would persuade his readers. However, overtly he reverses
the logic: he does not demonstrate or defend the identification of the many, but
instead he assumes its cogency and so draws the conclusion that this is no ordinary event but a sign of the final testing moment, and hence demanding of particular caution.

**[19]** His uncompromising identification of the antichrists was demanded by
the apparently much more problematic situation in which he found himself.
These "antichrists" had not emerged suddenly and without preparation but had
previously been members of "our group." The awkwardness of the author's language betrays the difficulty he faced in explaining what had happened. Previously he had denied that anything in the world could have its origin in, or
"belong to" (*ek*), the Father; now he denies that "they" truly had their origin in
or "belonged to (*ek*) us" (see commentary on 2:16). Yet if the former was self-
evident, the latter is not, for evidently "they" indeed had had their origin among
"us," although now they had "gone out," presumably irrevocably separating
from "us." The author's solution to this dilemma is to declare that any apparent previous common membership was illusory, falsified by its impermanence;
had it been a genuine belonging, they would not have separated but would still
be secure partners in the common fellowship.

This explanation provokes a troubling specter of insecurity and instability.
How could any group be totally confident of the authentic belonging of all its
apparent members if the only certain test was their continuing membership, which
might at any time be unexpectedly terminated? The author is compelled to address
this, but his precise meaning is unclear.[37] Probably he means that the purpose—
presumably of what had happened, although this is not made explicit—was that
*they*, the false members, might be exposed. The grammar of what follows is
clumsy; he may be elaborating what such exposure entails (or possibly its cause),
namely that (or because) none of *them* (lit. "they all . . . not") had any claim to
true membership. Alternatively, he is making a more far-reaching assertion, that
the reason behind their exposure was because not everyone, presumably who so
claims, belongs to "us"; so understood, the events were a dire warning, prompt-

---

37. Some manuscripts and versions have him conclude that the purpose was so that *it* (not
"they") could be made clear either that they (all) did not belong to "us," or that not everyone (who
might appear to) does belong to us; since this reads more smoothly in Greek it is unlikely to be
original.

ing vigilance lest there be other, still covert, alien members. Although this second alternative observes the Greek word order more closely, the wider context does not indicate that he is introducing such a theologically troubling possibility; a certain circularity and a lack of grammatical precision are characteristic of the author's style, and he tends to argue by constructing such closed circles as this without exploring the practical or theological dilemmas that might ensue: "they" left us because they were not genuine members of the group/their leaving demonstrated the truth of their nonmembership.[38]

It is commonly assumed that the group of believers to whom the author is writing had experienced some form of schism: a group had broken away on the grounds of differences in belief or practice yet to be explained; it might even be that the majority had refused to follow the route taken by the audience of 1 John and would, if asked, have declared the latter to be those who left. In this view the author is interpreting what would in any case have been a distressing experience, but one made more so by a prior belief in the complete security in faith of those who had shared a fellowship of experience of forgiveness and understanding (2:12–14). The only framework in which he can make sense of events is by recasting their expectation of eschatological tension and conflict, historicizing a quasi-mythological set of images. He would not have been alone in doing this: many would argue that actual historical figures, although in these cases on the world stage, may lie behind the vivid images of Mark 13 or of Revelation 13; our author would merely be somewhat more parochial in perspective.

However, the repeated use of "us" in contrast to the "you" of the following verse (v. 20) suggests that the problem has arisen not in the community to whom the author is writing but among those whom he has only identified as "we." In verse 18 he is not explaining to his readers the true meaning of their own experience but is warning them of something they may yet encounter. Those to whom they looked for authoritative teaching and as the source of their own understanding were fallible, or worse. In this setting, to describe those others as having "gone out from us" is heavily ambiguous: perhaps from their own mouths it would have carried a note of authority, as when Jesus uses the same language of his mission from God (John 8:42; cf. 3 John 7 and commentary). But there can also be a negative "going out," seen particularly in the Fourth Gospel's picture of Judas; he too is described as having "gone out" from the fellowship of Jesus and the other disciples (John 13:30, 31); in the narrative context there the verb is meant literally, but the terse "it was night" (13:30) offers a comment on the deeper significance of the event (cf. 11:9–10). Judas was one of the Twelve, chosen by Jesus, and yet was to be labeled "the one destined for [Greek: the son of] destruction" (*ho hyios tēs apōleias*) (17:12), an epithet given

---

38. A further alternative would be to read the second half of the verse as an exclamation, "But let them be exposed . . ."; this is possible in Johannnine Greek but seems least likely.

to the eschatological opponent in 2 Thess 2:3; this is clearly troubling for the Gospel's firm confidence in the security of those entrusted to Jesus by God (John 6:70–71; cf. 6:37–39; also the disciples who turned back in 6:66). The Gospel may be wrestling not only with the theological problem posed by the historical traditions concerning Judas, but also with more immediate conflict and division among those revered as continuing the discipleship and authoritative witness of Jesus' first followers, a situation analogous to that reflected by 1 John.

Other New Testament writers are also forced to respond to conflicting interpretations of the Gospel (2 Cor 11:4–6; Gal 1:6–9), and do so with impassioned anguish. In later texts (Jude; 2 Peter 2) the actual contours of the alternative positions are swallowed up in the vivid imagery and fierce polemic drawn from biblical and quasi-mythological eschatological tradition. In these cases it is impossible to reconstruct the opponents, or indeed to be certain of their existence: they may be straw figures of terror more designed to encourage the audience to watchful perseverance and fidelity. First John stands somewhere between these positions; the author is more interested in his audience's response than in delineating or challenging any alternative position, which is sufficiently rejected by the eschatological "antichrist" label. It is easier to trace how they fill a role within his wider task and intention than to describe them in their own terms, but this does not mean that they are just a figment of his imagination. He does not attack their moral standing or their motives, as do Jude and 2 Peter, but he does seem to consider their origin "among us" as something that might yet constitute a threat to his readers.

**[20–21]** The author meets this potential danger not with warning or with exhortation but with assurance. He does not want his letter to be taken as a sign of any lack of confidence in his readers as individuals or as a group: they (an emphatic "you") are *all* secure in their knowledge—an unmistakable contrast with the "all" of the excluded dissidents of the previous verse. What they know is not immediately stated, and the verb "know" (*oida*), which is used three times in these two verses, is not 1 John's preferred term (*ginōskō*). To ease the awkwardness some scribes altered the Greek to the grammatically easier, "you know all things,"[39] but this is not what the author wants to say, which will shortly be explained. A passing allusion to Jeremiah 31 (LXX 38):34, "they all shall know (*oida*) me," is possible but not what drives his thought (see below, v. 27).

First, however, he explains the source of their knowledge, namely their possession of an "anointing"; this word, *chrisma*, comes only here and in verse 27

---

39. Perhaps also encouraged by this phrase in John 16:30; 21:17. This reading became part of the Majority text and is accepted by the KJV, and it is still taken seriously by many text critics and commentators. However, although difficult, "all" as the subject is not impossible if vv. 20–21 are run on quickly together, while it also makes the desired contrast with v. 19.

in the New Testament, but it shares the verbal root "to anoint" (*chri-*) with "Christ" and "antichrist," both important in the immediate context. The word could refer to an action, like the similarly formed "bapt*ism*"; if so this would provoke the question whether a literal event is intended and whether such "unction" was an element in the liturgical life or initiation ritual of this community. Although in the ancient world literal "anointing" was usually with oil or some other unguent, some have even suggested that this may have been the term given to what elsewhere is called "baptism," a word not found in the Johannine Letters. This interpretation rightly recognizes that the image in mind is not the mundane or regular application of oil, but the formal practice of setting aside items and of empowering individuals for a specific task or purpose (cf. Exod 29:7; 30:25–32). However, while not enough is known about Johannine practice, or first-century variety in general, to rule out the possibility that baptism might be so named, or might be accompanied by or replaced by an oil-based ritual, the emphasis here is not on what they have experienced in the past, but on what they now possess. The *chrisma*, then, is better seen as representing that with which they have been anointed, the oil and/or, more properly, its metaphorical equivalent and its lasting effect.[40]

It is not surprising that many interpreters, ancient and modern, have seen here a reference to the spirit, particularly as Jesus as the *Christ* could be understood as the one "anointed" with God's spirit, specifically through his baptism (see especially Luke 4:18 quoting Isa 61:1, and Acts 10:38). Those addressed are, in this view, possessors of the spirit, set apart and kept secure thereby. Yet if the spirit were intended the author would surely have named it as he does later (3:24; 4:13), in those instances as evidence of divine indwelling rather than as the source of special insight or gifts. Indeed, he evinces a certain caution about the spirit, aware that authentic possession of the spirit needs testing (4:1–6). Here and in verse 27 the anointing is linked to knowledge and to teaching; it is most likely that the term does itself refer to the readers' possession of true understanding, an internalization of the teaching that had transformed and shaped them. Despite, and in tension with, his words in the opening prologue, where those addressed were the recipients of a message or word, understood without reference to any specific expression of it, here they are autonomously defined by it, just as the priest was defined by the anointing with oil (Exod 29:7).

Yet they are autonomous only in one sense (see below on v. 27); the anointing that they possess comes from "the holy one" (*tou hagiou*).[41] The epithet is not used elsewhere in 1 John, and since the letter does not label the spirit as

---

40. This need not exclude an actual practice. In the novel *Joseph and Aseneth* participation in "the bread of life and the cup of immortality and the ointment (*chrisma*) of incorruptibility" distinguishes Joseph from Aseneth until her conversion, but it is difficult to determine whether these presuppose actual cultic practices or are entirely metaphorical (*Jos. Asen.* 8.5; 15.5; 16.16).

41. This could be masculine or neuter.

"holy," there are no grounds for seeing a reference to the spirit here as the source of their teaching. Beyond this, it is impossible to determine whether the reference is to God (as in John 17:11) or to Jesus (as in John 6:69); the author could use the adjective "just" equally of Jesus and of God (1 John 1:9; 2:1, 29; 3:7), and no doubt he would have done likewise with "holy." Later, he will describe the anointing as "from him" or "his," characteristically failing to define the reference (see commentary on v. 27). Although the letter opens by emphasizing the mediation of "we" who heard and proclaimed in their reception of the teaching, here it is "from him"; the anointing is, perhaps, that teaching together with the capacity to internalize it, understood as a divine gift.

It is implicit to the argument that their knowledge will protect them from the danger posed by the appearance of the antichrists. This becomes explicit as the author specifies what it is that they all know: the truth. This is not just the truth about the character of the antichrists but the truth as the encapsulation of the God-given understanding of God and of what God has done; this is the truth whose presence, like that of the word, he denied was in any who misrepresented their past sin or who failed to keep the commandments (1:8, 10; 2:4). To say that they also know that no lie belongs to the truth is not merely stating the obvious; the truth represents a sphere of belonging or place of origin, like the world or the Father in 2:16, and the lie represents that which is opposed to God's truth and can have no part in it (1:10; 2:4). That the author has bothered to write, according to verse 26, "about those who might lead you astray" suggests that his protest of confidence here is in part a rhetorical ploy; in a manner familiar from ancient practice as well as modern, he is using praise rather than anxious threat to persuade them that they would be right to stay loyal to him and to resist any alternatives, even if such came from those claiming a similar authority.

Although in the first part of the letter potential false claims were identified and excluded by their relationship to the truth and the lie (1:8, 10; 2:4), this does not mean that those claims—"We have no sin," "we have known him"—had been made by those now identified as the antichrists, and can be used to draw their profile (see Introduction §2.2). In contrast to this common reconstruction, the argument of the letter nowhere suggests that those claims were being made by individuals or groups outside the community, and indeed, as has been seen, it supposes the opposite; 1 John works with antithetical categories, and it is not surprising that the same terms should recur in different contexts. Indeed, this demonstrates the lack of nuance or differentiation in his patterns of opposing types; the author would have no interest in discovering whether those he deems outside the truth were in any way related to one another or even whether they shared common ideas. As his attitude to the antichrists demonstrates, his scheme does not readily conceive of people changing their position or wavering in uncertainty, even though his main concern is to secure the steadfast allegiance of those to whom he writes.

**[22–23]** The false position is identified not by claims or behavior but by denial (*arneomai*) of belief statements. Two questions need to be addressed here: first, the nature of the belief that they are denying, and whether they are affirming a clear alternative; second, what the context of their denial is, namely whether it is a formal denial or refusal to confess, or merely a failure to believe as the author thinks they should. A formal denial might suggest a context of outside pressure, whether socially constrained or one of persecution. It is in such a context that Matt 10:33 warns that those who deny (*arneomai*) Jesus in a human setting will be denied by him in the divine court, while those who acknowledge (confess: *homologeō*) him will be acknowledged; it is possible that later experience is also in mind when all the Gospels record in sharp detail Peter's denial of any association with Jesus (Mark 14:66–72). Apparently closer to our passage, John 9:22 and 12:42 envisage a situation, probably long after the time of Jesus when the narrative is set, in which confession of Jesus as "the Christ" would lead to exclusion from the Jewish synagogue, provoking some putative believers to avoid any open acknowledgment of him. However, while 1 John's negative attitude to the world, and the very use of the vocabulary of confession and denial, might suit potential or actual persecution, the letter offers no hint that there was such;[42] if there were, it would be expected that the world would be portrayed more in the role of active aggressor. Instead, the author is concerned not with an absolute denial of allegiance but with a failure to make the only confession that he would recognize as valid. Anything that they might have affirmed is for him immaterial; but what they should have but have failed to say can be understood only within the framework of the author's own ideas.

On the surface the denial "that Jesus is the *Christ*" might appear to presuppose a traditional formula of belief in Jesus as the promised Messiah (= Christ) of Jewish expectation (cf. John 1:41). However, since those who made the denial once "belonged to us," they cannot have been Jewish opponents with no prior connection. On the other hand, since he does not accuse them of having given up their earlier beliefs, it is unlikely that they are former "Jewish Christians" who have surrendered their convictions about Jesus to return to their Jewish friends. An intriguing suggestion is that 1 John addresses a Jesus-believing group emerging out of a Jewish context and berates those erstwhile comrades who have failed to sustain that journey.[43] A number of features of 1 John might support such a scenario, and it has the virtue of making sense of the scriptural echoes and parallels with other texts usually deemed "Jewish." However, any

---

42. Some have found a reference to persecution at 5:21 but this is unpersuasive; see the commentary on this verse.

43. For example, O'Neill, *Puzzle of 1 John*; W. Nauck, *Die Tradition und Charakter des ersten Johannesbriefes* (WUNT 3; Tübingen: Mohr, 1957); also Introduction §3.4 for the "Jewishness" of 1 John.

such approach does not sufficiently account for the author's primary interest in Jesus as the Son of the Father, or explain why he regularly, as here, sets the term "Christ" in this context (see already 1:3; 2:1). It appears that what sounds like the traditional formula of belief in Jesus as Messiah has taken on a new dimension of sonship (see below). This confirms that the force of the correct confession is "that Jesus is the Christ," and not, as is grammatically possible, "that the Christ [about whom we know] is Jesus [rather than someone else or as not yet appeared]" (see note f).

The author's logic is simple and can be understood within its immediate context. His strategy is to start from what could be taken for granted, namely that one labeled "the anti*christ*" would reject the confession of (Jesus as) the *Christ*. How he elaborates this is what matters: the real charge is not about "the Christ," a term he does not use again until the topic of the antichrist reappears in 3:23–4:6. Rather, it is that the antichrist denies the Father and the Son: this is no longer denial of belief about ("that") but a refusal to acknowledge. Again the author justifies his charge by elaborating it: it is ultimately a question of acknowledging, or denying, the Son. It is evident that he is not referring to "Son of God" as a quasi-technical messianic term (cf. commentary on 3:8). Rather, the Son is Son only in relation to the Father, and the Father is Father only in relation to the Son; to reject the Son is to reject both, even if this was not the intention. That this is the heart of the issue is confirmed by the way these verses (2:22–24) act as a pivot in references to Father and to Son in the letter. Up to this point Jesus has been identified as "his Son" only twice, both in formulaic phrases (1:3, 7); in the rest of the letter rather more emphasis will be placed on the fact that God sent "his Son," as a means of dealing with sin and as the true object of faith (3:8, 23; 4:9–10, 14; 5:9–12). Conversely, references to "the Father" and to believers' relationship with the Father are more frequent in the first part of the letter (1:2–3; 2:1, 14–16; 3:1; 4:14). Partly this reflects the structure of the letter, with the second part being more concerned with belief and with the achievement of Jesus than the first; but that the author does not yet introduce here the importance of believing that "Jesus is the Son of God," something that will assume central importance later (4:15; 5:5), suggests that he is developing his argument with due caution. After he has explored the role of the Son of God in the intervening chapters he will repeat the substance of these verses with more force and confidence (5:10–12).

There is, therefore, no surprise that the author does not explain whether those who had separated held some alternative belief about God (for example, as sufficient for knowledge and salvation without the Son), or about Jesus (for example, not as Son but as . . .), or about the Son (for example, not Jesus but . . .). Variations of each of these have been suggested, but the first readers would have known no more than do contemporary ones, especially if the feared "antichrists" had not arisen among them. Indeed, this is the point of the argument, not to inform but to alert the readers, to put them on their guard lest they encounter something that, whatever it may appear, is a denial of the Son and therefore of the Father. Perhaps equally important, it prepares them for the author's own theological explorations, which, even if they included some novelties, have been authenticated simply by being dissociated from anything an antichrist might introduce.

To fail to acknowledge the Son—whatever that may indicate—is to fail also to hold on to or possess the Father; the verb is the common Greek verb "to have" (*echō*), and is another distinctive formulation of the relationship with God (see also 5:12; 2 John 9). This may just indicate the presence and support of the Father, as when Esther in her distress speaks of having no one but God (Esth 4:17 LXX; cf. 2 Macc 8:36). In the next verse, however, 1 John reverts to the language of remaining or indwelling (cf. 1 John 2:6, 14), and some have argued that "having" God similarly expresses a deep personal fellowship, perhaps best translated as "possess." There is a superficial similarity to when the Stoic philosopher Epictetus asks the anxious person, "Do you not have God there? Having him, what other do you seek?" (Epictetus, *Diss.* 2.8.17), but this arises from a very different understanding of God's presence as pervasive. As elsewhere, the *Testaments of the Twelve Patriarchs* offer a striking parallel: "keep from anger and hate falsehood that the Lord may dwell among [in] you . . . but you shall be in peace having the God of peace, and war shall in no way overwhelm you" (*T. Dan* 5.1–2); however, unlike this assertion, the focus in 1 John is here on the individual. Elsewhere 1 John speaks of "having" fellowship, life, boldness, and testimony; and the Gospel would add to the list "having" his word, light, love, peace, and others (1 John 1:6; 3:21; 5:10, 12–13; John 5:38; 8:12; 13:35; 16:33).[44] Although none of these is difficult to understand, the cumulative effect is to suggest that the verb carried far more weight in Johannine thought than its mundane potential, but that it cannot be restricted to a single idea. Although "possess" preserves the continuity from the affirmation "you possess an anointing" (2:24), the context here implies an ambiguity between "being faithful to," almost synonymous with confessing, and a more subjective experience of divine presence.

It is striking that a similar development of "Christ" is found in the Fourth Gospel, which both represents debate about Jesus as Messiah (= "Christ," John 1:41; 4:29; 7:26–31, 41–42), and pushes the term beyond that framework (17:3; 20:31 is particularly problematic in this context). Given that identifying someone (or oneself) as Messiah was not of itself an offense, it may be that in John 9:22 the Jewish decision to exclude those who "confess him to be the 'Christ'" has already been glossed by the evangelist by "as we interpret that." Certainly

---

44. Although not a rare verb, "to have" (*echō*) is proportionately far more frequent in John and especially in 1 John than in other NT writings.

John 5:18, again read back into the time of Jesus, suggests that rather more was at stake in conflict with "the Jews" than messiahship alone. There is nothing to suggest that 1 John reflects the same conflict as these passages of the Gospel, but it also presupposes that "Jesus is the Christ" is to be interpreted within the author's own framework of meaning as explained in each text as a whole.

The switch from the antichrist "who denies" (v. 22) to everyone "who denies" (v. 23) prepares the readers to examine themselves. The "antichrists" already identified by the author may have arisen from among those with whom he was associated, but they were not an exclusive group; anyone else could find themselves numbered among them. Watchfulness and protection were called for, and fidelity to an author who could so identify the danger.

### *1 John 2:24–28—The Call to Remain Faithful*

2:24 As for you, let what you have heard from the beginning indwell within you. If what you have heard from the beginning does indwell within you, you will yourselves indwell within the Son and within the Father.[a] 25 This is, then, the promise that he promised us,[b] eternal life. 26 I have written this to you concerning those who might lead you astray. 27 But as for you, the anointing that you received from him does indwell within you, and you do not need anyone to teach you; but since his anointing[c] teaches you about everything and is true and is not a lie, and just as he did teach you, do you indwell in him.[d] 28 So now, children, indwell in him,[e] so that if he is revealed we may exhibit boldness and not be put to shame at his presence.

a. A few manuscripts (including Sinaiticus) reverse the order, with the Father first, possibly correctly since the reading given echoes the order in the previous verse.

b. Codex Vaticanus reads "you"; although this could be in order to harmonize with the repeated "you" in the passage, it could be original and have been altered to conform to 1:5, where "we" are the recipients of the message.

c. The original scribe of Codex Sinaiticus wrote "his spirit," probably an early interpretation.

d. Or "it"; this could be a command or a statement (see commentary). The later Majority text, followed by KJV, reads the future, "you will indwell."

e. A few manuscripts omit the opening words of the verse, probably because of the repeated "dwell within him."

Attention now turns to the audience. The author treads a fine line between reassuring them that neither he nor they have any cause for concern, for they have all the resources they need, and urging them not to waver in their commitment. Reassurance and encouragement meet in fidelity to the past.

**[24]** An appeal to what has come to them "from the beginning" is a familiar strategy of this author, especially when faced with a possible threat (cf. 3:11).

The phrase makes its own claim to authority while obscuring precisely where that beginning is to be located, whether in their experience, be that individual or corporate, or in God's purposes, or before time (see commentary on 1:1; 2:7, 13). Presumably the aboriginality of the one whom they know both authenticates and is authenticated by the aboriginality of what they know. Earlier in the letter the focus of what they had heard was on the, as yet still unidentified, commandment, and after that on the coming of the antichrist (2:7, 18); here it is surely wider, but still unexplained. From the context one might assume that it included teaching about the person and role of Jesus, but to speculate about this would be to misunderstand the appeal, which calls attention not to *what* they have heard but to the journey they have taken from and through that hearing and to where they now are. In practice to reiterate past certainties in a new context or to apply them to new circumstances always involves interpretation, and the challenge lies in discerning authentic continuity. Often, behind the call to be faithful to tradition or to the past lies hidden a call to be faithful to the person or group who is claiming to represent that tradition, and so it is here.

Handing on and making sense of the message of Jesus and of the significance of his person, life, and death demanded constant reinterpretation, and, not surprisingly, produced conflict. Writing to the Corinthians, Paul recalls his readers to the basic form of the message as they had heard it, asserting that it was no different from what he himself had first received or from what anyone else might have preached (1 Cor 15:1–11). He uses the formal language of transmission and quotes the tradition in a form that has taken an almost creedal shape, although he undoubtedly has added to its kernel. On this basis Paul then argues that some understandings of resurrection are incompatible with that core belief, others are continuous with it, and he urges them to be steadfast, immovable (15:58). In a very different manner Paul's later disciple recalls his readers to what he calls "faithful sayings" (1 Tim 1:15; 3:1; etc.), frequently taking a rhythmic creedal form, and he sees "the faith" as something like good teaching from which people can be shaken (1 Tim 4:6; 2 Tim 2:18; 3:8). Clearly it gets its authority from the chain of teaching, which reaches back through "Timothy" to Paul himself (1 Tim 1:3; 2 Tim 1:11–14). Again, it is evident that merely appealing to these verities is insufficient; implicit is the assertion of rightly representing them, and this ultimately can be ratified by God alone (2 Tim 2:14–19).

First John shares the same problems as Paul and his successor, but the author differs from both in the way he addresses them. He does not spell out what it is that they have heard, nor does he even indicate that it could take on a creedal pattern; he does not argue from the basic principles of the message they have in order to demonstrate correct or mistaken positions. Neither does he directly appeal to their dependence on those from whom they heard it; if readers were supposed to remember the assertions of the letter's prologue they might have expected an echo of it here, but the context (cf. vv. 20–21) emphasizes rather their autonomy. Further, "that which you have heard" is not something to be presented, deviated from, or even denied (as is "faith" in 1 Tim 5:8); it is internalized. They are urged to let it remain or dwell within them in the same way as love, or the word of God, or even God's own self, may remain in or indwell them (1 John 2:14; 3:17; 4:12). This is very different from the superficially similar encouragement to Timothy, "As for you, remain in those things you have learned and put your trust in, knowing from whom you learned them" (2 Tim 3:14).[45]

Nonetheless, this may provoke the question how the "what" of belief relates to the "[in] whom" of belief. First John has not yet used the verb "to believe" (3:23), which could prompt such a distinction, but the idea of indwelling now comes close to provoking this. If what they have heard from the beginning does indeed indwell them—and the wording suggests that this needs positive action on their part and not mere passivity—then they will indwell the Son and the Father; the conditional wording allows for the possibility of the alternative to be avoided. The same favorite Johannine idea, "indwell" (*menō en*; cf. commentary on 2:6), in each part of the condition suggests that the indwelling in Son and Father is not simply a reward for faithfulness but in some way is coterminous with it. In 4:15 there is a reciprocity between being indwelt by God and indwelling in God; here the first element is replaced by being indwelt by what they have heard. The latter is understood not as something objective, patent of taking different forms or of being set out, discussed, and negotiated, but as something that has entered into their being. On the other hand, indwelling in God cannot be a purely subjective or mystical experience. This has already become clear from 2:5–6, where any claim to indwell God is proven spurious if it finds no expression in the way one lives; here it cannot be independent of what one holds on to.

Also important is the corporate context. In the previous verses the author had been speaking of the denial or confession made by an individual and their consequent "hold" on Son and Father. Continuity with that concern means that here indwelling is in the Son *and* the Father, and not, as elsewhere, in "him" or in God. But, as always, when the author addresses his readers directly he does so as a group: "you" are always in the plural. The holding on to what they have heard and the dwelling in Son and Father are not a purely individual experience, nor even the sum of many individual experiences, but are that which shapes and identifies them as a group, a group that, like the "we" of verse 19, retains its essential identity, or is called to do so, in the face of what might disrupt it.

[25] The author's deep concern will continue to shape the following verses, but it is interrupted here as he recalls for them the certainty that they can hold on to. Both the noun and the verb for "promise" (*epangel-*) come only here in

---

45. In contrast to Hans Conzelmann, who labeled 1 John the "Johannine Pastoral"; "Was von Anfang war," in *Neutestamentliche Studien für Rudolf Bultmann zu seinem siebzigsten Geburtstag am 20. August 1954* (ed. W. Eltester; Berlin: Töpelmann, 1954), 194–201.

the Gospel and Letters of John, although they share a common root with the various terms for announcement that 1 John used in the opening verses (1:5 [cf. 3:11], *angel-*; 1:5, *anangel-*; 1:2, 3, *apangel-*). Unlike these, "promise" carries a strong forward perspective, and the noun can refer not just to the act of making a promise but to its actual realization, to that which is promised; elsewhere in the New Testament it looks back to the reception of what had been "promised" in the Scriptures, for example of God's commitment to Abraham or the prophetically anticipated gift of the spirit (Acts 1:4; 2:33; 13:23); here it is defined as "eternal life" (see commentary on 1:2).[46] The author of the promise is in characteristic fashion "he," which could refer either to the Son or to the Father just named; although a reference to Jesus (cf. 1:5, "the message we heard from him") would make good sense, as often the author may not have looked for precision or for a distinction. In 5:11 eternal life, the content of the promise here, is given by God but is experienced "in" the Son.

Contrary to the explanation just given, the verse could be understood with the opening "this is" referring back to verse 24 (cf. 5:11). In this case that which they heard from the beginning and which is to remain in them (v. 24) would be the promise, which is then further defined as "eternal life." This might recall 1:1–2, where eternal life was also the content of what "we" proclaimed, and was in some way connected to "that which was from the beginning" (see commentary). On this reading, the argument would not be that in the face of possible alternative understandings of "the Son" they are to hold on to the internalized teaching they received, but that the promise of eternal life is what will keep them firm in the face of what might destabilize them. Closer attention suggests that this is not the intention. At least according to the best-attested text (see note b), despite the repeated emphasis on "you" in the surrounding verses, here the promise was "to us." The change of person must be deliberate: the author is not just including himself in its reception, but is returning to the distinction carefully maintained in 1:5 whereby "we" are mediators, recipients of the message and then sources of its proclamation to "you." This verse (and perhaps the other similarly formulaic "and this is" verses, 1:5; 3:11; 5:11) recalls the readers to their dependency on "us" for what they have heard; if the prologue, 1:1–3, drew on familiar patterns of claims to testimony, it may come from the same background. In his own way the author is after all making a firm statement about the personal authority that lies behind the exhortation to be faithful to the past.

[26] On the basis of this reminder that the group whom he has identified as "we" is the source of their understanding, the author reasserts his epistolary authority. Those to whom he writes are after all susceptible to being led astray, and he is in a position to identify both the source of the problem and its solution: it is firmly "you" who may be misled, not "us." The description of the

---

46. The "this is" points forward as in 3:11, but see next paragraph.

threat is ambiguous: the present tense, most simply "those who are leading you astray," sounds as if the problem is actual, and yet everything else in the section indicates that it is still potential. It would be possible to translate, "who are trying to lead you astray," although, again, it seems unlikely that even this is yet the case. The translation "who might lead you astray" appears to represent the situation, but the ambiguity of the Greek prevents the readers from dismissing this as a misplaced fear. This is a strategy the author will continue to use (cf. 3:7); however warmly he will now reassure them, they are to keep on their guard and heed his direction.

In the context of warnings about the antichrist, the threat of being led astray is not simply one of being led to draw the wrong conclusions or to take the wrong path (contrast 1:8). One of the characteristics of the end time was that "many would be lead astray" (Mark 13:6); this in particular would be the achievement of the "false christs and false prophets," and even the elect were not invulnerable to the danger (Matt 24:11, 24). The Apocalypse describes Satan as "the one who leads astray the whole world" (Rev 12:9), and later in this letter "the spirit of error"[47] is not only contrasted with "the spirit of truth" but is to be identified with "the spirit of the antichrist" (1 John 4:3, 6; see also 2 John 7 and commentary). As with the exposition of "the last hour" that opened this section (2:18), so also this description of the imminent threat marks the moment as one of decisive significance: to be led astray would not be a temporary aberration or easily corrected but would close off the promised eternal life.

[27] Yet, characteristically, the argument switches abruptly from warning to reassurance. They—again an emphatic "as for you"—already have all they need to withstand the danger. Again the author appeals to "the anointing" (*chrisma*), although now he emphasizes it as something they have "received" and do not merely possess (see above, v. 20). The verb (*lambanō*) is as appropriate for teaching (John 15:14–15) as for the spirit (John 14:17; 20:22); although a connection with the former still seems most likely, both the term and the emphasis that they have received it not from "us" but from "him" keep the emphasis not on a received body of material but on a divinely authorized capacity and insight. No longer do they have to make the effort to ensure that this, like what they had heard, indwells them; that it does so is its nature as given by him and on that they can rely. The verb is in the aorist, emphasizing the completion of their reception of this gift, although to see here a particular moment of reception, perhaps at conversion or baptism, is to read more than the context allows. As before, this gives them a certain autonomy: they have no need of anyone to teach them, not even those who might appear with new interpretations of the message. Does this also mean that they do not need the author

47. The noun comes from the same root as the verb (*planaō*), "to stray or lead astray," something difficult to express in English.

either? If it does, that does not prevent him continuing to tell them what to do and to warn them against mistaken conclusions. This may be because his assertions of confidence are actually taking the form of hyperbole, and everyone would recognize them as such: perhaps they are being invited to respond, "Oh, but we do need guidance, please. . . ."

On the other hand, despite the stress throughout the letter on what has been proclaimed and heard, the verb "to teach" appears only in this verse, and the noun "the teaching" is nowhere used; this is very different from the Pastoral Epistles, in which this is a favorite term for that which has to be held on to and which is "health giving" (1 Tim 1:10; 4:6, 13, 16, etc.). Perhaps the author would not have identified what he had done or was doing as "teaching." "Teaching" in this tradition may have been restricted to what comes from God; in the Gospel the spirit teaches the disciples, reminding them of what Jesus had said, and God teaches Jesus, so that his teaching comes from God (John 7:16, 17; 8:29; 14:26). Still only an echo, but sharper than in 1 John 2:20, there may be an allusion to the promise in Jer 31:34 that all will know God, and perhaps also to that of Isa 54:13, to which John 6:45 also appeals ("they shall all be taught by God").

By appealing to the sufficiency of what they already have, the author is implying that no one else would have anything additional to offer. The teaching they are given by the anointing is comprehensive, "about everything,"[48] but the present tense "teaches" here shows that this is an ongoing experience and so requires that they continue to be dependent on the anointing. This is not a license to say, "And now we've got it." Moreover, in this setting what is needed is not an encyclopedic knowledge about everything there is to know, but teaching about anything relevant to the present danger. Earlier, the author had contrasted the truth with the lie, the two opposing spheres with which they were faced. Now he reminds them that the anointing is true; it has nothing to do with the negative pole of the lie. By keeping centered on where they already are, on the understanding they already have, and by rejecting new influences and offered sources of insight, then they too will remain in the realm of truth. To question the past would be to go over to the side of the lie.

The final exhortation seems to sum it all up, but its translation is uncertain. The verb in the first clause might be translated "as it [i.e., the anointing] taught you," or "as he [i.e., God or Jesus] taught you"; the second verb could be translated as a statement, "you do dwell," or as a command, "dwell!"; further, the final phrase could be "in him" or "in it": they may be being told that they do remain in God, or in Jesus, or in the anointing, in accordance with how they were taught by any one (but not necessarily the same one) of these, or they could be being told so to do. Such ambiguities are entirely characteristic of this author,

---

48. This may have provoked the reading "and you know all things" in v. 20, but is not adequate grounds for accepting it.

and perhaps not even his earliest readers or hearers would have all agreed on what was intended. It is most likely that the final words refer to indwelling in God or in Jesus; although elsewhere the author does speak of indwelling in love, light, or death, what has been heard is always that which indwells within the believer and the relationship is not reciprocal; and it is unlikely he would think of indwelling in the anointing. Further, despite the absence of any indication of a change of subject, it would make good sense if God or Jesus were also the subject of "he taught"; "just as" (*kathōs*) similarly appeals to what God (or Jesus) had done in 3:23. What "he" taught them is no different from what the anointing continues to teach them; but since the anointing came from him, there is in the end little difference in meaning. Finally, the "just as" is most probably here, as it is in 3:23 and in 2:6, the basis for an exhortation: they are to dwell or remain within him.

[28] The final call of verse 27 could be read as the close of the section, so that this verse would introduce a new stage in the argument. Several translations and commentators do take it in this way (as does NA[27]). However, the author elsewhere addresses his readers as "children" at a key point within his argument, and not necessarily always to introduce a new stage (3:7; 4:4), while in 5:21 this address introduces the final verse of the whole letter. Here the address balances that which began the section in verse 18, although a different term is used (*teknia*; see commentary on 2:18). This verse provides links in vocabulary and idea with what precedes, while verse 29 introduces new terms that will be taken up in the following verses. Certainly verse 28 will provide something of a bridge to the new section, but it serves most to pull together and to trump the concern with the antichrists that has dominated the passage so far.

The opening "So now" summons them to a present response; all that has been said is not merely theoretical or relevant only to someone else, to somewhere else, or at some other time. It also recalls the "so now" of verse 18 that signaled the presence of "many antichrists": the decisive moment of the final hour is a present reality and demands immediate response. The response is, however, only what has already been urged, to continue indwelling in him: new strategies or beliefs are the least likely requirements. Paradoxically, such continuing has in view its own possible disruption; it is sustained in anticipation of "his" being revealed (*phaneroō*). The same verb was used in verse 19 of the exposure (*phaneroō*) of the antichrists as not being "of us"; if there such revealing was primarily negative, here it is positive. In retrospect, the manifestation of the antichrists was a sham imitation of the true revelation of the one expected. The "if" does not indicate some doubt as to whether he will be revealed but only keeps open its timing and nature.

At the end of the verse this revealing is described as "his presence." The word *parousia* could also be translated "coming," but the theme of boldness suggests that it is not the journey but the being present that is in focus. The "he" is not identified. Elsewhere in the New Testament *parousia* is used of the expected future revelation of the Son of Man (Matt 24:27, 37, 39) or of Jesus (1 Cor 15:23; 1 Thess 2:19; 3:13), at that moment which signals the fulfillment of God's purposes and the point of no return, the point of judgment. One of the roots of this idea is the Danielic vision of the Son of Man coming on or with the clouds of heaven (Dan 7:13); although his journey was *to* God, within the New Testament it is recast of his triumphant coming in judgment (Matt 26:64) to complete the work inaugurated, apparently inauspiciously, in the earthly ministry and death of Jesus. Yet another root of the idea was the anticipation of the coming of God's messenger in judgment (Mal 3:1–2), which was but a prelude to the coming of God and of "the day of the LORD" (Mal 4:1, 5). Since "the Lord" of scriptural references could be referred both to God and to Jesus in early Christian thought, there can sometimes be some ambiguity as to whose coming is anticipated (Jas 5:7, 8; 2 Pet 3:12). Thus the one whose presence is anticipated in verse 28 could as easily be God as the more familiar Jesus. Since the implied "he" of verse 29 will prove to be equally ambiguous, a close connection between the two verses would not decide the reference here, and the same may be true of 3:2 (see commentary). Neither does the rest of the letter provide a clear answer: the expectation of the coming of Jesus or of God is not developed elsewhere, and while 3:21 anticipates boldness before God, 4:17 is less precise. It is probable that John 14 offers a reworking of some such ideas (John 14:2, 23), but it does so in a very different direction from 1 John, and a shared prior conviction cannot easily be reconstructed.

Second Thessalonians 2:8–9 also uses *parousia* of the powerful coming or presence of Satan in a final onslaught against God's purposes and against those who believe in God, only to be destroyed by the yet more powerful presence or coming of the Lord (probably Jesus).[49] The author of 1 John has already appealed to some such pattern of expectation among his readers (v. 18), and he now returns to it in bringing the section to a close. Contrary to what might at first seem to be the case, the coming of Jesus or of God could be more to be feared than that of the antichrist(s). Yet fidelity and persistence are the sure protection against any such fear of shame.

Again 1 John draws on earlier Jesus traditions such as are now found in the Synoptic Gospels: in Mark the Son of Man when he comes will be ashamed of those who have been ashamed of Jesus ("me") and his words (Mark 8:37–38; Luke 9:26);[50] a parallel tradition speaks of confessing or denying resulting in being confessed or being denied (Matt 10:33; Luke 12:8–9). First John has already established the absolute choice between denial of the Son, which is the

---

49. The textual evidence at 2 Thess 2:8 is fairly equally balanced between "the Lord" and "the Lord Jesus," which reinforces the uncertainty regarding our verse.

50. Mark and Luke use the compound verb *epaischynomai*, 1 John the simple verb.

way of the antichrist, and confession of him (2:22–23); those who "remain in him" are those who do not in effect deny him and so will not be put to shame. Instead they will enjoy the open confidence of speech of those who have the freedom and right to be there, even in his presence. In Greek political thought such boldness (*parrēsia*) is the right of the free citizen, but in Wis 5:1 it is also the confidence that the righteous will exercise in the presence of their oppressors when God resolves all injustice. The frequency of the idea elsewhere in the New Testament suggests that such boldness was experienced as one of the benefits they had gained (cf. Heb 4:16). From here it will be a recurring theme in the letter with consequences for the present as well as for the future (see 1 John 3:21 and commentary; 4:17; 5:14).

In expressing the purpose, and so the consequences, of such fidelity, the author has moved back, without emphasis, into the first person plural, "we," now surely inclusive. This is a shared hope and goal; although there are no verbal links, it is an expression of the fellowship that was the avowed intent of the letter (1:3). Throughout this section the author has skillfully praised and reassured his readers, made common cause with them and yet also acknowledged their independent resourcing by God. This does not mean that he had no anxiety or sense of danger, for such expressions of confidence belong to techniques familiar in ancient letters; at times he also utters a quiet note of authority, intended to direct them to heed his warnings and his guidance, and, most of all, to remain true to the meaning of their faith as he interprets and explains it for them. The nature of the alternative represented by the antichrists remains obscure despite his casting of it in a stark eschatological framework. The author will return to this later in the letter, although even then he will not explain its error (4:1–6), and he never accuses it of the practices, strategies, and intentions familiar in the polemics of the wider eschatological traditions on which he drew. Positively, however, he upholds a conviction that faith is its own strength, and that the insight and understanding given by God are not easily corrupted or proved illusory; although he struggles to make sense within this framework of those who moved in another direction, that experience has not undermined his fundamentally God-centered understanding of religious experience.

## 1 John 2:29–3:12—The Identity of Those Who Are (or Are Not) Children of God

The anxieties and exhortation of the previous section now give way to assurance: the gaze toward the future introduced in the immediately preceding verse inspires a confidence that is rooted in the nature of the God to whom they are committed and through whom they have experienced a new level of being. To explore this a new set of metaphors is employed that centers around ideas of divine begetting and of the irreversible affinity between parent and child, both in nature and in activity. This does not, however, lead to complacency, for there remains a sense of something yet to unfold beyond this relationship. Moreover, the metaphor also generates its mirror image, an alternative affinity between those whose actions, and so whose origins, are antithetical to God. The dualism that has already emerged as characteristic of the thought of the letter is now expressed on a metaphysical or cosmic level as being rooted in the opposition between God and the devil. The fundamental identifying characteristics of the two forms of identity are presented in terms of doing justice and doing sin; these last become reciprocally exclusive categories, and appear to encompass more than merely particular actions or even their cumulative effect. It will become evident that this framework of thought is not congenial to ideas of repentance or forgiveness, and the passage contains a number of theological challenges.

Accompanying the change in metaphors and the dualistic theological framework there is also a change in style; embedded in this section is a series of assertions that follow the pattern, "Everyone who . . . does (not) . . ." (2:29; 3:3, 4, 6 [twice], 7, 9, 10; cf. 3:8, "The one who . . .").[51] Reduced to a basic structure, these can readily be arranged as a series of couplets:

> Everyone who does justice has been born from him;
> Everyone who does sin also does lawlessness (2:29b + 3:4a)
>
> Everyone who indwells in him does not sin;
> everyone who sins has not seen [or known] him (3:6a + b)
>
> Everyone who does justice is just;
> [every]one who does sin is of the devil (3:7b + 8a)
>
> Everyone who has been born from God does not do sin;
> Everyone who does not do justice does not belong to God (3:9a + 10b)[52]

When they are set out in this way a sharply antithetical structure emerges that gives expression to the fundamental dualistic division that, as outlined above, underlies the section of the letter as a whole. Some have suggested that this series represents a source adopted by the author; if this were so some of the challenges of this thorough dualism and of its consequences, particularly in its presentation of sin and of the possibility of not sinning, would be attributable to the source. However, although the author does seem at various points to have taken over earlier material some of which was possibly already familiar to his audience, it is not easy to see why he would have broken up such a balanced series resulting in the passage in its present form.

---

51. In the Greek the "Everyone who . . ." follows a consistent grammatical structure with the participle, and in 2:29; 3:4, 7, 10, using the participle from the verb "to do" (so also 3:8).

52. This analysis goes back to E. von Dobschütz, "Johanneische Studien I," *ZNW* 8 (1907): 1–8.

Moreover, despite the apparent patterns of both repetition and variation, the match within and between the couplets is not precise. In addition, while the other verses introduce new ideas, 3:6 (a + b) contains the already familiar themes of indwelling and knowing, which are part of the author's own thought. If this verse is excluded the symmetry between the stanzas is more balanced, especially once the lines are rearranged as follows:

> Everyone who does justice has been born from him;
> Everyone who has been born from God does not do sin (2:29b + 3:9a)

> Everyone who does sin also does lawlessness;
> Everyone who does justice is just (3:4 + 3:7)

> [Every]one who does sin is of the devil;
> Everyone who does not do justice does not belong to God (3:8a + 3:10b)

The focus in this series is consistently on the *doing* of justice or of sin,[53] that is, a primarily moral dualism. However, to adapt them to his argument the author has broken up the neat strophes, and has used them to provide a framework for further reflection: the first line has been brought forward to introduce this whole section (2:29b), the second couplet frames the first half of the next (second) subsection (3:4–7), while the two lines of the third couplet introduce the second half of the second subsection (3:8–10a), and the third subsection (3:10b–12), respectively. It will become apparent that the author is also taking up other traditions probably familiar to his readers as well. In this case it is his careful reconfiguration of the material that has intensified the theological implications of the earlier source, although the author may be also relying on its familiarity to persuade his readers. Such a reconstruction of the author's sources is inevitably hypothetical and not open to proof, and the task for a commentary must be to interpret the text that he created; still, on this account the author is not constrained by his sources but is deliberately reshaping and weaving them together to convey a new message.

### 1 John 2:29–3:3—The Confidence of the Children of God

**2:29** If you know that he is just, recognize[a] that equally everyone who does justice has been born from him. **3:1** See what sort of love the Father has given us,[b] namely that we might be called children of God, as indeed we are.[c] For this reason the world does not recognize us,[d] because it did not recognize him. **2** Beloved, we are at present children of God, but it has not yet been revealed what we shall be. We do know that if he is revealed

---

53. A further possibility is that originally the sequence of the middle couplet was reversed, i.e., 2:29b + 3:9a/3:7 + 3:4/3:8a + 3:10b; in this case doing justice would be the leading thought.

we shall be like him, because we shall see him just as he is. 3 So everyone who holds this hope in him purifies himself, just as that one is pure.

a. In form this could be a statement or a command, but is here taken as the latter.

b. There is considerable textual variation, although the most significant is the reading "you" (Codex Vaticanus), probably by harmonization with the previous verse, but
see note d.

c. This phrase is omitted by the later Byzantine tradition, followed by KJV.

d. Some manuscripts read "you," including the original hand of Codex Sinaiticus;
when taken with the variant in v. 1 (see note b), this may suggest that there was an alternation between first and second person in the earliest tradition, which has been variously
harmonized.

The first section introduces the theme of the unit, integrating future hope
with present reality. Despite the mention of "the world" in verse 1, there is no
hint yet of the dualism to come later, although, if the proposal offered above is
accepted, this has been achieved by splitting up an antithetical couplet, post-
poning the second half (2:29b + 3:9a). If the audience were aware of this, they
would be waiting for the negatives yet to come.

[2:29] It is easy to see why many commentators have attached verse 28 as
the opening of this unit: the section continues the theme of his future manifestation introduced there, while to begin with verse 29 produces an abrupt start.
However, it is better to see verse 28 as providing a bridge, bringing one section
to an end while provoking some of the ideas of what proves to be a new chain
of thought. A new idea is introduced by the opening condition of verse 29, but
it is one that recalls the assurances that opened the letter proper in its exploration of the consequences of sin. At that point the epithet "just" (*dikaios*) was
applied to God implicitly (1:9; see commentary) and also to Jesus (2:1), and
this provided the foundation for a confidence in forgiveness for those who sin,
as indeed they must confess that they do. In this verse the one who is just is
most probably God, who is certainly the "him" of its end. This confirms a disjunction with verse 28 if the "he" of that verse does refer to Jesus, although such
inconsistency is typical of this author's style.

That God is just is therefore something that they do indeed know; the conditional "if" is logical, not genuinely open. Elsewhere the formula "we/you
know that" appeals to certainties of conviction held by these believers: sometimes, as here, these have been affirmed earlier in the letter, on other occasions
they may recall traditional formulations (3:2 [→ 2:28; also John 14:9; 16:16];
3:14, 15 [→ John 5:26; 8:44]; 5:18 [→ 3:9]; 5:19 [→ 4:4]; 5:20 [→ 3:8; also
John 17:3]).[54] In this case the thought will move in a very different direction

---

54. It is clear that the echoes of the Fourth Gospel are not quotations or explicit allusions but
more probably go back to similar traditions.

from the earlier passage it recalls: here divine justice becomes the model and the origin of the activity of those who would claim a relationship with God.

What they already know about God's character forms the grounds for a further conviction: the word translated "recognize" can also be rendered "know," but with reference to facts or to convictions it indicates what they can come to recognize on the basis of argument or of the interpretation of events (2:3, 18). Although this could be a statement, "you do recognize," it is more probably a conclusion that they are being encouraged to draw, "recognize!" If the final clause of the verse, that which they are called to recognize, were drawn from a prior tradition (see above), and if it were one known to them, there would be an element of rhetorical artifice here; they would already agree with what follows, although possibly not as a consequence of the understanding of God just expressed. Their familiarity with the idea of birth from God would then predispose them in favor of what follows in the next verses, although these develop the theme in an unexpected direction.

Whether or not drawing on an earlier tradition, the defining character of the believer as born from God becomes a significant thread from this point—subsequent references establish that "from him" is "from God" (3:9; 4:7; 5:1; etc.). Yet the idea of God's producing offspring is a startling one and not easily paralleled. Certainly within the New Testament God is widely described as Father but without any implication that the relationship is a genetic one, and the idea that those who believe in God can be spoken of as children of God is not confined to the Johannine tradition (see Rom 8:16, 21; 9:8; John 1:12; 11:52). However—and not only within the context of the ancient world—there is more than one way of being brought into a filial relationship: Paul, for example, uses the language of adoption (Rom 8:15, 23). Within the New Testament 1 Peter probably comes closest to the Johannine idiom in describing God as the one "who has brought us to new birth," although a different verb is used (*anagennaō*, 1 Pet 1:3; cf. v. 23). Despite these, 1 John is distinctive in the use it makes of the language of birth from God and in the rich consequences it draws from it.

In its active form the verb used here (*gennaō*) properly signifies the role of the father, where English often has to translate "beget" (see Matt 1:2–16); the passive need not draw attention to the role of the parents and can simply indicate the fact and the consequences of having been born (see John 9:32 of the man *born* blind). Consequently while the active can also be used of the mother,[55] her role as the source and origin of birth is regularly expressed by the preposition "out of/from" (*ek*; Matt 1:3, 5, 6, 16). The same preposition, however, can also be used where the relationship is not strictly a genetic one, as when Jesus' interlocutors claim that they were not born as the result of (*ek*) an

---

55. The NT does not use a different form of the verb for the role of the woman, as is possible in Classical Greek; see Luke 1:13; 23:29.

illicit sexual relationship (John 8:41). It is still striking that 1 John and the Gospel share the consistent language of birth "from" (*ek*; John 1:13; 3:5–6; 1 John 2:29; etc.).[56]

Although the two writings share this common imagery, they apply it in different ways. In the Gospel Jesus uses the language of birth to replace that of entering the kingdom of God, also familiar from the Synoptic tradition (John 3:3–8). Only those who have been born "from above" or "from [*ek*] [water and] (the) spirit" will enter God's kingdom. Despite Nicodemus's incredulity there is no explicit contrast with the process of human birth, although if, as is possible, "from water" refers to the woman's role, the birth from (the) spirit is conceptually derivative from, and subsequent to, it; in any case, the antithesis with "that which [neuter] is born out of [*ek*] the flesh" (3:6) does not of itself denigrate flesh nor represent natural birth. The metaphor is one of a radical new beginning involving layers of discontinuity alongside elements of continuity. Most notably, in John 3 God is given no explicit generative role. This marks a distinction from the metaphor in the prologue of the Gospel, where those who do believe ("in his name") are those who have been born "from" (*ek*) God, and not from any other forces (John 1:13);[57] as a result they are children (*tekna*) of God, although this remains potential as much as actual, and it is not something innate but is the outcome of God's gift of the power or right to be such (1:12). Whether their believing is the condition of such birth, or is its consequence, remains ambiguous. In sum, although John 1:12–13 invites comparison with 1 John, it does not explain the origin of the metaphor nor does it share the framework of ideas and antithesis within which 1 John sets it.

The sources of the image remain uncertain. In Greek mythology, the gods do indeed beget children, sometimes through union with (and therefore "from") mortal women; such ideas presuppose some sort of parity between divine and human behavior, and even suggest that there is a continuum between them. This is fundamentally alien to the biblical thought-world where the distinction between God and humanity is sharply drawn and cannot be blurred. Even though Israel can be treated as God's son(s) (e.g., Isa 1:2–4;[58] Jer 3:14; Hos 11:1), this usually serves to emphasize God's care and Israel's disobedience, not any consanguinity between them. Psalm 2:7 might seem to challenge this: "You are my son, today I have begotten you"; in its original setting this may have been an adoption formula addressed by the Deity to the king, with earlier roots outside Israel's tradition. However, despite its christological use elsewhere in the New Testament (Acts 13:33; Heb 1:5), there is no indication that

---

56. On the Johannine use of *ek* see commentary on 2:16.

57. The excluded alternatives in John 1:13 cannot be discussed here, but it should be noted that whether they are negative is not certain.

58. Isaiah 1:2 LXX, "I begot sons," uses the same verb (*gennaō*) where the Hebrew reads, "I caused to grow" (Hiphil of *gdl*).

this psalm has influenced the Johannine tradition. Philo does contrast birth from a mother, which denotes enthrallment within mundane earthly matters, with birth from (*ek*) God, but the child of such birth is virtue or the sabbath (*Who Is the Heir?* 61–70; *Life of Moses* 2.209–10), and Philo's allegory draws on the negative associations in Greek ideology of the female with the body, a framework very distant from the thought of John or 1 John. The lack of obvious parallels means that the idea can only be interpreted within the framework in which each author uses it; only this can determine which aspects of the metaphor are either to be stressed or to be ignored.

An important question on which at this point 1 John is not clear is whether doing justice is the inevitable, and perhaps exclusive, *consequence* of birth from God or whether it is the prior *condition* for it (cf. John 1:12–13 discussed above). The second alternative means that those who do what is right earn for themselves a particularly close relationship with God: as imitators of God's justice they merit, or are given by God, the status of God's children; the language of birth merely gives this dramatic force. The former alternative gives priority to God's generative action, which ensures that those born do justice. A logical consequence is then that those who do what is right can claim no personal credit for it; yet it leaves unexplained why God births some and, presumably, does not birth others. A further question follows how God exercises such a dramatic effect on human behavior, namely how, when, and where such birth takes place—unless it is assumed that some are "from God," and others are not so, literally from their birth, itself a theologically difficult proposition. Such questions will continue to be provoked by this passage, and in particular by verses 7–10. To ask them may be to seek a logical transparency and theological lucidity on an issue that continues to exercise theological minds, perhaps from an author who does not intend theological analysis; for this is a dilemma that inevitably accompanies any belief in a powerful and just God who acts within and upon human lives. The practical and rhetorical message the author wishes to impress is evident: no one can claim divine birth without manifesting its fruits or its roots. On the other hand, for those uncertain of their status in the face of the expectation of a divine coming, as well as of the coming of the antichrist, and for whom divine justice might generate the anxiety of shame (2:28), there is the reassurance that being brought into a relationship with God is as irreversible as is birth.

First John does not explain what "doing justice/righteousness" entails, although clearly it is inseparable from "*being* just/righteous" (3:7). Inasmuch as for God the latter means a readiness to forgive sins for those who acknowledge them (1:9; 2:1), the meaning cannot be limited to adherence to a moral code alone, either to a Johannine one or to the Jewish law, which is nowhere mentioned. But "justice" (*dikaiosynē*) is not an abstract concept: in 1 John the noun is used only in the formula "[the/every-] one who *does* justice" (2:29; 3:7, 10), and the implied parallel between "doing justice" and "loving one's brother [or sister]" (3:10) suggests that personal relationship in action is integral to the idea. "Doing justice" is to be measured not by what one does when compared to a set of expectations, but by the relationships in which one engages and by the character of those relationships. The idea both defines and is defined by this unit of the letter,[59] marking its beginning (2:29), its center (3:7), and its climax (3:10).

[3:1] The author's voice becomes yet more urgent, and, as it does so, it becomes inclusive, switching to "we." Their status is not earned but is a gift, an act of unmerited and unimaginable generosity, founded not on any obligation felt by God nor on any expectation, but on love. The tense of the verb "has given," a perfect, emphasizes the completeness of the gift, recalling the earlier diagnosis of the completeness of love of God expressed in obedience (2:5). Here it is unambiguous that the love that comes from God is intended, not that offered to God (cf. commentary on 2:15). The content of that love (rather than its purpose, which would also be grammatically possible) is that God has named them God's children. The passive verb "be called" does not indicate that it was they themselves or others who called them this, but continues to keep the emphasis on God's act. What elsewhere is an eschatological hope (cf. Matt 5:9, "for they shall be called sons of God") is here experienced already. As the source of love, God is identified as "the Father," here without specific reference to "the Son" (cf. 2:15), linking back to the metaphor of begetting or birth in the previous verse. Therefore naming does not imply adoption, or a change of status (Rom 9:26), nor is it something of pretense, but is a declaration of what is irrefutably the case.

For the first time in the letter the term "children" (*tekna*) is introduced, to be distinguished from the diminutive *teknia* (also here translated "children"), which the author uses for addressing them (2:1, 28; 3:7). In contrast to the more familial "son," which is never used of believers, *tekna* perhaps stresses the dependency on and affinity with the parent;[60] dependency and affinity is taken up in the second part of the section, reaching a climax in the antithesis between "the children of God" and those "of the devil" (v. 10). At this point, then, there is no sense of the creation of a new family of God or of a relationship generated by the one who is uniquely son; only toward the end of the letter will the author suggest that the experience of being children incurs obligations toward other family members (5:1–2).

Initially, however, the only shadow on the horizon is cast by "the world" (*kosmos*), which the readers already know to be the order and system antithetical to God, seductive and yet forbidden (2:15–17). In the present passage "the

---

59. It is not found elsewhere in 1 John.

60. In contrast to Rom 8:14–17, where "sons" and "children" are synonyms, 1 John never uses "sons" of believers.

world" becomes active and personal, unable to recognize, able to hate (v. 13), but, later, not able to hear (4:5). Rhetorically the term sums up and dismisses those who are outside; they are differentiated from the erstwhile members, the antichrists, who can be identified, albeit under a code, although later it will become clear that there is an affinity between the two (4:1–5). Unlike Paul, who reflects on the problem, even if in stereotyped forms (1 Cor 1:22–23), this author has no interest in further identifying outsiders as Jew or Gentile, nor in their status, nor in explaining why they remain outside, except in what follows. The faceless label "world" betrays no concern for them or for their conversion to be other than what they are—although 2:2 and 4:14 reflect another stance (see commentary).

They/the world did not recognize "him," and therefore—"For this reason" looks forward, not back to the first part of the verse—they do not recognize us. The one whom the world did not recognize is still God, as throughout this section, and the reference is not to a specific event (such as the rejection of Jesus), but to the unassailable givenness of this failure: it is ultimately what makes the world "world." This affirmation may have been the more persuasive because it was a familiar refrain in earlier tradition: in the same way the Johannine Jesus contrasts the world's failure to recognize God with his own knowledge of God, while in the prologue the world did not recognize the *logos,* through which it came into being, in the world (John 17:25; 1:10, each using the same aorist tense).[61] These parallels show that it is not a case of the world's not recognizing *that* the addressees were children of God—what would this mean? Rather, as children of God they share God's experience, which is one of rejection, anonymity, or effective invisibility in other people's concerns and experience. If they are to all intents and purposes of no account, this is hardly a cause for anxiety but only what is to be expected.

**[2–3]** At this stage, however, it is not the opposition that matters but the readers and their hope. Unlike sonship, to be an infant can hardly be the final goal, nor can it be the ultimate intention of the begetter—confirmation that the motif of a new family is not in view. For this author, the metaphor of childhood invites not encouragement to growing maturity (cf. 1 Cor 3:1–3; Heb 5:11–14) but expectation of future transformation. Something more must lie ahead, although still veiled—veiled, or "not yet revealed,"[62] because the one who can effect transformation has yet to be unveiled. A few verses earlier (1 John 2:28), the expectation of the self-manifestation of God or Jesus evoked the possibility of hiding in shame; now the same expectation is recalled, "if he is revealed," but

---

61. Here 1 John differs from the Gospel, where Jesus is the mediating figure in the disciples' knowledge of God and their treatment by the world (John 14:7; 15:21; 16:3); see v. 13 below.

62. The same verb is used of his being revealed in 2:28 and later in this verse; it must be impersonal here, but the play on words is intentional.

the consequences are the reverse, not shame but sight. It is sight that will lead to transformation, likeness to the one seen.

If the one to be revealed and seen will be Jesus (cf. John 16:16), the transformation is presumably from being children to being sons. This might still be so if the one revealed were God, as may be the case in 1 John 2:28; although throughout the biblical tradition it is axiomatic that no mortal can see God and live, to be able to look on God does belong to the eschatological hope for the future (Matt 5:8), when the consequence will be not just full understanding (1 Cor 13:12) or adoration (Rev 22:3–4), but even being called *sons* (Matt 5:8–9); in Luke 20:36 being "sons of God" and like angels characterizes the resurrection age when mortal constraints are past.

However, the transformation that 1 John anticipates may be likeness to God: conversing with God had a transformative effect on Moses' face sufficient to strike awe in those who saw (Exod 34:29–35), and Paul recalls this tradition as he presents believers as those who look on the glory of the Lord and are transformed into the same likeness (2 Cor 3:18). In Phil 3:20–21 such transformation will be to the likeness of Jesus, whose work it will be at his revelation, demonstrating that precision and consistency are not to be expected in writers at this time.[63] Such ideas parallel and may draw on Jewish mystical traditions whose goal was to ascend to before the divine throne, and which described the transformation of those who achieved this. Although the developed sources for this (often called Merkabah mysticism) are late, it is now widely agreed that their roots are to be found in Judaism of the late Second Temple period;[64] they confirm that 1 John's thought is to be located within a Jewish framework and not within Hellenic notions of deification or apotheosis. If ultimately the language is too allusive to reach a firm conclusion as to what lies ahead, this is only what the letter itself acknowledges: the answer is not yet revealed and will only be revealed when "he" is revealed.

What lies ahead is not just a matter for speculation or for reassurance, however: it impinges on the present. The confident expectation of future likeness demands a commitment to being like him now, to purifying oneself. The language of purification originates in the cultic sphere, where the Divinity is pure and all that is associated with the Divine must be made so, for example through lustrations and through other rites. Those who are to approach God in worship must prepare themselves (cf. John 11:55), often by separation from contact or activities that were seen as defiling; in Exod 19:10, 14–15 such purification included abstinence from sexual intercourse. The common figurative sense of (moral) purity follows naturally, whether or not the association with preparedness for an

---

63. See also John 17:24, Jesus' prayer that "they may see my glory."

64. See the introduction, p. 23; also April D. DeConick, ed., *Paradise Now: Essays on Early Jewish and Christian Mysticism* (SBLSymS 11; Atlanta: Society of Biblical Literature, 2006).

encounter with God is retained (e.g., Jas 4:8), and the terminology may be used of innocence, of the consequence of forgiveness, or, as frequently, of sexual chastity. It is axiomatic in Jewish mystical traditions that extensive purification is a precondition of the ascent to God's throne, often involving a range of ascetical and other practices. For 1 John, purifying oneself is therefore not just a preparedness that may be expressed in avoidance of the inappropriate but an active discipline for those who would see God.

The one in whom hope is sustained—the expression indicates more than merely hoping[65]—must be the one who is seen and/or to whom likeness is promised in verse 2. Even if that be God, the one who is pure and who is their model is probably Jesus; the emphatic "that one" (*ekeinos*) regularly introduces affirmations about Jesus (see 2:6). This produces a bridge to the following verses, where the removal of sins by "that one," in whom there is no sin, provides the grounds for believers not to sin (vv. 4–6). That does not mean that the language of purity in verse 3 already presupposes ideas of sin or any particular form of inappropriate behavior; the image focuses on commitment and on readiness to serve and to encounter God. Although the Fourth Gospel does not use this term ("pure," *hagnos*), it uses a related one (*hagiazō*) to speak of how Jesus was set apart by and for God, and prayed that his disciples might also be dedicated in the same way (John 10:36; 17:17–19).

This section (1 John 2:29–3:3) has begun and ended with an affirmation about God or Jesus—"he is just . . . that one is pure"—sealing everything in between (and for this author a switch from God to Jesus does not spoil the pattern). Neither term is abstract or aesthetic, even if what it means for God to be just is not explained, for example by appeal to what God has done. Similarly, it is not the past, how Jesus acted in his ministry, that provides a model but that he now *is* pure, even if readers might deduce this from what they had heard about the former. These characteristics of God or of Jesus both make demands on and offer hope to those who would respond. God's children cannot seek to be other than what God is, but they are God's children not through their own efforts but through God's act. This reaches into the future: those who see God will see God as God *is*. The future may be transformative but it will not be anything that the present does not already prepare for. The elements of a future eschatology that 1 John retains thus do not fundamentally qualify or diminish the emphasis elsewhere on what is now assured and already realized.

### 1 John 3:4–10a—The Two Ways

3:4 Everyone who does sin also does lawlessness, for sin is lawlessness.
5 You already know that that one was revealed in order to remove sins,[a]

---

65. The verb is "to have" (*echō*); see commentary on 2:23.

and there is no sin in him. 6 Everyone who indwells in him does not sin; everyone who sins has not seen him or known him. 7 Children, let no one lead you astray. The one who does justice is just, even as he is just.

8 The one who does sin belongs to the devil, because the devil sins from the beginning. The Son of God was revealed for this purpose, to do away with the activities of the devil. 9 Everyone who has been born from God does not do sin, because his seed indwells him—indeed, cannot sin, because they have been born from God.

10a In this way the children of God and the children of the devil are exposed.

a. Although some manuscripts read "our sins," this is probably an addition.

If encouragement dominated the last section, urgent persuasion dominates this one. On one level readers are not being told to do anything, nor that they or anyone else has acted or believed wrongly. Yet the tone suggests that much is at stake, appealing to what they already know (v. 5), warning against being misled (v. 7), and reaching a climactic demonstration (v. 10). That demonstration, the contrast between the children of God and the children of the devil, highlights the new theme that emerges through these verses. Whereas the previous verses offered hope and assurance, with attention fixed firmly on the inclusive "we," author and readers of the letter together, this section addresses readers only twice, each time as "you" (vv. 5, 7); the predominant present tenses and the impersonal "everyone who" or "the one who" leave the readers to determine where they are to see themselves. The vigorous style and uncompromising assertions will stop as suddenly as they started, to be recalled only briefly at the end of the letter.

This is one of the most difficult passages of the letter. Interpreters have long wrestled with the dualistic language that seems to divide people into two camps, where origin determines behavior and behavior confirms origin, with no apparent way out of the cycle. Studies have also highlighted the contrast between the view of sin here as something that no one born of God can commit, and the rejection at the start of the letter of any claim not to have sin (1:8, 10). There have been a variety of attempts to soften the apparent contradiction (see below), although a final discussion will have to await the author's return to the theme at the close of the letter (5:16–18). That none has won total agreement suggests that there is a tension at the heart of this theme, itself so important for the letter. As suggested earlier, this tension may owe something to the author's adoption here of an antithetically worded source. Further evidence that the author is working with earlier material is provided by the number of echoes of John 8:41–47; these do not amount to quotations in either direction, and support the position taken throughout this commentary that the Gospel and First Epistle share common traditions rather than there being any literary dependency. This may mean that the author is citing familiar formulae in order to drive home what he wants to say, but unless there is evidence to the contrary we must assume that he cited only that with which he agreed, or which he felt could be shaped to his purposes.

Although the passage is best treated as a unity, it falls naturally into two subsections.[66] The first (vv. 4–7), with its two appeals to the readers (vv. 5, 7), uses a number of arguments to reinforce an implicit call "to do justice," whereas the second (vv. 8–10a) introduces the more metaphysical opposition between God and the devil. Links between them, however, mean that the one cannot be read without the other.

[4] While the evocation of the one who is pure in verse 3 provides a surface link to the obverse topic of doing sin, the language and antithetical form connect this verse more tightly back to 2:29 and forward to 3:7, which concludes this subsection.[67] The parallel between the closing words of verses 7 and 3, "as that one is just/pure," further tie this section into its context. In turn, "doing sin" will introduce the second subsection at verse 8. Those who read or listen to the letter are persuaded not by careful logical argument but by multiple interwoven threads, recalling earlier ideas, reinforcing and being reinforced by them.

If this is so, this verse cannot be read without reference to the earlier discussion of sin in 1:7–2:2. There the language was of "having/possessing (*echō*) sin" and of "sinning," while here (and in 3:8, 9) it is of "doing (*poieō*) sin"; it is, however, difficult to detect a clear difference in meaning, for example, as if "*doing* sin" indicated something more persistent than the other formulations. It is more probable that the expression has been generated as a parallel to "doing justice"— 1 John never speaks of "having justice" and there is no equivalent performative verb to match "to sin." At this point the main concern is to exclude any undervaluing of the significance of sin. By defining sin as lawlessness (*anomia*) the author's intention is not to identify it with transgression of the law (*nomos*), whether of biblical law (Torah) or of the norms of the community—which are never described as "law," a word absent from the Johannine Epistles. In 2 Thess 2:3–8 *anomia* and the adjective *anomos* are used of the eschatological manifestation of opposition to God. A similar association is implied here, particularly in view of the eschatological framework of "his coming" (2:28; 3:2) and of the earlier antichrist imagery, as well as of the figure of the devil in verses 8–10. As *anomia*, sin puts its perpetrator firmly in the camp of the archopponent of God, something that may not otherwise have been evident. Sin has a systemic and not

---

66. NA[27] gives a paragraph break between vv. 6 and 7, but this depends on a false assumption that the address to the readers (v. 7) marks a new beginning.

67. See the introduction to 2:29–3:12 for the suggestion that 3:4 + 7 formed a couplet in an underlying source.

a mere occasional character. Such redefinitions of sin may have been a Johannine formulary: in John 8:34, in a chapter with other parallels with 1 John 3, Jesus declares, "*Everyone who does sin* [the same formula] is a slave of sin"; again, the image is of sin personified as a power and as more than merely contingent error. Those words probably intentionally evoke Gen 4:7, where sin is represented as ready to control Cain, who must in turn rule over it; echoes of the story of Cain also provide a thread through the rest of this chapter of the letter. There are here glimpses of a more extensive reflection on and reworking of biblical traditions out of which the language and thought of both Epistle and Gospel arise, and which may have been familiar to the earliest readers.

Toward the end of the letter the author identifies "injustice" (*adikia*; cf. 1:9) with sin, and suggests that sin itself may need further definition (5:16–17). In all this, "sin" (*hamartia*) is the focal term, and the author does not again refer to lawlessness. He shows no interest in defining specific acts or attitudes as sin; sin serves rather as an emblematic element within the imagined world that he is painting, and his audience should be in no doubt that its threatening reach cannot be bypassed.

[5] Now that the scene has been set by the specter of lawlessness he changes tack with an appeal to a conviction with which he claims they are already familiar. The emphatic "that one" indicates a christological affirmation from their tradition (cf. 2:6; 3:3), as too does the characteristic "he was revealed" (*phaneroō*), which here looks to the past (so also 3:8; cf. 1:2; 4:9) and not to the future as in the previous verses (2:28; 3:2). As "that one" he is effective primarily as the one who is proclaimed and whose story is told. That Jesus dealt with sin is fundamental to nearly all early Christian preaching, and probably formed a central element in catechesis and in confession of faith. Frequently this is explicitly tied to the affirmation that Jesus died "for sin(s)" (1 Cor 15:3; 1 Pet 3:18), but this core conviction preceded any precise theory as to how Jesus' death was effective against sin, and a number of different models are already to be found within the New Testament writings. The verb used here, *airō*, "to take away (sins)," which can also mean to lift, carry, or remove, is only otherwise used of forgiveness in the New Testament by John (the Baptist) in John 1:29 ("Behold the lamb of God, who takes away the sin of the world"; cf. v. 36), although related words are found elsewhere.[68] A connection between the two passages is supported by John's subsequent explanation that his own activity was "so that he might be *revealed* to Israel" (John 1:31). Neither here nor in the Gospel is the taking away of sins explicitly restricted to Jesus' death, and the letter's "was revealed" would support a more general association with his presence.

Even so, there may be a passing allusion to Isaiah 53, a chapter that came to be interpreted of Jesus' death, although most intensively toward the end of the

68. Romans 11:27; Heb 10: 4 (*aphaireō*). It is used in the LXX at 1 Sam 15:25; 25:28.

New Testament period and beyond. Such an allusion has regularly been detected in the Gospel account, combining an allusion in the "lamb of God" to the servant "led like a lamb to the slaughter" (Isa 53:7) with one to the servant as one who "bears" our sins/the sin of many (53:4, 12), where, although the LXX does not use the Johannine verb *airō*, the Hebrew root (*nśʾ*) could have been so translated. As an explanation of John 1:29 and 36 this is not entirely persuasive: Passover echoes are more probable in the context of the Gospel, and the phrase may draw on a composite picture from within early Christian tradition. Despite this, there may be more in the context than the use of *airein* to sustain an echo in 1 John. The first clause of the last strophe of Isa 53:9 ("he did no violence") is rendered by the LXX, "he did not *do* lawlessness (*anomia*)," while the version in 1 Pet 2:22 reads, "he did not *do* sin (*hamartia*)," both expressions in the immediate context (1 John 3:4); the second clause of Isa 53:9, "neither was there deceit in his mouth," matches at least in structure the closing words of 1 John 3:5, "and there is no sin in him." Indeed, this may uncover another link with John 8, where Jesus demands, "Which of you convicts me of sin? If I *speak* the truth . . ." (John 8:46): here the Isaianic tradition has arguably been transformed into narrative.

Even if found at all persuasive, this remains nothing more than an allusion, and one may wonder whether readers would detect it without prompting. Such prompting may have been provided once again by familiarity with the scriptural reflection that is a major feature of Johannine creativity. Even so, detecting such scriptural echoes does not determine how, for 1 John, Jesus takes away sins, nor whether this is founded in Jesus' death or only in his manifestation. Rather than the picture being one of doing away with the sins of individuals (as in 1:9), the absence of a personal pronoun, "your/our," and the alternative expression, "do away with" in 3:8 (see below), suggest a more comprehensive removal of sins from the sphere in which he is active and of those who also belong to it.[69] Sins have no place here, even as sin itself has—the present tense—no place in him.

It would be wrong to see this last assertion as expressing an explicit doctrine of the sinlessness of Jesus, particularly as expressed in subsequent debates as to whether he was "capable of not sinning" or "not capable of sinning." Similar sentiments to here are expressed in 2 Cor 5:21 and in Heb 4:15, and there the concern is to affirm Jesus' complete participation in the experience of the human condition, but at the same time to maintain the conviction that the power of sin which is central to that experience could never be overcome entirely from within it. This has as yet nothing to do with later theories of the inherent sinfulness of the human body, especially as sustained through the normal pattern of human conception and birth. Earlier the author has considered the conditions

---

69. This may be clearer in John 1:29, where the singular, "sin of the world," is used.

of truth or of love being within someone, measured by their adherence to God's commands (2:4–5). Sin belongs to the opposite camp to these, and so can have no part in Jesus, even if, or not least because, his task is to take sins away.

[6] It follows that anyone who does have part in him cannot also actively participate in the sphere of sin; conversely, anyone who does exhibit the evidences of sin cannot really be said to be fully on his side of the great divide. The theoretical logic of this is easier to follow than its practical application. Moreover, the writer does not say that anyone who remains in him *cannot* or *should not* sin, but that they *do not* sin. What can this mean positively, except as the premise on which rests the conclusion that if someone is found engaged in sin, then they self-evidently cannot be engaged with him? It surely does not mean that whatever they do do, regardless of how others view it, is by definition not sin: any such idea is ruled out by the second half of the verse. The conundrum is further complicated by the exhortation to confess sins in 1:8, supported by the assurance of divine aid (2:1–2), and by the vehement denial that anyone can validly claim either not to possess sin or not to have sinned (1:8, 10). Subsequent verses will intensify the problem, but already the wording of this verse has given rise to a number of what will prove to be false solutions.[70]

Some have suggested that the present tense in this verse, "sins" (so also "does sin" in 3:4, 8, 9), refers to habitual and persistent sinning, while what is forbidden at the start of the letter is any denial either of a past, presalvation, state of sin, or of those occasional lapses that are an intrinsic aspect of living in the "not yet" (3:2). Yet it would be a hypersensitive reader who could so distinguish between the not-to-be denied "having sin," and the prohibited "doing sin," both expressed in the present tense (1:8; 3:9). Although "doing sin" (*poieō hamartian*, 3:4, 8, 9) is used only in order to exclude it, this is not because it means something different from the other expressions but because it appears only in this section of the letter, perhaps, as suggested, shaped by earlier traditions and by the contrast with "doing justice" (3:4–9; cf. 5:18).

Another proposal is that the solution to the problem lies in the description of *"everyone who indwells in him* does not sin": insofar as people do dwell within him, they do not sin, but in sorry truth no one does remain steadfastly in him without wavering, and to the extent that they waver, so are they susceptible to sinning, for which forgiveness must be sought. Theologically and experientially this may be the case, but it is hardly so in Johannine terms. The very force of the Johannine "indwell" (*menō en*) is that it denotes stability and continuity, such as also mark divine presence (4:12–15), not a constantly precarious relationship. The obverse confirms this: one could hardly say that not to

---

70. An easy solution would be to suppose that 3:6 is a quotation of an opposing view that the author wishes to denounce, and that the first audience would recognize it as such; but without any textual indication exegesis must first endeavor to make sense of the text as the author's own words.

have seen or known him, the description of the one who sins in the second half of the verse, is a changing state, into and out of which one moves.

A third suggestion offers a variation on the second and suffers from the same weakness: this is that even if "indwelling" is stable and persistent it is never complete; consequently all are caught between that indwelling, which they experience in part, and the incompleteness of their sight and knowledge. In these terms they may be said at one and the same time not to sin and to sin, and this is all the more the case if not sinning and sinning refer not to individual acts of obedience or of disobedience, but to the (un-)brokenness of a relationship with God. Once more, even if subsequent theology has appropriately used such dialectic to interpret religious experience, this bears little relation to the language and thought of the author of 1 John. The dualistic pattern of this verse as it is sustained through those that follow maps a division not within the individual, as these solutions suppose, but within the cosmic order.

Readings such as these are predicated on taking the sentiments of this verse out of the broader context and pitching them against the implicit assumptions of the earlier part of the letter, also taken out of their epistolary setting, and then seeking a theological harmonization of both. Yet this author is prepared to say apparently incompatible things about sinning even in close succession, as 5:16–18 demonstrates. Within the rhetorical context of each stage of the letter both sets of assertions make fully coherent sense. Indeed, 3:6 says little more than has already been argued earlier: 2:6 firmly stated that anyone claiming "to remain in him" must imitate "that one," while a couple of verses earlier an avowal of having known him is falsified by a failure in obedience (2:4). This verse reformulates these ideas in the antithetical form and with the language of sinning supplied by the couplets that, as suggested above, underlie the whole section. At the same time, it has already been shown that it is indeed possible and indeed appropriate to affirm, "we have seen" (1:1–3) and "(you have) known" (2:13–14); the combination of sight and knowledge here denied the one who sins, although not otherwise found in 1 John, was perhaps part of the same tradition (cf. John 14:7, "henceforth you know him and have seen him"). Such certainties are now shown to be grounds not for self-congratulation but for self-reflection. As so often, the "him" who is seen, known, and dwelt within is not identified; in the light of verse 5 a reference to Jesus is expected, although in another context it might equally be to God. At this point the verse is less a statement of fact than a challenge to those quick to utter such claims; when they are brought into the dualistically framed cosmic order the consequences are inescapable.

[7] However, sin is not the author's real concern; now at the climactic point of his argument he addresses his audience directly (cf. 2:28). It is even possible that he has reversed the order of the two members of the couplet (cf. v. 4; see n. 51 above) so as to end the subsection not with sinning but with doing justice. The solemn warning lest anyone lead them astray recalls his similar cau-

tion in 2:26. This does not mean that those whose departure was described in 2:19 also held and were propagating treacherous views on the present topic. The common suggestion that they failed to take seriously the reality or the consequences of sin is misplaced; if that were so this admonition would have needed to introduce verse 6, directly contradicting any alternative teaching about sin— a "misleading" alternative to the affirmative statement in this verse is difficult to imagine. Rather, the echo of 2:26 is rhetorically designed to conjure up the eschatological scenario of danger and the need for steadfastness that were established by that earlier passage.

This is also achieved by the way that this verse echoes 2:29, recalling its pivotal position in the tension between shame and eager anticipation. In these ways what may at first seem to be a tautological platitude, or, with verse 4, the straightforward description of two classes of people, becomes a summons to action. In the earlier source material the one "who is just" was perhaps God, as in 2:29; but now that it follows the similarly formulated comparison in verse 3 (*"just as that one is* pure," *kathōs ekeinos estin*), as well as verse 5 (*"that one* [*ekeinos*] was revealed"), the reference is surely to Jesus. The author is no more interested at this point in justifying the epithet "just" or in defining "doing justice" than he was in defining sin. It is in his framework self-evident that the two are entirely opposed to each other, without any possible ambiguity or contamination, one by the other. He is not establishing a basis for ethical decision making or for negotiating conflicting demands on human capacities and desires for justice. Instead, as throughout the letter, he is shaping for his readers a world of nonnegotiable choices, urging them to discover the consequences of the commitments they have already made. It is a world legitimated not only by a dualist understanding of reality, or by an apocalyptic vision of the ultimate opposition between light and darkness, justice and sin, but by the presence of the one whose manifestation has determined the final resolution of that opposition. In the face of this the statement of imitation ("just as") is in actuality a call to imitation (cf. 2:6), which will almost certainly be expressed not in moral rectitude but in manifest allegiance.

[8] The second subsection starts like the first (v. 4) but ratchets up the tension. This time it is not sin that is being redefined in eschatological terms but the person who performs it. The challenge to allegiance becomes an uncompromising statement whose backdrop is the relentless antagonism between God and the devil. By the first century the idea of the forces of opposition to God being embodied in or under the leadership of an archopponent was a familiar one (see commentary on 2:13). Although the Greek term *diabolos* was in common usage of slanderers (cf. Titus 2:3), it was used by the Septuagint as a translation of "Satan," who had himself developed from being a sort of cross-examiner of Job's fidelity (Job 2:1) to the instigator of human disobedience (1 Chron 21:1). Attempts to explain how such disobedience could emerge within God's good creation, something Genesis fails to do, struggled between

affirming human free will and propensity to wrong (Sir 15:14–20) and casting the blame on the primeval act of rebellion against God by an evil or fallen angel who could easily be merged with the devil (see *1 Enoch* 6). Such views, influenced perhaps by Persian dualisms, pushed the conflict between good and evil onto the metaphysical or cosmic stage (cf. 1QS III, 20–24, quoted above on 1:5). In this development humankind is caught up in an enduring battle whose final resolution lies in the future, sometimes cast more in the role of its victims or passive agents, sometimes called to take up arms and to resist infiltration (cf. Eph 6:11–17).

In 1 John the picture is not of attack and resistance but of established identities and allegiances. In 2:16 (see commentary) the preposition *ek*, "from, out of," expressed the utter incompatibility of that which owes its character to God (the Father) and that which takes its being from the world. Here the same preposition is used to relate the person who does sin to the devil, but because the devil is envisaged in quasi-personal terms the relationship is even more ambiguous. It is not that they merely belong to the devil, a state that could be overcome; something more intrinsic is suggested: they owe their being and their origin to the devil. However, whereas 1 John does speak of *being born* from God, it never speaks of *being born* from the devil; the antitheses of the letter and, most probably, those that underlie it, do not push the dualism that far. This might be to avoid ascribing to the devil generative powers equal to those of God—God alone can beget: the idea of a world peopled by two "races" of human beings with two different and antagonistic progenitors would severely challenge the fundamental biblical monotheism. The imbalance may also keep open the possibility that those who are identified by their relationship with the devil are not so indelibly; however, the language ensures that change cannot naturally come about through any potential of the human actors.

Sinning is the fundamental, perhaps the sole, characteristic of the devil. "From the beginning" may imply this—"intrinsically"; alternatively, it might refer temporally back to a beginning before time in the devil's original act of disobedience against God, or to the story of Adam and Eve. In an earlier form of this tradition the reference was arguably to Cain's murder of Abel, a story that puzzled Jewish interpreters, both because of internal incoherencies and because of the theological problem as to the origins of the impulse to murder (Gen 4:1–16): one line of interpretation attributed Cain's paternity to the devil.[71] This tradition likely lies behind Jesus' words in John 8:44, "You are of the father, the devil, and you long to do the desires of your father. He was a *murderer* from the beginning." First John refers to Cain later in this chapter, and

---

71. Aided by Eve's words in Gen 4:1; for this and what follows see Judith M. Lieu, "What Was from the Beginning: Scripture and Tradition in the Johannine Epistles," *NTS* 39 (1993): 458–77, especially 467–72.

also uses the distinctive word *murderer* (1 John 3:12, 15), showing his familiarity with this exegetical tradition. Once again this affords a glimpse of the scriptural reflection that in different ways influenced the language and ideas of both Gospel and Letter. However, the allusion, if present, will become fully apparent only as the chapter progresses. At this point there may be a clearer echo of the way that "from the beginning" has resounded as a refrain through the letter so far, in confidence and in encouragement (1:1; 2:7, 13, 14, 24). The readers are now being shown another trajectory "from the beginning"; the choice is not between faithfulness to the past and multiple other possibilities, but between two pasts, which shape two presents and two futures.

However, what could be told as a story of two battle lines confronting each other and stretching through time and humanity has been interrupted. Originally, that story may have awaited any resolution in the future when the conflict would finally be won. Instead, now the resolution has in effect already taken place, not by the supremacy of one of the protagonists but by the intervention of a new figure, "the Son of God." He "was revealed" (cf. v. 5), particularly appropriate here since his intervention was as truly eschatological as any future appearance will be, establishing a new situation in the standoff between God and the devil. He had but one purpose, a purpose that it can be assumed was achieved, to render ineffectual the activities and achievements of the devil. The verb (*lyō*) can mean to release or untie (Mark 1:7), but also to destroy (John 2:19); here the sense is perhaps more to annul the power of (cf. John 10:35). "The activities of the devil" do not need further definition, although the first audience may have detected another echo from an exegesis of the story of Cain (cf. John 8:41, "You do the activities of your father").

It is striking that this figure is identified only as "the Son of God," the first time that this phrase has been used in the letter. Although there is now some evidence that this could be used as a messianic title in Judaism of the time (4Q246), there is no suggestion of the fulfillment of scripturally defined hopes here. Rather, in this context and used without further identification, "the Son of God" is a title that might be described as belonging to myth, that is, to a story in which figures beyond the human sphere are the primary actors.[72] Taken on its own, the outline plot of this story emerges: the scene starts with that resolute confrontation, on stage stands the devil; off stage, but with a presence ever felt, is God; and perhaps in the shadows those who belong to one or other side. Now the Son of God has appeared and has successfully challenged the devil's apparent control of the stage, so what will happen next? It is easy to imagine how such a story could be told even in initial preaching; easy to imagine, too, how it could be illustrated from other stories taken from the opening chapters of Genesis.

---

72. So understood, "myth" makes no judgments about history.

Readers of the letter will not need to ask the identity of this Son of God, although there is no explicit reference to Jesus or Christ throughout this chapter until its end (3:23); those who heard the story for the first time may have needed to ask, and this would have been their passage to faith. When and where this victory, or "annulling," took place is not stated beyond the "revealed," and it is notable that there are no encounters with the devil or evil spirits in the Fourth Gospel as there are in the Synoptics.[73] Still, from this vantage point it is clear why to deny the Son would be to deny the Father (2:22–23), for without the Son the victory would not yet be won; it would still only be a story, awaiting realization. Yet if this is a foundational story, why has the author waited until halfway through his letter to recall it? Partly, perhaps, because it was foundational, experienced "from the beginning" (1:1–3), and so it needed no retelling; partly, perhaps, because the author wanted to introduce other ways of telling it, such as those that emphasized the relationship between Son and Father (2:1)—as just noted, up to this point there have been references to "the/his/the Father's Son," but only now is the title "the Son of God" used. The story also needed to be related to the direct experience of believers, to the realities of sin and forgiveness, as well as to the received traditions about the life of "that one" (vv. 3, 5), of Jesus. Within the framework offered by these, as will become clear, the story could become more than a path to conversion, and could offer new challenges to living in community, to envisioning and playing a part in the scenes that did after all stretch beyond that momentous intervention.

[9] Surprisingly, the author continues as if this dramatic interruption has not taken place, with the antagonism between God and the devil (v. 10). The description of someone as having been born from God, introduced at the beginning of this section (2:29, "everyone who does justice has been born from him"), is taken up again. In the original source suggested earlier this verse would have been the obverse partner of that statement, reinforcing rather than adding to it: "does sin" would be defined as the reverse of "does justice." In the author's reworking of the material this is no longer the case; doing sin has acquired an independent seriousness of its own (vv. 4–6). Moreover, in isolation from its lead clause, which established and defined its language, attention now focuses on the subject, "everyone who has been born from God." The concern is no longer with identifying people by their actions and with drawing conclusions, but instead with taking for granted the actions that will result not from their own choices but from a state for which they are not responsible. Offspring have no choice in their parentage and can take no credit or blame for it. Whereas in human society children are not automatons, their every thought or deed deter-

---

73. Although the devil or "ruler of this world" is still very much at work: John 12:31; 13:2; 14:30. In the temptation narratives Jesus' encounter with the devil hinges on his status as Son of God (Matt 4:1–11; Luke 4:1–13).

mined by their genetic inheritance, those who are born from God do not, it is assumed, have what it takes to sin.

This implication is reinforced by what follows, an expansion of the original line, which now gives this verse its own neat symmetry, the opening words repeated at the end. It is not simply that such as a matter of fact—or, more realistically, of aspiration—do not sin but that they do not have the capacity so to do, they "cannot sin." Why this is so is obscured, first, by the author's characteristic use of the third person pronoun "he, him, his": literally the Greek reads, "Everyone born of God does not do sin, *because his seed remains in him.*" In the context "his" and "him" could refer back either to God or to the one born from God, and might, but need not, refer to the same in each case. Thus the phrase might be translated: (a) because God's seed remains in God; (b) because God's seed remains in the person born from God; (c) because the seed of the person born from God remains in them; (d) because the seed of the person born from God remains in God. Second, "seed" (*sperma*) might indicate (i) something implanted, (ii) offspring (singular), (iii) offspring (plural). From these options the following explanations of why the one born from God *cannot* sin become possible:

1. because God's offspring (plural) remain in God (a + iii)
2. because what God has implanted remains in the person born from God (b + i)
3. because God's offspring (singular) remains in the person born from God (b + ii)
4. because what is implanted in the person born from God remains in them (c + i)
5. because what is implanted in the person born from God remains in God (d + i)

Although other combinations are theoretically possible, they make little sense. Further, option 4 would be difficult to distinguish from 2, since the author has given no hint of anything inherent in human beings, such as an immortal soul, independent of God's generative activity; and this also excludes option 5. The third option is certainly possible, and would refer back to the Son of God of the previous verse, whose indwelling presence now keeps believers from sin. Although elsewhere in the New Testament "seed" is used of Jesus through an exegetical play on God's promise to Abraham and his seed in Gen 13:15; 17:8 (Gal 3:16, 19), this scriptural tradition has left little trace in Johannine thought. Closer to the primary Johannine scriptural testimonies, Gen 3:15 with its anticipation of enmity between the serpent and the woman, between its seed and her seed, also invited messianic or christological interpretation.[74] The verse would

---

74. The verse came to be called the "Protoevangelium." A christological interpretation is first explicit in Irenaeus, *Against Heresies* 5.21.1.

then express an idea not dissimilar to the less ambiguous assertion in 1 John 5:18, "We know that everyone who has been born of God does not sin, but the one who was born from God [cf. God's offspring] protects them, and the evil one does not touch them."[75] However, the switch from the straightforward "son" to "seed" is sudden, and this option seems the least likely of the first three.

More attractive is a reference to something implanted by God (2), and this invites comparison with 2:20 and 27, where the possession and indwelling of the "anointing" (*chrisma*) provided an inalienable source of knowledge. The image has shifted, but the idea would be much the same, and the question would then be the identification of the seed God has planted. The seed or grain sown is a common image of the word of God (Mark 4:3–20), and elsewhere 1 John does describes the preservative powers of the indwelling of "that which you heard from the beginning" (1 John 2:24); this is a popular interpretation, although in this context the focus would be on teaching as received more than on the converting gospel. In the context of the birth metaphor, however, seed more probably evokes not grain but (human/male) generative power. The "word" might still be so understood (1:1; cf. 1 Pet 1:23), but 1 John has not elsewhere linked birth from God to "that which you heard." Similarly, the spirit as the divinely given source of life might seem an obvious candidate, but again this association is not one that 1 John anywhere makes, and the spirit serves other functions in the letter (3:24; 4:1, 13).[76] Perhaps the most that can be said is that although the metaphor of birth is becoming stretched—properly, the seed implanted in *the woman* is the source of conception—the language serves to emphasize that God's relationship to those born from God is not simply one of generation and origin but continues ("indwells" [*menō en*]) to be effective. God's seed is not to be identified with any particular agent of continuing energizing, but merely asserts its potency. Being born from God means to continue to be vivified by God's creative power; such birth cannot be lost or abrogated. The verse thus falls neatly into two parallel lines:

> (Everyone born of God)
>
> does not do sin          because God's begetting power indwells them
> and cannot sin           because they have been born from God.

While this goes some way toward explaining 1 John's abrupt introduction of this new term, "seed," it would also be at home within a tradition of exegesis of the story of Cain's murder of Abel. In Gen 4:25, after conceiving and giv-

---

75. See commentary on 5:18, where a change of tense indicates that "the one who was born from God" refers to the Son of God.

76. John 3:5 makes a connection in speaking of "being born from water and the spirit," but John does not use the analogy of seed, and it has been shown that the Gospel's development of the birth image follows different lines from that of 1 John.

ing birth to Seth, Eve declares, "God has raised up for me another seed [i.e., child, LXX *sperma*] in place of Abel, whom Cain killed." In later Jewish tradition, this provoked a dual response similar to Paul's exegesis of the promise to Abraham and his seed: on the one hand, two lines of descent ("seed") could be traced, one from the wicked Cain who embodied the characteristics assigned to the serpent, the other from Seth who, like Abel, was righteous (Josephus, *Antiquities* 1.52–9; Philo, *On the Posterity of Cain* 172–74). In the light of the promise of Gen 3:15 (see above), especially as interpreted in a quasi-messianic sense, Seth himself became a figure of speculation; while in Philo he represents "the seed of human virtue," for some, particularly in developing gnostic traditions, he became the continuator of God's image in Adam and revelation to him, the founder of a race ("holy seed") of the elect, sometimes entrusted with the knowledge that Adam and Eve had forfeited.[77] It is not possible to plot or to date the precise evolution of such speculation—nor is it necessary to label it "gnostic"—and clearly 1 John does not presuppose a developed schema of any kind. But behind it (and the Gospel) may lie the same fascination with what is not said in Scripture as well as with what is, with the gaps as well as with possible connections, whether or not intentional, and particularly with these perplexing early narratives of Genesis that wrestle with the origin and transmission of disobedience and of evil.

Such a background would explain the use of "seed" here, as well as the idea of something originating in God that sustains the identity and character of those whose true origin is with God.[78] It would also, however, give some support to the first proposed explanation, that God's offspring remain in God; they are "the seed" not only because they are born from God, but also because they represent the seed anticipated in Gen 3:15 and continued in Gen 4:25, passages that also already establish the relentless pattern of opposition in which they are caught. This would also develop what has already been said in verse 6, "everyone who indwells in him does not sin," except that now the power to remain originates in God. This interpretation also offers a very smooth translation, since it means that both "his" and "in him" refer to the same person, God, and that the subject, "his seed," is in effect the same as the subject of the other verbs, the one born from God who does not and cannot sin.

A final decision will probably continue to elude us because, once again, the wording seems to assume a familiarity among its earliest readers that is lost to later ones. Yet if the mechanics of what is being claimed are obscure, the consequences appear less so. It is not simply that those born from God do not commit

77. Among the Nag Hammadi tractates, the *Apocalypse of Adam* already reflects this, and it is developed in later documents that bear Seth's name. See next note.

78. This integrates the image in the wider context of 1 John 3 more firmly than do appeals to the Valentinian doctrine, according to Irenaeus, *Against Heresies* 1.6.1–2, that the elect or "spiritual" were possessed of a divine seed. See Introduction §3.4.

sin but that they are consistently (cf. "the seed remains") unable so to do. The dilemma that verse 6 already presented is here even more categorical. Even from common experience, quite apart from the affirmation of sin and forgiveness earlier in the letter, it would be natural to conclude either that no one truly has been born from God, except for Christ, who can hardly be in view here, or that the sinning that cannot be done has some limited sense.

The possibility of different types or levels of sin has nowhere been intimated, however, and when the author later does introduce such differentiation he does so with very careful explanation and without any backward reference (5:16–17). Although many interpreters do explain 3:9 by 5:16—the sin that those born from God cannot commit is the "sin that results in death"—it is highly unlikely that the author would fail to make this plain; if it was assumed to be self-evident, the explanation at 5:16–17 would be redundant. Moreover, it would be illogical to affirm what would then be implied, that people who either were God's seed or possessed God's seed *could* sin (i.e., those sins that did not automatically result in death). Interpretations that attempt to follow this route wrongly treat as anthropological an issue that for the author is cosmic. The point is unequivocal: God's presence and empowerment are antithetical to the presence of all sin.

This indeed is the conclusion to which the author's fundamental system has forced him. The repeated emphasis, his own expansion of an earlier stanza, leaves no doubt of his refusal to allow this tenet to be softened in any way. The world of meaning into which readers have been brought is one of inflexible alternatives, and for the moment they are not allowed to duck away from the consequences. If the words do not describe the reality of how things are then it is the reality that is flawed, not the words. So understood, the verse is neither an offer of false security—"you are born from God, therefore you do not sin"— nor a cruel rejection of their hopes—"you do sin, and cannot do otherwise, therefore you can never hope to be born from God." By maintaining the third person singular form it paints for them in sharp contrasts a landscape with which they are already familiar, and in which they know themselves to be placed, and it leaves them to determine what it means to be there. Yet they can do so in the light of the experience of confession and forgiveness, which the letter began by affirming in the strongest possible terms.

[10] The passage concludes by leaving them in no doubt that there are indeed children of God, just as it is the case that there are children of the devil. The characteristic "In this way" (cf. 2:3) that introduces the verse points back, summarizing the argument that began at 3:8 when the devil was first introduced. But whereas there it was a case of someone belonging to or coming from (*ek*) the devil, language that could be taken as only vehement disapproval, the intervening argument has prepared for a more intrinsic familial likeness and dependency. Although the author does not go so far as to speak of some as born from the devil, he comes but a few, albeit important, steps short of so doing. How some become

children of the devil, and whether there was a point in time when they became such or whether they were always so is not asked, or answered. That falls outside the writer's interest, which only concerns his audience. Further consequences of the scheme are that there is little room for a change of parentage and that there can be no third alternative or middle way, not even prior to choosing one or the other. This sharply dualistic model of the two parallel sets of children and their parents, as well as the different grammatical form—here (and at 5:2) both nouns have the definite article (*ta tekna tou theou*)—suggests that the metaphor has developed independently of the earlier acknowledgment of being children of God (*tekna theou*, without the article; 3:1–2). Still, readers will recall both the encouragement there and also the expectation of something yet more. The effect is to temper assurance with warning, but also warning with reassurance.

### 1 John 3:10b–12—Justice and Love as the Marks of the Children of God

3:10b Everyone who does not do justice does not belong to God, and likewise everyone who does not love their brother.[a] 11 Because this is[b] the message that you heard from the beginning, that we are to love one another,[c] 12 not like Cain—he was from the evil one and slew his brother. Why did he slay him? Because his own deeds were evil but those of his brother just.

a. The link with the story of Cain makes it difficult to add "or sister" here; see further on 2:10 and Introduction §5.
b. "This is" (*hautē estin*) looks forward; see 1:5; 2:25; 5:11.
c. Grammatically, the link between v. 12 and v. 11 is clumsy, but the sense is clear.

**[10b]** The final line of the original couplets provokes the third and last stage in the reflection. The milder formulation, literally "is [not] from (*ek*) God," is shaped by the earlier tradition (cf. v. 8),[79] but now has been fully informed by what was said about being children of God and born from God. Although in form the line parallels the opening of the previous two subsections (3:4, 8), sin is no longer the focus of attention; instead the negative formulation serves to reinforce the necessity of the positive: what matters for these readers is that they show themselves to be among those who do justice. For the first time this is given some tangible content, in love for one's brother (see note a). Earlier, such love or its failure, there labeled hatred, was aligned with belonging to the sphere of light or of darkness (2:9–11); now the author is integrating that identification into his discourse about birth from God. The metaphor of birth, which in 1 John

79. See also John 8:47, another example of the common traditions behind these two passages. It reemerges in the letter at 4:1–6; 5:19.

is always applied to an individual in the singular (in contrast to John 1:13), might direct attention only to the vertical relationship between believer and God. Even the picture of children of God and children of the devil is designed to emphasize more their filial likeness and derivation from a parent than the kinship thus created among them. The vertical has been the single thread running throughout this section, but how is it to be measured or evidenced? Only in the horizontal relationships that eventuate. It is not that justice is to be identified with love, and with love alone; rather, justice so far has been determined more by its Godward direction than by its content, but now love is its demonstrable expression. A failure in love inevitably means a failure in justice, the absence of the defining mark of one whose origin is God.

[11] At this stage, the author does not justify this move either by the nature of God or by the commitment siblings should have to one another; that will come later (4:7; 5:1). Instead he evokes again, and for the last time, the recurring theme of the first part of the letter, that which they have heard from the beginning (1:1; 2:7, 24); its identification as "the message" (*angelia*) deliberately echoes the opening of the body of the letter (1:5)—that which we heard and proclaimed now "you heard." Wherever his unfolding argument may lead, however much he may stress their inalienable status as begotten by God and as God's children, they will never leave behind the foundational message that created them as a community of those who had responded. The "because" that opens the verse must be given its full weight;[80] as at verse 7, the direct address, "*you* have heard," engages the readers with what might otherwise become a theoretical discussion about this sort of person or that sort of person, but not about themselves. This prepares for the incorporation of readers' own experience into the dualistic pattern that he has just established. Yet whereas in 1:5 the message was of God as light, here the content immediately shifts to the first person "we," which evokes the sense of the shared community.

The specific call to "love one another" appears again in 3:23, where it is labeled a command, and in 4:7, 11, 12, providing something of a leitmotif for the next two chapters;[81] each time the first person plural form is used.[82] Indeed, readers familiar with a distinctive Johannine tradition would have been expecting this ever since the reference to the new, yet not new, command in 2:7; this, as was noted, reflects the same tradition as when Jesus gives his disciples his (new) command, "that *you* [plural] love one another" (John 13:34–35; 15:12, 17). Superficially that formulation can be contrasted with the Synoptic Gospels, where the greatest commandment affirmed by Jesus is explicitly drawn from

---

80. Contrast the NRSV, which starts a new paragraph at v. 11 with a vapid "For."
81. Also in 2 John; see commentary.
82. At 4:11 the additional verb "we ought" provides the person, followed by the infinitive, "to love."

Scripture, and is a combination of the foundational love for God (Deut 6:4–5) and of the injunction, "you [singular] shall love your neighbor as yourself" (Lev 19:18; Mark 12:31, 33 and parallels). That these represent different lines of tradition should be acknowledged, but any contrast should not be overstressed. In John "one another" does have as its primary focus relations among themselves, not toward outsiders, but this is also how love of neighbor is mostly to be understood: the extension of "neighbor" in the parable of the Good Samaritan (Luke 10:29–37) is an exception even in the teaching of Jesus, as is shown in Matt 5:43–44 where love of neighbor can only be extended by including love also of enemy. Other New Testament writers appeal for communal harmony both with a call to "love one another" (1 Thess 4:9; 1 Pet 1:22) and also by citing Lev 19:18, love of neighbor, as supreme (Gal 5:14; Jas 2:8), while Paul explicitly justifies the former by the latter (Rom 13:8–9).

In contrast to these, 1 John here justifies the necessity to love one's *brother* in the previous verse (3:10) by the call to love one *another*, which is part of their received tradition. The particular formulation, love for a brother, is found only in 1 John in the New Testament (see commentary on 2:9–10; cf. 4:20, 21); the consistent grammatical structure—the singular participle or third person verb—and the repeated contrast with the possibility of hating, neither of which is found in the "one another" pattern, indicate that this represents a further distinct tradition. Although it may also be equally dependent on Lev 19:17–18, where (not hating a) "brother" parallels (loving a) "neighbor," 1 John never appeals to Scripture to give it authority.[83] However, the combination of the two forms need not have been newly coined by the author: a similar pattern is frequent in the *Testaments of the Twelve Patriarchs*: "Now, my children, let each one of you love his brother, and remove hatred from your hearts, loving one another in deed and word and the intention of the soul" (*T. Gad* 6.1). Although the narrative setting of the *Testaments* determines that the "brother" belongs first of all to the family of the nation, the generalized moral exhortation within which these calls come, alongside the virtues of integrity and generosity to others, here points toward an at least potential universalistic ethic. In the context of 1 John the author's concern is almost exclusively focused within the community for whom he writes, although this does not exclude the possibility that the "one another" might extend beyond its limits.

[12] Elsewhere the author regularly follows his exhortations with positive examples, introduced by "just as" (*kathōs*) (2:6, 27; 3:3, 7); a similar pattern follows Jesus' call to his disciples to love one another in John 15:12, "Just as I have loved you." But here it is the failure to love that threatens (v. 10), and a

---

83. Leviticus 19:17–18, "You shall not hate your brother in your mind . . . and you shall love your neighbor as yourself." In the LXX "brother" (*adelphos*) very occasionally translates Hebrew *rēaʿ*, usually rendered "neighbor" (*plēsion*).

negative example follows: "not like (*kathōs*) Cain." The story of Cain's murder of Abel invited reflection, although it is usually Abel who is the focus, remembered as righteous victim (4 Macc 18:11; Matt 23:35; Heb 11:4), while Cain more often appears as an example of greed or of unbelief (Jude 11). Here attention is directed to Cain the murderer, and Abel is not named; it is more important that he was "his brother," recalling "the one who does not love *his brother*" in verse 10. Genesis 4 does not state that Cain did not love his brother, but 1 John surely presupposes it by "he slew," a verb conveying the violence of the act itself.

But the murderous act itself is not the sole point. Cain belonged to, or had his origin in (*ek*), "the evil one." The expression recalls verse 8, "the one who does sin belongs to (*ek*) the devil," an assertion that was already shaped by the tradition of Cain (see commentary). The epithet "evil one" (see commentary on 2:13–14) now replaces "the devil," and so allows a smoother transition to the reference in the second half of the verse to Cain's *evil* actions. Readers, however, already know that they (or the youths) have conquered the evil one (2:13–14), and so they can be in no doubt where they stand. As throughout this passage, the question is left unresolved whether Cain's murderous act was the result of his diabolical affinity or whether it established it. The pattern so far has tended toward the former, but what follows suggests the latter. Although Genesis 4 ascribes Cain's act to his jealousy at God's preference for Abel's offerings, it never justifies that preference, and so it leaves the ultimate cause, as also the ultimate source of evil, unresolved. Subsequent interpretation sought to provide a tidier solution, including, as already noted, the reassignment of Cain's paternity. First John's explanation, although neat, has no real basis in the text of Genesis, other than that murder is evil; it relies on the simple logic that evil and justice are bound to be antagonistic, and that evil will respond murderously to justice.

The epithet "just" or "righteous" (*dikaios*) was already attached to Abel, perhaps originally meaning little more than "innocent," as a victim of murder (Matt 23:35; Heb 11:4). Although when used of Abel's "deeds" (*erga*) it may invite a more moral tone, the author has no particular act in mind. Both God and Jesus have already been labeled "just," as have those "who do justice" (1 John 2:29; 3:7); by contrast, the activities (*erga*) of the devil have been rendered void by the Son of God (3:8). There may also have been other Johannine resonances in the language: twice in the Fourth Gospel Jesus (or the light) exposes that "their/his deeds were/are evil" (John 3:19; 7:7). The author has brought together a traditional designation of Abel with the formulations that underlie and have acted as a thread throughout the section since 2:29. Against this background, Cain's murder of his brother is not simply an illustration of the threat that good poses to evil, and of the tendency of evil to destroy the good it cannot countenance. It is a paramount example of the dualism that runs throughout this passage; hence it is not just a statement of how things are but a summons to remain in solidarity with one another and as children of God.

This major section (2:29–3:12) ends as it starts, with the adjective "just," which has also run as a thread throughout it. This is merely one example of the artistry displayed throughout the passage. The first audience of the letter would have appreciated the skill with which the author has woven together traditions and ideas, and would have found the skill itself rhetorically persuasive. Those who have been sensitive to the echoes of the story of Cain in the preceding verses will respond to his naming in verse 12 with satisfied recognition. That will have alerted them to other more subtle echoes and connections, and, on subsequent readings, they would have drawn out the deeper resonances of the earlier verses. As the climax that brings these different themes together, the example of Cain and his brother shows that the challenge of being "born from God" is not abstract or spiritual, but can be played out in the concrete experience of human life; conversely, the call to love one another is not simply a desire for communal harmony, and its failure is not to be merely regretted, for it is this which embodies the decisive alternatives of being of God or of the devil. At 1:5 the message (*angelia*) was about God, at 3:11 it is about mutual love. This should not be seen as a contrast, nor as marking a division of the letter, between theology and ethics. Just as for God to be light cannot be independent of the lives of those who confess him, so here the call to love one another is not based on a common humanity or on a shared set of ethical values but on an understanding of God.

## 1 John 3:13–24—Love within the Community and Confidence before God

After the unequivocal assertions of the previous verses, the mood now changes, back to encouragement. First person plural verbs (e.g., "we know, we love") shape this section, and the two appeals to "you" (3:13, 15) are more expressive of support than of instruction. If there was a danger that the concepts of doing sin or justice could remain theoretical, here love is played out in action. Allusions to the story of Cain continue, providing another layer of continuity with what precedes, but they no longer support a dualism that cuts through human experience.

The passage falls into two parts, the first looking at the horizontal relationships between those addressed, the second at the vertical relationship with God. Horizontal and vertical are brought together at the end (v. 23), confirming, as has repeatedly been emphasized, that they cannot be separated. Readers may come to this passage with a sense of relief, and of knowing where it will lead them.

### 1 John 3:13–18—The Bonds of Love

**3:13** Do not find it surprising, then, brothers, if the world hates you. **14** For our part, we know that we have made the transition from death to life, because we love the brothers. The one who does not love[a] dwells in death. **15** Everyone who hates their brother is a murderer, and you know that no murderer has eternal life indwelling in them. **16** We recognize love in this way, because that one laid down his life on our behalf; we also ought to lay down our lives for the brothers. **17** Whoever possesses worldly livelihood and sees his brother in need and refuses to feel compassion for him—how can the love of God dwell in such a person? **18** Children, let us love not in word or in talk but in action and in truth.

a. Later manuscripts supply the object "brother" (so KJV).

[13] With Cain and his brother still in mind, the author addresses his readers not by his usual "children" but as "brothers."[84] In other New Testament letters the frequency of this suggests an almost casual reflection of the sense of being part of a new family of equals (e.g., 1 Cor 1:10; 2:1; Heb 3:1; Jas 1:2; 2 Pet 1:10). This is less evident in the Johannine corpus and, despite 1 John's distinctive form of the call to love (see above), "brother" (see note a to 3:10b) does not seem to have had any particular significance as a designation for members of the community.[85] After this passage (see vv. 14, 16) the author reverts to the more familiar "children" or "beloved," but at this point he wants to reinforce the sense that they all belong to the same tight-knit group standing over against what he once again labels "the world" (cf. 2:15–17; 3:1). The thought has moved from the inability of the world to "know us" at the beginning of the chapter (3:1) to its equally inevitable hatred. The logic is only implicit: the world takes the place of Cain, "we," who are brothers, take the place of his brother—although the analogy breaks down since "we" are not brothers of the world. Again, the connection may have been reinforced for the readers through its echoes of a familiar Johannine exegetical tradition: in John 7:7 Jesus says to *his* brothers, "The world cannot hate you, but it hates me, because I testify concerning it, that its deeds are evil," the same explanation as that just given for Cain's act of murder (1 John 3:12). The unpredictable and varied distribution of such echoes, particularly through this chapter, demonstrates that this is not a matter of literary dependence, but represents similar though independent reworkings of and reflection on a shared exegetical tradition. How such hatred

84. It would be natural to add "and sisters" to acknowledge the probable presence of women in the community, but the pattern of Cain and his brother controls the language; see also note b on 2:10.

85. Some have deduced a technical use from John 20:17; 21:23; see further commentary on 2:9. 3 John (3, 5, 10) represents a different situation; see commentary.

is expressed is not stated: elsewhere in the New Testament the anticipation of hatred from every side belongs to an eschatological expectation that is prefigured in the experience of persecution (Matt 10:22; 24:9), but there is no suggestion that the audience of 1 John were undergoing such opposition. At this point, unlike similar passages in the Gospel (John 15:18–19; 17:14), the author does not explain why the world hates them or why they should not be surprised by it; he will return to the world's response later (1 John 4:3–5), but at the moment he is more concerned to use it to reinforce the cohesion of the community of believers and the need to preserve this.

[14] The emphatic "*we* know" implies a contrast with the world, which presumably still belongs to death, and reinforces the common identity and convictions of the author and those he addresses. That they "have made the transition" (perfect tense) emphasizes that this is secure and irreversible, but how it has been made and what it entails remain unclear. The language draws on the idea of two spheres, death and life, with a moment of transition from one to the other, either at mortal death or at a future eschatological moment.[86] For the author this moment lies in the past for those who love, although presumably that is not incompatible with the hope of yet more to be revealed (3:2). His purpose is not to be precise about an eschatological timetable but to reinforce the implications of the dualistic scheme he has detailed. The love that binds them together both is the mark of their safe location outside the sphere hostile to God and dominated by the destructive power of death, and is that which has secured and sustains that position.

The author may not have wanted to decide whether their love "for the brothers" is the grounds for their certain knowledge or for their having made the transition, both of which are grammatically possible. The formula echoes the message that "we should love one another" (3:11, *agapōmen allēlous*), replacing "one another" with "the brothers" (*agapōmen adelphous*).[87] This maintains the link with the story of Cain established by the opening address (v. 13) and also recalls the formula, "the one who loves his brother," which has already evoked the contrastive possibility of hatred (2:9–11). Once again, themes familiar to the readers and explored in the letter are being woven together to shape new patterns. The transition is signaled as the author continues, "The one who does not love dwells in death." A number of later manuscripts supply an object, "the [or "his"] brother"; this is surely the sense, and yet the absence of an object conveys the underlying truth—that the failure to love is itself the hallmark of

86. Again, this is a Johannine formulation, and in the Gospel it is given its proper eschatological context and is integral to response to Jesus: the one who responds to Jesus and believes God who sent him "possesses eternal life and does not come to judgment, but has passed from death to life" (John 5:24).

87. In the first case the verb is a subjunctive and in the second an indicative, but the form is the same.

the sphere of death. Although 2:15 envisaged, only to reject, the possibility of loving the world, here, as generally in the letter, love is entirely positive, to be associated with the spheres of light and life: the author does not contemplate any love by the world for its own.

The possibility of "indwelling" in death experienced by the one who fails to love offers an alternative world to the certainty of indwelling promised to readers in the letter so far (see 2:6, 24, and commentary). It also recalls the earlier description of one who fails to love as "being in the darkness" (2:9, 11); death is not an event that befalls people but a realm, to which also belong darkness and hatred. At the same time the verb could be translated "remains," reminding the readers again that death and life, darkness and light, are not two static parallel types of existence, but that a passage from the former to the latter is possible, and that the former is doomed, its power already fading (2:8). The one who does not love is left behind, having failed to make that transition to life.

[15] The echo of the earlier identification of the one "who hates his brother" (2:11) is also refashioned by the prefixed "Everyone"; this recalls the repeated pattern that underlay the immediately preceding section, "Everyone who does justice/sin" (2:29; 3:4). Therefore it occasions no surprise that the author continues, not with "is in . . ." or "indwells in . . . ," but with "is a murderer." Readers are brought back again with a jolt to the story of Cain, the archetypal murderer. The word translated "murderer" (*anthrōpoktonos*) is rare, although easily understood (lit. man-killer); Philo uses the related "fratricide" (*adelphoktonos*, lit. brother-killer) of Cain (*On Cherubim* 15). Again this draws on a more extensive exegesis of the Cain story: Jesus similarly describes his opponents, "You are of the father the devil . . . he was a murderer from the beginning" (John 8:44). At this point the author is more concerned with the theme of brothers, absent from the Gospel, than with fatherhood, but the earliest readers would have been able to trace the thread that links this verse both with the identification of the children of the devil, and with the one who does not love his brother in 3:10. When the earlier verses and these are read in the light of one another it becomes clear that for all the eschatological framework of two realms, this is not merely a matter of imagined worlds or of a dualist outlook that remains in the field of thought. It becomes concretized in ruptured family or communal relations, in violence and in the destruction of life.

The appeal to what they "know" is not just an appeal to logic or to common sense but to this earlier exegetical tradition, which is being used to provide an interpretive template for the developing argument. A murderer does not only destroy life but thereby puts her- or himself outside its realm: just as love cannot truly exist outside the sphere that has its origin in God, so neither can life. To indwell or remain in death (v. 14) is the same as not to possess indwelling life (v. 15). Such life is eternal, belonging to the age to come, and lies at the very heart of the letter's message (1:2; 2:25); so anyone who falls under the strictures of this verse is excluded from the proclamation of the letter as a whole. The language is uncompromising: "no murderer"—literally "*every* murderer does not"—reaches beyond the example of Cain to the "*every*one who hates" at the beginning of the verse. There is for this author no middle ground between hatred and love, between death and life; he is not offering moral guidance in the face of the ambiguities or hurts of human experience, but neither is he portraying the ideal saintly life to which all are called to aspire. He is shaping a vision of what it means to be the community of those who have responded to God's action, in the midst of a hostile and uncomprehending world; it is a vision that proclaims both how it has always been (the example of Cain), and the transformation effected by the manifestation of the Son of God, and by the new possibility of experiencing in the present the life that belongs to God (3:8, 14).

As what follows shows, the author's purpose is to summon his readers to actively embody the love that should be their very nature, and the primary intent of the negatives has been to reinforce this positive goal. Whether there were those who "hated" those whom they should have loved as brothers—such as those who had departed according to 2:18—lies outside his concern. No doubt he would have seen such departure as a failure in love, and so by default as hatred, and he might have been anxious lest others follow their example. But his task is not to describe what has happened or might happen outside, but to create and sustain the very identity of the community of those he addresses.

**[16]** If hatred, the failure to love, is made concrete in the example of Cain, love is made concrete in the example of Jesus. The characteristic "in this way" looks forward (cf. 3:10). Despite the address "*you* know" in the preceding verse, here "*we* recognize" includes both author and readers, for this is the experience that binds them together, giving them a shared voice. This form of the verb, the perfect tense (*egnōkamen*, "we have come to know"), is elsewhere used personally, of knowing God (or "him") rather than things (2:3, 4, 13, 14; 3:6); the love that is known is not an impersonal object but is embodied in personal action.

As elsewhere, the example of Jesus probably comes from a traditional formula, identifying him not by name but as "that one" (*ekeinos*; cf. 2:6; 3:3, 5). The language of "laying down (his) life" (*tithēmi tēn psychēn*) is exclusive to 1 John and the Fourth Gospel in the New Testament. Although the reference is clearly to Jesus' death, in other Greek usage the metaphor means to take a risk, to hazard one's life rather than actually to sacrifice it: to put oneself on the line. How this is to the advantage of, or for the sake of, others is not specified; 1 John here makes no reference to sin or to the power of the devil, and does nothing to support any specific understanding of atonement. It is enough for him that "we" are the beneficiaries of what he did in risking his life, averting danger from us.

The Gospel understands Jesus' death in a similar fashion. Jesus' readiness to "lay down his life on behalf of" the sheep as the good shepherd, or Peter's on behalf of Jesus, are also more a matter of putting themselves on the line—the sheep would not benefit from a dead shepherd (John 10:11, 15, 17; 13:37–38). However, John 10:17 ("I lay down my life in order that I may take it again") probably does imply death, and the actual narrative reinforces this. How his death is on their behalf (*hyper*) is not stated, although in the shepherd discourse it is to protect the vulnerable from marauders, and in context Peter presumably hopes to defend Jesus against danger. Although the verse is not quoted, Jesus' readiness to give himself up at his arrest so that his disciples can go free could be seen as acting out his own injunction in 15:13 (John 18:8–9). Thus John's usage should not be assimilated to the more explicit "give his life" (*didonai tēn psychēn*) of Mark 10:45, even if at times it comes close to it. Although some have found in Mark 10:45 echoes of Isa 53:10 ("When you place his life as a sin offering"),[88] and the Hebrew verb (*śîm*, "place") could equally well be translated by the Johannine *tithēmi*, the absence of the crucial "as a sin offering" (or "ransom") means that the Isaianic image cannot be in mind in the Johannine formulation. Indeed, by contrast, Jesus' readiness to lay down his life can be, and must be, imitated: in a passage framed by the command that they should love one another, Jesus offers the readiness to lay down one's life for one's friends as the supreme example of such love (15:12–17).[89] This is particularly close to the passage in 1 John, and like it is constrained by the reciprocity that sets them apart as a closed circle of "friends" (*philoi*, John 15:13), although the latter is not a term 1 John uses.

In 1 John the metaphor may be abstracted from the immediate situations envisaged by the occurrences in the Gospel, but the latter already implicitly points to such an abstraction. "We" for whom he risked his life (v. 16) belong to another time and place, but are still part of a closed circle. It is not the danger averted that matters but that Jesus' self-offering serves as an example to be imitated. It also serves as a reason for imitation, the grounds for obligation; as in 2:6 and, in closer parallel to this verse, in 4:11, the way in which Jesus (or God) has acted leads into how we "ought" (*opheilō*) to act. Again, this is intrinsic to the Johannine understanding of Jesus' death: Jesus similarly tells his disciples that his washing of their feet means that they also *ought* to wash one another's feet (John 13:14). Here, however, the beneficiaries of our imitative action are not "one another," or "friends," but "the brothers," the third use of the plural in the passage, and the last in the letter. Fellow members of the community are still in view, but the term reinforces the earlier link with the story of Cain. As love is opposed to hatred, so is a readiness to put one's life at risk opposed to murder.

---

88. The line is obscure and the LXX translates differently.

89. A number of commentators on the Gospel see John 15:13 as a traditional formulation, while others would argue that both John 13:13–17 and 15:12–17 come from a secondary, redactional, stage in the Gospel's composition, although this is not incompatible with the possibility that they enshrine an older, traditional formulation.

**[17]** If what precedes some suggests self-sacrificial act in the face of the threat of danger and death, the example that follows will at first disappoint. Yet, for the first time in the letter, there is a glimpse of a real world of poverty and inequality, in the midst of which most early believers lived. Some, it is supposed, do have a worldly livelihood, literally "the life of the world": the words are carefully chosen, already setting something of a shadow over such a possession. "Livelihood" is *bios*, the word translated "life" in 2:16, which warned against the pride associated with it; there such pride was said to have its origin in "the world," and this is how such livelihood is qualified here. Life of this sort has nothing to do with the enduring life (*zōē*) promised believers in 3:14.

Evidently, despite 2:15–17, some might have such means, but whether they love it is now to be put to the test. Another in the community, a brother, might be in need. The economic realities of the early Roman Empire, particularly in urban settings, and the probable social location of the early Christians have been extensively studied. Society was steeply pyramidical and the majority of the population lived close to the breadline, particularly vulnerable to the uncertainties of employment or of food supply. Often they would have been dependent on the handouts organized by rich patrons within the city or by the various voluntary associations to which many, but probably not the most destitute, belonged. Like such associations, the early Christian groups offered members the benefits of mutual support. The demand to support the vulnerable poor is deeply ingrained within the scriptural tradition (e.g., Deuteronomy 15), and a regular theme of the prophetic writings is the neglect by the wealthy of their obligations (Mic 2:1–2; Isa 10:1–4). Jewish communities spread throughout the Roman Empire probably organized relief for their own members. The New Testament and other early Christian writings show how this tradition continued in the early church, and generosity and hospitality are dominant in lists of virtues and summons to their exercise (Heb 13:1–3). Also common, however, is the accusation of willful blindness by the wealthy toward the needs of the poor (Jas 2:1–7), reflective of how far such inequalities could be too familiar to prompt concern. Despite these, it does seem likely that the support by the early Christian communities for their own members—charity for others lay in the future—was an important aspect of their attraction, and it certainly was something that later apologists paraded.

Therefore, the situation envisaged here would not be an unusual one; indeed, it may have been the normal pattern. Someone would not have needed to be very wealthy in order to have the means to alleviate someone else in need. It is not the failure to provide for the needs of the impoverished member that the author condemns, although that is undoubtedly in view, but the failure in compassion that inspired it. In ancient thought the seat of emotion was not the heart but the guts, and the vivid image here is of shutting off the deep-seated emotional response as completely as closing a door in their face. Instead of identifying such action as the hatred that has been spoken of, the author ends with a rhetorical question that needs no answer. As elsewhere "love of God" might mean either love for God or the love that comes from God (cf. 1 John 2:4, 15). The former is the most straightforward—anticipating what will be explicit at 4:20, the person who has excluded all compassion for another in need cannot be supposed to be harboring any love for God, regardless of anything they may claim. Yet earlier the author has denied that eternal life indwells the murderer (3:15), and so perhaps here there is a parallel denial that God's gift of love, marked by self-giving, could be truly at work in one who shows themselves to be so untransformed by love. The rhetorical question acknowledges that the presence of God's love is itself invisible, but those who possess it must surely manifest its marks.

[18] Underlining the importance of his example the author turns to his readers, addressing them again as those in need of instruction, "children," but continuing the inclusive first person exhortation. The contrast between mere mouthings and actual action is an obvious one; although not making this contrast, the words of the *Testament of Gad* are not so very different, perhaps suggesting that this was a commonplace of ethical exhortation: "So now, my children, each of you is to love their brother and root out hatred from your hearts, loving one another in deed and word and the intention of the soul" (*T. Gad* 6.1). However, in their context in the letter other resonances may be sensed. That they are to love "in action" or "deed (*ergon*)" recalls the evil deeds of Cain and the just deeds of his brother, as well as the deeds of the devil destroyed by the Son of God (1 John 3:8, 12). "In truth" may just mean "sincerely," particularly since the preposition is not repeated and, only here in 1 John, there is no definite article; however, it is difficult to exclude entirely any association with "the truth" that is done, known, and indwells believers (1:6, 8; 2:4, 21), and the next verse will make this connection explicit. The love they are called to is not only expressed in action and integrity, but characterizes those who belong to the sphere of life and not of death.

This may seem a fairly weak conclusion after the urgent and uncompromising language of hatred and murder; the encouragement to fraternal concern, one feels, could have been reached on other grounds. This may underestimate the importance of maintaining the cohesion and equality of the early Christian groups, both pragmatically so as to ensure their survival, and theologically. This is a repeated theme for Paul also, and he likewise appeals to Jesus' self-giving in urging generosity and the preservation of unity (2 Cor 8:8–15; Phil 2:1–11). For both writers a theological understanding of the effects of Jesus' intervention has to be embodied in social reality. Although other voluntary associations did bring together individuals of varying social status, the early Christians still convey a sense of feeling countercultural in their determination to make this work. Beyond this, the mutual commitment of members to one another is evidently an overriding concern for the author of 1 John, and one about which he has considerable anxiety. Nonetheless, despite the evidence of skillful construction and the weaving of different themes together, the author also allows his thought to take him in new directions, not anticipated at the beginning of the argument, and this does seem to have happened here. He switches from confidence to anxiety, from assurance to exhortation, with surprising rapidity, endeavoring to hold them together in breathless sequence.

### *1 John 3:19–24—Confidence before God*

**3:19** Indeed, in this way we shall recognize that we belong to the truth and we shall reassure[a] our heart[b] in his presence, **20** that,[c] even if our heart condemns us, God is greater than our heart. **21** Beloved, if our[d] heart does not condemn we exercise boldness before God, **22** and we receive from him whatever we ask, because we keep his commands and do what is pleasing in his sight. **23** This, then, is his command, that we believe[e] in the name of his Son, Jesus Christ, and that we love one another, just as he gave us a command. **24** So, the one who keeps his commands indwells in him, and he in them. In this way, indeed, we know that he indwells in us, from[f] the spirit that he has given us.

a. Here, in v. 21 ("we exercise boldness"), and in v. 22 ("we keep"), some but not the same manuscripts replace these statements with verbs of encouragement, "we are to," "let us."

b. Many manuscripts read the plural "hearts," to match the plural "we," but the singular is to be preferred as the more difficult reading.

c. The translation of this verse and its connection with v. 19 is obscure, in part because the word translated "that" (or "because": *hoti*) at its beginning is repeated before "God." See commentary for discussion.

d. Omitted by many manuscripts but certainly to be understood; a number of manuscripts supply "us" after "condemn," and this is clearly the intended sense.

e. Manuscripts vary as to whether the verb is present or aorist (as in B [Codex Vaticanus], followed by NA[27]); see commentary for discussion.

f. This seems to be the only way of translating *ek* at this point, although the closely similar phrase at 4:13 will be translated "he has given us of his spirit" (see commentary there).

From the horizontal relationship with one's fellow believer, attention shifts abruptly again to the vertical relationship with God, of which the horizontal is the visible sign. That vertical relationship may appear to be particular to each individual, hidden in their inner being, but the individual is always part of the larger group, sharing in their experience and strengthened by it; so the author speaks of the heart (singular) and at the same time of "we/us." A sense of insecurity may strike the individual, but corporate reassurance lies in obedience, and—two new themes—in the answer to prayer and in the experience of the spirit. Although this general sense of the passage seems clear, the detail of the argument is less so, and in particular whether the opening verses carry a note of hope or of solemn warning.

**[19–20]** The catchword "truth" leads from the exhortation to love "sincerely" or "in truth" to our belonging to "the truth." The use of the article and the distinctive *ek*, indicating belonging or origin (cf. 3:8), give "truth" its full force as that which carries the integrity and authenticity of God's purpose (cf. 1:8). This means that the characteristic opening "in this way" (cf. 2:3; 3:10, 16) does not point back to verse 18 alone but to the whole of the preceding section, with its antithesis between the marks of love and life and those of hatred and death: it is with the former that truth belongs, and those who experience and demonstrate love and life can also be confident of their origin and identity. The phrase "belong to the truth" (*ek tēs alētheias*) has already been used in contrast with falsehood (2:21), but closer to this passage is the Johannine Jesus' assertion that only those who belong to the truth are capable of responding to what he says (John 18:37). There, such belonging is the prior condition for, and not the consequence of, response, and the question of why some do so belong and others presumably do not is left unanswered. Here the relationship is more ambiguous, although the author does not go so far as to say that loving action *determines* belonging: it is the inherent certainty of belonging that he wants to reaffirm.

This certainty is needed not against overconfidence, as may potentially have been the case in the first part of the letter, but against anxiety. Earlier the author has raised the specter of shame in the face of God's eschatological coming (2:28); here, despite the future "we shall know," it is an awareness of inadequacy before God in the present that is in view. The heart is the seat, not of the emotions (cf. 3:17), but of the conscience or of self-knowledge. Such self-knowledge can, the author is aware, lead to self-criticism and self-doubt, undermining the security of being God's children. In the face of this one can but rely on God's all-encompassing vision, which sees beyond the apprehensions of the individual.

This is to interpret the author as offering a strong note of encouragement, but it need not be the case that God's greater knowledge of the individual is ultimately a source of comfort; within the biblical tradition that God searches the heart and knows what is hidden from other people can also be grounds for warning and judgment (Prov 24:12; Luke 16:15; Acts 5:4). It is this fundamental attribute of God that makes petitionary prayer, including the prayer for forgiveness, both necessary and possible, while ensuring that the offer of forgiveness does not undermine but reinforces reverent trust in God (1 Kgs 8:39; 1 Chron 28:9; cf. Ps 139; Rev 2:23); it also means that God may act in ways that are not anticipated by human planning (Acts 1:24; 15:8).

The reminder of God's greater knowledge could, therefore, have a more ambiguous or even negative effect; that this is intended here seems unlikely, but the stages in the author's argument are difficult to trace and leave a number of details uncertain. These are provoked both by the ambiguity of the language—"reassure" (*peithō*) is neutral, "persuade," but must take its tone from the context—and by the imprecise relationship between the parts of the sentence, and they are aggravated by the textual instability they have occasioned. The main issues are these:

a. The opening "in this way" may refer (i) back (to v. 18) or (ii) forward (to v. 20).
b. The verb translated "we shall reassure (our heart) (*peisomen*)" may be (i) positive (= encourage), or (ii) negative (= admonish).
c. Verse 20 may provide (i) the content of that reassurance ("that . . ."), or (ii) its grounds ("because . . .").
d. The fact that God is greater than our heart may be a source (i) of hope, or one (ii) of anxiety.
e. In verse 20 "that/because" (*hoti*) appears twice, at its beginning preceding "if" and again before "God is greater"; if this is redundant duplication (i) the second could be ignored, or (ii) the first may be a mistake.

These alternatives might be paraphrased to offer the following possibilities:

1. "If we love in deed and truth (a [i]) we shall know that we are of the truth; and we shall reassure (b [i]) ourselves in his presence *that* (c [i]; e [i]) even if our heart condemns ourselves God, being greater, knows everything [i.e., we have done including our acts of love]" (d [i]).
2. "If we love in deed and truth (a [i]) we shall know that we are of the truth and shall reassure (b [i]) ourselves in his presence *because* (c [ii]; e [i]) even if our heart condemns ourselves God, being greater, knows everything [i.e., we have done including our acts of love]" (d [i]).
3. " If we love in deed and truth (a [i]) we shall know we are of the truth and we shall reassure (b [i]) our heart in God's presence, whatever it may accuse us of (e [ii]),[90] because (c [ii]) *or* that (c [i]) God is greater than our hearts and knows everything" (d [i]).
4. "If we love in deed and truth (a [i]) we shall know that we are of the truth; yet we shall admonish (b [ii]) ourselves in his presence because (c [ii]; e [i]) *or* that (c [i]; e [i]), all the more when our heart condemns us, God, being greater, knows everything (i.e., we have done including any insincerity in our love)" (d [ii]).

---

90. This requires reading the first *hoti* of v. 20 as *ho ti* ("that which") followed by *ean* indicating an indefinite "whatsoever."

5. "Because (a [ii]; c [ii]; e [i]) even if our heart condemns ourselves God is greater than our hearts and knows everything (d [i]), we shall know that we are of the truth and we shall reassure ourselves in his presence" (b [i]).

Of these, the fourth most clearly carries a note of warning; but if this were the author's intention he surely would have offered some further remedy or exhortation rather than immediately dismissing its implications with the positive note of verse 21. The fifth possibility is also unpersuasive since it grounds certainty of status ("that we are of the truth") only on the less satisfactory situation of self-condemnation, and provides no cause for the move into the greater confidence of the following verse. Hence a positive reading with a backwards reference to the preceding section seems most likely; the differences between the first three, namely whether the heart's condemnation is the content (1) or the context of the reassurance (2, 3), and whether that reassurance is absolute (2) or has its own message (1, 3), do not seriously affect the general thrust and can probably not be resolved. The primary intention is trust in God in the face of anxiety. Similarly, Peter appeals to Jesus to confirm the integrity of his love for him: "you know all" (John 21:17).

More immediately in the context, readers would have caught yet another echo of the story of Cain. There too God knew of the murderous act that Cain had hoped to hide (Gen 4:9–10); Cain's fear was that driven from God's presence he would become a target for others to kill him with impunity, something that God averts without, however, rescinding Cain's expulsion (Gen 4:13–16). How much more can those who have not shared in Cain's ways be sure that they will continue to enjoy the safety of God's presence.

[21–22] There is, however, another situation, which may even be more the norm—hence the attention-drawing "Beloved"—namely, that of the untroubled heart or conscience. Then, no reassurance is needed to claim what is theirs by right. Earlier (2:28), boldness (*parrēsia*) was promised as an eschatological certainty at "his" coming (so also 4:17, "on the day of judgment"). Such boldness is often associated with speaking in the open and with a readiness to be accountable, perhaps in contrast to the whispering of conspiracy or in fear of retaliation (John 7:13; 18:20; Acts 4:13, 20); in Greek thought it denoted the freedom of speech, which was the democratic privilege of the free citizen who had the right to be heard and who could expect a response. This is the picture in mind here (cf. also 1 John 5:14): God is, as it were, the potentate before whom people might tremble and hesitate to express their opinions or wishes; but there are those who, however limited their means of persuasion and however inferior in status or power, have the right to speak and to be heard. Believers possess this right—those manuscripts and translations that preferred a verb of encouragement ("let us have") realized but hesitated to repeat the enormity of the claim. Other references in the New Testament also show how such boldness was seen as a privilege not to be underestimated or abused (cf. Heb 4:16; 10:19, 35; Eph 3:12).

It follows that this boldness is best embodied in the confident expectation of a response to requests. For the moment the author does not elaborate this point, which will be taken up again at the end of the letter (5:14–16). The theme of asking in the certainty of the request being met is a common one, both within and outside the Johannine corpus (cf. John 14:13–14; 15:7, 16; 16:23–24, 26; Matt 7:7; 18:19; 21:22). Sometimes the promise of an answer appears to be made without qualification, but more often, as is surely implicit elsewhere, conformity of the request or of the person making it to the will of God is a necessary condition. Although "whatever we may ask," reinforced by the present tense, "we do receive," may seem to offer no restrictions, the setting envisaged of the petitioner in the court of the ruler already indicates that what may be granted would never be such as would undermine the authority of or counter the purposes of the one granting the request. More particularly, the absolute confidence with which the assurance started is immediately qualified by what is a statement but which acts as a condition: "because we keep his commandments" implies "on condition that we keep his commandments."

Such obedience was already established earlier in the letter (2:3–5; see commentary), and what was probable there is explicit here, that the commandments are God's just as it is God who will grant the requests; the same theme will be taken up again in 5:2–3. Here obedience is supplemented by the almost formulaic "and do what is pleasing in his sight" (cf. Heb 13:21; Rom 12:1–2; 2 Cor 5:9);[91] picking up the "before God" of the previous verse, it does, however, serve to remind again that such requests are only those that can also be made before God.

[23] The earlier reference to "his command" had not provided any definition, beyond assuring them that it was not unfamiliar to them, but that which they "had heard from the beginning" (2:7–8); at 3:11 this aboriginal message was elaborated as that "we are to love one another," and so it is no surprise that this is given as the content of the commandment here, again in the characteristic first person plural form (see commentary on 3:11, and the discussion of the relationship with John 13:34). More surprising is that this is preceded by "that we are to believe . . ."; this is not an additional commandment—the plural of verse 22 has been replaced by the singular in this verse—but part of the same one. Again, the vertical dimension of belief and the horizontal dimension of reciprocal love are inseparable: "we" and "one another" are those who so believe.

---

91. These (and other) passages use the compound adjective *euarestos*; 1 John's word (*arestos*) is also used by Jesus of his own relationship with God in John 8:29.

Although confession (or denial) of the Son, or of Jesus as the Christ, has already proved central to what the author assumes of his readers (2:22–23), this is the first reference to "believing" (*pisteuō*). The elaborate wording ("in the name of his Son Jesus Christ") sounds formulaic, and is picked up toward the close of the letter (5:13, although with a different grammatical construction). It is difficult in the New Testament to distinguish between the various construc-tions that can express a personal object of belief following *pisteuō*—the prepo-sitions *eis* (with the accusative, 5:10, 13, and frequently in John), *epi* (with the accusative or the dative, Rom 4:5; 9:31), *en* (with the dative, John 3:15) or the simple dative (as here, also John 5:24; 8:31; etc.).[92] Each of these might be trans-lated as "believe in," but the different nuances that would be expressed by the English "trust," "accept the veracity of," "have confidence in," or "make a per-sonal commitment (like that made to God)," are not easily distinguished and can-not be identified with particular constructions. The simple dative used here is also found in 5:10, where the one who "does not believe God [dative]" is con-trasted with the one who "does believe in (*eis*) the Son of God"—inviting a trans-lation "have faith in"—but where that failure is explained as a failure to believe "in" (*eis*) the testimony given by God (suggesting "accept the veracity of"). Sim-ilarly, in the more immediate context here, the decision as to which spirit(s) to believe (simple dative) is to be made after careful evaluation of the confession they generate (4:1–3). Here, however, such belief is not simply in the Son but in "the name of his Son"; this, but with the preposition *eis*, is also the formula used at 5:13, and at John 1:12; 3:18 (cf. 2:23), but not elsewhere in the New Testa-ment (although cf. Acts 3:16). However, many other aspects of the distinctive activity of believers are carried out in, with, or because of "the name of Jesus": baptism (Acts 2:38), petition (John 14:13), thanksgiving (Eph 5:20), preaching (Acts 9:27), exhortation (2 Thess 3:6), prophecy (Matt 7:22), miracles (Acts 4:30), exorcism (Acts 16:18), suffering persecution (Acts 5:41), and, in 1 John, forgiveness (1 John 2:12; see commentary). The name (*onoma*) thus represents the full significance of the person and their authority.

However, in this verse the weight lies not on Jesus but on his primary iden-tification as God's Son: God's command is directed toward the authority of God's Son, just as it is God's Son whose task was to render void the works of the devil (3:8). This is the first time in this chapter (and, indeed, since 2:22, the denial of Jesus as the Christ and, by implication, as the Son) that Jesus has been named. As in the similarly formulated anticipation of fellowship with "his Son, Jesus Christ" (1:3) that opens the letter, "Jesus Christ" functions almost as a proper name (cf. 2:1) that serves to identify God's Son through and with whom such benefits are experienced (so also 5:20, and cf. 1:7). Personal commitment

92. *Pisteuō* can also be followed by an accusative (see 4:16) or by a "that" clause (5:1, 5), and also, although not in 1 John, be used absolutely (John 20:8, 29).

to him is therefore implied, along with acceptance of that identification, and this will be made explicit in 5:5.

There is considerable variation among manuscripts as to whether the verb "believe" is in the present tense (as is "love") or in the aorist; the same variation is found in John 20:31, where it has led to heated debates as to whether the purpose of the Gospel is to encourage the maintenance of existing faith (present tense) or to inspire faith in nonbelievers (aorist).[93] Whether the tenses of the verb alone can sustain this distinction is debatable, and here, even if the aorist were original, it is unlikely that there is a distinction between the continuation of love (present) and the initiation of belief. Inasmuch as the letter is addressed to those already within the community, they are being urged to maintain the belief and love that is properly its primary characteristic.

The concluding explanation is not a redundant repetition of the opening definition of "his command." The familiar "just as" (*kathōs*) formula (cf. 2:6; 3:3, 7) points to a tradition about Jesus; the distinctive "that one" (*ekeinos*) of the other passages is not needed here because he has just been identified as the object of belief. If God's command is faith in his Son, then it necessarily includes the love for one another that the Son himself gave as his command; but this does not just belong to the past: it is *we* who are the recipients of that gift. Strikingly, in contrast to the Gospel, where "you [the disciples] are to love one another just (*kathōs*) as I [Jesus] *loved* you [them]" (John 13:34; 15:12), here "we are to love one another just as (*kathōs*) he [Jesus] *gave* us *a command*."

[**24**] As the passage reaches its climax it recalls again the exploration in 2:3–6 of the relationship between religious claim and keeping his commandments. Indeed, the first half of the verse would have fitted there well and would have provided a smooth transition from 2:4 to 2:6: it adopts the same structure of a nominative present participle ("the one who *says/keeps*"), the plural "commands," even though no additional ones are in view, and it introduces the possibility of "indwelling in him," which is taken up as a claim in 2:6 without preparation.[94] Whether or not this verse originally belonged in that context in an earlier source or oral refrain, now that it is placed at this point the various elements are imbued with additional resonances, and the alternative possibilities negotiated in 2:3–6 are both recalled and reinforced. The nature of his—probably God's, although the distinction is now of little significance—commandments has been made clear, as has been their community-building effect. The certainty of "indwelling in him" must be shaped at least in part by the confidence of receiving requests (3:22). Earlier such indwelling was contingent on being indwelt by the aboriginal message, itself hardly to be distinguished from the command to love one another (2:24;

---

93. There is a similar variation at John 13:19 and 19:35.

94. 1 John 2:5 only partly provides a transition, and it uses a different grammatical structure, "whoever keeps. . . ," an indefinite relative clause (see commentary).

3:11), and it was also made the condition of not sinning (3:6). Together this has constructed a closed circle of obedience, certainty, exhortation, and hope, in which the relationship with "him" (Son and Father in 2:24) is the consistent focal point of reference.

Reinforcing this, such indwelling is now seen to be reciprocal. Although the relationship is directly with God (cf. 4:12–13), however, it is not a mystical experience, nor a form of possession, private to the individual and separate from any social or practical expression. Earlier in the letter, the word, the aboriginal message, the anointing, and perhaps the seed have been said to indwell them (2:14, 24, 27; 3:9); more than these, God's all-pervasive and all-encompassing presence must be personal, but it is never independent of them. Again this is a broader Johannine conception: in the Fourth Gospel, however, Jesus' relationship with God, a relationship of obedience and of unity of will, is the model of that reciprocal indwelling that believers experience with Jesus (John 6:56; 14:20; 15:4–7; 17:23). First John does not share this characteristic christological focus, because the author's attention is firmly directed toward his readers, to their place in a wider community, but also to their unmediated experience of God.

Just at the point when the author appears to have brought his argument to a satisfying conclusion, he introduces a new, unexpected theme, which will be taken up in the section that follows. As so often in the way the letter is structured, a bridge verse both concludes what precedes it and prepares for what is to follow. The introductory "In this way we know" recalls the same testing formula in 2:3 and 5, but whereas the test there was obedience, here it is a further expression of divine presence. The spirit that God has given is evidence of God's indwelling. This is the first reference to the spirit in 1 John, and the following passage shows that there are other spirits (or at least an other spirit) than that which comes from God (4:1–3). The idea here recalls that of God's spirit as enabling specific individuals to speak in God's name or to achieve tasks set for them by God (Isa 42:1); it is a particular gift of God's presence and power, which can have a powerful and unpredictable effect (Num 11:26–30; 1 Sam 16:13–23; 1 Kgs 18:12). The expectation of a special outpouring of God's spirit as an eschatological sign exercised a strong influence on some early Christian thought as they reflected on their own experience (Joel 2:28–29, quoted at Acts 2:17–21). There too the spirit is specifically a portion of God's spirit and not in some way personal, independent of God (see further commentary on 4:1). First John does not betray any knowledge of the Fourth Gospel's developed understanding of the Holy Spirit, which is also identified as the Spirit of truth and as the Paraclete (a title used here of Jesus, 1 John 2:1) (John 14:16–17, 26; 15:26; 16:7, 13–15). Likewise, Paul's particular development of the presence of the spirit as marking the distinctive character of believers' lives, both in prayer and in behavior (Rom 8:13–17; Gal 5:22–25), should not be read into all other New Testament thought or into 1 John, although it does act as a reminder that the presence of the spirit was not associated with ecstatic behavior alone.

However, the idea that there are also other spirits comes closer to the passage from the *Community Rule* quoted earlier (commentary on 1:5; cf. 4:1, 6): that passage envisages a world of spiritual beings ranged on the side of God and against God, mirroring and influencing human choices. Yet, whereas there it seems that all human individuals have a share of the spirit of truth or of deceit by nature and birth,[95] here the spirit has been given by God at a precise moment, perhaps that of coming to faith. It is thus evidence of the divine indwelling, which also is not given to all but which is the mark of those who belong to the community of faith and obedience.

The author's purpose in introducing the language of the spirit will become clear only in the next section, where it provides him with a means of explaining why some may appear to manifest some signs of divine presence but do not belong to the "we" of this section. Before he can address the dilemmas which that will provoke, he has first reinforced for his readers what it is that binds them together and that provides them with the assurance that, if they but hold fast, they can be certain of God's enduring presence and protection. The passage has been marked by its confident statements and affirmative language; such confidence is rhetorically designed not to induce complacency but to persuade them to resist any tendency to neglect what holds them together with one another, with the tradition they have received, and, most of all, with the author.

## 1 John 4:1–6—Testing the Spirits

Leaving the confidence of the previous section and its characteristic inclusive first person plural, "we," the author abruptly turns his attention to his readers, challenging them with warning and direct address. The letter has brought its readers to a moment of decision. But there are continuities with what precedes: the spirit, which has just been a source of assurance, is now a potential source of confusion, for there is a spirit, or its manifestation, that misleads. This recalls the earlier concern with those who, although they might have seemed to be reliable members of "us," had departed, revealing their true nature (2:18–19). They had been identified as the embodiment of the antichrist anticipated at the last hour, just as the misleading spirit is here similarly traced back to the antichrist. Again, confession of Jesus lies at the heart of the deception (cf. 2:22), but this time the confession is expanded, apparently to leave no doubt that this Jesus shared the humanity of those who respond to him. The threat posed is a serious one, demanding vigilance, and yet it cannot undermine the fundamental

95. "Until now the spirits of truth and of injustice feud in the heart of man" (1QS IV, 23).

confidence of those who remain faithful; this is not a conflict between equally resourced parties with an outcome yet to be decided. To belong to God is to be on the side of victory, and the author has no doubt that that is where he and those whom he addresses stand. There is after all no serious possibility of mistaking what belongs to God and to the realm of truth, and what does not. Such clarity may reassure, but it also acts as a warning against wavering or considering any alternative. The section therefore ends with a return to the inclusive "we," giving readers little opportunity to do other than commit themselves to the author's cause.

For many interpreters this passage, along with 2:18–22, holds the key to the letter. The confession of the spirit from God in 4:2 has been seen as directly challenging the beliefs of those who had left the community, and much effort has gone into reconstructing those beliefs, and into attempting to relate them to ideas reflected or rejected elsewhere in early Christian literature. However, this is unnecessary: although the appearance of false prophets is the incentive for vigilance, the concern of these verses is entirely with the audience of the letter, and they must be understood not in relation to some external convictions but to those that shape its thought.

> 4:1 Beloved, do not put your faith in every spirit but test the spirits to see whether they belong to God, because many false prophets have gone out into the world. 2 You recognize the spirit of God in this way: every spirit that acknowledges Jesus Christ having come in flesh[a] does belong to God. 3 But every spirit that does not acknowledge Jesus[b] does not belong to God. This is the one of the antichrist: you heard that it was coming, and now it is present in the world.
>
> 4 You, children, do belong to God, and you have won a victory over them, because the one who is in you is greater than the one who is in the world. 5 They belong to the world; for this reason they speak of what belongs to the world, and the world listens to them. 6 We belong to God; the one who knows God listens to us, while the one who does not belong to God does not listen to us. From this we recognize the spirit of truth and the spirit of error.

a. Codex Vaticanus reads an infinitive in place of the participle; for the text and its translation see the commentary.

b. There are some significant textual variants at this point; see commentary.

[1] A switch in person, from first to second plural, and the direct address, "Beloved" (see 2:7), snap the readers out of any complacency the previous verses may have encouraged. The mention of the gift of the spirit, which climaxed the certainty of divine presence (3:24), provokes the caution that the idea

of the spirit can be an ambiguous one; having just reminded them of the command to "believe" the name of the Son of God (3:23; see commentary), he now urges them not to "believe" every spirit. The term itself, *pneuma*, carries a spectrum of meanings, from that which in the modern world might be understood as natural, "wind"; as biological, "breath," which denotes life; as psychological, whether "spirit" as the sentient and creative part of being human and that perhaps continues after the body's dissolution, or as responsible for extraordinary or aberrant behavior; through to the noncorporeal denizens of the universe. *Pneuma* may be integral to the constitution of the living human being, or may act upon it from outside; it may be a neutral force or actively good or evil. Of itself it lacks personality, but acting in or on human beings it can acquire personal characteristics. God, too, acts through God's spirit; since God is personal God's spirit may readily be understood in personal terms. What may now be perceived as distinct ideas belonging to different spheres, such as the natural versus the supernatural, were for the author and readers part of a single continuum, all belonging to the unseen and inexplicable phenomena of nature and of human behavior. It is a continuum that is also reflected in, as well as exploited by, Jesus' conversation with Nicodemus in John 3:1–8.

First John's call to test the spirits has to be set against the background of the various experiences of the spirit among the earliest believers in Jesus. A particular empowerment by God, or outpouring of God's spirit, was associated with the eschatological age (cf. 1 John 3:24 and commentary), and the early communities felt themselves to have entered into that experience. Paul sees the spirit as the defining characteristic of all Christian living and behavior (Gal 5:16–25), but he also has to deal with the apparently uncontrollable manifestations that might more easily earn indiscriminate admiration (1 Cor 14:13–16, 32). Paul similarly uses confession of Jesus as Lord as the sign of direction by the authentic spirit of God, although it is a matter of debate whether the alternative that he excludes, "Let Jesus be cursed," serves rhetorical effect only, or whether it does represent what some might have said either in ecstatic possession or to avoid persecution (1 Cor 12:1–3). The multiple ambiguities of the concept are demonstrated when Paul goes on to see acts of discrimination among spirits as one of the gifts of the one spirit (12:10).

Such discrimination or testing is not restricted to visible manifestations of the spirit but is an integral part of the new form of individual and corporate living. Since believers and communities were often thrown upon their own resources, and had not built up the structures of leadership or received guidance and instruction, it was for them to test and to discern (*dokimazō*) what was right and in conformity with the will of God (Rom 12:2; Phil 1:10; Eph 5:10). The summons to test was a sign both of their vulnerability but also of the autonomy given by faith (2 Cor 13:5).

This may seem close to 1 John's encouragement to "test (*dokimazete*) the spirits."[96] However, in Paul the context is that of the internal, in some cases the worshiping, life of the community. This is not the scenario in 1 John, where the testing ultimately serves to reinforce the distinctive identity and membership of those to whom the author writes; the broader arena is that of "the world," and the division between the spirits replicates that between the community of the faithful and all that lies outside. The concern, therefore, is with identifying people and not with the validation of spiritual gifts or of personal living. The relationship between the spirits and the individuals is not made clear: at the end of the section there are just two spirits, the spirit of truth and the spirit of error (v. 6), but the "every spirit" of the next two verses could suggest a multiplicity of spirits, although they belong only to two categories. There is nothing in the immediate or wider context to suggest that the setting is one of inspired speech or of individuals claiming the authority of charismatic gifts. The confessions that will distinguish the spirits are presumably being made with conscious conviction, and not in ecstatic acclamation but with the intent to persuade others—it is a matter of teaching, not of prophecy (vv. 5–6). However, conscious conviction does not mean that the spirits here are the minds and intentions of the people involved rather than any supernatural powers. This is probably not a distinction that the author would have made: his worldview is a dualistic one in which human allegiances and identities proceed in unbroken continuity from the antagonism between the sphere that is God's and all that opposes God; it is a worldview that is shared with other Jewish writings of the time (see below at the end of this section).

The author justifies his caution by the advent of many "false prophets" (*pseudoprophētai*). He is drawing on the same eschatological tradition as shaped his earlier discernment of the "last hour" in the appearance of those whom he identified as antichrists (2:18; see commentary), and this new label recalls the "lie" and "liar" that he had associated with them (*pseudos, pseustēs,* 2:21–22). Within the older biblical tradition the false or lying prophets were those whose message did not express the authentic word of God, although this might sometimes become apparent only in the outworking of events (Jer 23:28–29). There they are mostly encountered in conflict with the frequently solitary voice of the one who will eventually be remembered as a prophet of God, although whether their messages were invented by themselves or were inspired by a lying spirit, with or without God's connivance (1 Kings 22), remained an unresolved problem. The false or lying prophet was therefore both one who falsely claimed prophetic authority and one who propounded lies.

---

96. John's relationship with ideas in the Gospel is mixed. In John it is not obvious that the spirit is associated with unusual or ecstatic behavior. Instead, as the continuing guarantee of God's presence, a surrogate as it were for the physical presence of Jesus, the spirit is understood in singular and in personal terms (e.g., John 14:17).

Where prophetic powers were taken for granted there would always be those rejected as false prophets (Acts 13:6; Matt 7:15). The Johannine setting, however, does not seem specifically to envisage such powers; rather, these "many false prophets" echo the "many antichrists" of 2:18, and, like them, they evoke scenarios familiar from contemporary sources of a final intensification of opposition to God: "For there shall arise false christs and false prophets, and they shall perform signs and wonders in order to lead astray, were it possible, the elect" (Mark 13:22 = Matt 24:24; cf. 24:11).

For 1 John this almost fantastical tradition (cf. Rev 16:13; 19:20; 20:10) has become embodied: they have already gone out and are to be found "in the world." "Out" might refer to their departure from the community of the faithful or from that of the author—the same verb is used as at 2:19—but the emphasis of the perfect tense is probably more on the evident fact of their presence. "In the world" is not a neutral description of society outside the community, but has by now been sufficiently defined in negative and hostile terms (2:15–17; 3:13): there is no merit in being there. First John is not alone in applying this eschatological tradition to contemporary experience; 1 Timothy appeals to the Spirit's express prediction that "in the last times some will fall away from the faith, paying attention to deceiving spirits (*pneumasin planois*) and the teachings of demons," expanding that description in terms of the particular errors he was concerned to address (1 Tim 4:1–4; cf. 2 Tim 3:1–5; 2 Pet 2:1–3). In comparison, 1 John is notably restrained, although his account does not, any more than does theirs, directly reflect how those targeted viewed themselves or how other observers would have understood them. The effect of his words is dependent on the associated ideas they evoke, both from within the letter and from traditions familiar to the readers.

The warning against "many," however, encourages the readers to see themselves as "the few," vulnerable unless they are ever alert. There is no suggestion that without his intervention his readers may have been inclined to believe "every spirit," nor that they were in danger of being overawed by any charismatic behavior. The exhortation to discernment is conventional (Mark 13:21; 1 Thess 5:21); it encourages the audience to see themselves as those who consciously measure alternative ideas by their own standards and who remain always alert against any diminution of what they have learned in the past.

**[2–3]** Any criterion for such testing, therefore, would be unlikely to contain anything new or unexpected. The author is not giving them a command as to how they are to recognize any spirit that comes from God—although the verb could be so read ("know!")—but rather is making a statement of what is already the case. This is the standard pattern following the characteristic "in this way" (cf. 2:3), but instead of the regular "*we* know" (2:3; 3:24; 4:6, 13; 5:2 [cf. 3:16, 19]), the direct address, "you know," carries a note of instruction and of warning not to forget. The antichrist has already been characterized by the denial that Jesus is the Christ (2:22; see commentary). Here what matters is the positive, the recognition of the spirits that are from God (cf. v. 1), emphasized twice within verse 2. The second occurrence, "every spirit that acknowledges . . . does belong to (*ek*) God," indicates how the initial description, "the spirit of God," is to be understood, and confirms that it does not refer in exclusive singular terms to God's own spirit (or to the Holy Spirit). In contrast to the one who does not do justice in 3:10 (see commentary), the authentic spirit does belong to and does have its origin with God.

The authentic spirit is recognized by its acknowledgment of Jesus—in practice, presumably, by the expression of faith that it inspires. The actual wording of this confession is unparalleled,[97] and translators and commentators have interpreted it in a number of ways. The debate surrounds, first, the grammatical construction—the content of the spirit's acknowledgment—and, second, the intention of its distinctive emphasis, particularly if supposed to rule out an alternative expression.

As to the former, it is particularly striking that the grammatical structure does not put the emphasis on acknowledging facts about Jesus—who he is or what he has done. Although it has sometimes been translated in these terms, the wording is not the most appropriate way to emphasize either that the spirit from God (a) acknowledges *that* Jesus *is* the Christ (or Messiah) (who has) come in flesh, or that it (b) acknowledges *that* Jesus Christ *has come* in the flesh (KJV, NRSV). When the author wishes to express the belief or confession, or the denial, *that* Jesus is *the* Christ or the Son of God, the Greek construction—a "that" (*hoti*) clause and the article ("the") with the predicate—makes this plain (2:22; 4:15; 5:5). Indeed, both Codex Vaticanus here and, perhaps independently, Polycarp in his letter to the Philippians offer an alternative construction that would carry the second meaning explicitly; their readings are certainly not original but they indicate the difficulty early interpreters found in the text, and how they felt it could best express a straightforward statement of belief.[98]

On the contrary, the construction used here—"Jesus Christ" followed by the participle, "having come," itself qualified by the prepositional "in flesh"— serves as an acknowledgment of identification, with an emphasis on the person rather than on a fact about them: the true spirit "acknowledges Jesus Christ having come in flesh" or "Jesus Christ as having come in flesh."[99] The proper name

---

97. Except for the probably dependent formula at 2 John 7 (see commentary). See also n. 98 below.

98. Both Codex Vaticanus here and Polycarp, *Phil.* 7.1, read an infinitive ("to have come," *elēlythenai*) instead of the participle ("having come," *elēlythota*); the infinitive is a standard Greek construction for expressing belief or confession. In Polycarp the emphasis is on the negative ("do not confess"), and it is uncertain whether Polycarp is quoting 1 John or shares a common tradition.

99. It is not the case, as sometimes claimed, that the verb *homologeō*, "acknowledge," cannot be followed by a participle, but where it is it keeps the focus on personal identity, e.g., to acknowledge someone to be innocent; see LSJ 1226, s.v. II.2.

"Jesus Christ" takes up the identification a few verses earlier of Jesus Christ as God's Son in whom they believe (3:23; cf. 1:3; 2:1). This backwards reference excludes the further alternative that in this verse it is a matter of acknowledging Jesus *as* "the Christ having come" or *as* "the Messiah having come," both of which might be grammatically possible.[100] There is now something further that characterizes Jesus Christ: the one in whom they believe is one who has come. Again the form of the verb used, a perfect participle (*elēlythota*) rather than an aorist, focuses attention not on some past event but on its continuing impact. This is not just one thing among many that can be said about Jesus Christ; if Jesus Christ is not known and confessed as the one who has come, then he is not known and confessed at all. This is why when the author goes on to speak of the spirit that is not from God he describes it simply as not confessing Jesus. So understood, there is probably little difference whether in an English translation "as" is added.

But why is this coming said to be "in flesh" (*en sarki*)? At its only other occurrence in the letter, "flesh" (*sarx*) carries negative potential: "the lust of flesh" belongs to all that is *in* the world, and presumably shares its transience (2:16). To that extent "flesh" might seem to belong to the realm that opposes God and that is incompatible with what is "of God." Yet that opposition has been challenged: as will shortly be declared, God has sent (the perfect tense again) his Son not only as savior of the world but *into the world* (4:9, 14; cf. 2:2). This claim will confront the false prophets who themselves, it has just been said, have gone out *into* that same *world* (4:1). The same sense of confrontation is reinforced by the use of the perfect tense of the verb "to come/go" both of Jesus Christ and of the false prophets in 4:1–2; up to this point the verb "to come/go" has been used only of the antichrist and of its derivatives (2:18–19; 4:1, 3),[101] while "he" or the Son of God "was revealed" (3:5, 8). Any ambiguity about what such "revealing" or appearing entailed is now removed.

Yet to acknowledge Jesus Christ as having come in flesh is not merely another way of saying that he has come into the world. "In flesh" signals not destination but mode and location: the means by which and wherein his presence is known. The rest of the letter gives little hint of how the author understood this "in-flesh-ness." That in an even less translucent passage he can also describe Jesus Christ as one who came "in the water and in the blood" (5:6) perhaps warns against reading too much into "in flesh" alone. In the later passages in this chapter the concern remains for those who believe: only by his sending could they ("we") experience life and divine indwelling (4:9, 14–16; see commentary). This is also true in the immediate context, for the spirit is the guarantee of divine indwelling

---

100. See commentary on 2:22 and 3:23.

101. The verb in 4:1 is a compound, "to go/come *out*" (*exerchomai*), of the simple verb used of Jesus in 4:2 (*erchomai*).

"*in* us," and the discernment of that experience is the chief concern (3:24–4:1). This might suggest that "in flesh" here points to that which believers also share. Belief is not directed to an isolated event situated in the past but is interlocked with believers' own certainty of divine indwelling as also with their obedience to the commands.

For the first readers, acknowledging Jesus "in flesh" probably meant more than this, particularly when set against a certain ambivalence about the flesh in Johannine thought. The unexpected dynamic of testing the spirit by reference to flesh recalls two passages in the Gospel where spirit and flesh are held together in tension. First, birth from the spirit achieves what birth from flesh cannot, although that need not devalue the latter (John 3:6–8; see commentary on 1 John 2:29). Second, in John 6:63 it is the spirit that is the source of life, not flesh; and yet immediately preceding this verse Jesus has impressed on them the necessity of "eating his flesh" as the condition of reciprocal indwelling (6:51–56). Probably somewhat less important is another verse often cited in this connection, John 1:14, "the word became flesh"; contrary to the assonance of the English translations, "becoming" (aorist from *ginesthai*) and "coming in" (perfect from *erchesthai en*) represent very different processes. Clearly within the Gospel the inescapable particularity of Jesus and of the encounter with him are not to be done away with, although no conclusions are drawn about the "in-flesh-ness" of those who follow him. While the Gospel does not supply us with the clues for understanding the letter, it does suggest that early readers would have heard in the true confession of 1 John 4:2 not a regulatory formula but a host of associations. Similarly, in the Fourth Gospel Jesus is frequently described as one who "comes" or "came," and this coming can even be said to be "into the world" (John 1:9; 9:39; 16:28; 18:37); a shared tradition may have enabled the readers to identify a number of resonances.

Beyond the Johannine corpus, Ignatius describes Jesus in startling and characteristically extravagant terms as "one doctor, fleshly and spiritual, begotten and unbegotten, God having become [aorist from *ginesthai*] in flesh, true life in death" (*Eph.* 7.2); he too uses participial clauses to affirm the steadfast confidence that believers in Smyrna have in "our Lord, . . . truly crucified for us in flesh," and his own certainty of Jesus as "being in flesh even after the resurrection" (*Smyrn.* 1.2; 3.1).[102] Ignatius cannot be shown to be familiar with either the Gospel or Letters of John, but his language is often, at least superficially, similar. Other references suggest that "in flesh" could become formulaic with reference to Jesus, although differently nuanced as the context demanded: thus,

---

102. Although in *Smyrn.* 3.1 Ignatius uses "know and believe" rather than "acknowledge," the construction, "him being in flesh," is similar to that here; the deliberate itemizing of details, absent from 1 John, permits a translation "believe that," although his focus remains on the one in whom faith is held.

"who was revealed in flesh, justified in spirit" (1 Tim 3:16), and the repeated emphasis in the *Letter of Barnabas* that Jesus is the one who was "to be revealed in flesh (*en sarki*)" (*Barn.* 5.6, 10; 6.7, 9, 14; 12.10).[103] All such affirmations belong to the broader understanding of "flesh" as denoting the sphere of human activity and existence as created; if he had not so come "how could people see him and be saved?" (*Barn.* 5.10). Although using different terms, the author of 1 John would probably have agreed; he might have added that just as there is a specificity about circumcision, which is paradigmatically "in flesh" (Sir. 44:20; Rom 2:28; Eph 2:11), so was there a specificity in Jesus as one who came sharing the state of those who rightly confess him.

That the correct confession is imprecise and allusive is illustrated by early attempts to alter or to interpret it. Before long the verse was taken as an attack against alternative views, particularly that Jesus did not fully enter into the corporality of all human experience. Some such views could suggest that the physicality of his body was a sham, in appearance only, or that his body was of a different quality than others, perhaps not participating in some of its baser functions. Underlying this was the conviction that the Divine could not undergo the limitations of fleshliness, particularly its inevitable involvement in change, decay, and suffering. Ignatius seems to be countering some such views, perhaps within the congregations to whom he wrote (*Smyrn.* 2, "some unbelieving say that he appeared to have suffered"; cf. *Trall.* 9–10). The same conviction could be expressed by the rather different belief that the divine element was only present in part of Jesus' life, avoiding both birth and suffering and death, a view associated with a certain Cerinthus (Irenaeus, *Against Heresies* 1.26.1; see also commentary on 5:6–8).[104] Both ideas were to be found in the early church and are often labeled Docetism, although this is more accurately applied to the former. Before long early tradition did describe the apostle John as battling against such views, and specifically as repulsing Cerinthus (Irenaeus, *Against Heresies* 3.3.4, 11.1).

Although earlier commentators often accepted this tradition as an explanation of the circumstances behind 1 John 4:2, it is likely that it developed as an interpretation of the letters—there is little to support that there were such views in their background. The form of the confession here is not well suited to refute the idea that a divine being came in what was not human flesh, or entered into a fleshly body for a temporary period. In verse 3 an early reading, perhaps traceable back to the second century, offers instead of "does not acknowledge Jesus" "dissolves [*lyei*] Jesus"; although this verb could mean "empty of power" (as in 3:8), the formula is more probably intended as a reference to the separation

---

103. See Collins, *I & II Timothy and Titus*, 107–9, who decides on balance that in 1 Tim 3:16 the reference is to the resurrection.

104. See Introduction §2.2.

between the divine and the human in the second of the views described earlier.[105] If so, it, and perhaps also the variant in Codex Vaticanus (see note a), were attempts to make 1 John address a later concern with greater precision than the earliest form of the text did, or was intended to do.

That such attempts were needed suggests that our author's intention was not to refute specific views of this kind, and this is confirmed by his interest only in the correct confession, not in that made by the spirit not from God. This latter, as just noted, he tersely dismisses as not acknowledging Jesus: from his perspective, it is not that there are those who have an erroneous understanding of Jesus that he needs to identify and to attack or to correct but that there is no other conceivable way of confessing Jesus.[106] However, his antithetical scheme compels him to grant that there is a spirit that is not from God. This he identifies as belonging to the antichrist, reminding them of their expectation of its coming and of its actual presence "in the world." His language deliberately avoids suggesting that the antichrist is the source of, or gives, a spirit in the same way as can be said of God;[107] his intention is not to provide an account of the precise workings of the forces that oppose God. It is enough that the readers find themselves in a situation where the belief that shapes them can be challenged, and where they are being called continually to recognize that what forms them as a community and inspires their experience of God and of divine presence is their acknowledgment of the impact of the coming of Jesus. It might have been easy to ask, "Do we still need that initial story; does it matter?" Indeed, 1 John's own pattern of thought, with its strong emphasis on what God has done in identifying them as God's children, could lead to precisely such questions about the continuing relevance of Jesus. The answer is firm: that confidence is secure but it rests upon the point of intersection between their own context and Jesus, upon his having come in flesh.

**[4]** The challenge to that confidence has not come from within. An emphatic "you" at the beginning of the verse contrasts with "them" at the end of the same sentence, a contrast reinforced by the emphatic "you have won a victory." "They" (here "them") are not explicitly identified; although the masculine may point back

105. This would be more effective if it read "dissolve Jesus Christ" (i.e., into the component parts). Those who nonetheless argue for the originality of this reading translate "dissolve of power" and explain its replacement by "do not acknowledge" as due to its obscurity. Although this position has its attractions, the insecurity of the earliest attestation—restricted to the Latin translation of Irenaeus—favors the reading adopted here. It is easy to see why scribes would introduce something more precise than the general "not confess," but is less easy to see why the reverse process would take place. See Bart Ehrman, "1 John 4:3 and the Orthodox Corruption of Scripture," in *Studies in the Textual Criticism of the New Testament* (NTTS 33; Leiden: Brill, 2006), 221–46, reprinted from *ZNW* 79 (1988): 221–43.

106. Further evidence of early commentators' frustration with this abruptness is the expansion by a number of later manuscripts of "Jesus" in v. 3 by "Lord," "Christ," or "having come in flesh."

107. A simple genitive is used, lit. "the one of the antichrist," not the more emphatic *ek*.

to the false prophets of verse 1, these were symbolic figures, and the spirits (neuter) and antichrist have intervened since. More immediately, within the unit formed by verses 4–6 "them" here anticipates their description in the next verse (5): rhetorically, they (as object) are defeated before they (as subject) are identified. Victory over them is already a foregone conclusion, just as was the victory over the evil one assured to the young men (2:13). The parallel indicates that this does not mean that the readers have won the argument, or have merely succeeded in driving the other out; neither may have been the case. Rather, the confidence that those who presumably make the same confession as does the spirit also belong to and have their origin in God confirms that they share God's ultimate victory. This is not something for which they can take credit; rather, they are the place where God's own conflict with the powers that oppose is being played out.

The author does not identify the "greater" one who is in them, or the one in the world, but the masculine in each case serves to focus the conflict not as between abstract forces, nor as one between the spirits (neuter), but as a personal one in which the audience are also participants. The one who is in them is presumably either God (cf. 3:20) or Jesus—the author would have seen even less reason here than elsewhere to belabor the distinction. The continuity from verse 3 suggests that the one in the world is the antichrist, but now viewed not in terms of its manifestations in their immediate experience (2:18–19) but as the chief antagonist in a mythic struggle whose last stage is now being played out. That elsewhere the author can speak of victory over the evil one or even over the world (2:13; 5:4–5) does not mean that the antichrist *is* the evil one or the devil, nor that the world, as the place of all human experience, is itself inherently evil. In his scheme of things, these labels are different modes of expressing the same conflictual worldview, sharing the same allegiance and embodying the same hostility and danger that face the readers.

[5] The assurance of victory does not mean that hostility and danger belong to the past. There continues to be a division between those whom the author identifies only as "they" and those whom in the previous verse he labeled "you," as well as the "we" of the next. "They" have their origin in and belong to the world; first "you," then "we," are aligned with God. Why should this opposition continue to matter if the readers are already confident of what the final outcome will be? Apparently because the expected consequences of their supremacy had not been realized. Some forms of eschatological hope envisaged the final defeat of evil and the consequent acknowledgment of God by all: in Isa 2:1–4 the nations will stream toward Zion, while early Christian hope anticipated the universal confession of Jesus as Lord (Phil 2:10–11). Others were less optimistic: perhaps only the elect would be preserved (Mark 13:22–27); in the meantime, if the vast majority failed to respond, or even preferred other sets of ideas, this too might itself be part of God's purpose (2 Thess 2:11–12). For 1 John the outcome has yet to be realized in full.

Despite the apparent exceptions (2:2; 4:9, 14), the author never seriously qualifies his opposition between his audience and the world; he never tacitly acknowledges that they are "in the world," still less that they also have been sent "into the world" (contrast John 17:13–18). Yet they could hardly have been totally isolated from their immediate or wider social context. As a tiny minority their ordinary lives as individuals would have been lived out in what must often have been an extremely uncomfortable contradiction to the separateness and the confidence of the worldview of their shared convictions. Even if they did not engage in organized mission,[108] they could not have avoided some explanation of their beliefs or behavior, or at least have failed to observe the general lack of interest if not the ridicule. Such experiences could be explained by and would reinforce casting "the world" in thoroughly negative terms; if the world is inherently hostile to God, then no positive response is to be expected from it. Indeed, the next verse will suggest that the response of those who do already belong and of any new members is not to be taken for granted and itself needs to be explained (v. 6). Anyone who does respond positively must already not be genuinely characterized by "the world"; consciously or not, they must already have what it takes to respond.

However, it is not only the negative, the marginalization, that demands explanation. The world does listen to those who are determined by it, and whose message is equally determined by it. Just as "we" and "you" are not named, neither are "they": merely to so describe them identifies them as "other," not "us," and puts them outside the relationship that is being built between author and readers. This makes it difficult to know who they were, and how real. On one level they are to be identified with the false prophets of verse 1, but that description is shaped by the conventional imagery of eschatological expectation. Since the author does not ascribe to them specific teaching, however general, beyond the negative of verse 3, to attempt now to do so is not only speculation but may provide them with more substance and particularity than they possessed; his refusal to provide a negative formulation of the positive acknowledgment of verse 2 is deliberate (and a further reason for rejecting the variant reading in v. 3). To some extent these others serve as a rhetorical artifice, the product of the author's antithetical scheme, which demands their presence in order to confirm the readers in their opposing position.

However, they were probably more substantial than this: 2:18–19 implies a destabilizing threat that needed interpretation, and, although not explicit, the same situation is surely here in view; but now it is not their departure that is the concern but their apparent ability to belong at home "out there." That they "speak" and the world responds might suggest that they had an evangelistic

---

108. There is little explicit missionary interest in 1 John, in contrast to the situation apparently envisaged by 3 John.

message, which won a hearing, perhaps even converts; it is as likely, however, that "speaking" is simply what false prophets can be expected to do, and so belongs to the symbolic language on which the author draws. Certainly the self-chosen isolation of those represented by the author and his audience has been challenged, and his response is to turn the challenge on its head so that it becomes a source of reaffirmation. The absence of response and support that they experience does not undermine the validity of their beliefs or of their strategy, but rather reaffirms it, for it makes explicit those who are already not of God; for readers to change belief or strategy to a superficially more effective one would be to surrender the identity that is securely theirs.

[6] Although the author has sufficiently established the antithesis between "you" and "they" (vv. 4–5), he now sets up a further contrast between "they" and "we" (vv. 5–6). The latter could be identified with the author and his immediate associates; in this case, the readers (as "you") are confronted by "them" on the one hand, by "us" on the other. Since a dualist scheme such as the author has constructed cannot accommodate a tripartite division, they must choose with whom to ally themselves. The author warns that if they choose the former ("they") they will show themselves not to be of God: "the one who knows God listens to *us*." Yet the shifting person becomes part of the interplay between assurance and encouragement; the confident "you do belong to God" of verse 4 is echoed by the one who affirmed it, "we belong to God." The final "we recognize (the spirit . . .)" in this verse cannot refer only to the author but must include the readers as well. By this point the readers will find themselves compelled to identify themselves with "we," and in so doing they will affirm that they stand against all those others. The rhetoric of the letter has served to achieve the author's goal as stated at its start—to create shared commonality between "you" and "us" (1:3). From now on the author will speak almost exclusively of "us."

The "you recognize the spirit of God" of verse 2 is now transformed to "we recognize": once more, as those who can and do recognize the authentic spirit, they have no serious option but to spurn any alternative. The choice is now not between multiple spirits or their manifestation but between the fundamental alternatives, truth and error. The change from the language of falsehood to that of error (*planē*) recalls the warnings against being led astray (2:26; 3:7; cf. 1:8); this is not an intellectual decision alone but has lasting consequences. To choose error is not merely to make a mistake but is to succumb to the forces that oppose God in the final eschatological conflict (cf. 2 Thess 2:11); conversely, truth is not only what is in fact the case but is that which conforms to and is established by God.

In retrospect, this is why the author does not provide a balance to "they speak of what belongs to (*ek*) the world" (v. 5) by declaring that "we speak from (*ek*) God." Any active mission "we" might have could have no independent effect.

Only the one who in some as yet unacknowledged way "knows God" will respond ("listen") to those who themselves belong to and have their origin with God; the implication is also that such a person inevitably will respond. In this sense, 1 John does not have a concept of conversion, of the possibility of radical change; this is because of the letter's consistent dualism and of its tendency to think in terms of origin, not of goal. For 1 John eschatology is not the destination of a journey but the confirmation of its beginning; despite his adoption of eschatology he is more inclined to origins than to unexpected destinations.

In setting the spirit within this dualistic framework, this passage once again echoes other contemporary sources. Perhaps most striking verbally is a passage from the *Testament of Judah*: "Recognize, my children, that two spirits are active in humanity, that of truth and that of error. . . . Indeed, those of error and those of truth are inscribed on the human heart" (*T. Jud.* 20.1). Here, in contrast to 1 John, the two spirits appear to be conflicting dispositions or tendencies inherent in human beings, and elsewhere in the *Testaments* there are multiple deleterious spirits, although the spirit of error appears to be preeminent (*T. Reub.* 2.1; 3.2). Simeon ascribes his hostility to Joseph to "the ruler of error sending the spirit of jealousy," and Judah can look forward to the day when "there shall no longer be the spirit of error of Beliar, because he shall be cast into the fire forever" (*T. Sim.* 2.7; *T. Jud.* 25.3).

Such ideas have their roots in earlier Jewish thought: the passage from the *Rule of the Community* that, as already noted, parallels 1 John's dualism of light and darkness declares, "He [God] created man to rule the world and placed within him two spirits so that he would walk with them until the moment of his visitation: they are the spirits of truth and of deceit" (1QS III, 17–19; cf. commentary on 1:5; 3:24). Although here the two spirits again might be human inclinations, their effects overlap with the dominion exercised by the Prince of Lights and the Angel of Darkness, which appears to divide humanity into two irreconcilable camps until the final resolution of God's judgment. In the *War Scroll* the elect praise God, "from of old you appointed the prince of light to assist us . . . and all the spirits of truth are under his dominion. You created Belial for the pit, angel of enmity; his domain is darkness, his counsel is for evil and wickedness. All the spirits of his lot, angels of darkness, walk in the laws of darkness" (1QM XIII, 10–12).

It is this pattern of thought that supplies the setting for 1 John's thinking more than does the Fourth Gospel, despite the latter's (alone in the NT) use of the epithet, "the spirit of truth" (John 14:17; 15:26; 16:13); in the Gospel there is only the one spirit and this is not set within a dualist framework. Against the background of these other writings, the author probably would not have felt the need to determine whether there were many spirits or only two, or their precise relationship both with God or antichrist and with the human individuals in and through whom they acted. However, he is even less interested than they are in the origins of these opposing spirits and in their ultimate destinies, and he does not ascribe to them the decisions to love or hatred so important in the previous chapter. This contrasts with the *Rule of the Community*, which continues by itemizing what belongs to the spirit of truth—meekness, patience, generous compassion—and to the spirit of deceit—greed, sluggishness in the service of justice, wickedness (see 1QS IV, 2–14). Whereas these other texts at times envisage the continuing effect of the spirit of error in human lives in the present age, and urge resistance against it, for 1 John there is no room for ambiguity; his only interest in the spirits is in the unquestioned alignment of the division between them with the existing boundaries that determine the faithful, namely adherence to the convictions that they have inherited. If the readers live at a time of heightened security, it is the steps to be taken and their undoubted efficacy that concerns the author, not the precise identity of the threat.

### 1 John 4:7–5:4—The Love That Is God's

Once again the atmosphere changes abruptly: there is little sign of polemic and the tone is largely inclusive and encouraging. The author starts with the familiar encouragement to mutual love, but now "because love belongs to God," and he closes by repeating that God's love is inseparable from obedience. The noun and verb "love" are prominent in 1 John (46 times), but two-thirds of all occurrences come in the section 4:7–5:4; through them God's relationship with believers, believers' relationship with God, and their relationship with one another are skillfully intertwined. Therefore there is less of a break from the previous verses than there might at first seem to be. Love is centered on the community of those who believe; to believe that God sent God's own Son is to recognize the love that is at the heart of God's acting and so of God's being. It is this that would be lost if the challenges to belief represented by the spirit of error were to prevail. Yet a community that acknowledges the love at the heart of God's being must itself have love at its own center.

This theme is developed through four main paragraphs. The first (vv. 7–10) is a celebration of the love that has its source in God. The short balanced phrases have led some to describe this as a hymn to love, and in some editions of the New Testament it is set out in poetic form, although it is not technically verse. The second paragraph (vv. 11–16) develops the theme in prose, although not more prosaic, language. It continues to build a web of love, at whose heart is the love that originates in God, but that must bind members to one another and them to God. The third paragraph (vv. 17–19) again starts from the priority of God's love, now as the immovable source of assurance against all that may cause anxiety or fear. Finally (4:20–5:4) comes the reminder that the only and necessary articulation of responding to God's love with love is to direct that love to a fellow member, in order to maintain the integrity of that web of love.

Throughout the whole passage the author's own gaze, and so that of his readers, is fixed firmly on their common life. Those outside the community of believers, the "world" and the representatives of the antichrist, are outside his view. He is equally silent as to how such communal love is to be expressed, whether among those who lived in physical proximity, or as a genetic characteristic of all who believe wherever they might be. This he leaves for readers to decide.

### 1 John 4:7–10—In Celebration of God's Love

As just noted, many translations (and the standard edition of the Greek New Testament, NA[27]) set this passage out as verse, although the lines are of uneven length and follow no metrical pattern. Yet similar short balanced clauses are found elsewhere in the letter, and simply represent one of the techniques that the author uses to vary his style. Some of the clauses may echo phrases already familiar to the readers from their own traditions; in this case he may be weaving together affirmations to which they would all assent with his own commentary, but this also continues to be the case in the following section.

> **4:7** Beloved, let us love one another because love belongs to God, so everyone who loves has been born from God and knows God. **8** The one who does not love did not know[a] God, because God is love. **9** The love of God was revealed among us in this way, that God has sent his only Son into the world so that we might live through him. **10** Love consists in this, not that we have loved[b] God, but that he loved us and sent his Son as a means of forgiveness for our sins.

a. The simple past (aorist) in contrast to the present tense of v. 7: several manuscripts read either the present or the perfect (cf. 2:4; 3:6).

b. There is very strong support for the aorist ("we loved"), but the perfect is probably to be preferred since there would be a tendency for scribes to assimilate it to the aorist of the following clause.

**[7–8]** The address to the readers as those who are loved is by now a familiar one (2:7; 3:2, 21; 4:1), but it is particularly apposite to the theme of love on which the author now embarks. Here the apparently formulaic first person plural subjunctive (here translated "let us love"; see commentary on 3:11) serves to embrace author and readers in a common cause: the inclusive "we" continues emphatically through the rest of the chapter, and the author does not directly address his readers again as "you" until the letter draws to a close (5:13). The readers have already been reminded of love for one another as the aboriginal message and as God's command (3:11, 23). Here, however, the call to love rests on a more fundamental foundation: love is not simply something commanded by God but has its origin with God and so "belongs to" (*ek*) God—it should then be second nature for those who have themselves also just been described as "belonging to" (*ek*) God (4:6; cf. v. 2). The author does not distinguish between different kinds of love or different objects to which it might be directed, and this prompted some later scribes to provide an object ("God" or "a brother") for the "everyone who loves" of the following clause; the author would not have disagreed, but the absence is not an oversight (cf. also 3:14 and commentary). Although he does know that love can be misdirected (2:15), this is only a theoretical possibility and is almost self-negating. The nature of authentic love has already been defined (3:16), and it is this that enables him to say that love has its origin in God: hence his words are not a licence to claim that wherever love, however defined, is felt and expressed it originates in God.

This is equally the case when in a near-parallel phrase in the following verse (8) the author declares that God *is* love. These words have frequently been seen as the pinnacle of the letter, and even of the New Testament, and, as such, regularly have been abstracted from their context. But the author is not engaged in abstract definitions of God (so also 1:5, "God is light")[109] or of God's internal life; still less is he concerned with idealizing love—he does not say, "Love is God." Love is not an abstract idea but is known through what God has done toward women and men; it finds its goal in the shared life of those who are formed by what God has done and who define themselves in relation to God. It follows that attempts to contrast this God who is love with God as one who judges also fail to do justice to the concerns of the letter. The author will later address the place of love in the face of judgment (vv. 17–18), but he does not doubt the reality of the latter, and his thought has repeatedly made a resolute distinction between those who belong to the realm of both light and love and those who belong to the realm of darkness and of hate. Understanding God in terms of love does not lead to an undifferentiated universalism where none is excluded from the certainty of life, nor does it lead to treating as of secondary importance matters of belief or of faithfulness to the tradition of teaching received and to the community of those shaped by that tradition.

Hence in these two verses the statements that relate God to love serve only to reinforce ("because") the nonnegotiability of love as the mark of those who claim themselves to relate to God. That relationship is expressed in terms that by now are already familiar in the letter, birth from God (cf. 2:29; 3:9 and commentary) and knowing God (cf. 2:3–4; 3:1, 6 and commentary). The structure suggests that they may have been influenced by the earlier antithetical formulations or have come from a common source:

---

109. See commentary on 1:5 and cf. also John 4:24, "God is spirit."

Everyone who does justice has been born from him (2:29)
Everyone who loves has been born from God (4:7)

Everyone who sins has not seen him or known him (3:6)
The one who does not love did not know God (4:8)

The nonspecific or apparently absolute "love" is a characteristic of this formulaic style; it does not mean that the author expects to find such love elsewhere
than among those who believe. Likewise, this is no idealizing of love or a reduc-
tion of love to the impulses of the emotions. It is only the one who expresses
love as it has been urged throughout the letter, "let us love one another," who
is truly in relationship with God, who is love. Hence, completing the circle,
toward the end of this section a third formulation of the positive pattern will
declare, "Everyone who believes that Jesus is the Christ has been born from
God," and on this basis the author will deduce the absolute demand of loving
other such children of God (5:1).

Conversely, love would not be found outside that circle: it has been acknowledged already that "the world does not recognize us [the children of God] because
it did not recognize him" (3:1). Those scribes who in verse 8 altered "did not know
God" to "do not know God" missed these characteristic internal resonances. Yet
the language leaves unresolved the question already provoked by the debate over
sin, whether birth from God precedes loving or proceeds from it, and likewise
whether a failure to love is evidence of not having known God or is its consequence, and hence where ultimate responsibility lies (see commentary on 2:29).

These two celebrated verses are therefore embedded within the thought and
the argument of the letter as a whole. In order to trace the inspiration or sources
behind them there is no need to look outside the ideas and influences that have
shaped the letter so far, the Scriptures and later Jewish thought, as well as some
concepts and language shared with other early Christian writings, and others
distinctive to the Johannine tradition.

Within the Deuteronomic tradition it is axiomatic that God's love for Israel
is the foundation of their being chosen and guided by God; God's love is unmerited, inspired by nothing except itself, but it is not unfocused nor a general
beneficence to all, for the God who is creator and lord of all chose only Israel
and their ancestors to love from out of all the peoples (Deut 7:7–8; 10:14–15;
cf. Hos 11:1, 4; Mal 1:2). The LXX uses *agapan* here to translate the Hebrew
ʾhb; this is not the distinctive term of God's "covenantal or "steadfast love"
(Hebrew *ḥesed*, e.g., Psalm 136),[110] yet it does demand a response of love, and
Deuteronomy calls on the people to love God and to keep God's commands

---

110. The LXX translates *ḥesed* not by *agapē* but usually by *eleos*, which is comparatively rare
in the NT, and is not used in the Johannine literature except at 2 John 3.

(Deut 7:9). Here also belongs the fundamental confession, "Hear, O Israel, the LORD our God is one, and you are to love the LORD your God with all your heart" (Deut 6:4–5); that God is one is not an abstract philosophical truth but is known in the experience that God is "our God," and so requires a response that is not intellectual assent alone but is undivided commitment. The same is true of 1 John's confession that "God is love." Even though the Wisdom literature might recognize that God must "love all that exists . . . for you would not have created anything if you hated it" (Wis 11:24), the more general thrust in Jewish literature contemporary with 1 John is to emphasize alongside God's love for Israel (2 Esd 2:27, 32), God's particular love for the righteous. They are the true heirs of God's electing love, which they acknowledge by their response to God (see CD VIII, 14–17). Such a response, in a tradition reaching back to Exod 34:6–7 (cf. commentary on 1:8–9), acclaims God as a God of truth, compassion, and forgiveness, in an outpouring of the divine virtues:

> I will chant your kindness, I will ponder your might the whole day, I will bless your name continually, I will declare your glory among the sons of men, and in your abundant goodness my soul will delight. I know truth is in your mouth and justice in your hand, and in your thoughts all learning, and all glory is with you, and in your wrath all punishing judgment, and in your goodness, abundance of forgiveness, and your compassion for all the sons of your approval. (1QH XIX, 5–9)

Such passages provide the appropriate context for understanding 1 John's own declaration of God's nature, but they also underline its distinctiveness. As in the *Hymns*, it is the community of those who feel themselves to be formed by God's love who can celebrate it, and who recognize in it a summons to be shaped by that love in their response to God and to one another. On the other hand, 1 John does not pile up the multiple attributes of God, neither does it merely say, "God is loving," "God loves," "God is [you are] a God of love," or "your love, O God," but "God *is* love." That form of affirmation is open to being understood as asserting that all the divine attributes can be encompassed by this one attribute, so that all God's activity is characterized in particular by love. Subsequent interpreters would draw this conclusion, but in the present context there are no grounds for assuming that the author would have agreed with such a limitation, or that he would have relegated to second place that, for example, "God is truth."[111] His driving concern in the immediate context is the absolute nonnegotiability of love as the defining characteristic of those who would claim to know God. To fail to manifest love is to expose oneself as untouched by God. Thus Augustine was adopting a very different starting point when he saw in these words in 1 John the key to the understanding of the Trinity as modeled by Lover, Beloved, and Love (*On the Trinity* 8)—even though recent theological

---

111. Cf. 1QH V, 24 where "you are the truth" is a reconstructed reading.

reflection has found in Augustine's insight the necessary impulse for the nature of the church in its own life and in society as founded on loving relationality, a conviction 1 John would approve.

[9–10] By contrast, 1 John understands divine love not in abstract terms but in terms of what God has done for this specific group of people. The "love of God" here clearly refers to the love expressed by God (a subjective genitive, in contrast to the more ambiguous cases in 2:5, 12; 3:17; cf. below on 4:12; 5:3). The verb "was revealed," a favorite of this author, indicates a specific moment (aorist), and prepares for the description of the sending of the Son (cf. 3:5, 8; 1:2; contrast the future reference in 2:28; 3:2), but this past focus is modified by the addition of "among us." "Us" does not refer to Jesus' own immediate contemporaries or followers but to those who have appropriated that experience for themselves and who know themselves to be the recipients of God's love (cf. v. 11; 3:16 and commentary); so God's love was not just *for* but was experienced "among (*en*) us," "in us" not as individuals but as the community thus created (see v. 11). This specific focus also modifies the apparent public demonstration of God's love otherwise implicit in "revealed," and it recalls the Deuteronomic tradition where, as already seen, God's love is directed specifically to those whom God chooses and saves.

Hence, the world is the setting *into* which the Son is sent, but the purpose of that sending is that "*we*" might live. Although "world" (*kosmos*) may here describe the earthly realm neutrally, in contrast to the negative connotations that it carries elsewhere (cf. 2:15–17; 3:13; 4:4–5), when set alongside 3:8 it would be better to envisage the mission of the Son into hostile territory in order to rescue those who will count themselves among "us." Since the sphere of the world is that of hatred and death, that rescue leads to true living; the verb "to live" appears only here in 1 John, but even, as here, without the adjective "eternal" (2:25) the noun has been used of the life that belongs to God's realm (1:2; 3:14). The means of that gift of life is expressed only in the most general of terms, "through him" (the Son): 1 John is not committed to any particular understanding of what would elsewhere be called the atonement, and here it is the sending of the Son that is effective, not his death in itself (see 3:16 and commentary).

The author is apparently quoting a familiar formula, "God sent his only Son": this explains why the subject, "God," is repeated unnecessarily—following after "love of *God*," "*he* sent" would be adequate. The adjective "only"(*monogenēs*), here alone in 1 John, and the verb "sent" (*apostellō*), which is restricted to these two verses and to another formulaic phrase in verse 14, also point to derivation from earlier tradition. Confirming this is the similar (but significantly variant) formula in John 3:16–17, which commentators on the Fourth Gospel often consider itself to be derived from earlier tradition:

| 1 John 4:9 | John 3:16– | 17 |
|---|---|---|
| The love of God was revealed | God loved | For God |
| among us in this way, | the world thus, | |
| that God has sent his Son | so he gave the Son, | did not send the Son |
| the only one, | the only one, | |
| into the world | *(the world thus)* | into the world |
| so that we | so that everyone who believes in him | so that he |
| | should not perish but | might judge the world |
| | | but that the world |
| might live | have eternal life. | might be saved |
| through him. | | through him. |

If this does represent what is almost a confession of faith, it is difficult to be certain whether in its earliest form the world was the actual object of God's love (John 3:16) or only the setting of the sending (or giving) of the Son (1 John 4:9; cf. John 3:17). The positive idea is restricted to this verse in the Gospel, and God's love is otherwise usually directed to the Son (John 3:35; 10:17; 15:9; 17:23–26), and is promised to the disciples in the future (14:21, 23; 17:23). This may suggest that it was not the evangelist's own creation but that it already belonged in the tradition used by him.[112] However, it need not follow that the author of 1 John deliberately dropped a universal focus in favor of the more restricted object of divine love, since even such shared traditions and formulae probably reached each author independently and in different forms.

Nonetheless, the comparison with John 3:16 highlights the absence in 1 John of belief as the channel through which God's love is actualized as the gift of life. The perspective is not that of the potential available for "everyone" but that of those ("we") who, now that the moment of their response lies in the past, measure not what it has achieved but the present realization that *they* are the

112. Similarly, only here in John did God "give" the Son: elsewhere God *sent* the Son, but *gave to* the Son (works, disciples, etc.: John 3:35; 5:36; 6:37).

recipients of God's love. From their perspective God's love was for *them*, and God's sending of the Son was that *they* might enjoy the benefits of light and life of which the author has repeatedly assured them. That God's love had a wider potential and invited assent and commitment lies outside the author's concerns, whether or not it lay outside his vision.

The description of the Son as "the only one" (*monogenēs*), only here in 1 John, belongs to this same tradition (cf. also John 1:14, 18; 3:18). The adjective is often used of the only child in a family (Judg 11:34; Luke 7:12; 8:42; 9:38); in this sense it is sometimes associated with the adjective translated "beloved" (*agapētos*), which, as in other Greek sources, may carry the meaning of "*only* beloved" (Judg 11:34). When Isaac is described as Abraham's "beloved" son (Gen 22:2, 12, 16), the real issue appears to be that he is Abraham's *only* son, and this is how he is described in other retellings of the story (*monogenēs*: Heb 11:17; Josephus, *Antiquities* 1.222). On this basis some interpreters have discovered a link between the Johannine description of Jesus as "the only (*monogenēs*) son" and the heavenly words addressed to Jesus at the baptism and transfiguration in the Synoptic tradition, "my son, my (only) beloved (*agapētos*)" (Mark 1:11; 9:7; cf. also 12:6; 2 Pet 1:17). In this interpretation the emphasis falls on the "only" (*mono-*) element in the adjective. Other interpreters have argued that in the Johannine context, the second element (*-genēs*) should be given greater weight in view of the distinctive Johannine metaphor of begetting (*gennaō*) (see above 2:29 and commentary). It is this that prompts the translation "only begotten" (or, possibly, "begotten from the only one"): if this were the case it would establish some relationship as well as a contrast between the one who by loving shows that they are "born (begotten) from God" (1 John 4:7), and the divine exemplar of love, the "only begotten" Son who has been sent (4:9).[113] However, if, as argued here, the epithet is embedded in an earlier tradition, there is less reason to ascribe it a specific "Johannine" meaning derived from the context; when 1 John does correlate the one who "was born from God" with those who "have been born from God," the author uses the same verbal phrase in different tenses (1 John 5:18). Those who first heard the letter may have identified the repeated *gen-* element, but it is unlikely that this would have imbued a traditional formula with a theological resonance that is not otherwise developed. Equally, while it is possible that the story of Abraham, the father who offered his only son, informed some other

113. Cf. John 1:13, those who have been "born from God," followed by 1:14, "glory as of an only begotten (*monogenēs*: there is no word for 'son' here) with a father." Similarly, the broader context of John 3:16 is the need to be "born" from above/again. The issue is complicated by the textual uncertainty at John 1:18, where the earlier attested reading is probably "*monogenēs* God" rather than "*monogenēs* Son," although both may have developed from an (unattested) earlier, unqualified *monogenēs*. See also commentary on 1 John 5:1, 18.

early Christian reflection on God's giving of his Son (see Rom 8:32), it is nowhere in view at this point in 1 John.

These conclusions are reinforced by the verb "sent" (*apostellō*). That Jesus is the Son sent by the Father, God, is axiomatic for the Fourth Gospel's Christology (John 5:36, 38; 6:29, 57; 7:29; 17:3; etc.). It is widely agreed that the social background to this idea lies in ancient understandings of the messenger as the one who carries the authority of and so represents the person of the sender; in the Gospel it is particularly important that the one sent is not just any messenger but is the Son.[114] However, none of this can be read into 1 John: the three occurrences of the verb (4:9–10, 14) are formulaic and do not invite further theological reflection.

In words that recall the Deuteronomic emphasis that Israel's election was through no virtue of their own but founded on God's prevenient love (Deut 7:7–8), the author reiterates that love is expressed only in and is defined only by what God has done as an act of love. Love does not need to be qualified as "love from God" (as it is in v. 9), because God's love is the source and the measure of all love. The author does not say that people (believers) do not or cannot love God: that they do so, and how, will become the theme of the final section of this part of the letter (4:20–5:4). Rather, their ("our") love does not have any priority—hence the perfect tense, "not that we *have loved*." By contrast, God's love for "us" was particular and concrete: both verbs used of God's action in loving and sending are here in the aorist.[115] This time the author expands the purpose of the mission of the Son in terms he had already used earlier, "as a means of forgiveness (*hilasmos*) for our sins," although here there is no extension to those of "the world" as there was in 2:2 (see commentary). There is little difference between 2:2, where this is what Jesus *is* in the present in response to believers' recognition of their sins, and this verse, where the focus is on the past: 1 John does not draw fine distinctions between what Jesus (or "he") was or did and what he is and does now (cf. 3:3, 5). As there, the formula was probably drawn from the community's tradition, and no specific understanding of how sins are forgiven is implied—hence the translation "means of forgiveness" rather than the more precise "expiation" or "propitiation," which denotes a particular mechanism (see commentary on 2:2).[116] Here it is placed in parallel to "that we might live" (v. 9); the emphasis is not on the

114. Although there have been attempts to identify parallels in religious patterns of the time, sending is no more frequent than other modes of appearing in gnostic descriptions of the coming of a redeemer figure.

115. In v. 9 "God sent" uses the perfect tense: given the variation between perfect and aorist in John 5:36 and 38, or John 17:18 and 20:21, it may be wrong to overemphasize this; the perfect is used in v. 14 and may be the formulaic choice.

116. I argued in the commentary that the prepositional phrase, lit. "concerning (*peri*) our sins," is not an allusion to a specific sin sacrifice, for which the singular "concerning sin" is regularly used.

precise details of how believers benefit from God's love, but on that love as the enabling foundation of any response to God.

## 1 John 4:11–16—God's Love as the Source of Our Love

The author addresses his readers again, returning to the point he made at the beginning of the previous section, the summons for them to love one another. Yet once again he moves back to reflecting on the priority of God's love and on believers' experience of God's presence in their lives. Hence there is not a simple two-stage process, cause followed by effect—first God loves, then we love. Rather, God's love, demonstrated in what God has done, continues as the atmosphere in which they live, providing the air or life that they breathe.

4:11 Beloved, if God loved us in this way, we equally are bound to love one another. 12 No one has ever seen God. If we do love one another, then God indwells in us, and his love is made complete[a] in us. 13 In this way we know that we indwell in him and he in us: because he has given us of his spirit. 14 So, we have seen and we give testimony that the Father sent the Son as savior of the world. 15 Whoever acknowledges that Jesus is the Son of God, God indwells in them and they in God. 16 We, then, have recognized and are convinced of the love that God has among us. God is love and the one who indwells in love indwells in God, and God indwells in him.

a. Although here a periphrastic perfect (formed with the participle) is used, there is no difference from the normal perfect passive in 2:4.

[11–12] The readers would have readily assented to this celebration of the preeminence of God's act of love that the author has just rehearsed, especially if it drew on familiar formulaic phrases. Yet it is open to being understood and experienced in highly individual terms, an aggregate of individuals each of whom could claim, God loved *me*. Such an understanding would not act as the foundation for the conclusion that the author draws: that God's prior love creates the obligation of a responding love, not to God (although that will come later), nor indiscriminate or unspecified, but precisely to one another. God's love for "us" does not simply transform individuals and offer them the possibility of life, but it creates a community; indeed, retrospectively, God's love for "us" is for the community as a whole and not for its members separate from the community. Hence God's act of love does not only impose the obligation to love, but also determines to whom that love must be directed, namely toward those who are equally recipients of God's love along with "us." Love here is not emotion, neither is it to be defined in terms of particular virtues or acts of kindness; it is the lifeblood of the community, that which gives it its existence.

This goes beyond seeing reciprocal love as something commanded (3:11), and so as an act of obedience, still less as satisfied by a catalogue of individual activities, or even by a general affirmative concern for each other. Love is not one among a number of characteristics of those who believe; indeed, at this point, rather than identify them as those who believe, it would be better to identify them as those who are founded on love.

That it is not possible for mortals to see God was an ancient commonplace. This was not because of God's invisibility but because of the gulf that separates the human from the Divine—because of human incapacity rather than because of the nature of divine substance. There are biblical accounts of those to whom God did appear (Genesis 17; 18), although these troubled later interpreters, who would have been more comfortable with the allusive special experience afforded to such exceptional figures as Moses or Elijah, or even Isaiah in a heavenly vision (Exod 34:5–9; 1 Kgs 19:11–13; Isaiah 6). Admittedly, there were those who claimed to have had access to the heavenly realms, and so to have had a vision of the Divine, but it is not likely that the author is deliberately rejecting such claims. There was also a tradition that the name "Israel" meant "the one who has seen God," but this also is not in view here. The author assumes that his statement will be uncontroversial (so also 1 John 4:20), just as does the author of the prologue to the Gospel (John 1:18, where the verb "to see" is that used in 1 John 4:20). He probably would not be bothered by the potential contradiction with 3:6 (where Jesus may be the object of the sight that might be claimed), or with the promise of seeing "him" in 3:2.

However, the surrogate for sight of God is very different in 1 John from the revelation of Jesus Christ in John 1:18; here it is the indwelling presence of God that is the corollary of love for one another. The author is not asserting that God's presence will be a reward for love or even its consequence but that it *is* a present reality when those who are loved also love one another. This language of indwelling is by now familiar (see 2:6 and commentary), as is the idea that it is fully reciprocal, although here it is explicit that it is God who is the indwelling power (cf. 3:24). In the light of some of these earlier passages (e.g., 3:6), the image may be an individualistic one, God indwelling the individual believers; but in the present context it would be more effective if it is God's indwelling within the community as a whole (cf. v. 9). This ambiguity between individual and communal continues in the following expansion, although it is likely that the author would have seen no serious difference between the two: the self-aware and self-reflective individual isolated from their social context was not the center of conscious reflection in the ancient world as is now the case in Western thought.

If God is love, it follows that love is a, perhaps *the*, mode of divine presence. The love that comes from God then finds its fullest expression, "is made complete," in those who, as members of the community established by God's love, exhibit that love in their interrelationships. Almost the same sentiment is asserted in 2:4 of the one who observes God's word (see note a): as there, his (= God's) love refers not to their love for God but to the love whose source is God—not just God's love for them but the love that is thus generated. Whereas in 2:4 the argument focused on the individual who might fulfill the condition, here it is on "we" who love. Since such love can never be exercised by the individual in isolation, but is always the task of the group, it is, as just seen, in the group, and not just in its individual members, that the divine love finds its completion.[117] An alternative view would understand this as meaning that God's own act of love is not complete until it has created a community of love; even the divine love would be unfulfilled were it to be met with no response—although for the author of 1 John this would not even be a theoretical possibility. In this case the "in us" of the completion of God's love would have a different nuance from the "in us" of God's indwelling: it would mean something like "through our being and action" (cf. Luke 22:37 of Scripture being completed "in me" [Jesus]).

While there may be truth in this sentiment, it is unlikely to be the author's primary intention; his concern in this and in the verses that follow is that they may fully experience and embody God's presence. Despite all the assurances of victory and of being children of God that underlie the letter, there can in the present age be no unmediated direct encounter with God; their love for one another is an active assent to and participation in the community created by God's love and so the most certain experience of God.

**[13]** Unexpectedly, the author now offers a further expression of, and test of, God's indwelling presence. The wording, "he has given us of his spirit," directly recalls 3:24b, which also commenced with the same formulaic "in this way we know (that he indwells in us)." There are minor changes of wording, a characteristic of the author as just illustrated by the comparison of 4:12 with 2:4. Here the verb "he has given" is in the perfect tense, which potentially places more emphasis on the lasting quality of the gift rather than on the moment of its bestowal (the aorist in 3:24), although such variation is not uncommon in this author.[118] Slightly more perplexing, the same Greek phrase, "of/from the spirit" (*ek tou pneumatos*), requires a different translation in context; here it is that God has given "of (*his*) spirit," which might suggest that God distributed some portion of God's own spirit.[119] The point should not be pushed: 1 John does not have a clearly articulated understanding of the spirit, as has become clear from 4:1–3, 6, where "the spirit of God" (4:2) best identifies the (or more than one)

---

117. See above on 3:11: the "love one another" formula is always in the first person plural in contrast to the third person singular "love of brother."

118. See n. 115. In 4:13 "we know" the reciprocal indwelling, God in us, we in God.

119. This is because of the addition in 4:13 of "because/in that" (*hoti*), and of the personal pronoun, "his" (*autou*).

spirit sent by and originating from God, pitched against the spirit of error. There has been no sense that the spirit is a personal form of the presence of God, such as is developed in the Fourth Gospel (John 16:13–15), and it would be wrong to find such an idea in the terse phrase here. The author is, perhaps, deliberately reminding his readers of what he had already said, and is unconcerned that the different sentence construction has given the same words a different meaning. If so, there is an ironic twist: the first occurrence of this assurance immediately led to the warning to discriminate among the spirits (3:24–4:1). Just as the readers may have been getting complacent in a haze of self-affirming love, they are awoken to the dangers that still lie ahead. Logically, this might expose the argument as flawed: how can the experience of God's spirit be any more secure than the experience of indwelling in and being indwelt by God; how can the former be the grounds of knowing the latter? The beginning of the chapter had already provided something of an answer: the experience of God's spirit is established by the confession of Jesus. Now it has become clearer why all this should be so; the God who indwells and is indwelt is the God whose fundamental nature has been demonstrated by and experienced in the sending of the Son.

[14] Giving voice to this, the author moves from the more subjective language of indwelling and knowing couched in present tenses to the objective language of what "we have seen" and what God has done, both perfect tenses that hold together past act and present impact. The confidence of having seen enables the giving of testimony, reinforcing the external reality of what has taken place. The verse does not simply describe an act of testimony but is itself one: the formulaic "we have seen" belongs to a pattern of Johannine confession probably already familiar to the readers, and it is regularly followed by "and bear testimony" (1 John 1:1–3; John 1:34; 3:11; 19:35; see also 20:18). The particular verb, "see" (*theaomai*; translated "looked at" in 1 John 1:1 to distinguish it from the alternative *horaō* [see commentary]), is that used in verse 12, "no one has ever seen God." Whereas God has not been seen in God's own self, what God has done can and has been seen; this is the only means of seeing God prior to the hope of future sight (3:2). If this was a familiar confessional formula, evidently it was used by those who had not seen Jesus physically in his own lifetime. In the opening of the letter this is the particular claim of those who by their place in the tradition of the community assumed the authority to proclaim to the audience (see 1:1–3 and commentary). The author is not returning here to that exclusive note: by this point in the argument "we" embraces "you" (see 4:6). Yet, as the readers make this claim their own, they cannot help but reaffirm the confidence that inspired the letter at its start. However the original affirmation may have been generated, it has become something that subsequent believers can make their own and then extend to others in "fellowship with" (1:3) them. The subjective experience of divine presence is grounded in and measured by the objective fact of what God has done, but that objective

truth is subjectively appropriated. The subjectivity here is again not that of the isolated individual but of the community: "we" have seen and bear testimony as members of this group established by what God has done, although (v. 15) each individual must be an active part of that.

The particular formulation of the content of sight and testimony again apparently draws on images from elsewhere in the Johannine tradition rather than from the letter itself; perhaps the author is using what is familiar to his readers to keep them with him. The sending of the Son is the primary way of understanding Jesus' purpose in the Fourth Gospel (see vv. 9–10 above); here the one sending is named not as "God" (v. 9) but, balancing "the Son," as "the Father," and this is also the regular pattern in the Gospel (John 5:36; 6:57; 10:36). It is not, however, out of tune with the letter, which contains few references to the "Son" without God as Father in close proximity (see 1:2, 3; and commentary): God as Father is primarily Father of the Son (although see 2:1; 3:1 and commentary).

The particular confession of Jesus as "savior of the world" is made in only one other place in the New Testament, by the Samaritans in response to the woman's testimony in John 4:39–42. This is striking given that the term "savior" (*sōtēr*) is used only here in 1 John, while the verb "to save" and the noun "salvation" do not appear at all: generally, this is not a Johannine way of understanding Jesus' role, although it is well-established elsewhere.[120] Although God can be described as "savior" in Jewish thought (Deut 32:15; *Pss. Sol.* 8.33; Luke 1:47), the epithet is often seen as more characteristic of the move of early Christian preaching into the wider empire: hence its importance in the later New Testament writings, applied not only to God but increasingly to Jesus (1 Tim 1:1; 2 Tim 1:10; Titus 1:4; 2:13; 3:6; 2 Pet 1:1, 11; 2:20; etc). While this ascription may have been influenced by the title "savior" addressed to other deities of the time, it was perhaps even more prompted by, and therefore a challenge to, the claims of generals or of rulers, and most of all of the emperor, to be "savior." Josephus describes how the people of Tiberias welcomed Vespasian on his capture/liberation of the city as their "savior and benefactor," while according to Philo the youthful emperor Caligula was similarly treated (Josephus, *War* 3.459; Philo, *Embassy* 22). Although many of the New Testament examples acknowledge Jesus as "*our* savior," the more universal Johannine claim (cf. also 1 Tim 4:10, of God) is paralleled both by the description of deities as saviors of all people, and, most strikingly, by an oft-quoted inscription from Athens addressed to Claudius as "all-powerful, savior of the world" (*IG* II.3273).[121]

The singular Johannine usage in both the Gospel and in 1 John is made the more striking by the apparent contrast with the generally more negative attitude

---

120. Similarly, in the Gospel "salvation" and "savior" appear once each (4:22, 42 [see below]), and "to save" only occasionally (3:17; 5:34; 12:47; also 10:9; 11:12 [12:27]: "keep safe, protect").
121. See G. Foerster, "σωτηρία," *TDNT* 7:1003–12.

to "the world" (*kosmos*) in both writings. The world in 1 John is characterized by its inability to recognize either us or God/Jesus, by its hatred, and as the domain of everything that resists God (3:1, 13; 4:3–5; 5:19). In particular, a few verses earlier the Son was sent *into* the world, but that *we* might live, an apparently more uncompromising note than the Gospel's emphasis on God's love *for* the world (see 4:9 and commentary). A similar exception to the overall picture presents Jesus as a means of forgiveness "not only for our sins but also for those of the whole world" (2:2), words echoed without that expansion a few verses ago (4:10). In both cases there are hints that earlier formulaic or confessional traditions are being evoked, but it does not follow that the author failed to observe the implications of what he was saying. For most of the letter his focus is on those who have responded, and his concern is both to secure that response in the unfailing action and purpose of God, and to urge his readers to live out that security. Experience has combined with his dualist theological framework to project "the world" as the negative pole to those he addresses, provoking the question whether, if "the world" were to respond to God, it would still be "world." Yet an unqualified dualism, particularly where any eschatological resolution is poorly articulated, is incompatible with the ultimate authority and power of God, especially of a God experienced in terms of love—the reach of God so understood cannot be limited in its extent. Whether the author would have made all this explicit, or even perceived it, cannot be determined, but it is implicit; and these two affirmations in 4:14 and 2:2, even if provoked more by familiarity and tradition, attest to that.

The very different context suggests that the same confession appears in the Gospel (John 4:42) not from any literary influence in either direction, but from a shared background. Nonetheless, its broader implications in the Gospel are also relevant to the letter. Although the "savior of the world" might be seen as particularly appropriate on the lips of the "non-Jewish" Samaritans, it may also serve as exemplifying the Gospel's understanding of the sending of the Son "that the world might be saved through him" (John 3:16–17). Within the broader scheme of the narrative the epithet stands in creative tension with Jesus' declaration to Pilate that his kingdom was *not* "of this world," and with the explicit recognition that to acknowledge Jesus' kingship was a challenge to that of the emperor (John 18:36; 19:15).[122] Acknowledging Jesus as "savior of the world" likewise offers a challenge to the emperor's claim to that title. A similar political challenge is less overt in 1 John, though it may be potential. The language of bearing witness is probably primarily directed internally as it is in 1:2, but elsewhere in early Christian thought it comes to entail not only public

---

122. For the thought of the Gospel it is immaterial whether the earlier passages (3:16–17; 4:42) are pre-Johannine tradition, or that in the context of the trial it is Jesus' kingship over the Jews that is at stake.

affirmation but the suffering that might ensue (Rev 1:2, 9; 2:13; Acts 1:8; 22:15; 23:11). Although such a setting has been posited for 1 John, it is not supported by the tenor of the letter as whole. Still, there is enough sense of anxiety (3:13) to suggest that early readers would not hear "savior of the world" as an entirely spiritual, unworldly acclamation.

[15] This remains true as the author turns from the traditional formulation of shared experience to the particular expression of belief in Jesus that forms the underlying thread through the second part of this letter, as "Son of God." The inclusive first person plural, "we have seen," now gives way to the third person singular, "whoever acknowledges" (cf. 2:22; 5:1, 5), which opens up, and excludes for these readers, the possibility of failing to do so. The reciprocal indwelling by and in God assured in verse 13 is now an individual reality contingent upon acknowledgment that Jesus is the Son of God. This is the first time this particular confession has been expressed, but numerous steps have prepared for it, beginning with the initial rejection of the one who denied that Jesus was the Christ, matched by the assurance that the one who confessed the Son also possessed the Father, an image quickly followed by that of indwelling in *the* Son and *the* Father (2:22–23). Since then the implications of such a denial or acknowledgment have become clearer: God's command had been expounded as belief "in the name of *his Son*, Jesus Christ" (3:23), and this was closely followed by the confession of the spirit from God as of Jesus Christ (having come in flesh), and its antithesis as the failure to confess Jesus (4:2–3). All this has confirmed that the dispute is not (for example with other Jews) as to who, if anyone, is Christ/Son of God, asserting that Jesus fulfills the necessary criteria; neither are the confessions claiming these as opposed to some other title for Jesus (see commentary on 2:22–23). Within the earliest preaching both titles quickly evolved specifically as ways of expressing the focal place of Jesus, and in so doing acquired elements not attested in their original setting in Jewish thought. In 1 John this takes the form of treating "Christ" and "Son of God" as near-synonyms (see further 5:1, 5), and of insisting that the latter cannot be understood independently of the unique relationship between Father and Son. Although similar moves are found in the Fourth Gospel (John 11:27; 20:31; 10:36), they have their own logic in 1 John, a logic that emerges as this passage draws together a number of threads from the letter so far.[123]

Hence the confession here is not an intrusive aside disrupting the flow of a passage concerned with God and God's love. It is insufficient to predicate this interlocking divine indwelling only on the communal embodying of love (v. 12), or on the felt presence of God's spirit (v. 13): these may be deceptive, and the spirit itself needs authenticating. The author never doubts the impor-

---

123. To that extent the reading of Codex Vaticanus, "that Jesus Christ is the Son of God," captures the cumulative argument, but is probably too poorly attested to claim serious consideration.

tance of *what* is believed. Forgiveness is activated through *the Son* (1:7); the annihilation of the activities of the devil has been achieved by *the Son of God* (3:8); God's love has become tangible in God's sending of *his Son* (4:9–10, 14); all this can be affirmed to be the case only because Jesus, named and identified, is God's Son. Within the framework of 1 John's thought two different elements have to be maintained. On the one hand, forgiveness, victory, and the definitive expression of the love of God can come from God only if the one who mediates them is nothing less than God's Son. On the other hand, the tendency that the author of 1 John himself displays of speaking anonymously of "the Son" or "the Son of God" runs the risk of turning these models or metaphors of God's work into a form of myth (see 3:8 and commentary), a foundational story whose main function is to project the self-understanding of the community. This risk must be countered by recalling the embodiedness of the Son, the primary story of Jesus, for it was the preaching about Jesus and about him as the Christ that first gave shape to the claims made for what the Son of God had achieved. For 1 John the definition of "Christ" or "Son of God" is not something that could be decided independently of the story of Jesus. That identification has to be reclaimed or restored in the dynamic, which means that what is known about Jesus gives content to how God has acted, while that God has acted gives content to who Jesus is. Hence in the immediate context this verse reminds that the Son of God whose sending has been declared three times (vv. 9, 10, 14) is none other than Jesus.

[16] There is, therefore, no conflict between making the proper confession of *Jesus* the condition for divine indwelling and the declaration of this verse that makes God the true subject and source of all, and the ultimate object of knowledge and belief. For this author talk about Jesus, the Son, always leads back to God. The emphatic first person plural, "we have recognized," draws readers back from the potentially disputed confession to the convictions that define them; as in verse 14 this is inclusive and is not an authorial or (pseudo-) eyewitness plural. The grammatical form, with both verbs in the perfect tense, recalls the other Johannine first person testimony formulations (see v. 14 and commentary); here, however, the emphasis is not on the grounds for testimony, sight, but on its inner assurance, knowledge. This too was probably a familiar formulation from Johannine tradition—similar sentiments are voiced by Peter: "*We have believed and have come to know* that you are the holy one of God" (John 6:69; cf. Martha's "I have believed that you are the Christ," John 11:27). Their familiarity would reinforce the readers' sense of inclusion as the author brings this section to a close.

This background explains the distinctive grammatical form of the emphatic "*we are* convinced of" (the first person plural perfect) followed by the direct object, "the love . . . ," which differs from 1 John's usual use of the verb (i.e. *pisteuō*, see 3:23 and commentary; 4:1; 5:1, 5, 10–13). Both form and construction are determined by the confident "we have recognized," which takes first place, echoing the importance elsewhere in the letter of having known him (2:3 [see commentary], 13, 14; cf. 2:4; 3:6); belief does not imply something less secure than knowledge. Maintaining the theme of the section, here it is God's love that has been known and believed; this, of course, is equally not something less than having known God, for by now it has become clear that it is by God's loving that God is most properly and completely known. This is not belief that God does after all love but confidence in that love and conviction of its reliability. Therefore more is now meant than by the similar wording of 3:16, "In this way we have known love, in that he laid down his life for us," for that love has now been shown to have its source in God. Although made evident in the sending of the Son, God's love is not tied to the past; just as the perfect tenses of the verbs of believing and knowing point to the present reality of those convictions grounded in the past, so the love that God "maintains" (*echō*) is also in the present and is to be found "in us," within or among the community of belief (cf. v. 12).

Contrary to those translations (and NA[27]) that put a paragraph break at this point, midway through verse 16, the repetition in the second part of the verse of the cardinal affirmation, "God is love" (see v. 8), is an integral part of the declaration of the first part. It is only because of what "we" have known and are fully confident of that this statement about God's very nature can be made; at the same time, this is why to have known God's love is to know God and not just some incomplete aspect of God. However, the main task of the whole passage has not only been to meditate on the nature of God or even on God's bearing toward humanity or toward those who believe, but to call for the mirroring and embodiment of that love among those formed by it. This is how this section, like the preceding one, started, with the summons to love one another (vv. 7, 11); it concludes instead not with "us" and "one another" but with the individual, repeating the assurance of divine indwelling given in verse 15 to the one making the right confession, but now directing it to "the one who *indwells in love*." This is both a logical consequence of the identification of God as love, and rhetorically serves as an exhortation to all readers. The love in which one might, or must, indwell may refer to the love that God offers and that God is: to indwell in love is to indwell in God and to fully experience God's presence. However, to indwell in love could hardly exclude inhabiting a circle of love that is given to and received from others, just as love for one another has already been shown to be the prerequisite of divine indwelling (v. 12). The author probably would not draw too great a distinction between indwelling in God's love and indwelling in love for others, and certainly would not exclude one or the other. The latter may seem most important as the climax of the opening exhortations; the former will help shape what is to follow.

## *1 John 4:17–19—Confidence in Love*

Up to this point love has been rooted in God's prior love and comes to fruition in the love that binds together those who make a common confession. Now the author assures his readers that love also holds them secure in the face of the future, even of the expectation of judgment. The argument follows closely from what precedes, and this is best illustrated by repeating the latter part of verse 16.

4:16b . . . God is love, and the one who indwells in love indwells in God, and God indwells in them. 17 In this way love has been made fully complete[a] among us, so that we may maintain confidence on the day of judgment, because just as that man is so we are in this world. Fear has no place in love, 18 but complete love drives out fear; for fear has to do with punishment, and the one who fears has not been made complete in love. 19 We ourselves love[b] because he[c] first loved us.

a. The form of the verb is the same as in 2:4 in contrast to the periphrastic in v. 12 (see note a on 4:12).

b. Or, "let us love." Some Greek manuscripts add an object (God, him [KJV], the Lord).

c. A number of manuscripts supply "God."

[17–18] Again the author picks up an idea from the previous section that invites further examination. The complete realization of God's love in them, which in verse 12 was the correlate of their love for one another, is necessarily also the correlate of the interactive divine indwelling assured the one who indwells love. The characteristic "in this way" most probably points back, encompassing also the foundational "God is love"; therefore "love" does not need qualifying as "his" or as "God's" (as in v. 12 and 2:4)—that it is God's love is to be understood. In any case, by this point in the argument the love that God offers is inseparable from the love experienced and shared in the community of love. This communal dimension is emphasized by the replacement of "in us" by "among (*meta*) us," which may also remind the readers that they are not passive partners in this and perhaps recall the purpose of the letter, fellowship "with [or "among," *meta*] us" (1:3). Yet the arena of love is not limited to God's action in the past and to the present experience of those who believe; it also reaches into the future. For all the emphasis throughout the letter on the absolute confidence that comes from already being God's children and from belonging to the light, there remains a future whose precise contours are uncertain. It would not greatly alter this sense if "in this way" were taken to refer forward—love finds its full demonstration in the future—but this would create an abrupt disjunction from the previous verse and is less persuasive.

Earlier, the author had spoken of "his coming" or appearance, whether that be of God or of Jesus, and had assured them that they could face it with confidence or boldness (*parrēsia*) (2:28 [see commentary]; cf. 3:2); here he promises the same on "the day of judgment," grounded, as there, in their indwelling in God, but even more in the total integrity of love. That God does and will judge those disobedient to the divine will, not only in Israel but among the nations also, is pervasive in the Scriptures; inevitably, as the anticipation of the effective establishment of God's authority looked increasingly to the future so also did the expectation of a decisive judgment. The idea is widespread in early Christian thought, with the anticipated judgment encompassing all people, "the living and the dead" (1 Pet 4:5). The specific phrase "day of judgment" is not found in the Old Testament, but it arises under the influence of the prophetic notion of "the day of the Lord," and is used by Matthew and by 2 Peter (Matt 10:15; 11:22, 24; 12:36; 2 Pet 2:4; 3:7). It comes only here in the Johannine corpus, and may appear surprising in a letter with so much emphasis on the present reality of the gifts usually associated with God's kingdom, and on believers' transition "from death to life" (3:14).[124] However, 1 John does not totally surrender any future expectation (2:28; 3:2); even the recasting of "the last hour" in the present appearance of the antichrists (2:18) requires some eventual resolution. The author's concern at this point, though, is not with them; he has no interest in what impact the judgment will have on anyone other than the members of the community. The day of judgment is mentioned only to be effectively undermined: it is not the unknown, a source of anxious trepidation and urgent preparation. Confidence is possible even now because the outcome is already assured.

The assurance they have is the ultimate goal (or demonstration; see above) of their participation in the full completion or perfection of love. Completion or perfection is itself an eschatological concept (see 2:4), when the imperfections and incompleteness of present experience are overcome (cf. Phil 3:12), and it is determined by what belongs on the other side of judgment. The author gives further grounds for their assurance by appealing again to the parity between them and "that man" (*ekeinos*), his characteristic allusion to Jesus (2:6; 3:5, 16). As in 3:3 and 5 it is not what Jesus did or was, nor what Jesus will do or will be, but what he *is* that provides the pattern; but unlike those two verses, here there is no specific definition of what it is about him that acts as a model and so offers reassurance. It is also unclear whether "in this world" represents how he also is, or only their current situation. The former might recall the confession of 4:2, Jesus' having come "in flesh," sharing their situation, although to express this by "is" would be startling. The latter would be a reminder of 4:4,

---

124. However, that it is evidence of a "primitive eschatology" is mistaken: neither Matthew nor 2 Peter is "primitive," and, as I demonstrate in the commentary, 1 John's interest is firmly fixed in the present.

where the one "in the world" is (presumably) the antichrist; although they also are in the world they do not belong to it, in contrast to the one who properly belongs there but who has been defeated. The difference between the two possibilities is not great and a decision cannot be pushed. For 1 John Jesus' significance is not determined by his life or death in the past, nor by any position with God in the heavenly realm, nor yet by the hope of his future return; Jesus belongs to the present, to the here as well as to the now; his story is their story and he models for them the true meaning of their life.

One last argument establishes the author's point: the opposite of bold confidence would be fear, but fear can only be present if the outcome is uncertain and the attitude of the judge unpredictable. For fear is prompted by the expectation of being punished, whether deservedly or not. For those familiar with contemporary eschatological expectations the unspoken figure in the argument is surely that of God as judge; it is unlikely to be Jesus (*ekeinos*), since Jesus is not part of 1 John's circle of loving and being loved. The God who is judge can be faced with boldness because the relationship with God has already been defined by love. The love that drives out fear is the love that has its origin in God; by definition God's love is whole and complete in itself, but it needs also to be realized as such in those who believe. Consequently, as in the previous two verses, there is no need to further define either the lover or the loved. Moreover, this is not a general comment on the nature of human relationships, or a summons to ever-greater efforts to love out of one's own resources. The one who looks to the future in apprehension demonstrates that he or she has not been brought fully and completely into the sphere of love that is the sphere of the presence of God.[125]

On this reading, hidden behind this short section lies an unspoken question: How does the love of God relate to the judgment of God? The issue is widely discussed in Jewish and Christian tradition, often in terms of God's mercy and God's justice: does one imperil the other? Because 1 John's horizon of concern is almost entirely restricted to the community of those who confess and who have responded to God, the dilemma is muted; this is particularly so because a dualist framework and realized eschatology do not labor with a painful sensitivity to the failings and inadequacies of those who belong to God. Fear and the prospect of a negative outcome in judgment, it is implied, belong to the realm of death and darkness that they have left behind. First John would not use fear to persuade his readers into more complete obedience or commitment; their task is not to achieve the complete fulfillment of love but to allow it to be enacted on and in them.

---

125. Just as the author speaks of both indwelling in God and of being indwelt by God, so here he speaks of being perfected in love, but in vv. 12 and 17 of love being perfected in them. This simply reinforces the closed circle of mutually reinforcing love, and expresses no significant difference.

Indeed, the author may have adopted the idea of "the day of judgment" from elsewhere without drawing any such conclusions about the identity of the judge or the nature and timing of that day; although the similarity of language with 2:28 might identify this judgment as consequent upon "his" coming, it is striking that in this passage he does not speak of "boldness *before him*" (cf. 3:21). Certainly, it cannot be decided whether he would have seen the judgment as outside the normal course of history, and even as bringing that to an end, or as expressed within or through the events of history (cf. 2:18), something that is often ambiguous elsewhere in early Christian thought. Despite the future associations of the day of judgment, the real concern is with the present; all the main verbs in these two verses are in the present tense, except for the two perfects, "has been made complete," which also look to the present state. There is, therefore, no contradiction with 3:19–22, which also challenged the possibility of condemnation, and affirmed the "boldness we have before God" as a present reality in answered prayer, a theme that will be repeated in 5:14. Confidence is given to believers here and now, and nothing in the future, whether immediate or more ill defined, can change that.

[19] The section ends with repeating the theme of the last stanza of the first section (v. 10), although again there is here no object to the verb "we love." The confidence of the last two verses is rooted not in what believers have achieved or can achieve but in the prior act of God, here emphasized by "first," which as an adjective qualifies God and not God's action alone. God's love not only preceded any human responsive love, but has absolute precedence; God's love belongs to God's own nature as the source and fount of all. As throughout this section, however, God's love is not a general or unfocused concern: it is specific in time and in direction—it is for us. Nonetheless, this does not mean that whether "we do love" is immaterial; the statement masks an imperative, and the following verses will establish this.

### 1 John 4:20–5:4—Obedience to God and Love for Others

The final section of this extended reflection on love returns to where it began in 4:7, to love among those who believe. This structural symmetry is achieved out of bringing disparate materials together. Whereas the love experienced in the community has been in the form of love "for one another," here the formula is of love for "the brother," and this itself is identified as obedience to God's command, a theme that has not so far served as a motivation nor has it been needed as one. Other elements will also point to this section as working within a different framework of ideas, although not one that contradicts anything that has preceded it. As so often, the paragraph, and the section as a whole, conclude with a verse that also introduces the next section. It will be discussed here, and revisited at the beginning of the next section, where its main themes and language are taken up.

4:20 If anyone says, "I love God," and hates his brother,[a] he is a liar. Indeed, the one who does not love his brother whom he has seen cannot love God whom they have not seen.[b] 21 This very command we possess from him, that the one who loves God is also to love their brother. 5:1 Everyone who believes that Jesus is the Christ has been born from God, and everyone who loves the one who begot also loves the one who has been born from him. 2 In this way we recognize that we love the children of God, when we love God and perform[c] his commands. 3 Indeed, this is love of God, that we observe his commands—and his commands are not burdensome; 4 because everything that has been born from God conquers the world, and this is the victory that conquered the world, our faith.

a. Or "and sister"; see commentary and note a on 2:9.
b. A number of manuscripts phrase this as a question, "how can they love God . . . ?" (so also KJV).
c. A number of manuscripts read "and keep," the author's usual verb with "commands."

[20–21] The author reverts to a style more characteristic of earlier parts of the letter, proposing scenarios only to dismiss them as self-evidently flawed. Instead of engaging his readers by appeal to the shared convictions of faith and of experience of divine presence, he is drawing them into a pattern of logical necessity. It may be that he is appealing to traditions he had used previously, perhaps to recall the rhetorical consensus he had achieved then, that love or hatred of one's fellow community member was the acid test and the real demonstration of belonging to the light or to the darkness (2:9–11). In contrast to the "if we say . . ." of the debate about sin (1:6–10), however, the more neutral "if anyone says" carefully distances such a possibility from the actual experience of his readers; after the emphatic "we/us" of the previous verses they would not see themselves included in this hypothetical "anyone." The label "liar" given the person whose words were contradicted by their deeds has already located them on the side of all that denies God's truth (2:4); the same epithet has been applied to those who denied Jesus as the Christ (2:22). All this has contributed to the creation of a world in which what does and should characterize the community of readers is decisively distanced from any other possibility. The coherent world of the lie, which has nothing to do with the truth (2:21), is in the main a rhetorical antitype whose purpose is to establish the contrasting coherence of the belief and practice of the readers. It follows that an actual external match is not implied; there is no suggestion, for example, that the shadowy antichrists of 2:18 claimed to love God but self-evidently failed to love their faith siblings, perhaps simply by separating from them. The author does not need to rely on what anyone else did in order to prove his point, nor is it his intention to engage in apologetics to explain alternative behavior: the point has already been established by the argument of the letter, and the alternative merely serves as a rhetorical restatement.

This is the first time the letter has spoken explicitly of someone loving God, although it is implicit in at least some occurrences of the ambiguous "love of God" (see commentary on 2:5; 3:17; and especially 2:15); in 4:10 it had been denied that love is determined by "our" prior love of God, but that such love was possible was not denied. Here it is expected that believers do love God, and that in principle they are right to say that they do so. It is characteristic of the biblical tradition that those who love God are those who faithfully respond to God; this is particularly the case where Deuteronomy, already echoed by 4:10, is influential. There, the fundamental call to Israel, the Shema, is to "love the LORD your God with all your heart, and with all your soul, and with all your might" (Deut 6:5; cf. 5:10; Isa 56:6). Love for God is not defined in contrast to some other emotion or to the absence of any, but in contrast to allegiance to some other deity; hence it is axiomatic there that to love God is to serve God and to obey God's commands (Deut 30:19–20). Given this biblical background, it is improbable that there actually were people presently or previously associated with the readers who were in danger of separating an emotional response to God from an obedient commitment. It is also unlikely that anyone would have understood such love along the lines of later developments in Christian thought, where love of God comes to mean a deeply personal, inner, almost mystical experience,[126] which conceptually might be isolated from committed action. Yet the author does envisage a danger of separating response to God from response to one's fellow believer.

At 2:9–11, shaped by the dualist framework, love belonged to the sphere of light, hatred to the sphere of darkness, and there was no intermediate space, no neutrality; that the object of love or hatred was specifically one's fellow believer was crucial for the author but was not necessarily fundamental to the logic, except in so far as love might be expected to be operative only within its own realm. Here the focus is different; although the antithesis of love and hatred is retained, the argument turns on the necessary connectedness between the objects of love, God and fellow believer. Hatred is defined as not loving rather than by any positive demeanor or action. The first stage of the argument is more effective rhetorically than it is logically.[127] Again there is an antithesis, but it is one between God who has not been seen, and the fellow believer who has been seen. The former echoes 4:12 (see commentary), but the verb "seen" (*heōraken*), used in both clauses here, is that also used at John 1:18 (cf. 1 John 3:6).

---

126. Compare Augustine's oft-quoted, "Late have I loved you, beauty ever ancient ever new. . . . You have touched me, and I am afire with the desire for your embraces" (*Confessions* 10.27).

127. Although *gar* is sometimes translated consequentially ("for"), it is here better rendered as emphatic, "indeed"; see also 5:3.

Where love is construed in largely emotional terms it might be natural to retort that it is somewhat easier to love someone not seen than the visible person who confronts one with his or her inescapable needs and unloveliness; but where love is construed as active commitment and requires a recipient of service, the concrete immediacy of the fellow believer provides a tangible measure of the otherwise intangible.

At the second stage of the argument the necessary twofold love is mandated by the commandment whose source ("from him") might be either God or Jesus (cf. 3:23). Earlier, the command was defined as belief in Jesus Christ and love *for one another*, the latter, as noted, often seen as the characteristic Johannine form of the (new) love command (3:23; cf. 3:11 and commentary). Here the command combines love for God, which it takes for granted in the person addressed, with love *for one's fellow believer* ("*brother*"), the alternative formulation distinctive to this letter and largely limited to the phrase, "the one who loves" (see 2:9; 3:10b–11 [see commentary], 14–15). However, the linking of love of God with love of other recalls the Synoptic tradition of the Great Commandment, in which Jesus brings together the call to love the Lord in Deut 6:5 and Lev 19:18, "You shall love your neighbor as yourself" (Mark 12:29–31; perhaps closer is Luke 10:27, where there is no reference to first and second).[128] In relation to this tradition there has been much debate as to whether Jesus was the first to combine the two commands, love of God and love of neighbor, or whether this was already familiar in Jewish tradition. However this may be, there is no suggestion in this passage that the author is conscious of the earlier sources, either in the Torah or in the Jesus tradition, and the apparent parallel with the latter may be fortuitous. A similar combination is characteristic once again of the *Testaments of the Twelve Patriarchs*: "love the Lord with all your life and each other with a sincere heart" (*T. Dan* 5.6; cf. *T. Iss.* 5.2; *T. Benj.*; 3.3, 4); here too it is not at all certain that there is any conscious echo of Lev 19:18. It is very possible that in early Jewish and Christian traditions love of God and love of the other were being combined in different forms and in different settings, and 1 John achieves it through its own internal logic.

[5:1–2] The inextricable bond between love of God and love of sibling relies on something even more fundamental. The author has already described those who believe as born from God, not by their own effort but by God's begetting (2:29; 3:9). The opening words follow the same pattern ("everyone who . . ."), if not coming from the same source then modeled on it (see introduction to commentary on 2:29–3:12, and also 4:7–8). Although the image of begetting points to the individual and to their relationship with God, it necessarily carries with it the corporate; the metaphor forces attention on those others who also owe their being to God's begetting more than does the language of indwelling or possessing,

---

128. See commentary on 3:11 for the near equivalence of "neighbor" and "brother."

which can retain a restricted focus on the individual. The argument might appear to run that anyone who loves God necessarily loves a God who begets offspring; love of those others who like oneself are begotten by God follows inescapably. To fail in this would be to fail in love of God as the begetter even of oneself. The author does not see believers as a family, bound to exhibit familial affection to one another; he does not use the language of "brothers" alongside that of begetting, and he knows that brotherly relationships are not necessarily loving ones (3:12). The horizontal relationship is always mediated through God; it is as "children of God" (v. 2; cf. 3:1 and commentary) that believers love those also begotten of God, not as their newly discovered brothers or sisters.

However, the author adds yet a further layer to his argument. Rather than define the one who is born from God as the one who loves (cf. 4:7), as would well suit the argument of the last paragraph, he describes them in terms of their belief. For attentive readers this reinforces the description of the one who fails in love as a liar (4:20), for the liar is the one who denies that Jesus is the Christ (2:22). This serves as a reminder that the one to be loved is the one who shares in that confession. A further nuance reinforces this: although the verb is given no object, it is probable that God, who as begetter is loved, is specifically God as the one who begot Jesus; this is indicated by the aorist participle ("who begot," *gennēsanta*), in contrast to the perfect tense consistently used of those begotten or born from God (see on 2:29). The deliberate contrast in tenses is confirmed at the end of the letter where "the one born [aorist] from God," to be identified with "the Son of God" two verses later, is able to protect "the one who has been born," the perfect participle (5:18; see commentary). So understood, it is striking that the same verb is used of God's relationship with Jesus and with believers; this contrasts with 1 John's restriction of "Son" (*huios*) to Jesus and of "children" (*tekna*, always plural) to believers (see commentary on 3:1; see also 4:9, "only begotten," and commentary). On one level believers are brought into a relationship that they share with that between Jesus and God but that is not identical to it. However, although as a result of later christological controversy the terminology of this verse would become enshrined in the words of the Nicene Creed, "begotten not made," here there are no grounds for asking whether the aorist points to a specific moment of the begetting of the Son, either in preexistence or in Jesus' ministry. First John is not concerned with relations within the Godhead but with a set of relationships into which believers are drawn along with the one in whom they believe, the author of which is always God.[129]

129. Some patristic interpreters who recognized "the begetter" as a reference to the divine Father-Son relationship also interpreted "the one who is born/begotten" as a reference to the Son: believers are to love both Father and Son (e.g., Augustine, *Commentary on 1 John* 10.3). The verse was then used against the Arians, who argued that the Son was *created* like the rest of creation (Faustinus, *On the Trinity* 2.10–13). The Latin translation is more conducive to this interpretation, as it does not distinguish the perfect tense of the participle in the Greek.

Therefore, those who make this confession of faith in Jesus love God not in some general or unidentified way but as the God who is the origin of the object of their belief; their belief is not a chance bond that unites them, which perhaps could be replaced by some other shared practice or conviction, but establishes the framework within which love for God and love for fellow believer is made both possible and necessary. If their horizontal relationship is always mediated through God, it is equally determined by everything that is implied by the simple confession, "Jesus is the Christ." This means that that confession can be understood only in the light of the whole section that began in 4:7. This was already anticipated by the acknowledgment of Jesus as Son of God in 4:15, a confession that was imbued with a much richer content in the light of the previous celebrations of God's love in sending the Son (4:9, 14) than was possible in the earlier allusive confession in 2:23. For the readers, the epithet "Christ" did not refer to concepts that might be identified elsewhere, whether in Jewish or other patterns of thought, but specifically evoked the story of what God had achieved through him (see commentary on 4:15).

There follows one of the reversals of expectation characteristic of 1 John's style. The logic of the preceding verses would suggest that love shown to fellow believers helps confirm love for God. Instead the opposite is stated: love for God confirms—it is how "we know" that we show—love for those who are also children of God, for it provides the context where ("when") such love is exercised. The effect is to set love for God at the center from which all else radiates. The description of fellow believers as "the children of God" rather than as brother/ sister belongs to the set of ideas associated with God as begetter (2:29–3:2; 3:9–10), but it also recalls the uncompromising opposition expressed in the last use of that phrase—the incompatibility between the children of God and the children of the devil (3:10; see commentary).[130] Hence it serves to exclude as much as to include, and to that extent so does love. Love is measured at this point not by what it does but by the cohesive bonds of unassailable unity that it forges; the unity is, however, determined by a status of being children of God, which is given not to all humankind but only to those who recognize in one another that they share the same convictions.

This does not mean that love, including love for God, is nothing more than warm feelings of devotion or even than consuming rapture; "and perform his commands" is not a further requirement nor a pragmatic afterthought but is intrinsic to the same intentional commitment. As elsewhere (2:3–4, 7–8; 3:22–24), the plural "commands" does not specify anything in addition to the one command to love (and to believe, 3:23). If the author had been aware of several commandments, no doubt he would have said that they are all encompassed in that one. However, the same variation between plural and singular is

---

130. As in 3:10 (contrast 3:1), both nouns have the article.

found in Deuteronomy, whose language he echoes several times in this section
(Deut 30:10–11); there too love to God both precedes and ensues from obedience to God's commands—love is the expression of and is expressed in obser-
vance (Deut 30:6–8, 16). Like Deuteronomy, 1 John does not make distinctions
between willing ("believing") and doing (emphasized by the specific choice of
"perform" [*poieō*] here), between commitment and its expression in action;
each is implicated in the other. The reader experiences this unity as the argument returns again to the point at which this paragraph started (4:21); the literary structure reinforces the theological argument.

**[3]** The issue is sufficiently important to require restating, reinforced by a,
for this author rare, "Indeed" (*gar*; otherwise only at 2:19 and 4:20 [see note
b]). Elsewhere the characteristic formula, "and this is," recalls readers to the
certainties they have heard and the confidence they experience (1:5; 2:25; 3:11,
23; 5:4, 11, 14); its effect is achieved not by careful logical deduction but by
inviting their assent to something they recognize as true to their experience. The
potentially ambiguous "love of God" (see 2:5) here can only mean "love for
God" (contrast 4:9); the author does not say that love for God *leads* to obedience as if these were two separate activities (as might be suggested by the similar John 14:15, where Jesus is the object of love), but that the latter, obedience,
is the content[131] of the former. This does not diminish love to a mechanical ser-
vility but infuses obedience with total commitment. Unlike those parts of the
New Testament and Christian tradition that have struggled to relate "faith" and
"works," this author would not comprehend any attempt to separate between
"love" and "doing" in order then to endeavor to correlate them; here again he
is close to the Deuteronomic tradition. At the same time, the resumption of his
standard formula, "observe his commands" (e.g., 2:3), offers a reminder that
such doing is always in relationship with God.

That God's commands are not burdensome again echoes Deuteronomy (Deut
30:11); therefore there is no contrast with the Jewish law, nor is it setting one easily comprehended command—since the plural is used here—against a plethora
of obscure ones. In Deuteronomy the command is accessible because it is not
arcane or the prerogative of the priests alone but is internalized within the people as the people of God. First John does share the idea that all have knowledge
of the truth (2:20, 27); however, even if the echo from Deuteronomy were identified, the following verse indicates that much more than that is intended here.

**[4]** The author abruptly drops the themes of love and of God's command(s),
neither of which appears again in the letter. This might suggest that this verse

---

131. This is the distinctively Johannine explanatory use of the conjunction *hina* (cf. 3:23); the
less likely alternative would be to take "and this is" as summarizing the previous verses, and "that
we keep his commands" as expressing purpose ("in order that . . .").

marks a new section, and it will be continued by verse 5; however, it is also connected with what precedes, both in language and as providing the reason (*hoti*) why God's commands are not burdensome. According to verse 1, love is restricted to those who have been born of God, and is determined by that state; it serves to identify them and to set them apart. Therefore, such love belongs to the new sphere of existence to which they belong, a sphere of existence that already manifests the eschatological goals. In general terms it might follow that if love, like truth, belongs to the sphere of God and of those who belong to God, then just as they already know the truth, so surely must they already be assumed to love both God and one another; God's commands will be entirely natural to them and hence not burdensome. The author is less direct than this, however, and instead he recalls earlier themes from the letter; once again the effect is to use structure and language to mirror the interconnectedness he wishes to create among his readers. Chapter 3 and the first part of chapter 4 have framed the existence of those who believe and love in sharply dualistic terms, chiefly against the world (*kosmos*). This dualism has been largely absent from the long section on love that began at 4:7, but now it reemerges in the image of victory over the world. In 4:4 the author assured them that they had already gained a victory over those who opposed them; they belong to God, and against them are arrayed those whose source and origin is the world. The world, they have previously been reminded, is not only opposed to God but is also associated with hatred, and is not to be loved (2:15; 3:13). Here he reiterates that victory; this time, however, the verb "conquers" is in the present tense, perhaps signaling that this is something in which each can participate. Obedience and love are possible because of such participation.

The winner of victory in this verse is not "you," but is "everything that has been born from God." The repetition of the perfect passive participle "born" or "begotten" provides a satisfying conclusion to verse 1, where God's begetting was what bound the one who loves and the one who is loved together. Yet characteristically a subtle change draws the attention to a new note. Whereas a simple resumption of verse 1 would require the masculine form, "*everyone who* has been born/begotten" (cf. 3:9; 5:18), here any neat symmetry is disrupted by the unexpected neuter, "*everything that* [*pan to*] has been begotten." Taken on its own the neuter "everything" might encompass love and truth, and even God's commands, which, it would follow, are not burdensome because they are means of victory; this would offer a partial parallel to the second half of this verse, where "faith" is identified as the conquering victory itself.

However, the image of begetting or birth seems best suited to persons, and elsewhere in the letter the perfect passive participle is used always of a believer (masculine singular). It seems most likely that the reference is the same here: in this case the neuter is best understood in a collective sense, in place of an implied plural ("all those who have been begotten"), a form 1 John nowhere employs. A similar unexpected neuter singular is found in the Gospel of John, in places where the context again implies a reference to believers (John 6:37, 39; 17:2, with the perfect of the verb "give"); it seems that this form was a familiar stylistic peculiarity. Here it enables the author to ascribe victory to them in their totality, as opposed to suggesting that believers conquer the world as individuals. The neuter also indicates that the source of their victory does not lie in they themselves but in the re-creative power of God manifested in them. If birth from God defines the circle in which love is demanded, it also defines the circle in which love and obedience are made possible. Outside that circle, in the world, God's commands would not be merely burdensome; they would be incomprehensible and ineffectual.

Although it has been possible to trace a logic in the connection between verses 3 and 4, it is not an immediately self-evident one; despite the connective "because" (*hoti*), the impression is given that the author's mind has jumped to a new thought, which now takes him in a different direction. The second part of the verse goes further down this route and will be discussed in the next section of the commentary. Yet in speaking of "faith" (*pistis*) it recalls 4:1, which identified the one born from God as the one who believes (*pisteuō*). For 1 John, belief and love for God and for one another are not separable from each other; one cannot be given priority over the other.

Although 1 John's great affirmations that God is love and that to dwell in love is to dwell in God have sometimes been accorded ultimate authority, overriding any other criteria of distinction or of judgment, this is not how the author wished to apply them. For him their realization could be conceived of only within the community of those who steadfastly held to the same beliefs, and who refused any compromise. His world was not one of an all-embracing and equalizing love, but one of sharp distinctions, between light and darkness, truth and falsehood, God and the world, love and hatred. If God as love cannot be understood apart from the story of the sending of God's Son, identified with the story of Jesus, then that love always remains tied to commitment to that story. In the context within which 1 John was written, what mattered was to maintain the vision of a community of those who, united in their belief, are also united at every level with one another; it was a vision that was sustained by the conviction that they were surrounded by forces that opposed them but that would never triumph. In other circumstances later generations might have the freedom to recognize that a vision that looks only inward can be as destructive as it can be creative, and that what has been experienced of God through faith must be true of every aspect and relation of God. Yet 1 John offers the challenge of holding together confidence in God as the ultimate creative and procreative source, with a serious recognition of the reality of the forces that oppose and that deny any confession of God's love.

## 1 John 5:4–13—Belief in the Son of God

The importance of right confession or belief has not been absent from the long section about loving that began with 4:7 (cf. 4:15; 5:1), but it now becomes the dominant theme of this section. Whereas up to this point it has seemed enough to emphasize that Jesus must be acknowledged as the Christ or as the Son of God, now that description appears to need further explanation. In 4:2 a different expansion of the core confession was provoked by the need to distinguish between "the spirits." Here there is no explicit alternative position in view, no reference to the antichrists or false prophets. This has not prevented many interpreters from detecting a polemic behind the confession in verse 6, although the lack of consensus as to how this is to be explained would imply that the author is being even more allusive or enigmatic than elsewhere. I will argue here that although the passage is obscure, a reasonable sense can be made without an appeal to an implied alternative position, and that this simpler approach is not only preferable but also accords best with the general ethos of the letter. The author's concern is not only with the precise identification of the core belief, but also with why that belief is to be held. As in 4:1–3, authentic belief is found in the presence of the spirit, but here there is no suggestion that there might be more than one spirit, or that the spirit is not to be trusted without discrimination. However, the ultimate authority for believing in Jesus as Son of God lies in God: belief does not move from Jesus to God but from God to God's Son. Any relationship with God is by definition a relationship with God's Son; there can be no relationship with God that excludes God's Son. The importance of this section is marked by the last of the author's references to his own intentions, where he also repeats the offer of eternal life made in the prologue to the letter. Although a general outline of the passage is possible, the train of thought is very dense and allusive, so that details are bound to remain debated; in addition, the passage has provoked a variety of textual variants, and these have been of considerable importance in subsequent thought.

### 1 John 5:4–8—Jesus, the Son of God

This passage does not argue, or offer alternative views, neither does it command; it makes a series of statements, which move in rapid progression from believers and their faith, to Jesus as the object of their faith, and to the grounds of confidence—the testimony on which they rely. At the heart of this is the affirmation of precisely who this Jesus is; he is Son of God, but this means that the Son of God is none other than the one through whose human life they experience life and forgiveness. Verse 4, which provided a climax to the previous section, also initiates this new one, and so will be repeated in the translation.

**5:4** For everything that has been born from God conquers the world, and this is the victory that conquered the world, our faith. **5** Who is the one who conquers the world? Only the one who believes that Jesus is the Son of God. **6** This is he who came by means of water and blood,[a] Jesus Christ, not only by[b] the water but by the water and by the blood.[c] The spirit is that which testifies, because the spirit[d] is the truth. **7** For there are three who testify,[e] **8** the spirit, and the water, and the blood, and the three are in agreement.[f]

a. A number of manuscripts add "and spirit," probably under the influence of John 3:5 and in the light of vv. 6–8.

b. Or "with" or "in" (see commentary).

c. Although this is undoubtedly the earliest reading, there is considerable textual variation in the order of the terms, some manuscripts adding (or substituting) "and by the spirit."

d. The Vulgate reads "Christ"; cf. John 14:7.

e. Within the early Latin tradition vv. 7–8 provoked the addition of a reference to the three witnesses, Father, Word (or Son), and Spirit, sometimes specified as "in heaven" in contrast to the three original witnesses "on earth" (an expansion known as the *Comma Iohanneum*). This addition subsequently entered the Greek text and thence the text followed by KJV. See further the commentary.

f. Those who expanded the text understood this as "are a unity," but this, although possible, is less persuasive.

**[4–5]** As already noted, verse 4 provides a transition from the previous section with its emphasis on love as the defining mark of those who are in relationship with God; such a relationship is, however, inseparable from belief in the true identity of Jesus. Just as love bound them together with one another and with God, and in so doing decisively separated them from all that opposes God, "the world," so too does the belief that they share. Earlier in the letter the author had assured his readers that victory over the world was already theirs (4:4). The metaphor was drawn from the common idea of a final battle at the end of time between God and the forces on God's side, against all that opposed God; this picture is even more evident in his previous encouragement to the "young men" that they had conquered the evil one (2:13, 14; see commentary). The victory did not lie in their own achievements but in the superiority of the one who indwelt them, and so they were encouraged to see their own struggles as the scene or articulation of a conflict of cosmological dimensions.

In 2:13–14 and 4:4 the perfect tense emphasized their complete possession of victory, no longer a future hope but a present certainty. In the first part of verse 4 the present tense, "conquers," pointed to the expression of that victory in their own experience and situation, while the subject, "everything that has been born from God" (see above), made clear that the source of victory ultimately lay not in themselves but with God. In the second part of the verse both subject and tense change, and attention focuses inward, on their response, as where victory is to be found. The subject of the verb is now "victory": although this noun (*nikē*, only here in the NT) might refer to the means by which the victory was won, the personification of victory itself (herself) was a common visual motif particularly celebrating the emperor's achievements, for example on coins; perhaps readers are being invited to visualize their own alternative symbol of triumph. This is their "faith" (*pistis*), a noun that covers a spectrum including the subjective emotion, whether directed to a person (trust, commitment) or to something about them (faith that), and the personal quality (faithfulness, loyalty, but also reliability) that expresses or inspires such commitment, as well as that which is believed (cf. Jude 3); at times elements of each of these come together to represent the proper response to God as revealed and known (cf. Luke 18:8; Hebrews 11). Although important elsewhere in the New Testament, *pistis* appears only here in the Johannine literature, but already in 1 John the verb "to believe" (*pisteuō*) has included confidence, commitment, and trust, as well as indicating a specific content (see commentary on 3:23). While no doubt the author would have agreed that the facts in which they believed, the true identity of Jesus, proclaimed how the victory over the world had been won, it is their response and commitment that has embodied and realized that victory, and that is labeled *pistis*.[132] The aorist tense ("conquered") draws attention to the completed achievement, the moment of victory, although this need not be limited to a specific event, such as the conversion or the baptism of the original readers (see 2:7, 27 and commentary). Where faith is found, so too is the triumph over all that opposes God, but this is not some generalized faith or trust, but a faith that has a particular expression and content.

From the neuter or abstract language of verse 4, the author turns (v. 5) to the individual who believes, and who in believing also participates in the victory over all that opposes God, again summarized as "the world." Here the author repeats for the last time his core confession of belief, that Jesus is the Son of God (cf. 4:15); after expanding it (v. 6) he will not again mention "Jesus" until the letter's end (v. 20), but "the Son of God" becomes the focus of each remaining section of the letter ("Son of God/his Son," 5:9, 10 [2 times], 11, 12, 13, 20 [2 times]; cf. "the Son," 5:12). As has become evident, for the author acknowledgment of Jesus as Son of God gives shape to and properly defines the belief that Jesus is the Christ (2:23; 5:1; cf. 3:23 and commentary on 4:15). On one level, then, this declaration might be read as completing the circle that began in the first verse of the chapter: everyone who believes that Jesus is the Christ = has been born from God; (v. 4, everything born from God) = conquers

---

132. We may compare and contrast John 16:33, where Jesus declares that *he* has conquered (the perfect tense) the world.

the world; (v. 5, the one who conquers the world) = is the one who believes that Jesus is the Son of God. This imagery of birth/begetting has offered a possibility of exploring a new nuance in the framework within which both "Christ" and "Son of God" are to be understood (see 5:1); but the author has not yet finished such exploring, and this verse, therefore, does not only look back but drives forward.

**[6]** Underlying the author's thought thus far have been two apparently separate ways of speaking about Jesus as Son. On the one hand there is "*the Son,*" each time mentioned in close connection with God, designated as "the Father" (1:3; 4:10, 14; cf. 2:22b–23), and named, without any hint of controversy, Jesus Christ (1:3; 2:1; 3:23).[133] The second pattern, the title or role "*the Son of God,*" first appeared in chapter 3 as a quasi-mythical figure whose task was the destruction of the similarly quasi-mythical devil (3:8; see commentary), but he was not yet further identified. Subsequently, the author stipulates the cardinal belief that Jesus is the Son of God, just as he is *the* Christ, itself also a title (2:22; 4:15; 5:1, 5). The third person form of these confessions, "the one who . . . ," reflects the author's concern to use them as benchmarks for identifying those who truly belong. Already in chapter 4 these two patterns were implicitly brought together, at least to the extent of setting "our" certain experience of God's love in the (Father's) sending of *the Son* alongside the affirmation of "the one who acknowledges" Jesus as *the Son of God* (4:10, 14–15). Despite the unequivocal demand that Jesus be so identified, there is only a limited sense of what further ideas or stories either "Jesus" or "Jesus Christ" would evoke for author or for readers; references to "that one" have shown that they knew something of his life and death (2:6; 3:16), but that it was his exemplary or present significance that was of greater impact (3:3, 5; cf. 2:1). This impact, however, would only be effective because Jesus Christ "having come in flesh" is one who unmistakably belongs to the sphere of human experience (4:2; see commentary).

A similar point seems to be at issue in this verse, but the author's choice of words is obscure, most probably echoing formulae that would carry more meaning for his first readers than they do for contemporary ones. It is not enough to say that Jesus is the Son of God (v. 5), for from this follows something rather more precise. If this Son of God is Jesus Christ, he does not only belong to the divine sphere, or to the cosmic or "mythical" stage on which the devil is at work (3:8); in specific circumstances he "came"—the same verb as in 4:2 (*erchomai*) but here used in the punctiliar aorist tense.[134] The manner or means of this coming demands particular emphasis: first the author describes this as "by means

---

133. In these cases "Christ" is part of the name, not a title.
134. As in 4:2 in a participle, although here with the article.

of" water and blood, and then, as if to exclude any doubt, reiterates that this is no less "by the blood" than it is "by the water." Quite what is at stake here is disputed, as also is whether there is any significance in the change of preposition, from "by means of" (or "through," *dia*) to the repeated "by" (or "with," "in," *en*), as well as in the introduction of the article, "the," with the latter, or whether they are only for stylistic variation.

Among the questions to be answered are: What do "water" and "blood" represent, and to what does "to come by means of" these refer? Do they signify actual, physical, water and blood or are they symbols for something else? Does their meaning change either with the change of preposition or when they are joined by "the spirit" to form the three witnesses (v. 8)? Does the emphatic "not only by the water" suggest that some might have thought that this was the case? If so, is the final emphasis primarily on "the blood [*also*]" or is it on the two components in combination with each other? Is the main thrust polemical, against those holding alternative views, or is it primarily making an affirmative point for the readers?

Proposed solutions to the dilemma may be loosely grouped as belonging to one of three types, although the possibility of a switch in reference between verse 6 and verse 8 could allow for a combination of these.

1. A *christological solution* identifies the concern as to do with the nature of Jesus Christ's human identity.

a. Understanding water and blood as physical realities, some would identify them with the male and female components in the conception of the child (as understood in ancient science), or else with the processes (or associated phenomena) of actual birth from a mother. So understood, the coming of this Son of God was not extraordinary or extraterrestrial but bound by the conditions of all human conception and birth. Seen as polemical, this affirmation would be targeted against any who held the human embodiment and experience of Jesus to be a matter of appearance only, a view often labeled docetic (see commentary on 4:2).[135] Against this interpretation, however, is that the wording appears to be a very allusive way of emphasizing something that easily could be more clearly expressed—such as by Ignatius's "of the race of David, of Mary, who was truly born" (*Trall.* 9). Indeed, "through" or "with" might itself allow something less than total identification with the human processes.

b. One widely accepted symbolic interpretation of water and blood refers them to the baptism and to the death of Jesus: so understood, the Son of God's participation in human experience encompassed both his baptism and his death. The baptism practiced by John, and in the Synoptic Gospels undergone by

---

135. An alternative suggestion is that it is targeted against those who believed that Jesus was not Son of God from birth but only after his exaltation, though this faces the same objections.

Jesus, is "by [or "in," *en*] water" (Mark 1:8; John 1:26, 31, 33).[136] This interpretation has often been supported by reference to the view held by some early
Christians, especially associated with Cerinthus, the legendary opponent of the
apostle John, that the divine element (here "Son of God") descended upon the
ordinary human Jesus at his baptism and departed prior to his death, thus ensuring that the impassible Divine was in no way implicated in suffering (see commentary on 4:2 and Introduction §2.2). Alternatively, Ignatius appears to be
combating a less developed view of this kind when he denounces those who say
that "he appeared to suffer" (*Trall*. 10). While this reading rightly recognizes
that "Son of God" is the leading subject of the verb "came," the polemical effectiveness of the author's riposte is weak. In particular, while the specific emphasis on "by the blood" (i.e., that he did experience death) may be so explained,
it implies that the author did accept that the human story of the Son of God
began with the baptism (i.e., "by the water," which is affirmed). Such an understanding, often described as a form of adoptionism, was held by some in the
early church, and it may lie behind early versions of the baptism story and of
God's words there (Mark 1:11), but on this reading the author accepted both it
and his (supposed) opponents' use of it.[137] One solution to this difficulty would
be to take "water" as referring not to Jesus' baptism but to his human birth, in
parallel to the suggestion sometimes made at John 3:5, being "born out of water
and spirit"; the emphasis would then be on his real participation in death as well
as in birth. Even so, the positive point could have been more directly expressed;
although the initial formula "came by means of/through (*dia*)" could be understood as indicating the manner and moment of his manifestation, the alternative "by" is particularly imprecise for either meaning. For example, Ignatius
defends his position by a more effective repeated "truly born . . . truly crucified
and died" (*Trall*. 9; cf. *Smyrn*. 1–2). Although this view and the similar interpretation of 4:2 ("having come in flesh"; see commentary) might be taken as
reciprocally reinforcing, the differences between the two expressions and the
indirectness of both make this a precarious alliance.

2. A *soteriological solution* identifies the concern as not so much with the
past person of Jesus Christ but with how the saving effects of the Son of God's
advent were brought about and are now appropriated. This focus is in accord
with the letter's general interest in what has been achieved through the sending

---

136. John does not explicitly refer to Jesus' baptism, although it can be inferred from John's
mission and testimony (John 1:31–34). In some manuscripts at John 1:31 and 33 the article "the"
is added ("in the water"), providing an even closer parallel to 1 John 5:6, but this may be due to
influence from the latter passage. See further below.

137. See further below; in a framework other than a polemical christological one this may be
less unlikely.

of the Son and in what is available for believers now (3:8; 4:10). A present sote-riological interest is also the context of the only other mention of "blood" in the letter: *"the blood* of Jesus his *Son* cleanses us from all sin" (1:7).

a. Understood from this perspective, Jesus' baptism ("by water"; see above) signals his identification with the human situation; but for the author forgiveness is not brought about by this alone, independently of his death ("by blood") also. The primary emphasis, therefore, is on the salvific nature of Jesus' death.[138] This view is easily combined with a christological emphasis on Jesus' death (cf. 1b); how is redemption possible if not by the true death of the redeemer?

b. An alternative interpretation of this type would not take "by water" as bear-ing baptismal associations—for which an accompanying appropriate verb or noun might be expected. Although "water" does not otherwise occur in the Johannine Letters, the first audience may have associated it with "life," as in the Gospel (John 4:10–15; 7:38), or with cleansing and forgiveness, as elsewhere in the scriptural tradition (Ezek 36:25), both important themes in 1 John. At 2:2, where similar phrasing is used, *"not only* for our sins" is not separate from or of lesser value than *"but also* for the whole world," but may even be the determi-native element without which the latter cannot be the case. In the same way here the real emphasis may be on the life-giving (or cleansing) water within whose symbolic significance Jesus' death is also to be understood: paraphrased, he came as a means of, or to bring, life, and this is also available through his death; or, perhaps, he came as a means of, or to bring, life ("water"), and also to offer forgiveness ("blood"), on which the former depends and through which it is real-ized. The attraction of this solution is its conformity with the author's overall interest in believers' appropriation of what Jesus or the Son makes available; its weakness is that it does not adequately account for the aorist participle "came" or for the curious choice of prepositions ("by means of/by").

3. A *sacramental* approach interprets "in water" as a reference not to Jesus' baptism but to that undergone by believers. Once this association is made it is easy to conclude that the second element, "blood," refers to the eucharist: the benefits brought by the Son of God are appropriated not by baptism alone but by both baptism and eucharist. This seems the least persuasive reading: while some have seen allusions to baptism elsewhere in the letter, for example in the "anointing" (2:20, 27), these are tenuous, and it would be extremely difficult to identify any eucharistic overtones. Moreover, while there are occasions where "bread" on its own may indicate the meal commemorating Jesus' death (Acts 2:42, 46), that the wine or cup, and still less the blood it represents, would do so is without parallel. Neither does this interpretation adequately account for

---

138. This is sometimes then used to understand the coming "in flesh" of 4:2 as a reference to Jesus' death (see John 6:51).

the emphatic "he who came." However, some interpreters who reject a sacramental reference in verse 6 do find one in verse 8 (see below).

One difficulty in reaching a certain conclusion is the suspicion that the author is alluding to phraseology or formulae that were familiar to the first audience but that elude later ones. The prepositional phrases that strike us as obscure and oddly chosen for them may have been entirely unproblematic. There is probably some support for this supposition in the curious incident found only in John's account of Jesus' death, when a soldier stabs Jesus' side with a spear, "and immediately there came out blood and water" (John 19:34)—although the reverse order should not be ignored. This obscure passage has been subject to a similar range of contested interpretations to that in 1 John, so that neither one can throw definitive light on the other. However, that there is some relationship between them may be confirmed by the presence in the broader context in the Gospel of the themes of the spirit and of witnesses, which are also developed in the following verses in 1 John (John 19:30, 35).[139] A similar conjunction of language occurs in the account of John's witness to Jesus, where the one sent to baptize "in water" saw the "spirit" descending on him and "bore witness" that "this one is the Son of God" (John 1:32–34); although there is no reference to blood here, some would see it implied by John's description of Jesus as "the lamb of God who takes away the sin of the world" (John 1:29, 36; see commentary on 3:5).

These passages do not provide the solution to the meaning of 1 John 5:6, but they do confirm that the author was appealing to ideas that readers would recognize and affirm. That in the Gospel these ideas were tied to the actual ministry of Jesus and, together, specifically to his baptism and death, does not demand that the author of 1 John used them in the same way; divergence in application and reference of shared language and concepts has been the main characteristic of the relationship between the two writings. On the other hand, particularly if he were not opposing alternative views, the author may well have only considered to be relevant (or may only have known) the story of Jesus that began with his baptism; the Fourth Gospel, similarly, has no interest in the physical birth and origins of Jesus. In addition to a background within Johannine ideas, here, as elsewhere, 1 John's language also echoes a more extensive early Christian vocabulary. The prepositional phrases "by means of (his) blood" and "by (his) blood" are used by other New Testament writers of the saving effects of Jesus' death, without being tied to any one understanding of this (*dia*: Acts 20:28; Eph 1:7; Col 1:20; Heb 9:12; 13:12; Rev 12:11; *en*: Luke 22:20; Rom 3:25; 5:9; 1 Cor 11:25; Eph 2:13; Heb 10:19; Rev 1:5; 5:9). Their combination with the verb "to come" is not paralleled, but in the Gospel of John it

---

139. Although this is weakened if John 19:30 is understood as Jesus surrendering his breath (*pneuma*).

is as "the one who comes/came" that Jesus is most often characterized (cf. also 1 John 4:2; 2 John 7, and commentary). This strengthens the probability that the author's intention is to reinforce the achievements and effects of the whole story of the Son of God, including his death, a story they know to be that of Jesus Christ.

Therefore, if the author was evoking a familiar set of images, the force of the verse is not to tell them something they did not already know about Jesus, nor necessarily to challenge an alternative understanding that only accepted it in part; he is emphasizing that the one with whose story they were familiar, and whose significance for them was encapsulated by this set of images, is the Son of God. As seems to be the case with 4:2, the actuality in Jesus of the story of the Son of God necessarily entails his intersection with the conditions of the life lived by those who believe in him. To confess Jesus as Son of God is to affirm as Son of God the one who so came, and whose coming brings the benefits of his death.

Against this broader background the abrupt introduction of the spirit as that which bears witness is less unexpected than it first appears. Earlier in the letter the spirit is God's gift, which authenticates the experience of divine indwelling, which itself accompanies proper confession of Jesus (3:23–24; 4:13–15). Although the spirit does not provide testimony in these passages, the second incorporates the declaration, "We ourselves have seen and *testify* that the Father sent his *Son* as savior of the world" (4:14). This parallel might suggest that the spirit's testimony is given to outsiders, as is probably the case in the promise in Jesus' farewell to his disciples in the Gospel, that the Paraclete "will testify concerning me, and you testify because you have been with me from the beginning" (John 15:26–27). However, in what follows it seems that the testimony is given to believers themselves, to confirm them in their belief. Moreover, it does not belong to some past occasion, either in Jesus' life or in that of believers, but is a present reality (cf. also v. 7).

Here, in contrast to 4:1, there is no suggestion that the evidence of the spirit must be subject to scrutiny, or that what appears to be spirit may fail to make the proper confession of Jesus Christ (4:1–3; see commentary). Whereas there "the spirit of truth" was contrasted with "the spirit of error" (4:6), here the spirit is without qualification identified as "the truth." The formulation, rather than "the spirit is true," is typical of the author, echoing "God is light" and "God is love" (1:5; 4:7). "Truth" in 1 John is not an abstract idea (any more than is love), but is most fully expressed in who God is and what God has done (1:8; 2:4). The spirit is not truth in some absolute or independent sense but only because it expresses and embodies God's truth in those to whom it is given.

Although the idea of the spirit in 1 John is far less developed than that in the Gospel, the identification with truth does recall that of the Paraclete as "the

Spirit of truth" in the passage already cited (John 15:26; cf. 14:17).[140] Other passages in the Gospel also confirm that the associations between the spirit and truth and between testimony and truth were familiar within the Johannine tradition (John 4:23–24; 5:32; 8:14; 18:37; 19:35; 21:24; 3 John 3, 12). It is probable that the apparent discontinuities in thought that perplex modern readers would have delighted the first audience as the author anticipated without prompting the more subtle associations that they instinctively made.

[7–8] The next move appears to an even greater extent to be provoked less by any clear logic than by a prior collocation of images. The spirit as the source of testimony is now joined by the water and by the blood. As noted above, some interpreters refer the last two to baptism and to eucharist, which, along with the gift of the spirit, mediate and make real for believers the salvation brought by Jesus as the Son of God. It remains unlikely, however, that blood would bear a eucharistic reference, and a more persuasive solution would allow some continuity with the meaning that water and blood carry in verse 6. The spirit, and life, symbolized by water, and forgiveness, symbolized by the blood, are all given by God and experienced as realities in the lives of those who believe, but are no less grounded in the life and death of the Son sent by God.[141] Each represents a separate and necessary aspect, and yet they are not independent of one another, nor can one be affirmed without the others. This is why they are described as resulting in one thing; it is the testimony they give that is a shared one, not what they are in themselves.

I have already suggested that there is a connection with the scene at Jesus' death in the Fourth Gospel where Jesus' surrender of the spirit/breath is followed by the emission from his side of blood and water (John 19:30, 34–35). There the testimony is borne not by these but by "the one who saw," but the emphasis on the truth of the testimony and on the intention "that you may believe" reflects a similar set of concerns to this passage.[142] A common pattern of reflection, perhaps arising out of traditions of Jesus' death or out of scriptural interpretation (cf. John 19:36–37), has been developed and applied in two different directions.

---

140. The difference between this and the same phrase in 1 John 4:6 was noted above; see commentary.

141. So already Clement of Alexandria (*On the Second Letter of John* [see p. 26]) commented, "'there are three who testify, spirit,' which is life, 'and water,' which is regeneration and faith, 'and blood,' which is understanding, 'and these three are one.' For in the Savior these virtues are agents of salvation, and life itself subsists in his Son himself."

142. Interpreters differ as to whether "the one who saw" is the soldier, the Beloved Disciple, an anonymous witness, or an intertextual allusion to John's testimony (John 1:34). The last possibility and/or also the later repetition "that you may believe *that Jesus is the Christ the Son of God*" (John 20:31) would strengthen the nexus of connections between Gospel and Epistle.

This process of association and reinterpretation or expansion did not halt with the author of 1 John. Once the doctrine of the Trinity began to develop, the presence of the spirit and the final phrase of verse 8, understood as "and the three are a unity," were bound to evoke the unity of the three persons of the Godhead. This was perhaps aided by the fact that the "three who testify" (v. 7) and "the three" (v. 8) are expressed in the masculine plural, despite "spirit," "water," and "blood" all being neuter nouns in Greek, and in contrast to the neuter of the spirit's testifying in verse 6. The simplest expansion of the text merely appended at the end of verse 8 the words "Father, Son, and Holy Spirit, and three are one"; subsequent forms addressed the ungainly effect this has by contrasting the (initial) three who testify "on earth" with the (additional) trinitarian) three who testify "in heaven." Such expansion of the text can be traced back to the early third century, and perhaps earlier, but it was initially restricted to the Latin tradition. Even there it was not unanimous—there are several textual variants, including the alternative of "Son" and "Word"—and it is not found in the main Vulgate manuscripts. Even where there were doubts about its authenticity, however, the value of a scriptural testimony to the Trinity ensured its survival and perhaps prompted its eventual inclusion in a few Greek manuscripts and subsequently into the Received Text (cf. KJV).[143]

Although in retrospect the process of expansion is readily understandable, it does not represent 1 John's understanding of God. Despite the frequent ambiguity as to whether "he" (*autos*) refers to God or to Jesus (e.g., 2:4, 6, 28), and despite the affirmation that only by experiencing or confessing the Son can the Father also be experienced (2:23), 1 John does not reflect theologically on the relationship between them. Moreover, the spirit is not part of this relationship between Father and Son; the spirit is God's spirit and God's gift to believers, but, as has been seen, the concept is still a fluid one (3:24–4:6). This passage brings together God and God's Son in verses 9–12 entirely independently of the mention of the spirit, and instead it sets the spirit alongside water and blood in verses 6–8; this shows just how far 1 John is from the trinitarian understanding of the spirit that later scribes credited to him. Rather than attempt to conform his thought to later doctrinal developments, his own insights should be allowed their voice. The "spirit" was for him, perhaps, no less (or no more) material and no less a symbol for a deeper truth than were "water" and "blood"; each was a way of expressing the means of experiencing a relationship with God, and each was grounded in the reality of the sending of the Son of God, and in his death.

---

143. See W. Thiele, "Beobachtungen zum Comma Iohanneum (1 Joh 5 7f.)," *ZNW* 50 (1959): 61–73, who does not exclude a Greek original, and sets it alongside other expansions in the Latin text (cf. below on 5:9, 20; 2 John 11); also H. J. de Jonge, "Erasmus and the *Comma Johanneum*," *ETL* 56 (1980): 381–89.

## *1 John 5:9–12—God's Own Testimony to the Son of God*

Although the author has appealed to testimony to the meaning of Jesus as God's Son, putting trust in it is not something additional to or independent of the act of faith in God, even less something that can provide the grounds for such faith. To set trust in human testimony over trust in God's own self-witness would be nonsense. Yet ultimately the authentic witness that God gives to God's own Son can only be known in the life-giving relationship with God. There it becomes evident that God's gift of life is inseparable from knowing God's Son.

5:9 If we accept human testimony, the testimony God gives is greater. For this is the testimony God gives, that he has testified concerning his Son.[a] 10 The one who believes in the Son of God has the testimony[b] in himself;[c] the one who does not believe God[d] has made him to be a liar, because he has not believed in the testimony that God has provided concerning his Son. 11 So this is the testimony, that God gave us eternal life, and this life is in his Son. 12 The one who possesses the Son possesses life; the one who does not possess the Son of God does not possess life.

a. Some Latin manuscripts have a lengthy addition here tying God's testimony to the Son's fulfillment of the Scriptures and to the testimony born by the "we" of the prologue to the audience; cf. 5:20 note b.

b. Some manuscripts add "of God"; but see commentary.

c. There is strong textual support for "in him"; this could still be reflexive, but would more correctly refer to God or Jesus (see n. 148).

d. There is strong but not persuasive textual support for "the Son [of God]," probably added because the Son is the usual object of belief.

**[9–10]** The argument that anyone who trusts in human testimony has no reason not to trust in God's witness is a style of logic than moves from a lesser to a greater case: if God is greater and presumably more reliable than humans, so must be the testimony that God gives. In that sense the reliability of human testimony is a general truth, and "we accept" need not refer specifically to this author and audience. Within this logic, the objection that humankind and the evidence they supply are rather more tangible and susceptible to testing, and hence are more readily accepted than are God and God's testimony, would carry little weight. However, it is more probable that, as elsewhere, the author is referring specifically to his audience, who, he knows, do accept human testimony. This would still allow the latter to be a general truth, in which case the "greater" testimony that God gives is to be identified with, or at least includes, the testimony of spirit, water, and blood just mentioned. Alternatively, this threefold testifying may in some sense be "human testimony," so that God's own witnessing is something additional to these. In the former case, "this is the testimony" in the middle of verse 9 refers back to the preceding verses; in the latter case the clause refers forward, so that the distinctive form of the testimony that God bears is elaborated by verses 9b, or 10, or 11.[144]

Given his emphasis on them it seems unlikely that the author would dismiss the testimony of spirit, water, and blood in so summary a fashion, but in what follows his concern is undoubtedly on the testimony given by God and its accessibility to believers, and this has not been exhausted by the threefold witnesses, which are not mentioned again. Once more, some of the difficulties of the argument arise from the fact that the author was drawing on patterns of ideas that were familiar to his readers. Evidence of this is the switch to the perfect tense with reference to the testimony given by God (vv. 9–10) in contrast to the present tense of the testimony given by spirit, water, and blood (vv. 6–7). Although the perfect no less has in view the present and lasting impact of God's act of witness, this formulation seems to have been a traditional one in Johannine thought and so to have carried a particular authority (John 1:32, 34; 3:26; 5:32–33, 37; 19:35; 3 John 12 and commentary). Among these passages John 1:32–34 and 19:35, at the moments of Jesus' baptism and death, have already been seen to reflect the same network of ideas that lies behind this section of 1 John. More specifically, in John 5:31–40 Jesus challenges his audience to recognize the multiple testimony to which he can appeal: there is the testimony of John (the baptizer), which, although Jesus himself would not "accept testimony from a man,"[145] they may acknowledge; then there is the "greater" testimony that is constituted by Jesus' works, which originate in God; in addition, the Father "has himself testified concerning me," a statement not further elaborated; finally there is the testimony borne by the Scriptures. The overlap of similar ideas and even of some of the same phraseology, although put to very different purposes, in 1 John and the Gospel suggests that this was part of the distinctive pattern of Johannine thought and language.[146] Within these circles, the convictions they held and the confidence with which they held them could be summed up in the language of testimony; God offers testimony but so do those who have experienced what God has done, and so too do the symbols of that experience. The idea is a distinctive one, but it may have had its roots in reflection on passages in Isaiah where God's people "who are blind yet have

144. See commentary on 1:5 and 2:25 on 1 John's use of the "this is" formula, and also v. 11 below.

145. See also John 8:17–18, where Jesus refers to the reliability in Jewish law of the testimony of two men.

146. "Accept" (*lambanō*): 1 John 5:9/John 5:34; "human" (*anthrōpōn*), lit. "of men," 1 John 5:9/cf. "from a man" (*para anthrōpou*), John 5:34; "greater": 1 John 5:9/John 5:36; "has testified concerning" (*memartyrēken peri*): 1 John 5:10/John 5:37. This does not exclude the possibility that in the Fourth Gospel, where it is combined with other law court imagery, it helped address a specific context.

eyes, who are deaf yet have ears" (cf. 1 John 1:1; 2:11), are witnesses, almost in spite of themselves, to whom God is (Isa 43:8–13). Here these echoes from earlier tradition help authenticate the testimony of God, but what that testimony consists of is not yet defined.[147]

The community of believers is founded on and lives by testimony. At its heart is the testimony that God alone gives, and the central testimony of God is given to God's Son: it is God alone who can and who does authenticate his Son. The belief in Jesus as Son of God, with which this section started (v. 5), ultimately rests on God's own affirmation of that truth. As in the Gospel, this affirmation is not restricted to the specific instants of Jesus' baptism and death; although there these did provide significant narrative moments, those moments point beyond themselves. God's testimony is given and is irreversible, and yet it also becomes actualized as it is accepted. To believe is to accept that testimony and so presupposes it; but believing also means internalizing God's testimony and experiencing its validity.[148] The positive act of belief is defined as belief "in (*eis*) the Son of God": in the context of the previous verses this might indicate belief that Jesus is that Son, or belief that as Son he brings life and forgiveness even through his death; however, the distinctive "in" ("into," or *eis*), used for the first time here (cf. 5:13),[149] is probably not limited to this. The different constructions after the verb "to believe" are not always easy to distinguish (see commentary on 3:23), but the focus is perhaps on commitment and allegiance. It is significant that the object of such commitment is not Jesus but "the Son of God": this is not a personal cult of Jesus but an identification with what God has brought about through God's Son.

Hence the negative alternative is not "the one who does not believe in the Son of God" but "who does not believe God." Although, given the fluidity of constructions the verb "to believe" can take, it would be mistaken to overemphasize the simple dative used here, the implication appears to be that to refuse to acknowledge and respond to God's Son, whose status relies on God's own testimony, is nothing less than to refuse to *trust* God. It is to treat God as a liar—within the dualistic framework of this letter this is to place God firmly alongside all that opposes God's own truth and light (1:10; 2:21–22). This is not, then, merely a misapprehension or an erroneous judgment; it is not a failure to believe a secondary article of faith nor an understandable if mistaken difference of opinion. It is a fundamental denial—the perfect, "has made"—of who God is and what God

---

147. To interpret that the content of God's testimony is that God has given testimony produces a tautology; to avoid this the later text read, "*which* God testified," clearly a secondary reading but closer to the author's meaning.

148. The well-attested variant, "has the testimony in him," can only mean "in himself"; testimony "*to* him" would not be expressed with the preposition *en* ("in").

149. The construction is more characteristic of the Fourth Gospel (John 3:16, 36; 9:35).

has done and does do. The sonorous tones of the final clause of verse 10 reinforce the seriousness of this. The two perfect verbs, one negative ("has not believed"), the other positive ("has testified"), set in a sustained opposition those two fundamental acts of commitment, and they effectively exclude the one who does the former from the benefits of the latter. The verse climaxes by repeating the final words of verse 9; there is no attempt to argue or to persuade, no appeal to specific evidence or support: God's testimony has been given concerning God's Son and there is no room for its reversal, for negotiation, or for debate.

[11–12] Characteristically, the author switches from the language of objective reality to that of the subjective appropriation that embodies that reality. The formulaic "this is (the testimony)" (cf. 1:5 and commentary) anticipates what follows; the "that" clause that follows is not the content of the testimony (i.e., what someone asserts) but constitutes the testimony itself. It also repeats the unfulfilled definition of verse 9b ("For this is the testimony of God"): God's gift of life is God's testimony giving. On this occasion "the testimony" is not explicitly defined as "God's," perhaps because that is by now self-evident, or perhaps because the preceding verses have excluded any suggestion that this appropriation in "us" exhausts the sum total of God's testimony.

The letter began by identifying the core of the proclamation as "eternal life" (1:2), and the theme of life will dominate its conclusion (vv. 11, 12, 13, 16, 20). Possession of life has already marked believers, those whom the author identifies as "we," over against those who belong to the realm of death (3:14–15). Now it is made explicit, not only that the source of that life is God, but that it is made available (only) in God's Son. Possession of life is possible only through a relationship with the Son, and, it is implied, that relationship presupposes acknowledgment of the Son and of his true identity. Although the idea of "eternal life" has its roots in the hope of an age to come, it is here, as regularly in the Johannine tradition, a present possession because it is the inevitable corollary of a present relationship. That relationship with the Son is expressed with the verb "to have" (*echō*), which is also used, more naturally, for the possession of life and, in verse 10, of the testimony. With a personal object the formula is unusual, but the author has already used it in 2:23, where "to have" the Father is contingent upon confession of the Son (see commentary).

There is, then, a circle: life (in its true God-given sense as eternal life) has been made available through God's Son and what he has achieved; it is, therefore, experienced only by those who acknowledge God's Son in the specific story that can be told about him, the story of Jesus. God's Son can be acknowledged with confidence because it is God who has given the ultimate testimony to him. Yet in the last resort that testimony is embodied in the reception and experience of eternal life. Conversely, those who reject (Jesus as) God's Son have already excluded themselves from being the recipients of the life that would testify to his truth. The division between those who do and those who do not share the divine life of God's eternity does not lie in the future but is established in the present. Seen from outside, this relentless self-fulfilling logic might seem to offer little opportunity to those approaching from an agnostic or questioning perspective, and little incentive to witnessing to those outside. This, indeed, is the position from which the author argues, but for the most part because his intention is to reinforce the allegiance of those to whom he writes and to make clear the stark consequences of withdrawing.

### *1 John 5:13—"This Is Why I Have Written"*

It would be possible to see this verse as the climax of the letter as a whole, and, as will be seen, such a view has created difficulties in understanding the relevance of the following eight verses. Its primary role, on the contrary, is to bring to a conclusion the section that began in 5:4. That those to whom the author writes are already in possession of eternal life is not in doubt, but neither should they forget that this certainty is always dependent on their faithful adherence to the one acknowledged as the Son of God.

5:13 I have written these things to you[a] so that you might know that you possess eternal life, to you who believe in the name of the Son of God.

a. There are numerous textual variants;[150] most significantly, a number of manuscripts add here the words that come at the end of the verse ("to you . . . son of God"), and some turn that phrase into a purpose clause, "in order that you might believe. . . ." This is partly an attempt to smooth out the grammar but it may also be influenced by John 20:31.

[13] Not least under the influence of the similar John 20:31 (see below), this verse has often been read as the conclusion of the letter as a whole. Verses 14–21 then become something of an appendix, tagged on awkwardly. Along similar lines the Greek critical text NA[27], followed by some English versions and commentators, identifies a major break between verses 12 and 13, and treats verses 13–21 as a single final section.[151] However, the reminder that they are hearing or reading what he has written to them ("to you") does not introduce a new section but serves to sum up and drive home the significance of what has preceded, just as it does at 2:1, 21, 26. "These things" (cf. 2:26) refer back specifically to verses 4–12 and not to the letter as a whole, even if the aspiration is not inap-

---

150. The Editio Critica Maior lists 26, although most are minor variations in word order of the accepted text or of variants described in the notes.
151. Made up of four paragraphs, vv. 13–15, 16–17, 18–20, 21. The NRSV sets out v. 13 as a freestanding verse.

propriate for it.[152] The section has repeatedly used the indefinite third person, "the one who believes/has life" (vv. 5, 10, 12); at a few points a passing first person plural, "we/our/us," has betrayed that this is no impersonal or theoretical discussion but is true because it is true of those who share the convictions claimed by the author (5:4, our faith; 5:9, we accept [?]; 5:11, God has given to us). Since 4:6 "we" has systematically included the audience; this is the first second person plural address, "you," since 4:4, and its reintroduction abruptly claims their attention, positioning them once again as those who have first to decide how they will respond. This is not an occasion for complacency.

Yet, as on previous occasions (2:21, 26), it is also not an occasion for doubt as to where they do after all stand. Unlike John 20:31, with which this verse is so often compared, and unlike the modifications introduced by later scribes (see also KJV), the author does not write in order that they might believe and/or have eternal life, but with the assumption that they already do so. His purpose is that they might *know* that they possess this life, the theme of the previous two verses. This need not imply that their confidence had been shaken in any way; there is no suggestion that they do not already know this. Just as throughout this section his concern was to tie the assurance of life to right acknowledgment of God's Son, so it is here. "You" are precisely those who do now believe, and the object of that belief is expressed with studied emphasis: first, there is the use of the preposition "in/into" (*eis*; see v. 10); second, there is the redundant use of "the name" (or reputation; see 3:23, where, however, it is in the simple dative after the verb). The position of the clause at the end of the verse, and not immediately after "you" as might be expected (and as was emended in some manuscripts), also draws attention to it. The author does not say, "if" or "so long as you believe," for he refuses even to consider any alternative possibility, but the implication is clear: if "you" are to be the recipients of this letter and its assurance, you have no choice but to be those who continue—the verb (participle) is in the present tense—to maintain that belief.

As throughout this section, the focus is not on statements about the identity of Jesus, nor about his identification as the Son of God. By now the author has established this identification as inescapably part of the package of believing in the Son of God. The real emphasis lies on the conviction that the assurance of victory and the possession of eternal life have been made possible through the coming at a point in the past (4:2; 5:6) of God's Son; this is no sideshow, nor is it one means of salvation to be set alongside others, nor can it be discarded when the goal has been attained, for God's own testimony has established it as the exclusive source of life and as the only setting in which life is known.

This might be seen as the point to which the whole letter has been working, and that is why it is not inappropriate to see verse 13 as in some sense referring

---

152. It is unlikely that the verse recalls 1:4, "we write . . . our joy. . . ."

back to the letter as a whole. There are still further consequences to explore, however, and, although this is the last time that the writer refers to his own authorship (other than his gloss in v. 16), it is not yet the sum of what he has to say.

## 1 John 5:14–21—Exercising the Privileges of Life

The assurance of life is not merely theoretical, neither is it only a matter of inner personal experience. It is discovered as a reality in what even this author would have to acknowledge are the ambiguities of life in the present. Moreover, this reality consists of the continuing relationship with God as made possible through God's Son, and within the common life of those who share that relationship. It has, throughout, been at the heart of the letter that life, divine indwelling, and all the other expressions of belonging to the realm of God's light are not primarily individual but are communal (see 2:18; 4:9, 12). This is why love for one another or for the brother has been a repeated theme as offering the true test of sharing fellowship with God.

Here, however, as the author returns to demonstrating the practical outworking of life in the community of those who believe, it is not the network of love that he identifies. Instead, he returns to the issue that at the beginning of the letter represented for him the most testing challenge to the assurance of life, sin. Sin, however defined, surely belongs to the realm of death; but it will emerge that the divine gift of life can, sometimes, overcome even the natural propensity of sin. Moreover, it is here that the gift of life truly becomes a communal reality. However, the author does not intend to end on a note of anxiety, and this passage is replete with declarations of confidence: "we know." Readers who have identified themselves in verse 13 are brought in to share those triumphal declarations. A final abrupt parting shot challenges them to recognize the journey on which the letter has taken them, and to choose life.

### *1 John 5:14–17—Seeking Life*

5:14 This is the boldness that we maintain before him, that if we ask for anything according to his will he hears us. 15 And if we know that he hears us, whatever we ask, we know that we possess the requests that we have asked of him. 16 If anyone sees his brother[a] committing a sin that is not death-bound, he shall ask and he[b] will give him life, for those who sin but not bound to death. There is sin bound to death. I do not say that one is to ask concerning that. 17 All unrighteousness is sin, but there is sin that is not death-bound.

a. Or "and sister"; see note a on 2:9; only by retaining the masculine can the ambiguity that follows (see note b) be retained.

b. See commentary for the ambiguity of the referent here.

[14–15] Throughout the letter boldness before God has been a recurring symbol of the relationship with God shared by those who believe (2:28; 3:21; 4:17). The boldness (*parrēsia*) is the freedom of speech granted the citizen, but it also implies being in the presence of an individual or group of greater power and authority (see commentary on 2:28). The confidence in being able to exercise such boldness is at the same time an acknowledgment that anxiety might be a more instinctive reaction. Hence in its previous occurrences the possibility of merited condemnation has hovered in the background; even if experienced in the present there has been an element of looking to the future. Already in 3:22, the present experience was expressed in the receiving of answered requests; here, where there is even more emphasis on the present, the example the author will give (of prayer for someone who commits sin) shows that the context continues to be one of approach to a God in whose presence only light and truth belong.

It is fundamental to the biblical tradition that those who call upon God will be heard—and the anguished protests against God's apparent silence are themselves evidence of this expectation (Pss 86:1–7; 102:1–2). Such asking is not the privilege of religious functionaries or of the particularly pious, but is open to all, and this is an important theme in the Psalms as well as in narrative (1 Sam 1:12–17). This does not mean that men and women can coerce God, for it is axiomatic that God will respond only according to God's own nature. Hence in Matthew Jesus' unconditional invitation, "Ask and it will be given to you," climaxes with the assurance that "your Father in heaven will give good things to those who ask him" (Matt 7:7–11). Neither does asking imply that God would otherwise be ignorant (Matt 6:8). Rather, asking is the practice of a relationship with God, and this explains the importance of the marriage between asking and confidence (Mark 11:23–24). The frequency of the theme in the New Testament reflects its significance in the experience of early Christian communities (cf. Jas 1:5; 4:2–3). This was, of course, no different from other religious traditions outside the biblical Jewish one; perhaps one of the most common aspects of the religious life of ordinary people for which there is evidence in the Greco-Roman world (as elsewhere) is the making of requests to the deity, often accompanied by vows or offerings, together with the subsequent expression of thanks.[153] Hence the importance of accompanying the assurance that this was a God to whom requests could be made in confidence of a response, with the reminder that requests must be shaped by the nature of God and by God's purposes. At the same time, where prayers were not answered in the manner

153. See commentary on 2:2 for dedications dealing specifically with sin.

expected, the implication is that the failure must lie not with God but with the request or with the one making it.

Here 1 John therefore qualifies the request as "according to his [God's] will." This is not a throwaway phrase; in 2:17 the one who does the will of God is the one who overcomes the transience of the world. In John's Gospel one of the defining characteristics of Jesus and of his oneness with God who sent him is that he fulfills God's will (John 4:34; 5:30), whereas elsewhere in the New Testament the will of God is the lodestone of Christian behavior (Rom 1:10; 12:2; 1 Thess 4:3; Heb 10:36). What God wills is not unpredictable and liable to change but is determined by God's total purposes; it is, therefore, not to be privatized, limited to contingent circumstances (as in "God willing"), and therefore unknown, but is set within the declared goals of all God's working.

Throughout this passage 1 John uses the ordinary word "to ask" (*aiteō*).[154] This is characteristic of the Johannine literature as a whole, which nowhere uses the technical language of prayer. This too, perhaps, is part of the way the authors demystify prayer, setting it within a relationship in which request and response occur naturally, and with no embarrassment that the most fundamental element in that relationship is petition. However, 1 John differs from the Gospel by never qualifying these requests as made "in his [Jesus'] name" (John 14:13–15; 15:16; 16:23–26). For this author believers who ask according to God's will have a direct access to God similar to that which Jesus enjoys in the Gospel (John 11:22, 42).

It would be enough to affirm that God *hears* requests made according to God's will, for the verb "to hear" (*akouō*) regularly implies active response (cf. 4:6). But the author now secures that affirmation as one of the foundational certainties that unites the readers with him and with all who share their world, "if we know." Such certainties have already been signaled by the confident "you/we know" (2:20, 21; 3:2, 14, 15), which was a Johannine testimony formula (John 3:11; 21:24; cf. 19:35); it presupposed that no argument was necessary, although on occasion it may have referred back to an earlier demonstration (e.g., 3:22). It is not surprising that at the climax of the letter a repeated "we know" (*oidamen*) becomes the leitmotif of the passage and holds together the different elements within it (vv. 15 [twice], 18, 19, 20). Here the shared knowledge that God hears their prayers is at the same time a shared knowledge that they already possess those things that they have requested. For God to hear is for God to act. The present tense ("we possess") leaves no room for doubt or for hope alone: confidence anticipates reality; the perfect tense "we have made" also acknowledges that this relationship of request and response is a repeated one.

---

154. See below on the change of verb in v. 16.

The requests are received "from God." The author, in company with most people in his time, has no interest in the mechanics of answered prayer, but he has no doubt that it is God who acts—contemporary concerns with seeing human beings as coworkers or as agents in the answering of their own prayers is far distant from his worldview. Neither would it occur to him to wonder how or whether God will contradict the workings of the natural universe that was created by God, although his restriction of any real discussion to the issue of sin effectively circumvents this problem. He lived within a world where divine intervention was no less natural than human action, and in some cases no more predictable. As already seen, the contemporary concern in his situation was not whether God or the gods intervene in human affairs, but on whose behalf they will intervene, and, sometimes, how they can be persuaded so to do.[155] That (their) God exclusively acts on behalf of and responds to those who proffer their allegiance would surprise no one. First John's task is both to affirm that conviction, and yet also to establish its parameters.

**[16–17]** These last comments suggest that the requests that 1 John has in mind primarily concern the community of those who make them. His general outlook makes it unlikely that he would be concerned with intercession for outsiders (2:15; see also John 17:9), although elsewhere in the Scriptures this is encouraged, albeit in the ultimate interests of those who must live among them (cf. 1 Tim 2:1; Jer 29:7). The example he gives, however, is firmly located within the community; indeed, it appears not to be a random example, but the real reason why he returned (cf. 3:22) to the theme of answered prayer. The problem is not primarily how to deal with sin, which was already addressed in the first part of the letter (1:9–2:2); rather, it is how to respond to encountering a fellow member of the community committing sin. If sin has no place in the community of those who believe in God's Son, who belong to the light, and who share the assurance of eternal life, what happens when it does occur there? The picture of someone *seeing* this and the use of the term "brother" highlight this as disruptive of the relationships that constitute the community; the proper relationship with a brother is one of love, and, although using a different verb, an earlier verse had condemned any failure to respond when *seeing* a brother in need (3:17).

The author is treading difficult ground; despite the initial call to confession, the logic of the story told in chapter 3 had ruled out sin as having any place among those who have experienced the birth that comes from God (3:4–10; see commentary). He indirectly acknowledges this difficulty here by drawing a distinction between sin that is irrevocably death-bound (*pros thanaton*) and sin that is not. Only the latter can conceivably be committed and still permit of prayer. Such is the gravity of the former that the author does not say that prayer for

---

155. See commentary on 2:2 for dedications specifically dealing with sin.

someone committing it will be ineffective but that it is not to be made: the Greek is ambiguous as to whether he is actively telling them *not to pray* ("ask") concerning such sin, or merely *not telling* them to pray concerning it, but the result is little different. (Although a different verb is used for ask [*erōtaō*], it is unlikely that he is discouraging them from asking *questions* about such sin: both verbs of asking are used in the Fourth Gospel of prayer.[156])

The author does not explain the difference between the two forms of sin, nor how they are to be identified. Different categories of sinning are already to be found within the biblical tradition and continue thereafter, with a distinction between that for which forgiveness is possible and that for which it is excluded. Whether the difference lies in the act committed or in the intention of the person committing it remains inconsistent. For example, the biblical laws about a sin offering specifically address wrongs committed "unintentionally," even though in some of the examples it is unclear how the act could be inadvertent (Leviticus 4–5); opposed to these are those offenses that result in being "cut off from the people" without apparent means of mitigation (Lev 7:19–27).

Within the Jesus tradition, a distinction is drawn between "blasphemy against the Holy Spirit," for which there is no forgiveness, and other sins, although, once again, the specific content of the former is opaque (Mark 3:28–30; Matt 12:31–32; Luke 12:10).[157] One source of the dilemma becomes evident in Hebrews: if believers (through baptism) experience the once-for-all forgiveness for sins won through Jesus' death, what room for continuing sin can there be in their lives? Would not a repeated need for forgiveness undermine the completeness of that given through the initial act of conversion and commitment, and the absolute effectiveness of Jesus' death? Hebrews appears to rule out any further restoration for those who fall away, presumably primarily addressing the problem of apostasy (Heb 6:4–8), but the principle could be extended to all sin. Hermas apparently distinguishes between the sin of lust and the actual deed, which brings death upon the perpetrator, and is even more exercised over those members of the church who sin after their initial conversion (*Mand.* 4.1.1–2; *Similitude* 7–8). Later church pastors and writers were to introduce a distinction between those sins that could be forgiven a believer who confessed and showed appropriate repentance, and those that could not, at least in the normal liturgical cycle, that is, between venial and mortal sin.

Some such distinction is perhaps inevitable where the attempt is made to maintain with equal seriousness the gravity of sin, understood as the denial of God's will, and the unmerited primacy of God's forgiveness. The tension is exacerbated when God's eschatological judgment and pardon are believed to

156. *Aiteō*: John 14:13, 14; 15:7, 16; *erōtaō*: John 14:16; 17:9, 15 (always by Jesus).

157. The variations between the parallels suggest that Matthew and Luke were already trying to clarify an obscure earlier tradition.

have been anticipated and to be made available in the present, and where the cost of that forgiveness is the death of Jesus. Then it is not easy to make sense of evident acts of wrong by those who have experienced forgiveness and entered into the sphere where sin no more holds sway. In each case, the solution offered needs to retain the potential of some flagrant acts to mar fatally the relationship with God, while holding out the willingness of God to offer a forgiveness that overcomes the otherwise inevitable consequences. Hence in 1 John the assurances that "we" have passed out of death and that it is the one who fails to love who remains in death (3:14–15) surely entail that all sin is death-bound. Since God's capacity is to give life, however, that life may even be effective where death is otherwise inevitable.

For all this, the grounds of the distinction that the author wishes to make are not evident; neither is it certain whether they were evident to the earliest audience, for he has to explain that, although all unrighteousness (*pasa adikia*) is sin, there is both sin that is "death-bound" and sin that is not. The explanation does little to illuminate, especially since earlier he had said that all sin and "all unrighteousness," the same phrase, are forgiven through God's faithfulness (1:9). The label "death-bound" does not provide further information but is self-fulfilling: it is death-bound because there is no possibility that it can be overcome by prayer and by God's favorable response.[158] One explanation of the dilemma would be that the sin that inevitably results in death is the sin that the perpetrator refuses to acknowledge; although the present passage speaks only of the intercession of another and not of the attitude of the person committing the sin, on this view intercession is effective only where it adds support to the person's own penitence. The distinction would then lie not so much in the nature of the act but in the attitude of the actor. This makes reasonable sense and reinforces the importance of the community: the prayer for and the gift of forgiveness are experienced only within the community of those who believe. The difficulty with this explanation is that the author does appear to be emphasizing a distinction between sins and not only between attitudes to sin by the perpetrator; he has shown himself well able to condemn any refusal to acknowledge them (1:8, 10).

An alternative solution would be that it is the deliberate separation from the community that is the sin that irrevocably remains in the sphere of death. This, perhaps expressed in the refusal to love fellow members and in the schism lying behind 2:18, is willfully to put oneself outside the realm where life can be given, and even beyond the prayers of the most compassionate of one's former colleagues. Retrospectively, this would lessen the dissonance with the assertions

---

158. Hence the apparent parallel at *T. Iss.* 7.1, "I am 122 years old and I am not aware of having committed a sin unto death," is of little help except perhaps to indicate the currency of the concept; for Issachar the following lines appear to define such sin as sexual infidelity, drunkenness, and covetousness, which are the routine dangers of the *Testaments* but not of interest to 1 John.

that the one born of God cannot sin (3:6, 10; cf. 5:18 and commentary), for such a person would be demonstrating that they were not born of God; conversely, it would follow that it is only the sin that is death-bound that the one born of God cannot sin, while other sins are those that are to be confessed and forgiven (1:8–2:2). This is a neat solution, both to the present passage and to the apparent contradictions within the letter; it is, however, hardly how the sharp binary scheme in chapter 3 is most naturally read, particularly since that pattern is immediately repeated (5:18; see below). Moreover, the implication of the present passage appears to be that one might see someone who is still a "brother" committing the death-bound sin. Furthermore, if the remedy for sin is the life that God ultimately bestows (see below), then the death-bound sin is made so by God who does not there give life, and not by the self-chosen location of the individual.

As the various attempts to categorize sin in other traditions (see above) illustrate, it is probably wrong to expect too rigorous a consistency; apparently contradictory consequences do follow within different frameworks of considering the problem, while the puzzling dilemmas of community life challenge the neat certainties of theological models. The author may have expected his readers to identify with relative ease those situations where prayer was both possible and appropriate, but he may also have felt that this would become obvious to them. More important, the emphasis here is not on the inevitable consequences of the choices made by a member of the community, the sinner, but on the exercise by the community as a whole of the privileges of having the ear of God. Within the biblical tradition particular individuals are able to act as intercessors before God for the people as a whole (Gen 18:22–33; Exod 32); here that possibility is available to any member of the community. Here too, as in those earlier examples, they may be forbidden to intercede, because God is determined to let the punishment run its course (Jer 7:16; 11:14).

In verse 16 the identity of the one who will give life when the request is made is unclear; the echo of the similar phrase in verse 11 might indicate that it is God whose gift of life is assured for all who believe, although that life needs reaffirming in this potentially destructive situation. However, this would introduce a sudden and unmarked change of subject from the immediately preceding verb; grammatical continuity would suggest that it is the one who makes the request who also gives life. Grammatical discontinuity would not be unusual for this author, and ultimately, of course, that life does come from God to whom the request has been made, and who alone can reverse the propensity for all sin to result in death. Nonetheless, since those who believe do themselves possess life (5:12), the second interpretation would be a powerful image of how that eschatological life is made effective within the experience of the community, even while showing that it is never independent of God. Although interpreters have often concentrated most on the identity of the sin that leads to death, at this point in the letter it is rather this more celebratory affirmation that the author wishes to make.

## *1 John 5:18–21—The Ultimate Confidence*

**5:18** We know that everyone who has been born from God does not sin, but the one who was born from God protects them[a] and the evil one does not touch them. **19** We know that we are from God and that the whole world lies in the power of the evil one. **20** We know that the Son of God has come[b] and has given to us insight to know[c] the one[d] who is true, and we are in the one who is true and in his Son, Jesus Christ.

This is the true God and eternal life. **21** Children, guard yourselves against idols.

a. Lit. "him"; there is strong manuscript support for "himself" (so KJV); see commentary.

b. In some parts of the Old Latin translation there is an addition, "and put on flesh for our sake and suffered and rose from the dead and took to himself [or "redeemed"] us."[159]

c. The earliest manuscripts read an indicative and not the expected subjunctive.

d. Some manuscripts specify "God" here.

**[18]** The letter reaches its powerful conclusion with three confident affirmations, "We know" (*oidamen*; cf. v. 15). As a confessional formula familiar within the Johannine tradition, these appeal to shared certainties, even if at times they have been argued earlier in the letter (2:29 and commentary; see John 3:11; 21:24). Within the rhetoric of the letter the "we" by now includes the readers who can make these certainties their own: in saying "we know," the author is not stating the obvious, but is inviting his audience to acknowledge these as truths for them and to acknowledge also the consequences. If they were recognized as formulaic these readers would be aware that they were participating in a tradition that did not originate with them and was not limited to them; the unexpected direct address of verse 21 will reinforce both this and their position of dependency and their need to commit themselves. However, the certainties that follow recall in particular the story of the Son of God that underlay chapter 3 together with the sharply dichotomous world that it shaped (see commentary on 2:29–3:12); this means that the "we know" equally works as an internal

159. See Bart Ehrman, *The Orthodox Corruption of Scripture: The Effect of Early Christological Controversies on the Text of the New Testament* (New York: Oxford University Press, 1993), 235–36, who sees this as one of a number of readings, perhaps from a Greek original of the end of the second century, directed against Docetism; see also n. 143 above.

cross-reference, taking the audience back to the earlier argument to which they have implicitly assented.

The first certainty, the denial that the one born from God does sin, seems deliberately chosen to contrast with the immediately preceding encouragement to intercession on behalf of the fellow member who does sin—the author can hardly have been unaware of the contradiction, particularly since in both cases the present tense of the verb "sin" is used.[160] Since he does not here qualify "does not sin" by "death-bound," a phrase that he has been careful to specify four times in the last two verses, it is unlikely that here he is only denying this restricted sense of sin. Rather, he is juxtaposing the reality of their experience and struggle alongside another reality that to some extent they have accepted as no less authentic—most directly when the same sentiment was made at 3:9 (cf. 3:6 and commentary). Within the narrative world that is evoked by this imagery and within which they are invited to place themselves, the one who has been born of God simply does not sin. So doing may engender a high degree of dissonance, which will be intensified as the passage continues and which will prepare them to make a final response at its end.

In the earlier passage in chapter 3 their genetic heritage seemed to ensure this freedom, but here the field of conflict also hinted at there is brought fully into the picture. Sin would bring them into the realm opposed to God, which belongs to "the evil one." The story line of chapter 3 identified the opposition as "the devil," and the one who sins as belonging to "the devil" (3:8), but then proceeded to describe Cain as belonging to "the evil one" (3:12), and it is clear that the two epithets have come to be synonymous. There it was the task of the Son of God to destroy the works of the devil (3:8); here those who are born from God are kept safe from the baleful influence of the evil one by "the one who was born" or "begotten from God." The aorist tense of the participle distinguishes this one from those whom he protects (represented by the perfect participle), and identifies him as the Son of God;[161] the description is unexpected, but the use of the same verb together with the prepositional formula "from God" acknowledges some degree of consanguinity between them. A similar strategy was probably already implicit in 5:1, and it was argued there that, despite the later church's christological use of the epithet for the Son's eternal relationship with the Father, 1 John is neither interested in the nature or the occasion of this begetting, nor concerned with the inner being of God (see commentary). On the contrary, it is the relationship that the Son shares with them as born from God

---

160. In contradiction to those who try to ameliorate the tensions by appeal to the tenses in chaps. 1 and 3; see pp. 61, 131.

161. This is lost in the widely supported reading, "keeps himself," probably because scribes failed to recognize the unusual expression.

that enables them to share in the benefits that he has achieved. Without this connection, the imagery of believers as having been born of God could suggest that they possess in their own right all the benefits this brings, leaving no meaningful role for the Son of God, whose importance the author has been at such pains to assert.

The present tense, "protects," acknowledges that this is a continuous necessity; the reach of the evil one would otherwise remain a threat. This stands in tension with the assurance given the "young men" that victory over the evil one was already securely theirs (2:13, 14). By now such tensions in the thought of the letter are familiar, and as they are repeated in the following verses they will maintain the dissonance just established. The author is in no doubt that what the Son of God has achieved is irreversible, and that believers already share in the complete certainty of the life that God gives; at the same time those same believers continually face the possibility of rejecting that life, and the power of the evil one is still to be experienced in the world (v. 19). Hence there is need for explicit or implicit exhortation, but also need for the assurance that the battle that has been won can be won. Once again, if the wording draws on familiar affirmations among the readers (cf. John 17:15), they would have been accustomed to struggling with these tensions in what they "knew."

[19] The second affirmation repeats the assurance that brought readers and author together in the face of the threat of the false prophets (4:4, 6). As there, to be "from (*ek*) God" signifies more than to belong to God or to come from God; it has been shaped by the images of birth and of being children, and so it means to have one's origin and one's being in God (3:10; see commentary). This is not something that can be said of just anyone, but only of those who have declared their common allegiance. Who they are is determined by the opposition that they face; over against them is "the whole world," which as so often in this letter represents all that is opposed to God (2:15–17). The author now makes explicit what so far has been implicit, that in his dualistic scheme the world is inextricably tied to the evil one. Yet he does not say that the world is "*of* the evil one," but that it lies under or in the power of (*en*) the evil one. Perhaps this offers a glimmer of hope that the world may at some time be wrested from the grip of the evil one; if so, the apparent contradiction would be softened with the author's earlier declaration that Jesus is a source of forgiveness even for (the sins of) "the whole world" (2:2; cf. 4:14). However, the author has repeatedly shown himself not uncomfortable with such contradictions in his own thought, and his real concern at this point in the letter is not with whether the world will also come within the realm of God (and cease to be "world"), but with those whom he invites to share this affirmation. By making these words their own they will effectively be distancing themselves from any contamination from the world, where the power of the evil one is at work.

As in 4:5, success in the world and its pursuit can hold no attraction for them. Nonetheless, that they need the protection of the one born of God against the evil one (v. 18) shows that they have not left the world behind; it remains a place of danger.

[20] The third affirmation, "We know," again alludes back to the story that shaped the narrative world of chapter 3, "the Son of God was revealed . . . to do away with the deeds of the devil" (3:8). The author does not directly identify the Son of God with the one who was born of God two verses earlier (v. 18), because each of these affirmations independently evokes the significant themes of his letter. It is as one also born of God that he protects those who share that dependency; it is as uniquely Son of God that he acts on God's behalf to overcome all that opposes God and to bring into the realm of life those who belong to God. That he "has come" is decisive, for only by that intervention into the situation could the victory be won; the tense of the verb (*hēkei*, only here in 1 John) puts the emphasis on that coming not as a past event but as something whose effects can neither be reversed nor surpassed. So it is "we" who are the direct beneficiaries of his coming, and those benefits are expressed not in terms of some change in the past (such as forgiveness) but as the gift of a new understanding and relationship.

That new understanding or mind-set (*dianoia*) results in knowledge of "the one who is true." The adjective (*alēthinos*) is used only here in 1 John—a different word is used at 2:7, 27—but although not made explicit, the rest of the verse indicates a reference to God (so also John 17:3; 1 Thess 1:9). The epithet frequently carries an implied contrast with what is spurious or nonauthentic (cf. John 6:32; 15:1), and, when applied to God, it sets God over against all other claimants to ultimate power and authority. Already in 1 John, knowing God is one of the gifts that believers share, although such knowledge needs to be demonstrated in the way they live (2:3–4, 14; 4:7–8). That the Son of God has given the faculty to do this means that knowledge of God is not a natural human capacity, nor can it be taught, for it requires a transformation of the mind. Such knowledge is not abstract or factual but implies a relationship; knowing the one who is true does not mean to be intellectually persuaded of God's existence, or to know what God is like and has done, although it must presuppose these, but to be brought into a relationship with God. As in 2:20, 27, there may be embedded here echoes of the promise of Jeremiah 31 (LXX 38):31–34 that God would give the laws in the people's "understanding (*dianoia*) and write them in their hearts" so that all would know God. However, the author of 1 John immediately goes on to say that this relationship is in fact a present reality: reverting to imagery that by now is familiar, "we are in (God)" (cf. 2:5, commentary).

At this point the author's language becomes more allusive, setting ideas alongside one another by association without explaining the connections, perhaps because he is moving toward an almost doxological climax. The one in whom "we are" is "the one who is true," an epithet just implicitly applied to God. However, here that adjective is immediately followed by "in his Son, Jesus Christ." In the absence of a connecting "and" the two phrases are most naturally taken as in apposition, so that the one who is true is this Son, although the pronoun "his" is left without any explicit referent. This is possible: within the Johannine tradition Jesus is the *true* (*alēthinos*) bread or vine (John 6:32; 15:1), although this is not quite the same as the unqualified "the true (one)" (*ho alēthinos*). For good reason, however, most interpreters prefer to maintain the reference of "the one who is true" to God and to understand "in his Son" as indicating that it is through the Son, or by being in the Son, that "we" are in God.[162] Although the author does not seek to explain the nature of the relationship between God and God's Son in terms of the divine being, he has no doubt that there can be no human experience of God independently of the Son.

This conviction apparently drives him to compress his ideas and language together as he makes a final declaration, "this is the true God (*alēthinos theos*) and eternal life." Grammatically and logically the sentence continues the difficulties that immediately preceded it: "this" most naturally refers back to the last-named person, Jesus Christ, yet nothing in the letter so far prepares for his identification with God, while the addition of "and eternal life" immediately also undermines any straightforward identification. Despite these difficulties, the language of these final declarations does evoke earlier themes in the letter as well as in the Johannine tradition familiar to the readers. This verse introduces the conclusion both of the letter as a whole and of the immediate section: the section has been an expansion of the declaration that God's gift of *eternal life* is present in, and only in, *God's Son* (5:11–12); the whole letter has been directed to demonstrating that the opening proclamation of "the *eternal life* that was in the presence of the Father and was revealed to us" (1:2) is nothing less than the proclamation of the *Son of God, Jesus Christ*. Within the Gospel narrative these same certainties are expressed in Jesus' own identification of himself as the life (John 11:25; 14:6); even closer to this verse are the opening words of his prayer to God: "This is eternal life, that they know you the only true God (*alēthinos theos*) and Jesus Christ whom you have sent" (John 17:3). Jesus may be the exclusive medium of access to and knowledge of God, but God's primacy is never compromised;[163] even 1 John's tendency to speak indiscriminately of "he/him" does not lead to an ultimate confusion of their roles.

---

162. There are no textual variants to suggest this, although as noted in the apparatus of NA[27] A. von Harnack conjectured a missing "(we) *being*" in his Son.

163. Although Thomas can acknowledge the risen Jesus as "my Lord and my God," the "my" is crucial (John 20:28); difficult is John 1:18, where the oldest surviving manuscript evidence reads "(the) only begotten God" (see commentary on 4:9, *monogenēs*).

None of these difficulties would arise were the words "in his Son, Jesus Christ," omitted. Verse 20 would then use a threefold repetition incorporating a final acclamation to counter any challenge from the evil one, the world, or (v. 21) idols—". . . that we know the one who is true, and we are in the one who is true. This is the true God!" Yet for the author of 1 John there can be no knowledge or experience of God independently of the Son of God, Jesus Christ, and it is through this and this alone that others can experience God's gift of life. By modifying a perhaps familiar acclamation with the addition of "in his Son," he now invites his readers either wholeheartedly to endorse everything he has been urging upon them throughout, or to risk rejecting both God and eternal life. Indeed, it was the incorporation of Jesus Christ into the praise of God who is at work and known through him that was to lead toward speaking of Jesus alongside God in the language reserved for God.[164]

[21] Dramatically verse 20 would have been a powerful closing assertion. This author, however, sees himself not as an orator but as a pastor. The confident sequence of "we know"s has created an implied community of shared convictions and intentions, just as the creation of such a community of commitment has been the letter's strategy from the start. Yet even the most apparently unshakable affirmations have been swiftly followed by words of warning and encouragement as the author again adopts the mantle of the teacher addressing his "children" (cf. 2:28; 3:7). That he does so again here, reverting to the second person plural, which distances his readers, leads readers to anticipate a final injunction that will bring together all that has gone before. Yet just where his parting shot might be expected to be the most direct and pointed, it leaves modern readers perplexed, and wondering just what their first counterparts would have made of it. Why does the author suddenly warn them against the attraction or the power of idols?

Taken on its own the contrast between the true God and idols is not unexpected. The term "idol" (*eidōlon*) was a standard way in Jewish, and subsequently in Christian, thought of referring to the representations of deities other than the one God whom they worshiped. Although in the Septuagint it was used to translate a number of different Hebrew terms, its semantic range in Greek particularly evoked ideas of appearance and of insubstantiality. In the ancient world deities were routinely represented by statues or other three-dimensional artifacts—although the term *eidōlon* was not used for these in non-Jewish Greek sources—and the absence of such in the Jewish tradition was the occasion of incomprehension and mockery by outsiders. Conversely, although no polytheistic worshiper would have supposed that the image they worshiped was identical with the deity it represented, such an identification is a commonplace

---

164. In a similar fashion the doxology at Rom 9:5 could grammatically be read as identifying Jesus Christ with "the God over all," but is most probably an independent acclamation.

in Jewish and then in Christian polemic: the gods are as insentient and incapable, and as much the result of human imagination and creativity, as are their "idols" (Isa 44:9–20; Jer 10:1–16; Ps 115:3–8). To acknowledge God as "true" is, therefore, to imply a contrast with the insubstantial deities or "idols" that others might worship: "You turned toward God from the idols to serve the living and true (*alēthinos*) God" (1 Thess 1:9).

Converts from a non-Jewish background would have internalized the implications of the vocabulary of "idols" (1 Cor 12:2), but in the ancient city, where religion did not belong to a separate enclosed area of life, it was difficult to avoid all social activities in which the representations of other deities were encountered. Paul's advice to the Corinthian church shows how attitudes toward the worship of or just association with these could become the touchstone of the precarious balance between integration in society and the absolute demands of faithfulness to God and to Christ (1 Corinthians 8; 10). The issues, therefore, were not necessarily primarily intellectual, such as the merits of polytheism or the existence and power of the gods others worshiped, although these were not unimportant (1 Cor 8:4; 10:19–20). Rather, "idolatry" could become a cipher for the attractions of integration in contemporary society, and for assimilation.

This was already true among Jewish communities. So, for example, the Epistle of Jeremiah, written perhaps not long before the second century B.C.E., apparently seeks to counsel a diaspora community to avoid "becoming like the foreigners" (Ep Jer 5), and 2 Maccabees takes its message to be that they should "not . . . forget the commandments of the Lord or . . . be led astray in their thoughts" (2 Macc 2:1–3). Yet the letter achieves this goal by taking the form of a pastiche of polemic against idols heavily dependent on the earlier biblical models, and it ends in a manner not dissimilar to 1 John 5:21: "Better is the righteous person who does not have idols, for he shall be far from reproach" (Ep Jer 72).[165]

In a different development from the biblical roots, straying after idols can become a way of expressing and explaining deviation from the community. Deuteronomy 29:17–20 promised curses on those in Israel who would "serve the gods of the nations";[166] the *Community Rule* subsequently rewrites those curses, directing them against the erstwhile member of the covenant who fails to live by its demands, "Cursed be he who transgresses by the idols of his heart."[167] Such a one is separated from God "because of his idols," although, since this was an inner-Jewish conflict, these probably existed only within the

---

165. Sometimes printed as Baruch 6, the Epistle of Jeremiah survives only through the LXX but probably stems from a Semitic original.

166. This follows a reference to the "abominations and idols (LXX *eidōlon*)" of Egypt.

167. Or perhaps, "cursed by the idols that his heart serves"; the Hebrew term is that used at Deut 29:16, *gillûlîm*.

rhetorical world of polemic (1QS II, 11, 16–17; cf. IV, 5, where the spirit of truth "detests all unclean idols"). Outside the Scrolls, in other writings directed internally, idolatry becomes part of a catalogue of vices, and even the archetypal vice to which all others lead or from which they issue (1 Cor 6:9; *Did.* 3.4; 5.1); as such, to label something "idolatry" is the ultimate condemnation, perhaps particularly for those who would otherwise have viewed themselves as loyal members of the community and as worshipers of the one God. Partly aided by the conventional association of worship of other deities with sexual infidelity, idolatry is often closely linked to sexual offenses: "Fornication is the destruction of the soul, separating from God and bringing near to idolatry, because it is this that leads astray the mind and understanding" (*T. Reub.* 4.6; cf. Col 3:8, "Put to death . . . fornication . . . and envy, which is idolatry"). It is not surprising when warnings against idolatry can become the reverse side of exhortations to faithfulness and obedience: "Therefore let us repent from our whole heart, that none of us perish. For if we have commands in order that we also do this, to separate from idols and offer instruction" (*2 Clem.* 17.1). The Shepherd of Hermas even declares that "someone who asks a false prophet about some matter is an idolator, empty of the truth" (*Mand.* 9.4).

These scattered examples illustrate how warnings against idols could become a trope for exhortations to members of the community to avoid anything that might be construed as a failure in commitment. Here idols and idolatry retain their real reference, although the shift toward a more metaphorical meaning is beginning. They provide the framework within which 1 John's own exhortation must be understood, although none quite matches it either in climactic position or in abruptness and apparent lack of continuity with anything earlier in the letter. Two interpretive attempts to introduce some continuity are not finally persuasive.[168] One is to identify the idols with the false teachers and their teaching; this interpretation appeals to the association of idols with wavering commitment in the Dead Sea Scrolls, and to the ideas of insubstantiality intrinsic to the Greek term.[169] However, this entails giving the term a higher metaphorical content than other parallels support, and it also depends on the false teaching being more central to the letter, including to its final sections, than I have accepted. Since the author has twice used the highly effective term "antichrist," he might have been expected to warn his readers to avoid these. A very different solution understands "idols" in its most straightforward sense, as the representations of Greco-Roman deities, in whose worship readers may be in danger of participating. This involves envisaging a context of actual or antic-

---

168. For an extensive discussion see Terry Griffith, *Keep Yourselves from Idols: A New Look at 1 John* (JSNTSup 233; Sheffield: Sheffield Academic Press, 2002), 12–28.

169. So R. E. Brown, *The Epistles of John: A New Translation with Introduction and Commentary* (AB 30; Garden City, N.Y.: Doubleday, 1982), 627–29.

ipated persecution; within such a setting the pervasive language of witness or testimony, of victory, and of confession or denial of Jesus as Son of God, a title sometimes claimed by the emperor, would readily belong.[170] However, it has become apparent that the general tenor of 1 John does not suit a context of looming persecution, and that the language of testimony is used with outsiders but with insiders in view. Were this the setting, the intended point could have been made much more forcefully: "Do not worship idols!"

Both these explanations fail because they isolate verse 21 from the immediately preceding affirmation of "the true God," to whom idols are the conventional counterpart. Taken together with that affirmation, the warning against idols must be a warning against falling outside the place where that God is known and where eternal life is experienced. To that extent the idols are synonymous with "the world" just as are "the desire that pertains to the flesh, and the desire that pertains to the eyes, and the arrogance that pertains to life" (2:16). This does not mean that the idols are a metaphor for some other specific thing that they are to avoid. As in the passages quoted earlier, within a rhetorical tradition founded on the Scriptures idols police the boundaries of the community. To keep away from idols is no less than to "remain in God" (2:28). Although the verb (*phylassō*) could be translated as "avoid," a stronger phrase, "guard yourselves against," conveys the intended sense of threat better.

Modern readers may continue to find the last verse of 1 John a perplexing anticlimax. Although one may doubt whether any would have remembered that in Ps 115:7 (113:15 LXX) the idols "have hands but do not *feel*" (*psēlaphaō*, the same verb as in 1 John 1:1; see commentary), those earliest readers who recognized in the letter's prologue the Isaianic roots of the claim to have seen and heard that which was from the beginning (1:1; Isa 43:13; cf. commentary), would have enjoyed the skill with which the letter culminated in the related Isaianic theme of the failure of the idols.[171] Returned once more to the position of "you" after the inclusive "we" of the preceding verses, the readers are, as in the letter's prologue, those who are challenged by what others can proclaim.

The task of the letter has been to construct an imagined community in which they find themselves fully a part, in fellowship with the true God, enjoying the victory over all that opposes God, which has been won by God's only Son. That imagined community has been given a shape and an identity by echoes of earlier familiar traditions from Scripture and elsewhere. Such echoes have made

170. See, for example, E. Stegemann, "Kindlein, hütet euch vor den Götterbildern," *TZ* 41 (1985): 284–94, although he adopts a more nuanced position, arguing that in the face of persecution Christians would have to identify the extent to which their faith in Jesus distanced them from the Jews. See also the commentary on "savior of the world" in 4:14.

171. As argued by Julian Hills, "'Little children, keep yourselves from idols': 1 John 5:21 Reconsidered," *CBQ* 51 (1989): 285–310, who persuasively sets 1 John 5:21 alongside 1:1–3 and the Isaianic framework, but concludes only that the idols are the negative counterpart to Jesus Christ.

them feel at home, able to find their way around and to identify the perplexities of the challenges that face them. The alternatives to this home are uncompromising: antichrist, false prophets, the devil, the evil one, and, more abstractly, falsehood, darkness, and death. If these seem intangible, figures from myth or from abstract thought, idols would convey something much more real and immediate. Readers are faced with an uncompromising choice—idols or fellowship with us . . . with the Father and with his Son, Jesus Christ; this is the only true God.

# 2 JOHN

## 2 John

Although modern readers of the New Testament may remark on the brevity of 2 John, in the context of its time it meets many of the expectations of a letter: it opens with a greeting from sender to recipient, not initially in the first to second person, but both in the third person; it closes with hopes of a future visit and with greetings from a third party; and it would fit onto a single sheet of papyrus. The same features and overall length, which are also found in 3 John but with significant differences, can be paralleled in countless letters that have been preserved from the rubbish heaps of the towns and villages of Egypt of the Greek and Roman periods.[1] Despite this, a number of distinctive features of 2 John and of its language suggest that it is not a simple personal letter that has survived by chance. Even the standard epistolary features, the address, greeting, and closing messages, take a highly unusual and self-conscious form, and I will argue in the commentary that these are utilized to create an appropriate framework within which specific instructions can be given.

Particularly in the first part of the body of the letter the language is strongly reminiscent of 1 John, yet its relationship with the latter is different from that between the Gospel and 1 John. Whereas the Gospel and First Letter used the same traditions in distinctive and creative ways, here it is a matter of close literary dependence. Some have argued that 2 John may be a rough draft for the more polished and thought-through 1 John, or perhaps an initial hasty response to an urgent situation (2 John 7), to be followed by a more considered one in the longer letter. While this could explain the allusiveness of 2 John, I will argue that the letter is more probably deliberately reusing key phrases from 1 John to give weight to a particular concern. The result is that the logic and precise reference of the phrasing are not easy to determine, and it seems likely that the main purpose is their rhetorical effect in establishing sympathy and persuasion. This is particularly the case in the description of the "many deceivers" in verse 7. On this reading the primary creative element in the letter is to be found in the instructions on how to respond to those who may visit the community but who fail to demonstrate that their teaching is "approved" (vv. 9–11). If this is so, 2 John reflects a situation, known also from other sources, where small communities of those who believed in Jesus were dependent on the teaching brought

---

1. On these see the examples of letters given in the commentary on 3 John.

by visits from members of other communities or from traveling teachers. This situation provoked the need for means of accreditation, and an appeal to a figure of recognized authority as providing these was a natural response. However, conflicts might readily arise between different individuals who felt themselves responsible for the various separate communities, as appears to be in view in 3 John.

Like many letters where the immediate context is well known to all parties, the details are only hinted at and any reconstruction is inevitably hypothetical. This is exacerbated by the elements of artificiality and of imitation already described; to the Johannine ones may be added an awareness of the formal "Christian" letter tradition that begins with Paul but soon spreads much more widely. If 2 John is self-consciously imitative it is less likely to reflect a specific local situation. Instead it is using the letter format as a cloak, a strategy that is not unusual in the ancient world.[2] When this is combined with the studied anonymity, shared with but differently developed than in 1 John, the primary task of the commentary has to be to explore the world created by the author of the text, and the way that the recipients are placed within it.

## *2 John 1–3—The Greeting*

1 The elder to the elect lady[a] and her children, whom[b] I love in truth—indeed, not only I but all who have knowledge of the truth—2 because of the truth that indwells[c] in us[d] and shall be with us forever.[e] 3 There shall be with us grace, mercy, peace from God the Father and from[f] Jesus Christ the Son of the Father, in truth and love.

a. Although possible, it is unlikely that a personal name is given, either "the elect Kyria" or "the lady Electa" (contrast v. 13, "elect sister").

b. The relative pronoun is masculine plural, although referring to the lady (fem.) and children (neut.).

c. Codex Alexandrinus reads a different verb here, "dwelling in" (*enoikeō*) instead of *menō*; because it is not the expected Johannine (or NT) term it might have some claim to being original.

d. In vv. 2–3 some manuscripts read the second person, "you," as might be expected in a letter prescript, but the first person has the best support.

e. The grammatical construction changes in the middle of the verse, but the sense intended is clear.

f. The repetition of the preposition is unusual. Some manuscripts add here "the Lord," as in the Pauline greetings (see KJV).

2. See further, Introduction §1.2.

**[1]** The author identifies himself only as "the elder" (*ho presbyteros*), a term that might be translated as simply indicating greater age, or as a semitechnical designation of authority. In either case it would be very unusual for the sender of a letter to fail to identify himself also by name. The anonymity of the sender is matched by that of the recipient, "the elect lady" (see note a), and is sustained throughout the letter (cf. v. 13). This introduces an artificial note, which could suggest that the contrast between "the elder" and "the lady" is deliberately chosen as appropriate to a letter of concern and direction; the letter format was commonly used in antiquity as a fictional device and as a vehicle for teaching, for example of a philosophical nature, although the recipient is often named even in these.[3] Undoubtedly the letter format, once established as a Christian medium, was readily exploited, as witnessed by Revelation 2–3 or by the pseudonymous letters that quickly emerge. However, 3 John, with its address to Gaius and the personal details it supplies, shows that the author's epithet was a meaningful one in a real communication to a particular individual and that it probably indicated more than his greater age. Second John adds little to the picture that can be deduced from 3 John, and it may nonetheless be exploiting the potential of the label in a different context.

Since there are no external sources that can either account for the anonymity claimed by the author or identify him, he can only, at least initially, be profiled from the letters themselves. It is evident from both letters that the author claims some authority for himself, but—especially from 3 John—that this authority could be challenged. It also seems that he writes at a distance from his readers and in 3 John from what he labels "the church" (3 John 9), but, if this is not simply a conventional pleasantry, that he anticipates visiting them (2 John 12; 3 John 10). He hears news of the associates of those to whom he writes, including from some who had visited them (2 John 4; 3 John 3). He would therefore appear to be involved in, and at least sees himself as a focal figure in, a network of groups. To some extent his reference to those he addresses as "children" (vv. 4, 13; 3 John 4; see commentary) reinforces his seniority as someone of greater age and experience, but it is unlikely that this alone explains his anonymity. Yet he makes no other claims that might buttress his assumption of authority; indeed, although at key points he does use the first person plural "we," this does not carry the same overtones as it does in 1 John and it is generally not clear who is included in it (see 2 John 4, 8; 3 John 8, 10).

---

3. For example, among the pseudonymous Cynic letters roughly contemporary with 2 John there are brief ones to Hipparchia from both Crates and Diogenes. See A. J. Malherbe, *The Cynic Epistles: A Study Edition* (Society of Biblical Literature Sources for Biblical Study 12; Missoula, Mont.: Scholars Press, 1977); C. D. N. Costa, *Greek Fictional Letters: A Selection with Introduction, Translation and Commentary* (Oxford: Oxford University Press, 2001).

This initial sketch does not closely parallel other occurrences of the term "elder" in early Christian literature. Within the early church elders appear as a group holding some sort of responsibility for a local congregation (Acts 14:23; 20:17, 28; 1 Pet 5:1); such a structure, where the "elders" are, initially at least, chosen from among the older men, was, unsurprisingly, widely found among different types of organization in the ancient world, but in particular it seems to have been a regular feature of Diaspora synagogues. Their responsibilities would have varied according to the group of which they were a part. However, this was a local and usually a corporate form of office, in contrast to the context suggested above for the author; membership of such a collective would not explain his anonymity, neither is it obvious why someone would retain the title if he were no longer in this collegial context. This does not mean that he is outside any particular community—it is possible that he speaks from the community of "the elect sister" (2 John 13).

Another use of the epithet "elder" emerges in the second century among Christian writers (Papias and Irenaeus) who refer to some members of the previous generation as "the elders"; they appeal to these primarily as mediators of a tradition of teaching that ultimately goes back to the apostles, and not as men holding defined positions of structural authority in the church.[4] Irenaeus, possibly drawing on a written source, quotes "a certain elder" on the interpretation of scriptural passages (*Against Heresies* 4.27.1–28.1, 30.1–31.1); he also describes "the elders" as "disciples of the apostles," and even specifically associates them with "John the disciple of the Lord" whom he identifies with the apostle.[5] Earlier in the second century, Papias, alongside a general appeal to "the elders" on whom he ultimately depended, specifically names "the elder John," who is himself also a "disciple of the Lord," but the passage, transmitted by Eusebius, leaves his precise relationship with the other "disciples of the Lord," Andrew, Peter, Philip, Thomas, James, John, or Matthew, obscure: "If perchance someone came who had followed the elders, I asked the words of the elders: what Andrew or what Peter said or what Philip or what Thomas or James or what John or Matthias or some other of the disciples of the Lord, and the things that Aristion and the elder John, the disciples of the Lord, were saying."[6]

---

4. The sources are much discussed; see Judith Lieu, *The Second and Third Epistles of John* (SNTW; Edinburgh: T. & T. Clark, 1986), 55–63.

5. *Against Heresies* 2.22.5; 5.5.1, 30.1, 33.3; the identification with the apostle may not have been explicit in his sources.

6. Eusebius, *Ecclesiastical History* 3.39.3–4. Among the many questions provoked by this passage, it is unclear whether the sequence of questions, "What. . .?" are those asked by Papias, in which case all who follow from Andrew to the elder John are included in the first reference to "the elders"; alternatively "what. . ." may be the content of the elders' words, adding a further stage in the chain of reporting. It is also uncertain whether the change from "said" to "were saying" implies that the last two were still alive, and why John is separately named "elder."

Again, the value of the "elders" for Papias is what he can learn from them, albeit at second- (or third-) hand. Still, it is not surprising that there have been many attempts to locate "the elder" of 2 and 3 John among these shadowy figures, although Papias's interest in them bears little relationship to the profile obtained from the letters. More specifically, some have followed Jerome's lead in identifying the anonymous author of 2 and 3 John with Papias's "elder John," and have thus explained the letters' (mistaken) eventual attribution to the author of the Gospel, while others have gone further, suggesting an early confusion between the two Johns, or even that the elder was the disciple of the apostle.[7] Such reconstructions rely entirely on conjecture, however, and have no support either in the sources or in the character of 2 and 3 John themselves (see further Introduction §4.1).

Equally without foundation is the suggestion sometimes found that these "elders" held a regional authority grounded in their own charisma and/or in their place in the line of authoritative tradition. The sources do no more than indicate that the epithet "elder" was accorded by a later generation to shadowy figures who had no official status but who were believed to stand at a crucial point in what was a developing theory of unbroken tradition. Already toward the end of the second century, someone like Irenaeus valued the tenuous personal links through Polycarp, whom he had heard possibly only once, for he felt that these connected him to the apostolic age (Eusebius, *Ecclesiastical History* 5.20.4–8, 24.14); yet in practice he evidently had very little secure knowledge about the patterns of church life and the transmission of traditions across the period that separated him from that age. The picture modern scholars have is inevitably no less patchy and equally dependent on imaginative reconstruction. In addition, in these sources "the elder" is not a self-designation, rendering it even more unlikely that 2 and 3 John are illuminated by or can illumine this situation.

Neither is there any help from elsewhere in the Johannine tradition: the apparent lack of interest in church structures evidenced by the Gospel and 1 John does not provide a clear framework within which "the elder" can be set, and this is reinforced by the threefold pattern in 1 John 2:12–14, of little children, young men, and *fathers* (see commentary). Indeed, it may be the absence of any attempt to address problems through appeal to fixed guidelines and structures that does most to explain the challenges the elder evidently faces (3 John 9–10). Presumably for the first recipient(s) at least of 3 John there was no mystery surrounding the author, and 2 John, even if imitative, also presupposes that

---

7. Jerome, *On Illustrious Men* 9; 18. Jerome was building on the tradition reported by Dionysius of Alexandria in the third century that there were two tombs "of John" in Asia, although Dionysius concluded that one of these was the author of the Apocalypse (Eusebius, *Ecclesiastical History* 3.39.5; 7.25.16). The picture is complicated when scholars, doubting the apostolic authorship of the Gospel, rely on a similar hypothesis and ascribe the Gospel to the "Elder John." It is even less likely that 2 and 3 John are fictions dependent on the tradition from Papias of an "elder John."

the epithet will carry a note of authority; even so, it may not have been long before subsequent readers had no certain knowledge of him.

The identity of the "elect lady" is equally obscure, although "lady" (*kyria*) is a common epithet in letters, whether used of a mother or sister or of someone more exalted. The profile at first presented by 2 John is of a woman with her children, of their responsibility for a home to which visitors may come, and of her sister, who is well known to the author. However, this is hardly sustained throughout the letter: the lady plays no real role and the letter lacks any personal details such as characterize 3 John; the second person plural address quickly takes over from the singular (vv. 8, 10, 12; see also v. 5); the children are sufficiently numerous for the author to have encountered "some" of them (v. 4); and that he knew only the female siblings (v. 13) seems unlikely. On these grounds it is frequently assumed that the "real" addressee of the letter is a church, while the "sister" and her "children" represent another community.

One way of bridging the gap between the "narrative" established by the letter[8] and the real recipient would be if this particular community were indeed presided over by a woman, as was the neighboring one. Verse 11 likely presupposes a relatively small community located within the "house," perhaps of its patron or coordinator/leader, and there is plentiful evidence that such household communities might be under a woman's oversight (Acts 16:11–15, 40). Some have suggested that the presence in the Fourth Gospel of women playing key positive roles may reflect their prominence in Johannine circles (John 4; 11; 19:25–27; 20), although a more skeptical observer would note that none of these women remains among Jesus' circle beyond the immediate narrative in which they star. However, this hypothesis does not adequately address the deliberate if superficial construction of the family model of mother, sister, and their children. The last may *represent* members of the community, but it is not a natural label for them.

Certainly there is good precedent for the female personification of a community: in political contexts cities could be addressed as *kyria*, while coins depicting the Roman defeat of the Jewish revolt portrayed the captured Judea as a woman. More specifically, Zion/Jerusalem is represented as a mother in the Scriptures, often widowed or bereft of her children (*tekna*) (Isa 54:1–6; 62:4; Ezekiel 16; Bar 4:10–16). Ephesians 5:29–32 represents the church as the wife of Christ, and Revelation 21 offers the vision of the new Jerusalem "prepared like a bride for her husband" in brutal contrast to the woman of Revelation 12. The Shepherd of Hermas is peopled with female representative figures including a woman, first young, then old, who is the church (Hermas, *Vis.* 1.1–2.4); more specifically, the idea of "mother church" becomes a commonplace at the end of the second century (e.g., as a "virgin mother" in the letter of the churches

---

8. That is, the initial profile as sketched earlier; see below.

of Vienne and Lyons, cited in Eusebius, *Ecclesiastical History* 5.1.45).[9] However, all these personifications belong in contexts or in literary genres where one expects a degree of symbolism, and none fully explains such imagery in a letter. While it is possible that at least some of the women in the Fourth Gospel carry a symbolic significance that goes beyond their narrative role, this is more likely to be through their evocation of scriptural themes, of which there is little evidence in 2 John.[10]

All this suggests that 2 John is not simply an ordinary letter, as is also evident from the high degree of artificiality when compared with 3 John. A consequence is that any reconstruction should give priority to 3 John as to what appears to be a genuine letter from someone who could identify himself only as "the elder," an epithet whose potential 2 John then exploits. Second John initially has to be read as creating its own narrative, independently of questions as to the intended audience of the text; within this, the "narrative recipient," the lady, is not to be dissolved as a symbol of a "real recipient": to seek to identify a "real recipient" who might justify the personification as an "elect lady" fails to recognize that the letter creates its own, self-contained narrative world. This need not mean that 2 John is not by the same author as 3 John: their brevity means the question cannot be decisively answered, but it may also give little persuasive reason for doubting common authorship.

There may be a further inspiration for 2 John: 1 Peter 5 opens with the author addressing the elders as a "fellow elder" (*sympresbyteros*), and closes with greetings from "the fellow elect" (5:13; fem.: *syneklektē*) in Babylon.[11] An intriguing possibility would be that the author of 2 John is deliberately imitating the language of this chapter to give authority to his own writing, just as he also echoes the language of 1 John. There is, however, insufficient evidence confidently to substantiate this, and perhaps an easier alternative would be that these two examples provide a glimpse of a more widespread use of terminology, especially in the adoption of the letter format for encouragement and direction.

The adjective "elect" (*eklektē*) (also v. 13) is not otherwise found in the Johannine literature;[12] formed from the verbal root "to choose," it is, however,

9. Tertullian, *To the Martyrs* 1, refers to the church as "lady mother church."

10. For example, the mother of Jesus (John 19:25–27) has often been seen as a symbol of Israel, or as being in some sense an Eve figure. Both the well scene in John 4 and the woman in a garden in John 20 carry scriptural resonances. Some interpreters have seen Mary Magdalene in John 20 as representing the community that has to learn to live when their master is no longer visible, but again it would be a long step from this claim to a letter written to an anonymous woman.

11. This echo is presumably responsible for Clement of Alexandria's statement that 2 John "was written to virgins (*virgines* = Greek *pros parthenous*) . . . to a certain Babylonian, Eclecta by name, but signifies the election of the holy church" (*On the Second Letter of John*, surviving in Latin only). This is undoubtedly related to the tradition found in the Old Latin and repeated by Augustine that 1 John was "to the Parthians" (= Greek *parthous*). See further the introduction §4.1.

12. Except as a variant reading in the testimony of John (the Baptist) to Jesus at John 1:34.

widely applied elsewhere to those who believe in Jesus, most commonly in the plural (Rom 8:33; Col 3:12; 2 Tim 2:10). Perhaps not distant in time from 2 John, Ignatius does use the term in the singular when addressing the church at Tralles as "elect and worthy of God" (Ignatius, *Trall.* prescript). The scriptural background shows that they are chosen by God, and 1 Peter's opening greeting to "the elect sojourners of the Diaspora" deliberately echoes the description of Israel (1 Pet 1:1; cf. 2:4, 9; Isa 43:20; 45:4), although this cannot be transferred to 2 John. The lady is joined by her children, just as the final greeting will come from the children of her sister (v. 13). As in 3 John, the usual word *tekna* is used, not the diminutive with which the author of 1 John addresses his readers (*teknia*, e.g., 1 John 2:1): 1 John reserves *tekna* for "children of God" or "of the devil" (1 John 3:2 [see commentary], 10; cf. John 1:12; 11:52). Unlike 3 John 4, however, they are not the author's (metaphorical) "children," and the picture sustains the initial image of a woman in a family context. "Children" is not commonly used for members of a group, and to identify them directly with the receiving congregation would again be to confuse the world created within the letter with a supposed "real audience."

This far the third person form of the address, "A to B," follows the standard pattern of Greek letter prescripts. This pattern is disrupted as the author emphasizes in an emphatic first person his own "love" for the lady and her children, a love that is no ordinary love but is characterized by belonging to the sphere of "truth" (cf. 1 John 3:18 and commentary). Although warm expansions of the opening greeting are not unexpected in a letter, both "love" and "truth" are key terms in Johannine vocabulary, while "truth" is especially prominent in these two letters.[13] Particularly noteworthy is the frequency of the dative construction "in truth" (2 John 1, 3, 4; 3 John 1, 3, 4); although this could be translated as a conventional "sincerely," the Johannine resonances of the term do seem to be evoked even if a lack of depth or sharpness is producing something of an internal catchphrase. A further expansion includes in the circle of love "all who have knowledge of the truth"; who and where these others are is not and does not need to be explained, for the main effect is to intensify this appeal to a more extensive and shared code. Whereas in John 8:32 Jesus promised those who maintained the integrity of their discipleship that they would know (future) the truth, here such knowledge is already an assured possession (perfect); it is the mark of those who share the Johannine vision that transforms the meaning of everything they look at—God's dealings, themselves, the world.

[2–3] A third appeal to truth puts a final seal on the all-encompassing sense of reality that holds them together. Both the Gospel and 1 John had described

---

13. "Love": 2 John, 2 (noun) + 2 (verb); 3 John, 1 + 1; 1 John, 18 + 21; John, 7 + 36. "Truth": 2 John, 5 (3); 3 John, 6 (3); 1 John, 9 (1); John, 25 (4); (parentheses indicate the dative with "in"). See further commentary on 1 John 1:6; 2:4, 21.

truth as "being in" the obedient or faithful (1 John 1:8; 2:4; John 8:44); here, drawing on another distinctive Johannine image, truth becomes an indwelling force (*menō en*; see 1 John 2:6 and commentary), both now and also a promised presence for the future.[14] The contrast between the elder, or "I," and the elect lady and her children is now resolved into a plural "we," which unites them, with the "all" of the preceding verse, as those who together experience this certain possession.

This bond is reinforced as the author reformulates the greeting that conventionally characterized the opening formalities of a letter, and does so in a way that betrays awareness of a distinctive developing "Christian" letter style. When Paul developed the extended letter form to maintain his relationships with the communities he founded and his direction of them, he apparently also coined his own greeting formula that reflected both his theological convictions and the function of the letter in worship and direction. Instead of the standard Greek greeting, *chairein*,[15] he reworked the Greek translation of the Semitic greeting formula, "peace (be) to you," and added to that formula his own "signature" term, "grace" (*charis*), as well as identifying its origin: "grace and peace to you from God . . . and from Jesus Christ" (1 Cor 1:3; Gal 1:3). This pattern is taken up by other letter writers (Rev 1:4), and, perhaps further influenced by Semitic models, is also modified—for example, by making the wish explicit, "be multiplied" (1 Pet 1:2; 2 Pet 1:2; cf. Jude 2), or by the insertion of "mercy" (1 Tim 1:2; 2 Tim 1:2).[16] Second John uses this same threefold formula of "grace" (*charis*, which occurs only in the Gospel prologue, John 1:14, 16, 17), "mercy" (*eleos*, otherwise absent from the Johannine corpus), and "peace," but the elder replaces the wish with an emphatic assertion: these blessings "shall be with us." This is no longer a hope expressed by the sender for the recipient's benefit, but another declaration of shared confidence. The result is a remarkable, but probably fortuitous, echo of Wis 3:9, "Those who put their trust in him will understand truth, and the faithful will remain in him in love, because grace and mercy are for his elect ones."

For all this the greeting remains rooted in the tradition of Johannine language: the preposition "from" is not that used in the Pauline greetings (*apo*), but a particular favorite of the Johannine Jesus when he speaks of his origin "from" God (*para*, John 6:46; 7:29; 17:7–8).[17] Second, there is a repeated emphasis not only on God as Father but also on Jesus Christ as the Son of the Father, an unusual and emphatic formula: resonant of the central concerns of

14. For "remain . . . forever" cf. 1 John 2:17 (see commentary); John 8:35. See note e on text.

15. Among NT letters, *chairein* is used only by Jas 1:1 (cf. also Acts 15:23), although in the early second century Ignatius takes it for granted. See commentary on 3 John 1.

16. Jude 2 is distinctive in adapting the formula in its own terms: "mercy to you and peace and love be multiplied." "Be multiplied" does follow Semitic precedent.

17. *Para* is not used in 1 John.

1 John, it will be recalled as the letter reaches its main goal (v. 9). The "Father" is therefore Father of the Son, although when addressed to a woman and her children the epithet does also reinforce the familial pattern. Finally, the elder concludes the greeting with a formulaic "in truth and love," thereby integrating it into the Johannine ethos he has already established.

The overall impact is to give the letter considerable presence, inviting readers to expect an authoritative and significant message. It is the more striking that, unlike the prologue of 1 John, the author does not recall his readers to any specific Johannine images that might support the authority he personally claims. Instead he claims the implied authority that comes not only with Johannine appeals to the truth but also with the Pauline (and possible Petrine) letter tradition. The effect of all this careful crafting is still to exclude any possibility that the "elect lady" would not respond to the instructions that will follow later, and also to exclude any who do not already belong to "the truth" from demanding a hearing; the prescript rhetorically establishes the inviolable security and the tight borders which bind those who read together with the writer.

### 2 John 4–8—Encouragement to Steadfastness

4 I was greatly pleased that I discovered some[a] of your children walking in truth, just as we received a command from the Father. 5 So now I ask you, lady, not as if writing a new command for you but one that we have held from the beginning, that we should love one another—6 this, then, is love, that we are to walk according to his commandments: this is the commandment, just as you have heard from the beginning—that you walk in it.[b] 7 For many deceivers went out into the world who do not acknowledge Jesus Christ coming in flesh. This[c] is the deceiver and the antichrist. 8 Watch yourselves, so that you do not bring to ruin[d] that for which we have labored, but receive a full reward.

a. "Some" is implied by the use of a partitive genitive.

b. A range of textual variants witness to the difficulty in making clear sense of this verse; see commentary.

c. The switch to the singular prompted a range of scribal emendations.

d. There is some textual evidence for reading the last three verbs in this verse as the first person plural, "we" (so KJV), and rather more for reading all three verbs as the second person plural, "you"; although considerably less well attested the alternation represented in the translation given would explain both variations as attempts to harmonize and has a good claim to being original.

[4] An expression of thanks for news received is a common epistolary device for moving the letter from the opening formalities into its actual substance or

body (see commentary on 3 John 3–4). Whether the elder made his discovery personally, either from visiting the community or from encountering its members elsewhere, or whether he received news of them (cf. 3 John 3), is not explained. That he speaks only of "some" does not mean that there were others who were less commendable, but it does undermine the implied model of a small family unit even allowing for the extended classical family. After the repeated references to truth in the opening verses of the letter it is self-evident that the behavior for which he praises them, "following a path [lit. "walking"] in truth," indicates adherence to the norms that shape the author's vision of reality. Unlike 1 John's metaphor of "walking in the darkness" or "in the light" (1 John 1:6–7; see commentary), here "walking" (*peripateō*) is used in its well-established sense of "living," modified by an appropriate manner (cf. 1 Thess 4:1, 12; 2 Thess 3:6, 11). Although this would permit the translation "loyally" or "in sincerity," it is in context more likely that "truth" carries stronger Johannine echoes, even if it functions as a catchphrase in these two letters (cf. vv. 1, 3).[18]

The measure of this praiseworthy behavior is the command given by the Father. In the following verse the author will invoke the command that "we should love one another," and it is natural to assume that this is what is in view here. They were already demonstrating that close-bonded reciprocal loyalty that he will shortly reaffirm. How they demonstrated this is unimportant, for the expression of pleasure serves more as a placatory introduction to the elder's subsequent plea: he will not be asking of them any more than what the best of them already exhibit. The description of the command as received by "*us*" (and not by "you") reinforces this group-building and affirming strategy, but it also leaves open whether those whom he met would themselves have explained their behavior as a response to the command. More surprisingly, this command has come "from (*para*) the Father": in the Fourth Gospel the command is emphatically Jesus' own for his followers (John 13:34; 15:12), although 1 John was rather more equivocal (1 John 2:7–8; 3:23; see commentary). For 2 John "the Father" is consistently the primary point of reference for the behavior and standing of the lady and her children (vv. 2, 9), and the parallel with John 10:18 ("this command I received from my Father") may be fortuitous.[19]

**[5–6]** Since members of "the lady's" family are already, at least implicitly, adhering to the command, it follows that in introducing it now he is not imposing any new demand on them. The careful wording, however, indicates that the letter is moving away from its opening pleasantries to the real matter at issue, although the author continues to tread carefully. The repeated first person plural verbs, "we have held," "we should love," soften the authoritative request that

---

18. In 3 John 4 the article is added, "walking in *the* truth," which is less likely to be intended adverbially.

19. Although it is not the only point at which 2 John is closer to the Gospel; see also n. 17.

opens verse 5 and that will be reinforced by the closing second person plural verbs of the next verse; they allow no sense of distance or of difference in position between author and audience. The association of the command with "the beginning" was evidently formulaic (cf. 1 John 2:7, "*you* have held"; cf. 3:11 and commentary), and leaves no room for determining greater precision—for example, the beginning of their faith experience or that of the Johannine or Jesus tradition; instead the reminder reinforces the existing bonds between them and with the past. Nonetheless, the sharp denial that it is a new command contrasts with the Johannine Jesus' own identification of his command that they love one another as "new" (John 13:34), although the careful qualification of the epithet in 1 John 2:7–8 (see commentary) suggests that the formulation may have needed sensitive handling. Although what was novel on Jesus' mouth was no longer so among his followers, 2 John's tracing of the command to the Father suggests that this is not the primary logic at play here: antiquity was valued more than novelty in the ancient world, and when faced with challenges it is always preferable to be able to claim to hold the original tradition.

What the elder is requesting is obscured by the complex grammatical structure through to the end of verse 6, exacerbated by the numerous textual variants that reflect scribal attempts to clarify their own solutions. Most English translations assume that his request is "that we love one another" and finish the sentence at the end of verse 5 (KJV, NRSV).[20] However, elsewhere the introductory "that" (*hina*) consistently expands the content of the command (1 John 3:11, 23; 4:21; John 13:34) and is an inseparable part of the traditional formula, "that [*hina*] we [John 13:34: "you"] are to love one another."[21] If that is so here, the author finally explains his request only at the end of verse 6, after further, somewhat circuitous, attempts to reinforce its authority; in contrast to the "we" here, the second person plural there gives support to this interpretation and is reflected in the translation given. The author's intention is the same in both readings; whether he is deliberately voicing his request in an inclusive first person, or reaches it only after repeated appeals to an earlier heritage, the effect is similar: they are to remain faithful to the understanding and pattern of life that has formed them as a community and held them together in the past, and that is also the pattern that he himself represents and can interpret in a new situation.

This is why he explains what love is, not in terms of their behavior to one another as one might expect, but in terms of their obedience to "his commands." The wording recalls 1 John 5:3, "Indeed this is the love of God, that we keep

20. This is probably how the text has to be read if "in order that" (*hina*) is inserted before "just as you have heard" in v. 6 (so KJV, but not NRSV). Although this has strong textual support, including Sinaiticus and Alexandrinus, it is probably an attempt to clarify the more difficult reading without it.

21. See commentary on 1 John 3:11 on the Johannine form of the love command and the implications of "one another."

his commands"; there the definition of love as "of God" produces a clearer logic (see commentary), whereas here the love just identified (v. 5) has been that directed to one another. It is possible that both verses are echoing formulae familiar to a Johannine audience, but more likely that the author of 2 John is specifically echoing the language and more detailed argumentation of the First Letter. In either case, within a Johannine context the step from reciprocal love to love for or from God, and so to obedience, is not a great one—they are implicated in each other. The parallel suggests that the commands are God's, and, as in 1 John (see 3:23–24 and commentary), it is unlikely that by the plural the author has in mind anything specific beyond the single foundational command of love. The metaphor of "walking according to" (*peripateō kata*) the commands here, rather than "keeping" them as in 1 John (*tēreō*, not used in 2 or 3 John), picks up his earlier delight at finding the "children walking in truth" (v. 4). Although only here in the Johannine literature, the idiom ("walk *according to*") is found elsewhere of adherence to a norm (Mark 7:5; 2 Thess 3:6). The elder does not want his audience to think that love for one another can be continually redefined, or that it need pay no heed to inherited patterns of behavior.

Where verse 5 has been read as already completing the elder's request (see above), the last part of verse 6 must simply reinforce the importance of following the command. Even so it is uncertain whether the emphatic "*this* is the command" anticipates what follows or explains what precedes it. If it points forward (as at the beginning of this verse and at 1 John 2:25), the command is that they should walk "in it";[22] as a feminine pronoun, "it" refers back either to love at the beginning of the verse—making good sense but grammatically clumsy—or to the nearest feminine noun, the command: this is grammatically much smoother, and although the apparent meaning—that the heart of the command is to live by it—appears redundant, it would serve the elder's relentless reinforcement of his call to faithfulness to the tradition received. If the initial "this" points backward, it is apparently defining the command as to walk according to God's commandments, which themselves are the expression of love.[23]

The translation offered assumes that the elder does not finally make his request until the end of verse 6, "So now I ask you, lady, not as writing a new command for you . . . that you walk in it!" The switch to the plural "you" includes the children with the lady (or the community, where one is assumed), and follows better than a request voiced in the first person plural, "that we love one another." Between introducing the request and articulating it he has piled

22. So apparently KJV (see n. 20), but without clearly indicating how "it" is understood. On 1 John's use of the formula see commentary on 1 John 2:25; 5:3, 11. In addition to what follows, identifying "it" as the commandment involves a change from "walking according to," a recognizable idiom, to "walking *in* a command."

23. The NRSV implies a backward reference but turns the last clause of v. 6 into a new instruction, "—you must walk in it"; grammatically this is improbable.

up echoes of familiar commandment-related formulations, twice repeating its aboriginality, and excluding any possible separation between love and obedience; if what they have "heard from the beginning"—another familiar Johannine refrain (1 John 2:24; 3:11; see commentary)—is to love one another, it is no less to walk according to his commandments, for that love can only be understood in terms of obedience. The move from first person plural ("we have held," "we are to love," "we are to walk") to second person plural ("just as you have heard," "you are to walk") binds his audience to himself and then puts the onus on them to respond, while also suggesting that this is something that arises out of their own past experience.

On any reading of these verses, with a greater or lesser degree of clarity the author is most concerned to evoke familiar concepts and phrases—"from the beginning," "the command," "love one another," "this is"—packing them together to create a close-knit framework defined in terms of obedience and of continuity with the past. The specific identity of the lady and her children becomes unimportant for those readers who instinctively identify themselves in these terms and so find themselves invited to situate themselves along with the author. The reason why emerges as he continues.

[7] The elder explains the specific call to faithfulness, "For" (*hoti*). This is a connection that is obscured when verse 7 is printed as commencing a new paragraph (as in NA$^{27}$, NRSV), and especially when the *hoti* is ignored in translation (NRSV). The reason why the author has so emphatically reinforced the network of Johannine ideas that provide the readers with their sense of identity is because he fears the impact of alternative interpretations. The announcement of the many who have gone out into the world closely follows that in 1 John 4:1, "because (*hoti*!) many false prophets have gone out into the world," where it justified the rather different call to test the spirits. The echo is reinforced both by the definition of the problem in terms of the acknowledgment of Jesus Christ and by the epithet "antichrist," a neologism in these two writings (see 1 John 4:1–3 with commentary). This verse is so succinctly formulated that it would be difficult to understand its intention without reference to the passage in 1 John alongside the earlier explanation of the antichrist in 1 John 2:18–19 (see commentary); this, and the close similarity of wording together with some notable variations, suggest that 2 John 7 presupposes and has been formulated in the light of the longer letter. It is much less probable that the author here introduced an unfamiliar idea, which he subsequently had to explain in 1 John.

In 1 John 2:18–19 the "many antichrists" were described as having "gone out from among us," and this sense of their origin within the author's group or community may be carried over to the false prophets going "*out* into the world" in 1 John 4:1. Whereas in both those passages the perfect tense put more stress on the fact of their departure and their consequent presence "out there," the simple past (aorist) in 2 John 7 would allow more of a focus on the moment of their going, although it may be little more than a stylistic avoidance of the perfect tense. Second John does not state that they have left the community, however, and the anticipation in verse 10 of "anyone coming" makes this less likely. What matters is that they are active "in the world," a sphere whose negative associations probably have to be assumed from 1 John and the Gospel since the term is not used again (see commentary on 1 John 2:15). This is different from the more common pattern in warnings against false teachers, where the main danger is that they will infiltrate and be active in the community (Acts 20:29–30; 2 Tim 3:6; 2 Pet 2:1)—although that will come shortly.

Whereas 1 John described the "many" who went out as false or lying prophets (*pseudoprophētai*, 1 John 4:1), here they are those who go or lead astray (*planoi*). This noun appears only here in the Johannine literature, although the key passage in 1 John continues with an identification of "the spirit of error (*planē*)" (4:6), and elsewhere warns his readers against being led astray (*planaō*: 2:26; 3:7). A *planos* may be an impostor but is also one who leads others astray (Matt 27:63; 2 Cor 6:8); the image is particularly apposite in 2 John, after the appeals to proper, and directed, "walking," and might even fit the anticipation of anyone who comes (v. 10): such a one is a "wanderer." However, the advent of those, or of an arch-figure, who would lead others astray also belongs to eschatological expectation (Matt 24:4–5, 11, 24; Rev 12:9; 19:20: *planaō*). Without precisely identifying any particular individuals or their own claimed credentials, the elder evokes the possibility of being dislodged from the secure framework he has just constructed.

The only definition he gives these figures is their failure in confession. Again the wording appears to be drawn from 1 John 4:2, "every spirit that acknowledges Jesus Christ having come in flesh does belong to God." Here, however, it is the absence of right confession that matters ("do not acknowledge"), and this serves only to exclude; even more than in 1 John, it is impossible to determine whether this masks some alternative confession about Jesus that was being made. As is the case in 1 John 4:2 (see commentary), the construction using a participle is not an acknowledgment of a fact *about* Jesus ("*that* Jesus . . ."), but a confession *of* Jesus as he can be further described as (the) Christ and in terms of his coming. Particularly striking here, however, is that the present participle "coming" (*erchomenon*) replaces the perfect participle of 1 John 4:2, "having come," while the prepositional "in flesh" instead of preceding the participle follows it, although it is a moot point whether this gives it less significance. A number of translations ignore this present tense and treat it as if it were a past, "has come," merely repeating 1 John 4:2 (NRSV); this, however, is not what the participle means, and to translate so fails to explain why the author, if dependent on the passage in 1 John, has made the change—even if he had an aversion to the perfect he could have used an aorist tense. Similarly, attempts to suggest that the present tense expresses a timeless truth or continuous reality clash both with the inherent idea of the verb and with the precision implied by "in flesh."[24]

It is, however, of the nature of the verb that the present participle can have a future reference: "Jesus Christ (as) the one *to come* in flesh." The earliest known writer to cite 2 John, Irenaeus, used a chain of Johannine passages—2 John 7; 1 John 4:1–3; John 1:14; 1 John 5:1—to make this precise point: "knowing the same Jesus Christ, to whom were opened the gates of heaven because of his enfleshed assumption, who also in the same flesh in which he suffered, will come [future] revealing the glory of the Father" (*Against Heresies* 3.16.8).[25] This future fleshly coming was a common concern of the period, more frequently made by an appeal to Acts 1:11 ("in the same manner").[26] Although rarely taken up by translations and less favored among modern commentators, a continuing line of interpretation has seen in 2 John 7 a defense of the expectation of a fleshly parousia.[27] Such a reference cannot be excluded, and might cohere with the warning against eschatological loss of a reward in the following verse. It would, however, be difficult to imagine the author of 1 John expressing this concern, given his rather different expectation of future manifestation and transformation (see 1 John 2:28; 3:2; and commentary); this might then suggest that a different author, the elder, is reusing the perhaps familiar warning of the earlier letter to address a new danger. If this were the case, however, it is surprising that the elder has not signaled rather more emphatically what he was doing and why, perhaps by turning the confession into a statement *that* Jesus will come, by asserting the positive confession (as in 1 John), or even by evoking the coming Jesus as the one who would judge those who failed to recognize him.

A more persuasive explanation is that the author is again evoking familiar Johannine formulae without being particularly concerned about their precise reference. In the Fourth Gospel Jesus is identified as "(the prophet/the Christ, the Son of God) who *is to come* (*erchomenos*) into the world" (John 6:14;

24. See A. E. Brooke, *The Johannine Epistles* (ICC; Edinburgh: T. & T. Clark, 1912), 175: "the writer regards it as a continuous fact. The Incarnation is not only an event in history. It is an abiding truth." But he then describes the union (of Deity and humanity) as "permanent and abiding." It is hard to see how all this is expressed by "coming in flesh."

25. However, only the Latin survives of Irenaeus's quotation of 2 John 7, and this follows the Old Latin in reading a past tense (infinitive), so it is not certain that his future statement interprets 2 John 7. By contrast, Clement of Alexandria, although also only extant in Latin, interprets the verse in the words of 1 John 4:2–3.

26. Ignatius emphasizes that Jesus was "in flesh" even after the resurrection (*Smyrn.* 3.1); Tertullian, *On the Incarnation* 24, adds John 19:37 to Acts 1:11: he will not be recognizable to those who pierced him unless he has the same flesh.

27. So already Pseudo-Oecumenius, *Commentary on 1, 2, 3 John* (PG 119, 691–92); recent commentators include Gore, Loader, Strecker, Westcott; Brooke (p. 175) footnotes this as an attractive simpler explanation but misleadingly cites *Barn.* 16.9 (see below).

11:27). Moreover, a widespread earlier tradition spoke of Jesus simply as "the one to come," drawing on a variety of scriptural passages (see John 1:27; 12:13; Matt 3:11; 11:3; Ps 118 [LXX 117]:26; Dan 7:13 Theodotion). The idea was a malleable one, and its very familiarity in contrast to the perfect tense of 1 John 4:2 may have prompted the elder to elide it with the still opaque confession in that verse. This means that the warning is effectively against those who fail to confess Jesus as the broader Johannine tradition confesses him, namely as "the Christ who is to come"; the additional "in flesh" qualifies this by alluding to 1 John's conviction that this is the Jesus Christ who had indeed come. One consequence, but not necessarily one of which the elder was conscious, is a striking contrast with the Gospel, where Jesus is the one "[who comes] *into* the world" (*eis ton kosmon*, 6:14; 11:27; also 12:46; 16:28; 18:37), a destination that in 2 John is reserved for those who lead astray (cf. 1 John 4:1).[28]

A Johannine framework sufficiently explains the elder's formula, although it is intriguing that, entirely independently, a number of passages in the *Letter of Barnabas* read a similar emphasis on "in flesh" back into prophetic expectation of a future figure: "Learn what knowledge has to say, 'Hope on the one about to be revealed to you in flesh, Jesus'"; and quoting Ezek 36:26: "For this one was about to be manifested in flesh and to dwell in/among you" (*Barn.* 6.9, 14; cf. 5.6, 10, 11; 6.7; 12.10). The future perspective has misled some interpreters into seeing an eschatological reference in these passages (see n. 27), but the language is evidently formulaic while the emphasis is not on rejecting some other, less corporeal, form of coming but on Jesus' presence in the human sphere.

The elder's intention is not to set out a precise delineation of correct and incorrect confession but to evoke the specter of something that is indubitably wrong but may nevertheless mislead. It would therefore be a misunderstanding to speculate as to who there were "out in the world" and what beliefs they may have, or have not, held. For the elder's purpose it is enough for him to persuade his readers that there are those "who do not acknowledge" but who may nevertheless seek to exercise influence over them. Although he has anticipated the extent of the danger—"many"—they effectively count as one, as "*the* deceiver and *the* antichrist." The article here is not generic but specific, presupposing the idea, recalled a little more precisely in 1 John 2:18, of the final opposition to God embodied in a single figure (see commentary). At the same time, since this connection is presupposed but is not made explicitly, the possibility is kept open of identifying this figure with "anyone" (v. 10).

**[8]** The passage reaches its natural climax in an urgent command. The call to take heed or to watch out for themselves maintains the sense of eschatological urgency (Mark 13:9). The danger may not only be of *losing* the reward they

---

28. Elsewhere 1 John also preserves the tradition of the sending of the Son "into the world" (1 John 4:9).

might otherwise gain, one possible meaning of the verb *apollymi* (cf. Mark 9:41), or of undoing all that so far has been achieved; they may actually *destroy* it, assigning it, and by implication themselves, to the realm of destruction that in the eschatological divide is opposed to that of life and salvation (John 6:39; 17:12; 18:9; cf. Luke 9:25). The unexpected switch to the first person plural, "that you do not bring to ruin that for which *we* have labored,"[29] reinforces the seriousness of the moment. The effort has not been all their own; although the elder has endeavored to maintain a sense of the autonomy of the lady and her children, he cannot resist reminding them that they are part of a wider network and perhaps even dependent on it. This need not mean that behind the "we" stands only himself, anxious lest his own efforts go to ruin—he is well able to use the first person singular when he so wishes (vv. 5, 12); nor is he referring to an authoritative group such as has sometimes been held to stand behind the "we" of the prologue of 1 John (see commentary on 1 John 1:1–3), and whose "labor" is the creation of communities of believers. A similar alternation between first and second person plural in verses 5–6 set the audience within a larger community of the author and others ("all who have known the truth," v. 1), bound together by their common heritage of belief and its expression. Their loss would be to the loss of all those.

The reminder of what does lie ahead if they persevere returns the gaze to the audience again: no doubt "we" also may hope for a reward, but here it is the promise of that for "you," the readers, which will be most effective. The language of reward confirms the eschatological framework of this exhortation; the term (*misthos*) carries overtones of that which has been earned, "wage" (Rom 4:4), but is still used, even by Paul, of God's future recompense (1 Cor 3:8, 14; Rev 11:18; 22:12). Here it will have been earned by avoiding being distracted from the path along which they have already been traveling. It would be uncharacteristic of the author and of a letter as brief as 2 John to expand on how and when that reward would be experienced, and this is not a theme central to the other Johannine writings, which tend to focus more on the present experience of divine blessing. Its persuasive force is its primary function here.

The encouragement to the lady and her children to carry on as they have already been doing, in a manner that meets the approval of the elder and for him reflects the tradition that he represents, is thus reinforced by and reinforces the specter of the threat of being led astray from this tradition. His dense use of evocative and formulaic terms and ideas makes it impossible to discern the specific details of the danger that he feared, or, indeed, whether he could have supplied anything more specific. So far his instruction has also avoided anything too precise; however, the actual application of his anxieties will become more apparent in what follows.

29. See note d on text.

## 2 John 9–13—Holding on to the Teaching

Only at this point does the elder appear to reach the main purpose of his letter, as he envisages a potential situation and offers some harsh advice, whose rigor is only justified by the context in which he has set it in the preceding verses. Anyone seeking to join the community who does not acknowledge the same message is to be unequivocally excluded. That done he swiftly brings the letter to a close, and as he does so he reinforces the place of these "children" in a wider network.

> 9 Everyone who goes ahead and does not remain within the teaching of Christ[a] does not possess God. The one who remains in the teaching, that person possesses both the Father and the Son.[b] 10 If anyone comes to you and does not bring this teaching, do not receive him into the house and do not offer him a greeting.[c] 11 The person who offers him a greeting has fellowship in his evil deeds.[d]
>
> 12 Although I have much to write to you, I did not wish to do so by paper and ink; instead I hope to visit you and to speak face-to-face, so that our[e] joy may be made complete. 13 The children of your elect sister greet you.[f]

a. Or "the Christ/Messiah."

b. There is some manuscript evidence for reversing the terms, i.e., "possesses both the Son and the Father," but this may be in assimilation to the wording (but not the sense) of 1 John 2:23–24.

c. Literally, "Do not say, 'Hail!'"

d. Some witnesses of the Old Latin have an addition here, "Behold, I have told you in advance so that you may not be put to shame on the day of the Lord." Cf. 1 John 5:9, 20 for similar additions.

e. As frequently elsewhere, a number of manuscripts read the second person plural, "your" (cf. 1 John 1:4 note a).

f. As commonly happens at the end of NT letters, later manuscripts supply an ending, "Amen," and/or "Grace be with you [singular]."

**[9]** The elder maintains the image of making one's way: someone might forge ahead but in so doing might not so much go astray as fail to stay within the confines that have already been laid down. However, he is not concerned to define what such going forward might mean, and, contrary to some interpretations, the verb (*proagō*) does not imply that there were those claiming to be spiritually or intellectually "advanced." Again, although with an object the verb (*proagō*) can mean "to lead" or "to precede," there is no suggestion here that this is aimed against anyone claiming some sort of leadership in the community (as in 3 John 9). The structure of the verse, "everyone who . . . ," follows that used in 1 John to explore the consequences of an antithetical worldview (1 John 3:3, 6, etc.; see commentary), and, as there, need not suggest that there was such a case.[30] It appears instead that it is not the going forward that is at fault so much as the failure to remain; although perhaps the author would have thought that the latter was the inevitable consequence of the former, it is remaining that he intends to highlight. The verb (*menō*) is an important one in Johannine thought, and it represents a significant ideal in 1 John (2:6, 10, 24, etc.; see commentary). There, although inanimate objects could remain in or indwell the believer ("the word"; "what you heard from the beginning": 2:14, 24), where an individual is the subject of the verb the relationship is usually a personal one, indwelling in God or in Jesus.[31]

None of this quite parallels 2 John's ideal of "remaining in the teaching"; indeed, the noun "teaching" (*didachē*) is not found in 1 John. The idea is not totally foreign to Johannine thought: Jesus refers to his own "teaching" in the Gospel, and urges those who believe to remain in his "word" (John 7:16–17; 8:31), while 1 John does claim that "his anointing teaches you about everything" (1 John 2:27; see commentary). Nonetheless, 2 John's formulation still accords the idea of "the teaching" with a greater sense of fixity and regulation.

This sense is reinforced by the description of the teaching as "of Christ." It is unlikely that this means the teaching given by Christ, since the author has understood even the command as coming from the Father (v. 4); it is the teaching about (the) Christ that he wishes to safeguard. This must include the oblique formula in verse 7, although that itself functioned chiefly as an echo of other expressions of Johannine belief.[32] A potentially closer parallel in ethos is the Deuteronomic curse against whoever fails to "remain within (*emmenei en*) all the words of this law" (Deut 27:26 LXX); still closer is the injunction to Timothy to "remain in what you have learned and believed" (2 Tim 3:14; see further below). The idea is one of faithful allegiance to an inherited body of instruction that is becoming authoritative. The identification of what has been received as "teaching" (*didachē*) is found elsewhere, with the same sense that despite its apparent self-evident character, inherited teaching is always vulnerable to alternative interpretations (Rom 16:17). Such anxieties also have their place in eschatological frameworks: the injunction to Timothy just quoted follows immediately after a formulaic and imprecise warning against the "evil men and charlatans [who] will advance[33] to the worse, leading astray and led astray (*planaō*)" (2 Tim 3:13). This last example indicates that the frame-

---

30. However, given the distinctive use of "teaching," it is unlikely to come from the same (putative) source.

31. Although see 1 John 2:10, "indwells in the light"; 4:16, "indwells in love"; 2:27 is ambiguous; see commentary.

32. Hence "of the Messiah" would miss the internal reference.

33. *Prokoptō*; 2 John 9 uses *proagō*.

work within which 2 John moves remains one of conventional language, using both urgent warning and exhortations to faithfulness in order to serve a common goal.

That these conventions have been assimilated to a Johannine mind-set is apparent when the elder continues that anyone who so fails to remain "does not possess God." Similar language was used in 1 John in the context of the proper confession of Jesus: "the one who denies the Son does not possess the Father either; the one who acknowledges the Son also possesses the Father" (1 John 2:23; see commentary). In contrast to the close interconnection there between a relationship with God as *Father* and the acknowledgment of the one who is God's *Son*, here the association between "teaching" and "God" is both less integrated and less inherently personal and relational.[34] This is only slightly ameliorated in the antithetical second half of the verse, where the one who does remain in "the teaching," now not qualified, possesses both Father and Son. Instead of the confession effectively bringing someone into the necessary interrelationship between Son and Father, as in 1 John, here it is "teaching," something that can become objectified and formulated, that makes such a relationship possible. This means that, even less than in 1 John where "possessing" (*echō*) can be enriched by the other models of the close relationship a believer can expect with God such as "abiding" and "being in," a more precise description of how the emotive nature of this relationship is experienced is not possible.

**[10]** Against this background of warning and of encouragement to loyalty the elder finally turns to specific admonition. Here is something they can and must do, presumably his main concern all along. Someone may come—the "if" suggests not that this is only a vague possibility but that it is a very real one— but may not bring with them the core teaching that the elder has impressed upon his readers. The implication is not that these would be outsiders who have nothing to say but that they will bring some alternative to "*this*" teaching." Such a person is not to be given the slightest opportunity of infiltrating the group and, in the imagery of the earlier verses, of leading them astray. More than this: not only are they to be refused hospitality, they are even to be denied the courteous greeting (*chairein*) that would convey goodwill and might lead to further conversation.

The injunction that they should not accept this feared visitor "into the house" might simply denote the refusal of any domestic hospitality; however, it might equally reflect the situation of a community structured around a single household, perhaps even one under the patronage or leadership of a woman (see commentary on v. 1). Although not the only framework for meeting, the Pauline tradition witnesses to the importance of the household as the nucleus of groups

---

34. See commentary on 1 John 2:23 for other examples of "having God," although none is particularly close to that here.

of believers and as providing a place for meeting (Rom 16:5; 1 Cor 1:16; 16:15, 19). On the other hand, within the "narrative" created by the greeting the warning also plays on conventional ideas of the vulnerability of households and of women and children to the infiltration of unscrupulous and unauthorized teachers.[35]

The elder is clearly not envisaging merely a casual visitor. It could be a member of a group with a different interpretation of the Christian message ("teaching") whose mere presence in the enclosed circle of the elect spelled danger, but it is more likely that it is someone expressly seeking actively to share their teaching. It is easy to imagine how this might happen. Many of the early groups of believers were relatively small groups, perhaps founded, as were the Pauline churches, by someone who then went on elsewhere, or perhaps originating as a splinter group from a larger body, or as one set up by a former member from a different community. Their knowledge of the central teaching and practice would be derivative, and they would not necessarily have the resources among themselves to add to it or to determine how to apply it in different circumstances. At the same time itinerant teachers were a feature of the early church, as they were of other religious and philosophical groups. The account in the synoptic tradition of the mission of the Twelve envisages them seeking out a worthy house, and giving it their greeting, with a harsh warning against those who would not receive them (Matt 10:11–14); those traditions may have been preserved as a model not only for evangelistic mission (contrast 3 John 7; see commentary), but also for where direction and teaching were felt to be needed.

Other sources from the early decades of the church testify to comparable situations. In very similar words to these the *Didache*, claiming the authority of the twelve apostles, instructs, "Whoever comes and teaches you all these things that have already been described, receive him. If, though, the teacher himself turns and teaches another teaching in order to destroy, do not listen to him; but if it is to the increase of righteousness and knowledge of the Lord, receive him as the Lord" (*Did.* 11.1–2).[36] This passage continues with further provisos: anyone who stays too long or requests money for their onward journey is deemed spurious, as also is anyone who, although exhibiting charismatic gifts, acts in a way that undermines their claims. Yet those who are genuine are to be warmly welcomed, supported during their stay, and listened to. The *Didache* implies that

---

35. So, Celsus complains, "We see, indeed, in private houses workers in wool and leather, and fullers, and persons of the most uninstructed and rustic character, not venturing to utter a word in the presence of their elders and wiser masters; but when they get hold of the children privately, and certain women as ignorant as themselves, they pour forth wonderful statements" (Origen, *Against Celsus* 3.55).

36. Masculine language has been retained as most probably in view. There is a similar warning in Ps.-Clem. *Homilies* 9.35.4 against receiving "an apostle or teacher or prophet" without first having checked their teaching credentials with James.

such itinerant teachers, including those whom it labels apostles and prophets, play an essential role in the growth in understanding and in the encouragement of settled communities of believers. Indeed, while it encourages its readers to appoint their own leaders, "bishops and deacons," there is a sense that these need particular commendation because they were less readily granted respect, perhaps because they represented something of a novelty, or perhaps simply because they did not offer the stimulus of the visitor from elsewhere (*Did.* 15.1–2).

From the other side the verse is a reminder of the importance of hospitality within the early Christian movement. This was not only a social necessity but also established or reinforced bonds between different communities, building up the networking that was such an important feature of the growth of the early church. Hence encouragement to welcome strangers becomes a recurring theme in early teaching (Rom 12:13; Heb 13:2). Even an outsider noticed this characteristic of the Christians: in the mid-second century the satirist Lucian describes how the sophist–holy man Proteus Peregrinus, whom he denounces as a charlatan, came across the Christians, impressing them by his understanding of their beliefs, and by his own teaching and interpretation, to the extent that they supported him even when he was imprisoned (*Peregrinus* 13). Lucian mocks their gullibility, but still implies that this was a visible feature of Christian communal practice, at least in the Palestine of his time where he sets these events.

The harshness of the elder's response in 2 John 10 is paralleled elsewhere. Ignatius, who feared the threat of those who undervalued Jesus' humanity, warns, "Guard yourselves against beasts bearing the form of human beings; not only must you not welcome them, but if possible not even meet with them, but merely pray for them in the hope that they might repent, however difficult"; and, "it is right to keep away from such and certainly not to speak privately or in public about them" (*Smyrn.* 4.1; 7.1). In Ignatius's terms, influence from outside was fraught with danger, and was to be addressed by reinforcing internal structures, by the focal authority of the bishop (*Smyrn.* 8).

Looked at from another perspective, this response might represent the tension between the autonomy of the local community, often perhaps valuing distinctive aspects of the Christian message, and the consequences of the nature of the early Christian movement as emerging out of intersecting networks; although the latter, leading to mechanisms of achieving consensus, would ultimately determine its future shape and priorities, the former was never completely surrendered. Unlike Ignatius, the elder has no alternative structures to suggest, although this option will be important for understanding 3 John; instead he is able only to thunder the seriousness of any deviation from the pattern that he has evoked.

[11] Unable to propose any certain safeguard against the danger, or any penalties to ensure that his directions are followed, the elder powerfully evokes

the catastrophic consequences of even offering such a visitor a greeting. To do so is not a casual or empty gesture but establishes a relationship of acknowledgment and acceptance; such a relationship is formed not merely with the person but with what they represent. For his readers the elder's words would be reinforced by their Johannine resonances. Although the verb "have fellowship" (*koinōneō*) does not occur elsewhere in the Johannine literature, the related noun *koinōnia* expressed the unifying relationship with one another and with Father and Son that was the goal of 1 John (1 John 1:3, 6–7; see commentary). The one type of fellowship would surely exclude the other. Moreover, although the potential visitor's fault seems to be not a moral one but his failure to represent the teaching tradition championed by the elder, what those who acknowledge him will participate in is not his alternative message but "his evil deeds." The phrase recalls 1 John's explanation of Cain's murder of his brother, "because his own deeds were evil," itself explained as due to his origin from "the evil one"; in the Gospel it is those "whose deeds were evil" who preferred darkness to light, while the world's hatred of Jesus stems from his testimony that "its deeds are evil" (1 John 3:12; John 3:19; 7:7). To participate in evil deeds is to join the side of darkness and death, to go over to the world, which belongs to the evil one, and to surrender the victory won over him (1 John 2:13; 5:18–19). If the first readers had identified the earlier Johannine echoes no doubt they would have made some of these connections as well; at the very least they would have recognized that this was more than a threat of moral failure— they might well indeed bring to ruin all that had been achieved.[37]

The elder's injunction remains disturbingly rigorous. For vulnerable Christian communities within the wider society the balance between integration and isolation was a delicately balanced one, but more troubling would be the effect of the varying levels of transformation among the individual members. The elder was not alone in fearing the contaminating effects of inappropriate association (1 Cor 5:9–13; 1 Tim 5:22). For him, as for Ignatius, belief that deviates from the norm that he recognizes is most to be feared and avoided, and this is a pattern that would continue in the early church. The difficulty with 2 John is that his references to the approved norm are so cryptic and formulaic as to make the precise nature of the threat equally obscure. Indeed, it could even be the case that he was no more certain, and that his intention was chiefly to vigorously enjoin unity and loyalty in any eventuality.

[12] His purpose achieved, the elder brings his letter to a close in a conventional way: there are other things that would be better said, or perhaps can wait to be said, in person. It was a truism in ancient letter writing that a letter was a

---

37. The addition found in some Vulgate manuscripts, "Behold, I have told you this beforehand so that on the day of our Lord (Jesus Christ) you should not be put to shame," understood the point.

poor but sometimes necessary substitute for a face-to-face conversation.[38] This need not mean that his hope of a visit is a polite but unrealistic courtesy.[39] Second John and, even more, 3 John convey a picture of a man connected to these communities by other travelers, so why should not he himself also make the journey? The hope perhaps does ameliorate the authoritative note he has just adopted by anticipating a more open and equal encounter, but it also reinforces his status as one who would not be accorded the treatment he has just enjoined. This is further strengthened by the same phrase with which the author of 1 John closed the opening prologue, "that our joy may be made complete" (1 John 1:4; see commentary): as elsewhere the change to the first person plural, "our," serves to unite author and audience, but might also extend to locate them in a wider circle. More particularly, as another Johannine catchphrase (John 3:29; 16:24; 17:13), its use here, and not at the equivalent place in 3 John, is appropriate in a letter that has achieved much of its effect by echoes of language familiar to the readers.

**[13]** Conveying final greetings from a third party was equally conventional in ancient letters, where it testifies to their place in maintaining the only possible lines of connection between people. With the singular "greet *you*," the "elect sister" and her children reestablish the familial framework of the epistolary narrative. As with the opening address, it is therefore confusing two levels of the letter to speculate whether this is a further community headed by, or meeting within the house of, a woman. Implicitly the elder claims some association with the sister, but this does not settle the question of his status—for example, as a member of "her" community—or of his use of the epithet. To move too quickly from lady and sister to two communities is to assume that 2 John belongs to a setting of the local church, but the letter has done little to suggest specific contingent circumstances.

It is not surprising that subsequent readers have found little of note in 2 John; where it was quoted in the early church it was particularly for its usefulness in providing guidelines for relations with those rejected as heretics (vv. 9–11).[40] These are precisely the verses that more recent readers may find most difficult; yet the elder was not alone in proposing such measures, and they reflect the situation of the emerging and unstable communities prior to the development of other structures for maintaining stable norms of belief and practice (see above). They also arise out of a sharply eschatological interpretation of the current

38. Here lit. "mouth to mouth"; this is not the normal expression but is found at Num 12:8, although it is unlikely that the elder is echoing that verse.

39. See 1 Tim 3:14 for its use within an argument.

40. See Introduction §4.2; Lieu, *Second and Third Epistles*, 30–36, especially p. 33 on the appeal to vv. 9–11 in the dispute about the rebaptism of schismatics.

situation, although recognition of this should not ignore the destructive consequences that would ensue from such a rigorous division between "those like us" and "those who see things differently." Interpretation is not helped by the impossibility of reconstructing a clear context for 2 John; indeed, its use of formulaic language almost deliberately prevents this. This characteristic could suggest that the letter was not intended for a specific community but claimed a more "encyclical" character, and this would also explain the artificiality of the address. This may be so, but the world the elder addresses remains the Johannine world, which does not appear to have been an extensive one. Second John remains something of a mystery, offering a glimpse into a world and a reminder of the incompleteness of our knowledge of its time.

# 3 JOHN

## 3 John

More than any other New Testament writing, 3 John displays many of the features of the ordinary letters surviving from the ancient world, including the framing epistolary conventions such as a health wish (v. 2), a thanksgiving (v. 3), a promise of a visit to compensate for the brevity of the letter (vv. 13–14), and the sharing of greetings with a third party before a closing farewell (v. 15).[1] Other details are familiar in standard letters of its age—a request (v. 6), a commendation of someone known to both parties (v. 12), and the casual reference to other named individuals known to writer and recipient—and it probably would have fit on a single papyrus sheet. We might compare a letter from a recruit in the second century:

Apollinarius to Taesis, his mother and lady, many greetings. Before all I pray that you are well, as I myself am well and make supplication for you to the gods here. I want you to know, mother, that I arrived in Rome on the 25th of the month Pachon and was posted to Misenum, although I did not yet know my company. For I had not reached Misenum when I wrote you this letter. I ask you, therefore, mother, take care of yourself and do not worry about me; for I have come to a good position. Please write me a letter concerning your welfare and that of my brothers and all your people. And whenever I find someone I shall write to you; I shall not delay writing. I greet my brethren at length and Apollinarius and his children and Karalas and his children. I greet Ptolemaeus and Ptolemais and her children and Heraclous and her children. I greet all who love you by name. I pray for your health.[2]

Third John shares some of these features with 2 John but it lacks the latter's studied anonymity and much of the artificiality of address as well as the numerous echoes of 1 John and earlier Johannine tradition that make 2 John so difficult to place. Indeed, its relationship with 2 John is uneven, and, although the canonical order means that I will make numerous cross-references to the commentary on 2 John, it is 3 John that represents a more normal letter style and perhaps provided the model that 2 John has imitated. This does not prevent 3 John from also presenting something of an enigma: the elder is evidently fighting to retain the loyalty of his addressee, Gaius, and he rails against the harsh treatment

---

1. See commentary on these verses and Lieu, *Second and Third Epistles*, 37–51.
2. From A. S. Hunt and C. C. Edgar, eds., *Select Papyri* (LCL; repr. London: Heinemann, 1970), 1:303–4, no. 111 (= *CP* 22 [1927]: 243).

he has received from an otherwise unknown Diotrephes. Presumably Gaius knew the circumstances well enough not to need further clarification, and the same allusiveness is true of most ancient letters (see below on v. 15). Whatever they may have been, these circumstances were quickly forgotten; there is no substantial evidence that those who transmitted 3 John within the early church also retained any memory of its original situation, and yet despite its allusiveness and its brevity it did survive. References to it in the early centuries are rare, and its authorship and status are doubted as soon as it is first mentioned,[3] something that makes its survival all the more perplexing. All this has not prevented a wealth of vivid reconstructions from more recent readers. Inevitably any interpretation must seek to make the best sense it can of the details of the letter against the background of the other Johannine literature and of the early church, and must also suggest why the letter survived. However, it would be a mistake to allow an imagined scenario to control attention to the details of the argument.

### 3 John 1–4—Opening Pleasantries

1 The elder to the beloved Gaius, whom I love in truth.

2 Beloved, in every respect I pray that you are prospering and are well, just as your soul does prosper. 3 For I rejoiced greatly when brothers[a] came and bore witness to your truth, just as you do walk in truth. 4 I have no greater joy[b] than this, than to hear of my children walking in the truth.

a. On the problem of translation see Introduction §5 and commentary.

b. Some manuscripts, including Vaticanus and the Vulgate, read, "thanks" (*charin* instead of *charan*).

[1] In contrast to 2 John, here the letter's recipient is named, Gaius, although no more is known of him than the letter supplies; the name is a very common Roman praenomen but little can be concluded from this or from its use on its own—in this period such names had entered the lexicon of Greek personal names, and, contrary to Roman practice, Greek writers were more likely to use them on their own (cf. Rom 16:23; 1 Cor 1:14, hardly likely to be the same individual). The elder counts him among "his children" (see v. 4) and is in a position to receive news of him and perhaps to plan a visit; Gaius has the means to support other visitors (v. 6), so he may be a householder, although not necessarily of considerable means. "Beloved" (*agapētos*) is a common epithet for a fellow believer both outside and within the Johannine tradition (Rom 12:19; 1 John

---

3. By Origen, according to Eusebius, *Ecclesiastical History* 6.25.10, although the wording may suggest he had heard of but not seen either 2 or 3 John; see Introduction §1.1.

2:7; see commentary), and on its own need not indicate a particularly close relationship, which may be why the elder adds a further endorsement; it is, however, a distinctive variation on the epithets more common in secular letters, such as "dearest" or "most honored" (see below). The elder's own identity is no clearer here than it is in 2 John (see commentary on 2 John 1); indeed, the anonymous use of the epithet alone is even more striking in this apparently personal letter, and confirms that this was how the author would have been recognized within his own circle, without the label necessarily denoting any specific form of authority. Again, his position has to be deduced from the letter itself: he is evidently at a distance from Gaius but in receipt of news about him; he assumes a degree of authority and expects his words to be taken seriously, but this does not always happen, an eventuality that is part of the provocation of this letter.

The third person naming of sender and recipient follows the conventional epistolary pattern and would usually be followed by an expression of greeting, which in contemporary letters consistently uses the infinitive, *chairein*: "Irenaeus to Apolinarius his dearest brother, many greetings."[4] While other New Testament letters have largely abandoned this form (except at Jas 1:1; also Acts 15:23; [23:26]), Ignatius, probably writing not far distant in time from 3 John and despite claiming to write "in apostolic fashion" (*Trallians* prescript), does use it, although richly embellished. Third John, however, omits any greeting, an absence that is not without parallel in contemporary letters, but is apparently more characteristic of official ones. Only in comparison with 2 John is 3 John's failure to adopt the distinctive "grace to you and peace" formula that emerges from the Pauline tradition striking (see commentary on 2 John 3). This adds support to the supposition that it is 2 John that is secondary, turning to the developing epistolary tradition to supply the lack in its model, 3 John.

Instead, 3 John (here followed by 2 John) expands the almost conventional "beloved" with a more personal "whom I love in truth," thereby disrupting the third person style of the standard letter prescript. This is the single use of the verb "love" in 3 John and only in a broader Johannine context does it evoke the significance of love as a bond of unity; indeed, in the first person it contrasts with the author of 1 John's insistent positioning of love as the bond between believers and with God.[5] Similarly, "in truth" need not but can—and here probably does—presuppose a distinctive Johannine usage, as well as the tendency of this to become formulaic: five of the six occurrences of "truth" in 3 John are in the dative, three after the preposition "in," suggesting that while meaning more than "sincerely" it does have almost adverbial force as a Johannine norm (see commentary on 2 John 1). Although formulaic, the words inject a personal relationship

---

4. *Select Papyri*, 1:307, no. 113 (= BGU 27).

5. Despite the epithet "beloved" (e.g., 1 John 2:7), the author of 1 John never claims to love those to whom he writes, although the Johannine Jesus did love his disciples (John 11:5; 13:1; 15:9).

into the conventional letter opening, and this prepares for the elder's strenuous efforts to sustain that relationship in the rest of the letter.

[2] It was standard practice for the greeting to be followed by a health wish, as in Apollinarius's letter quoted earlier, "Before all I pray that you are well." The familiarity of "I pray" (*euchomai*) in such contexts militates against giving this any particular liturgical context, and it is perhaps the absence of any such health wish elsewhere in the New Testament or Apostolic Fathers that is more notable. The verb "to be well" (*hygiainō*) is also common in such formulae and should be taken in its prosaic sense of physical and material well-being (contrast Titus 1:13). Adding a further verb is not unusual, although "prosper" (*euodousthai*) does not yet appear to be attested in any contemporary letter; literally meaning "to journey successfully," it does suit the elder's predilection for the imagery of walking. Apollinarius in the letter quoted earlier follows a common convention of giving his health wish a more earnest introduction, "before all (*pro pantōn*)."[6] Third John's "in every respect/concerning all" (*peri pantōn*) is not otherwise attested but might be a personal or regional variant of this formula; it makes better grammatical sense, however, to understand it as qualifying the two infinitives: the elder expresses his hope that Gaius is flourishing in every respect before identifying the respect that he holds to be of prime importance, and where he is confident that Gaius is indeed ("just as") making good headway. Although here translated "soul," elsewhere in the Johannine tradition *psychē* represents the life that, like Jesus, one might lay down for others (1 John 3:16; John 10:11, 15, 17–18; 13:37–38; 15:13); the elder is not contrasting bodily prosperity, for which he can only wish, with a more certain, "spiritual" success. Yet the *psychē* does represent that aspect of being human that is not transient, and that provides the point at which one might center oneself toward God or away from God (John 12:25). Although the formulation is unusual, its import is clear: if Gaius continues as he is already doing, he will fulfill every aspiration that the elder has for him, and will have nothing to fear beyond.

Because most evidence of the conventions of ordinary Greek letters comes almost entirely from Egypt, there is no way of determining whether the elder's divergences are personal idiosyncrasies, deliberate modifications, or regional variations. It would be easy to set the whole verse in a religious light, but it would be mistaken to overdo this. The opening greeting probably demonstrates that the elder is conscious of the Johannine tradition from which he writes, and which will continue to color his language, but he develops his argument more within the framework of convention than by subverting it.

[3–4] The expression of joy over news received about the recipient is another conventional element in contemporary letters, forming a transition from the opening formalities to the body of the letter itself (cf. 2 John 4), here made

6. A variant is "I pray continually (*dia pantōn*)," as in *Select Papyri*, 1:307, no. 113 (see n. 4).

explicit by an explanatory "for." The elder uses the standard verb, "I rejoiced" (*echarēn*), and not the rather more liturgical "I give thanks [to God]" (*eucharis-teō*) favored by Paul (Rom 1:8; 1 Cor 1:4). The source of his knowledge of Gaius's good standing is more explicit than in 2 John: he has heard direct testimony of it. Those who brought the report are called "brothers,"[7] but their relationship either to the elder or to Gaius is not stated. Later Gaius will be commended for his bearing toward those described both as "brothers" and as "strangers" (v. 5)—the same people as those who subsequently testified to it (v. 6)—and so at that stage personally unknown to him. Whether the term is a general one for other members of the (Johannine) network or identifies a particular group by their specific task (see v. 7 below) is unclear. In either case the term carries a different sense from the relational one of 1 John (usually singular, "*his* brother," but see 1 John 3:13–14 and commentary), and a closer parallel is provided by John 21:23, "This rumor went out among the brethren." Yet *adelphoi* is also used widely outside the Johannine literature both for members of the same community and for believers in general (Acts 15:3; 28:14, 15; 1 Cor 6:5–6; 16:11, 12; Jas 2:15; Rev 19:10).

In verse 6 their testimony was given "in the presence of the assembly," ascribing to the occasion a sense of public formality. Here the present tenses do not suggest a one-off event: the elder may have received such news on more than one occasion or he may be exploiting the impact of that event and emphasizing his own place in it. However, he does not expand on what they said about Gaius, only that they testified "to [his] truth." When the author qualifies this in his more customary terminology, that Gaius does walk "in truth" (see below), it is likely that "truth" acts as a shorthand for fidelity to the norm recognized by the elder, and probably articulated through the Johannine tradition. The language of witness or testimony is also used in the Johannine tradition to establish norms and authenticity (see commentary on 1 John 5:9), and will be taken up toward the end of this letter (v. 12). The elder and his circle, but also members of the wider Johannine circle, are connected and held together by witnessing: although viewed from outside this may appear a self-fulfilling process, giving testimony, accepting it, and being its subject create the continuity with the past and with one another that defines those who belong, and that will exclude those who do not.

The elder does not want to allow any suggestion that without this evidence he would not have been confident of Gaius's fidelity, and this he affirms by a second "just as" (*kathōs*) clause. In his terms such fidelity is best described as

---

7. Greek *adelphoi*, which might equally be translated "brothers and sisters," since women also moved between communities and carried news; the NRSV "friends," while helpfully inclusive, obscures the difference from v. 15 and the question of how this relates to other Johannine uses of *adelphos*; see also Introduction §5.

"walking in truth"; as in 2 John 4 this could simply mean "acting honestly," but it is better to see "truth" as the sphere in which they walk or the standard by which they live. This sphere or standard is provided by the wider Johannine tradition in which "truth" plays such a central role. Confirming this interpretation, he repeats the image with the article, "walking in *the* truth," which is less open to an adverbial interpretation.[8] There is more here than a repetition of his pleasure at the news he has received of Gaius; he looks beyond Gaius to those whom he calls "my children." Gaius is reminded of his place among a wider group, and that his appropriate behavior will preserve it. Although the same term is used as in 2 John (*tekna*; see commentary on 2 John 4), and not that favored by 1 John in addressing readers (*teknia*), the children here are the elder's own; the epithet might suggest that he was responsible for their conversion (cf. Gal 4:19), or, more probably, that he is adopting the style of the wisdom teacher or mentor (cf. 1 Tim 1:2). This is different from 2 John, where the children belong to the familial metaphor, and perhaps the community model, created by the lady and her sister, although it may be the inspiration for it. There is nothing to indicate how widespread or numerous were his "children," and the carefully chosen "my" reinforces Gaius's obligation to him and the priority that loyalty to him should take. The elder deftly holds together encouragement and confidence in order to leave no space for Gaius to make some other choice.

### 3 John 5–12—The Test of Loyalty

The preliminary pleasantries have prepared for the main substance or body of the letter, signaled by a renewed appeal, "Beloved" (cf. v. 2). Although the details of what follows are obscure, it is evident that there is conflict between the elder and a certain Diotrephes; this has created a far-reaching division, and the elder is determined to keep Gaius on his side. Although he complains about the rejection he has experienced, he has limited means of self-defense or of retaliation. Instead he presents Gaius with a stark choice, between evil and good, as embodied in Diotrephes and in another man, Demetrius. Any attempt at a fuller interpretation has to suggest the precise status held by each of these individuals and also the nature of the issue that has divided them. Most suggestions approach the former from other information about structures in the early church, and from the attitude presumed by the Johannine literature; as to the second, the primary question is whether the problem is doctrinal (as in 2 John 7) or only structural. In the commentary I will explore these questions as I examine the text.

8. See on 2 John 4; this is a different form of speech than 1 John's metaphorical, "walk in light/darkness" (1 John 1:6; see commentary).

5 Beloved, you act faithfully in whatever task you undertake for the brethren, strangers as they are; 6 they bore witness to your love in the presence of an assembly, so you will do well to send them forward in a manner worthy of God. 7 For they went out for the sake of the name, accepting nothing from the Gentiles. 8 We ought, therefore, to support such as these, so that we might be helpers of the truth.[a]

9 I did write something[b] to the assembly, but Diotrephes, who enjoys first place over them, does not accept us. 10 That is why, if I come, I shall bring up the deeds he is doing, talking nonsense about us with evil words; indeed, not satisfied with that he does not even accept the brothers, and he forbids those who wish to and ejects them from the assembly.

11 Beloved, do not imitate what is wrong but what is good. The one who does good is from God, the one who does wrong has not seen God. 12 Demetrius has testimony borne to him by everyone and by the truth itself.[c] We also give our testimony, and you know that our testimony is true.

a. Both Codex Sinaiticus and Codex Alexandrinus read "of the assembly," but without wider support this is unlikely to be original.

b. Some manuscripts read "would have written," and some omit "something"; these variants probably arose because the letter does not survive.

c. The original scribe of Codex Alexandrinus apparently again wrote *ekklēsias*, "the assembly," rather than *alētheias*.

[5–7] At the heart of the elder's concerns is the attitude toward those described as "brothers and strangers"; for him this is the fundamental measure of loyalty both to himself and to what he labels "the truth"—and thus far Gaius has proved his worth. As "brothers" they are fellow members of the wider circle to which the elder belongs, and Gaius is being encouraged to view them in the same light even though they were strangers to him. Any more precise relationship with the elder is not clear—he does not claim to have sent them, although later he will associate their rebuff with the rejection of himself. From where "they went out" is not said, and their motivation "for the sake of the name" only determines that they were not casual visitors. The phrase is used of Christian suffering (Acts 5:41; 9:16; 21:13), but nothing in the letter suggests that they were fleeing persecution. More probably they were traveling preachers, and "the name" is both the motivation for and the content of their activity. Elsewhere, "the name" (*to onoma*), usually identified as that of Jesus, is the means of forgiveness (1 John 2:12), the cause of hatred (John 15:21), the source of miracles (Acts 4:30), the object of faith (John 1:12; 1 John 5:13), the means of life (John 20:31), the framework within which requests can be made (John

14:13), and that into which believers are baptized (Acts 2:38; 10:48). In all these settings it represents the person, and carries with it their authority—the early believers were defined by being brought under Jesus' lordship and with access to his power. However, "the name" can also be that of God, and the Johannine Jesus in particular defines his ministry in terms of making known the name of God—revealing the true nature of God, and so revealing God in God's own person (John 5:43; 17:6, 11–12, 26). Whether the elder would have specified "the name" as that of Jesus, who is not otherwise mentioned in 3 John, or that of God is not certain: there are Johannine parallels for both possibilities, but the call to treat them "in a manner worthy of God" perhaps suggests that it was for God's name that they embarked on their journey.

These brothers have already had occasion to discover that Gaius is a potential ally. As strangers their first need would have been hospitality, but whether this is what he offered them is not clear. The elder's language is remarkably circuitous and imprecise: their past testimony has only been to Gaius's "love," a central Johannine virtue but one that could have been expressed in a variety of ways. "Whatever task you [Gaius] undertake for the brethren" is, according to the elder, a faithful deed, but his choice of wording resists being tied down to a specific act in the past: he is, perhaps, trying to build up whatever Gaius had done into a positive commitment from which he cannot renege. Hence he swiftly follows with a particular request,[9] although he carefully presents it as a natural consequence and as nothing new.[10] He wants Gaius now to be prepared to "send them forward"; the verb (*propempō*), only here in the Johannine literature, elsewhere refers to the formal provision of support, financial or in kind, and perhaps also of credentials, on which traveling preachers relied as they continued their journey (Acts 15:3; Rom 15:24; 1 Cor 16:6, 11; Polycarp, *Phil.* 1.1). That Gaius is to do this in a manner "worthy of God" provides no further details, but reinforces the credit in so doing, again in terms with widespread currency (cf. 1 Thess 2:12). The brothers are in particular need of such support because they have resolved not to beg from outsiders (*ethnikoi*)—if they were missionaries, those to whom they were appealing (see below). The term is not the usual word for "Gentiles" (*ethnē*); in Matthew, the only other usage in the New Testament, it identifies those who are outside the new community (Matt 5:47; 6:7; 18:17), and its appearance there may reflect the need for a new term once Gentiles were also to be found among believers. Within this short letter, however, the term cannot determine how the elder and his assembly or that of Gaius saw themselves, or the nature of their ethnic composition.

---

9. "You will do well" (*kalōs poiēseis*) is translated "Please" in Apollinarius's letter cited earlier.

10. Literally "You act faithfully . . . toward the brethren . . . who bore witness . . . whom you send forward."

Evidently the brothers have already visited Gaius or his community, and subsequently have visited the elder. There they have made their report in the presence of an, or the, "assembly" (*ekklēsia*). This is a surprising term to find here: although common elsewhere in the New Testament of the believing community or "church," it is not found in the Fourth Gospel or in 1 or 2 John. In 3 John, however, the term appears without comment as the local gathering: in verses 9 and 10 it refers to another group to which the elder has no access, and one which clearly has a degree of organization and formality. Here the absence of the article leaves open whether it represents the community to which the elder is attached or whether it more loosely describes their witness before an open gathering of other members. The translation "assembly" best indicates that developed structures are not clearly in view.

[8] The elder caps his request by a general exhortation: to help people like this is an obligation creating bonds of unity. He does not appeal to any authoritative maxim that would support this obligation—unlike the author of 1 John who says, "we ought to lay down our lives for the brothers," or "we ought to love one another" (1 John 3:16; 4:11); however, a fifth appeal to "the truth" leaves no doubt as to the implications of failing to respond. Although the Greek could indicate that "truth" is the sphere in which Gaius, the elder, the brothers, and others who share their cause will cooperate, it is as likely that truth is to some extent personified—they will be cooperating with the truth. Although this precise formula is not found, such cooperation is, again, particularly valued within the Pauline tradition (Rom 16:3, 9, 21; 1 Cor 3:9; 1 Thess 3:2; etc.). Whatever the precise relationships between the brothers, the elder, and Gaius, their actual practice has become a touchstone of true fidelity even in Johannine terms.

Although allusive, the situation presupposed can be broadly sketched. There is plentiful evidence from the early church of the importance of people traveling between communities of early believers, carrying news, offering support and teaching, perhaps sometimes claiming or being accorded a degree of authority and leadership. This was an important aspect of the Pauline mission, which evidently relied on more than the work of Paul alone (2 Cor 7:13–16; 9:3–5). Whereas Paul vouched for his associates, 2 John anticipates the arrival of those bearing teaching who were not already known; that passage can be illustrated by the picture presupposed by the *Didache* of itinerant teachers who undoubtedly wielded considerable influence in the communities they visited but who also needed careful monitoring (see commentary on 2 John 9). Such traveling teachers would not have been unusual in ancient cities, and would have been found among other religious or philosophical groups. The determination of this group not to rely on the support of outsiders contrasts with evidence of others who expected to be given at least a bed for the night and some food. Apollonius of Tyana, who was also celebrated for being unusual in rejecting offers of wealth, mocks a certain Euphrates for having convinced himself that he was a philosopher simply by taking "money rewards" from all quarters (*Ep.* 51).[11] Gospel traditions, too, assumed that the itinerant apostle should expect to find support along the way (Matt 10:9–12). Such parallels confirm that this particular group were more concerned with preaching to such outsiders than with centering their activities within the community, although the two are not incompatible with each other.

It is remarkable that such a concern with outsiders contrasts with the ethos of 1 and 2 John: indeed, "going out" (*exerchomai*), which is here commended, is in 1 and 2 John the activity of the false prophets or antichrists, and there their success in the world (*kosmos*)—a term not used by 3 John—is evidence of their error (1 John 2:19; 4:1; 2 John 7). However formal a gathering "assembly" (*ekklēsia*) may indicate, this too is a term notably absent from the rest of the Johannine corpus, which generally betrays little interest in communal structures. Several of the other key terms of these and the following verses are also otherwise absent from the Johannine literature, but do provide links with other traditions within the early church. Besides "send forward" (see above), Paul also is very conscious of the contribution of his "helpers" (or "fellow workers," *synergoi*: Rom 16:3; Phil 2:25; 4:3); he would have Phoebe welcomed in a manner worthy (*axiōs*) of the saints, and has urged the believers at Thessalonica to live in a manner worthy of the Lord (Rom 16:2; 1 Thess 2:12). Paul similarly sets great store on how he and his fellow workers are received, the concern to which the elder now turns (2 Cor 7:15; Gal 4:14; Col 4:11). The scenario is readily imagined; it is its relationship with the rest of the Johannine tradition that is less straightforward.

[9] The elder needs to recruit Gaius to the cause because other avenues have been firmly closed off. The assembly to which he had written was presumably not that before which the brothers had made their report,[12] but the elder does nothing to further identify it. It is unlikely to be the community to which Gaius belongs and which the elder hopes to visit, but its identity is self-evident to Gaius and it may have been of some size or status since the elder is particularly distressed by what had happened. The letter that he had written does not survive,[13] but presumably he had been seeking support for the brothers or explaining his own position, which is evidently very vulnerable. Its apparent failure he blames on a certain Diotrephes, who is not otherwise known; the elder dismisses him as overly ambitious, using another new coinage (*philoprōteuō*)— although contemporary writers use the cognate adjective of a desire for tyranny

11. Epictetus, *Diss.* 3.22.10, also criticizes those who assume that setting out with a staff and begging will make them a Cynic philosopher.

12. Grammar alone cannot determine the significance of the absence of an article in v. 5 and its presence in vv. 9, 10.

13. It would hardly fit 2 John, although some have tried to make this identification.

(Plutarch, *Solon* 95B). It is, however, evident that Diotrephes did not simply hanker after a position of leadership but was also able to exercise it.

The complaint that Diotrephes "does not accept *us*" (*ouk epidechetai hēmas*) is ambiguous. Some have suggested that the elder is slipping into an authoritative "we" to underscore the extent of Diotrephes' arrogance, perhaps even echoing the strategic use of the first person plural elsewhere in the Johannine literature (see commentary on 1 John 4:16), and this probably lies behind the translation "does not acknowledge our authority" (NRSV). This is not a meaning that the verb itself carries, and in verse 10 it must mean "to accept" or "to welcome." Although this particular compound form of the verb (*epidechomai*) is not found elsewhere in the New Testament, the importance of receiving or welcoming emissaries, and thus showing them support, is a repeated theme (2 Cor 7:15 [*dechomai*]; Rom 16:2 [*prosdechomai*]; Acts 17:7 [*hypodechomai*]; 18:27 [*apodechomai*]), particularly associated with the idea that to receive the messenger is to receive the one who sent them (Matt 10:40; see also 10:14, "Whoever does not receive you . . ."). The same meaning makes sense here. Even if he has not sent them the elder is evidently associating himself with the brothers and those who do support them, and, by implication, he is inviting Gaius to include himself with them as well. Using the present tense, the elder implies that this is not limited to a single event in the past but is a current state of affairs, although he can only ascribe it to misplaced ambition and not to any more serious cause. The cloudiness of the picture may be because Gaius knew the details well, but it may equally indicate that the elder is baffled by what has happened.

[10] This certainly appears to be the case as he makes three further charges against Diotrephes. First, Diotrephes "talks nonsense" (*phlyareō*, another word found only here in the NT) against or slanders the elder and his supporters—the first person plural "us" again probably includes more than the elder himself. The description of Diotrephes' behavior as "deeds" (*erga*) expressed in "evil words" provides a vague echo of the "evil deeds" warned against in 2 John 11 (see commentary) and characteristic of Cain (1 John 3:12), but if the elder wishes to imply such an association he has left it remarkably opaque. More striking is his failure to find any more powerful accusation against Diotrephes—1 and 2 John would have provided a useful arsenal of damning labels. This may suggest that he is not fully cognizant of what Diotrephes holds against him, or even that he is unable to deny some of the things being said.

The second charge is that Diotrephes himself does not welcome (*epidechomai*) the brothers either—using the same verb the elder suggests that Diotrephes' objection to them arises from that to himself. Evidently Diotrephes had refused to offer the sort of support that the elder has been seeking from Gaius, but in practice it may have been because it was them and what they stood for that he disliked rather than their association with the elder.

Third, Diotrephes imposes his own reading of the situation and his response to it on other members of his community; he forbids anyone from offering a welcome and goes to the extent of expelling them, presumably if they persisted in challenging his ruling, from the gathering. The term is a strong one (*ekballō*) but it could refer to physical ejection from a building or assembly rather than to a more formal exclusion or excommunication from "the church."[14] There is a possible parallel with the ejection in John 9:34 of the man born blind and now able to see, but it is equally unclear there whether this represents an anachronistic formal ban (cf. 9:22) or the violence of the moment. The continuing present tenses may suggest that all this is Diotrephes' intention, at least as the elder perceives it, and not something he has conclusively put into effect. Nonetheless, the elder at least believes that there were those who did support both him and the brothers: the issue has split the community, but Diotrephes would appear to be in the ascendant, at least for the moment.

In the face of all this, all that the elder can offer is his own intention, if he is able to visit—about which there is some uncertainty—to make an issue of the whole affair. How effective such an intervention would be depends on the status of the elder. Those who identify the author with the apostle John or another senior figure see this promised visit as full of foreboding and suppressed power. So, Paul's own visits to his communities could be occasions of considerable tension (2 Cor 1:23–2:3; 13:1–4). Without the assumption of such a powerful voice behind them, the elder's protestations sound somewhat less confident; it is not at all clear what he can or what he hopes to achieve. "Bringing up" (or "reminding," *hypomimnēskō*) carries no note of admonition; it would even suit a scenario where the elder only plans to visit Gaius and to provide him with more details, but this does less justice to the "That is why" that links the anticipated visit with Diotrephes' behavior.

Such uncertainties underline the sense of frustrated impotence in the elder's response. It is striking that he does not interpret events, as the author of 1 John 2:18–19 might have done, as the desertion of Diotrephes and his cohort from the truth, or even as a failure "to abide" (2 John 9). Yet equally striking is the similarity of his experience with the response that the elder himself advocates in 2 John 10–11, where the visitor who does not supply the accredited teaching is to be refused hospitality or even the courtesy of a greeting; from that it would readily follow that anyone who disobeyed that injunction and was thus tarred with the same "evil deeds" would themselves be denied entry or greeting. Diotrephes would seem to be meting out to the elder or at least to the brothers the treatment that the elder himself is represented as advocating. Since other evidence suggests that 2 John was not earlier than 3 John, such policies might

---

14. See above on v. 9 and n. 12 on the difficulty in deciding whether the article gives *ekklēsia* a more formal sense here.

already have been in circulation: Diotrephes, perhaps, was dubious of the teaching the brothers were proclaiming, and was not content with the elder's commendation of them, or he may even have considered it safer to apply the measures to all comers rather than run the risk of letting in the unsuitable.[15] Yet if the elder had been aware of any such policies one would have expected him to insist that they did not apply to him or to the brothers; surprisingly he fails to assert either their or his own credentials.

It is this unexpected reticence that has inspired somewhat more imaginative reconstructions. Some have seen the issue as a matter of governance: Diotrephes represents the authority invested in the local community (*ekklēsia*), whether the informal power that one individual, perhaps the household head, could claim, or that of the single local bishop which Ignatius would defend so vehemently (*Phld.* 7.2, "The Spirit proclaimed saying this, 'Do nothing without the bishop'"). The elder, in this view, represents an alternative pattern, perhaps rooted in the heritage to which he could appeal, or based on a network of relationships characterized by those like the itinerant prophets and apostles of the *Didache* (see commentary on 2 John 9).[16] Other evidence, too, indicates that some viewed the development of authority in the hands of local figures with considerable disquiet (Hermas, *Mand.* 11.12). The Johannine tradition might seem conducive to an ethos of this sort: the Gospel and 1 John lack even those anticipations of subsequent authority and its transmission that may be detected in the other Gospels (Matt 16:17–20; 18:15–22; 19:27–29; Luke 12:41–48); there are few resources to address the inevitable need for developing structures of governance, and rather more to sympathize with an appeal to heritage and spirit guidance (John 15:26–27). The careful attempt in 1 John to preserve the independence and integrity of its readers (1 John 2:20–21, 26–27) would undermine any attempt to assert a superior authority, but might also provoke the need to develop more practical ways of dealing with the routine running of the community.

Although all this may contribute to a general context within which conflicts over the exercise of power could arise, it still does not decide the specific position of the elder or of Diotrephes. The question is complicated by 3 John's uneven relationship with the rest of the Johannine literature, which otherwise is characterized by a consistent worldview and set of language patterns; although undoubtedly Johannine, and appealing to those values, 3 John uses its own vocabulary, some shared with other, and perhaps particularly with

15. The threatening framework in which it is set and the concern with whom is to be excluded, not who can be welcomed after all, make it unlikely that 2 John 10–11 is an attempt to ameliorate a blanket exclusion.

16. See commentary on 2 John 1 on "elder" for older arguments that the author held an authority based on his place in tradition, and even one that had regional effect, and for the lack of supporting evidence.

Pauline, traditions. The intra-Johannine "dialect" was perhaps reserved for internal purposes and would be inappropriate for a normal letter; the consequence is that the elder appears less introverted and isolated than is sometimes supposed for the Johannine tradition as a whole.

All this presupposes that the problem is organizational; does it bear any relationship with the doctrinal debates that undoubtedly trouble 1 and 2 John? The elder does not accuse Diotrephes of any failure to confess, neither does he describe him in the colors of the eschatological opponent of God. Some have suggested that it was the elder's views that were judged deviant,[17] and that he can protest but not prove his innocence. This is unpersuasive, for surely he would have labeled anyone who rejected his witness as the antichrist. Certainly the elder believes that he has "the truth" on his side, but he does not categorize the opposition as "the lie"; neither does he evince any interest in the status of Jesus Christ, a name that, along with "Father" and "Son," is missing from the letter. If there were doctrinal issues at play, perhaps in Diotrephes' view, the elder does not understand them; they are nothing but nonsense, evil words. All this suggests that, far from rejecting Diotrephes and his "assembly," the elder wants to regain his relationship with the latter.

[11] However, he has to start with Gaius, to whom he turns once again, for the first time in a direct command. The encouragement to imitate (*mimeomai*) good rather than wrong might sound like a truism, but it is set in a framework that will demand that Gaius choose between the elder with his protégés and Diotrephes. Imitation is not an ethical category elsewhere in Johannine literature, but it is one within the Pauline tradition, where it is individuals—Paul himself—not qualities, that are to be copied (1 Cor 4:16; 11:1; 1 Thess 1:6; 2 Thess 3:7, 9; cf. Heb 6:12; Ignatius, *Smyrn.* 12.1).

The couplet that follows, "The one who . . . , the one who . . . ," certainly sounds Johannine, and is presumably intended to reinforce the seriousness of the decision that Gaius must make. Superficially, it recalls similar formulations from 1 John: "every*one who does* justice has been born from him. . . . Everyone who sins *has not seen him* or known him," or "The one who does justice is just. . . . *The one who does sin* is of the devil. . . . Everyone who does not do justice *does* not *belong to God*" (1 John 2:29 + 3:6; 3:7–8, 10b). It shares the same antithetical structure of two types of doing, which demonstrate the opposed belonging of their subjects (see commentary on 1 John 3:4–12). Within that tradition the antitheses were not only rhetorical; they projected a view of reality as dualistically constructed, the division combining human actors with their cosmic counterparts, and they were entirely nonnegotiable. Here they

---

17. Most creatively by E. Käsemann, "Ketzer und Zeuge," *ZTK* 48 (1951): 292–311: the elder, there assumed to be identical with the author of the Gospel, is both heretic and witness.

sound rather more formulaic, serving a useful paraenetic purpose but hardly inviting any deeper theological reflection. "Being from God" (*ek tou theou einai*) is a distinctively Johannine expression of origin, derivation, and dependency (see 1 John 3:10; 4:6 and commentary; John 8:47), but here it is simply a form of commendation. The antithesis "has not seen (*heōraken*) God" provides an effective counterpart and has some precedent in the antithetical tradition (see 1 John 3:6 [using the same verb but with "him"] quoted above and commentary), but a more thoroughly Johannine theme would be that no one has ever seen God anyway (1 John 4:12, 20; John 1:18; 5:37; 6:46). Moreover, the language of doing good and wrong, used to describe the two types of person, is not Johannine; the Johannine tradition prefers *ponēros* ("evil": John 3:19; 7:7; 17:15; 1 John 2:13, 14; 3:12; 5:18, 19; 2 John 11; 3 John 10), not *kakos* as here ("wrong": John 18:23 only), while the antithetical tradition uses *dikaiosynē* ("justice, righteousness": 1 John 2:29; 3:7, 10), not "good" (*agathos*: John 1:46; 5:29; 7:12). The elder has chosen terms that do not belong to the fixed Johannine dualism of identity but to a more generalized lexicon of moral virtue and beneficence: in standard usage the one who does good (*agathopoieō*) is the person who does what is right by any standards, but also what is of benefit to someone else, just as the one who does wrong (*kakopoieō*) is the person whose actions will not be beneficial but may bring harm (Mark 3:4; 1 Pet 2:12, 14–15; 3:6; 4:15, 19). If Gaius is not swayed by the superficial Johannine resonances of the rhetoric, the appeal to the "obvious" virtue of giving help to others will perhaps be more effective.

[12] If Diotrephes was an example of the wrong behavior to be avoided, then presumably Demetrius serves as an example of virtue. Again, nothing is known of him outside this verse, which reveals even less than did the earlier passage about Diotrephes. He is extolled in terms that provide the elder with another happy marriage between Johannine echo and contemporary encomium. It is difficult to think what could gainsay a testimonial (*memartyrētai*) corroborated not only "by everyone" but even "by the truth itself." The language is that of the law court, where the case for or against someone is—so it is argued—beyond questioning: Aeschines declares that the evidence stacked against Timarchus, "testified against (*katamemartyrēmenos*) by his own life and by the truth," must override any biased support he might claim (Aeschines, *Against Timarchus* 90), whereas, closer to the time of 3 John, *1 Clement* declares that those who "have testimony borne to them (*memartyrēmenos*) by everyone" should not be deposed from office (*1 Clem.* 44.3). Such expressions, especially using the passive voice of the verb "to testify" (*martyreō*), become a commonplace in early Christian literature, applied to those who are honored, and who perhaps are to be imitated or to be given due office: no further investigation or support is needed (Acts 6:3; 10:22; 1 Tim 5:10; Ignatius, *Phld.* 11.1). The Christians were

not innovating here; this vocabulary of testimony as a mark of honor is familiar from inscriptions from Asia Minor.[18]

This undermines the suggestion sometimes made that Demetrius was the letter carrier, or, indeed, that the whole purpose of 3 John was to ensure a warm welcome from Gaius for this particular "brother." Certainly recommendations did play an important role in networking in ancient society, and in enabling a traveler to find support in a new location; these could take the form of a paragraph added to a longer missive (e.g., Rom 16:1–2), or could constitute the whole of the letter:

> Theon to the most honoured Tyrannus, many greetings. Heraclides, who is bringing you this letter, is my brother. Therefore I beseech you to treat him as *recommended*. I also asked Hermias the brother to inform you about him by letter. You will give me the greatest pleasure if he can gain your approval. Before all I pray that you are well and succeeding without adverse fortune. Farewell.[19]

However, there was a recognized vocabulary for such recommendation, using, as in this example, the verb *synistēmi* ("I commend"), and this appears to have been maintained by the early Christians (Rom 16:1; cf. 2 Cor 3:1; 5:12; Polycarp, *Phil.* 14). The language of testimonial (employing *martyreō*) belongs to a different context, giving weight not to the person making the recommendation but to the unquestionable character of the one named. Of course, there might be points at which the two occasions coalesced: at the close of his letter to the church at Philadelphia, Ignatius reminds them of two of his companions, a certain Philo, "a man well testified to" (*anēr memartyrēmenos*), and Reus Agathopus; the Christians at Philadelphia had welcomed them, and the two had borne witness to this (lit. "to you"; cf. 3 John 3, 6), while Ignatius had given thanks to God. Yet there were others, whether in the same or in another church, who had dishonored them (Ignatius, *Phld.* 11).[20] Both the language and the scenario hinted at are surprisingly close to 3 John. The elder may be defending Demetrius if he had been, or if the elder feared he would be, rejected by Diotrephes; Demetrius may even have received some preliminary help from Gaius and now needs more. In Ignatius's case, it is explicit that neither of the two men is bringing the letter; whether this was the case here is less clear.

---

18. For example, *MAMA* 8.410, an inscription honoring a certain Dionysius who had successfully fulfilled a number of offices, "as testimony has already been born (*memartyrētai*) to him through the majority votes"; *MAMA* 8.414 is an inscription honoring a recently deceased young man, Praxiteles, who had lived life well (*agathos*), so the city council and people had decided that he should be recorded as "worthy (*axios*) of all praise and testimony (*martyria*)." See the discussion of these by L. Robert, *Hellenica* 13 (1965): 207, and also idem, *Hellenica* 3 (1946): 21–23.

19. *Select Papyri*, 1:296, no. 106 (= P.Oxy. 292).

20. In a (for him) conciliatory note, Ignatius hopes that they may be forgiven for this by the grace of Christ.

Therefore, when the elder adds his own testimony, this is not so that he can recommend Demetrius, but rather so that he can confirm that here is a man who needs no commendation. Again he speaks not only for himself but uses an emphatic "we also"; at this key point, as also in verses 8–10, the elder wants to remind Gaius that he is not speaking as a lone voice: although those who support him are shadowy and have to be taken on trust, Gaius is encouraged to make common cause with them, as—within the rhetoric of the letter—he surely will.[21]

The elder's confidence produces a final rhetorical ploy: Gaius perhaps does *not* know for certain whose view to take most seriously, but the assertive "you know" ascribes to him the certainty that the elder wishes him to adopt. The effect is underscored by a further seemingly Johannine turn of phrase. The final chapter of the Gospel closes with a very similar affidavit: "This is the disciple who testifies concerning these things and has written them, and *we know that his testimony is true*" (John 21:24; cf. 19:35). Such language draws on a more pervasive motif in the Gospel: Jesus declares, "If I testify about myself my testimony is not true. There is another who testifies concerning me, and I know that the testimony is true that he testifies about me" (John 5:31–32); there a decision about the truth of Jesus' self-testimony is a point of radical division (cf. 8:13–18). Divorced from that christological context its use at this point sounds somewhat banal, a talismanic platitude that relies on the associations it evokes; but perhaps it was precisely those associations that made these words an insistent rallying call, transforming a personal antagonism into a moment of choice as decisive as any other that a Johannine Christian has faced. It is possible that it was the elder's declaration that inspired the affidavit of the anonymous "we" of John 21:24, perhaps suggesting that its authors believed the elder to be or to represent the mysterious disciple, although if the influence is the reverse, the elder is adding another note to his claims.[22] In either case the elder concludes the letter in control of the situation; the humiliation implied by his account of Diotrephes' treatment of him is forgotten in this unassailable statement of authenticity. He can now close the letter as the same authoritative figure who first addressed Gaius.

### 3 John 13–15—Closing Formalities

The final pleasantries follow the conventional pattern of contemporary letters, looking forward to a future encounter and reinforcing the network of bonds by exchanging greetings, even if no individuals can be named.

---

21. Whether he did is unknown, but perhaps suggested by the preservation of the letter.

22. A connection is further supported by the use of "the brothers" in John 21:23 (see above on v. 3); see Introduction §1.1.

13 I did have much to write to you but I do not wish to write to you by ink and pen. 14 I hope to see you very soon and we shall speak face-to-face. 15 Peace be with you. The friends[a] greet you. Greet the friends by name.[b]

a. Codex Alexandrinus here but not in the next clause reads "brothers."
b. Compared with 2 John there is less manuscript evidence for any closing "Amen" and none recorded for a grace formula, reflecting the different reception history of this letter.

[13–14] Apologies for the brevity of a letter could be formulaic, echoing the convention that a letter was a poor substitute for a face-to-face meeting, although most letters were also constrained by the size of the sheet of papyrus used, and 3 John is already longer than many. In this case, however, the elder has already anticipated a possible visit (v. 10), so his hope for a personal conversation may be more than a formality.[23] Within the Pauline letter tradition the promise of a visit could act as an assertion of authority and carry a warning note (2 Cor 12:14, 20–13:4), but there is little sense of that here. Indeed the hope of "seeing" Gaius is less precise than that in 2 John 12, and may suggest that it is Gaius who should make the journey. Nonetheless, the elder assumes that Gaius will respond to the requests that he has made and that the letter will have served its function of cementing the relationship between them.

[15] Not all ancient letters come to a clearly marked closure, but where they do the sending of greetings is common. The letters cited earlier in this commentary capture well the importance of such greetings in maintaining the network of relationships between friends and family, and the need to make the most of the opportunity afforded by finding a suitable person to deliver a letter. The elder precedes his greetings with a simple farewell wish. The form this takes is unusual: instead of the standard "farewell" (*errōso*), his "Peace be with you" has a more Semitic flavor. It may, however, reflect a developing Christian convention; Paul closes a number of his letters, "The grace of our Lord Jesus be with you," echoing his distinctive introduction of "grace" in the opening greetings (Rom 16:20; 1 Thess 5:28; etc.), but 1 Peter similarly finishes, "Peace to all of you who are in Christ" (1 Pet 5:14; cf. Eph 6:23), while later letters have a variety of hybrid forms (Ignatius, *Smyrn.* 12.2–13.2). Given these parallels, the echo of the Johannine risen Jesus who greets his fearful disciples, "Peace to you" (John 20:19, 21, 26), may be one of those fortuitous resonances that have characterized this letter.

Similarly, the exchange of greetings among those named only as "friends" (*philoi*) is a commonplace in ancient letters, and cannot be used as evidence that the elder is conscious that Jesus had said to his disciples, "You are my friends if you do what I have instructed you" (John 15:14–15). In the letter cited earlier Apollinarius had written to his mother, "I greet those who love you (*phileō*)

23. On this see commentary on 2 John 12, especially n. 39.

*by name,*" without actually naming them; the elder does the same, and this need not indicate that they were sufficiently few in number to do so, or that he is deliberately excluding those who had failed to demonstrate their goodwill. On the contrary, the rarity of the term "friends" in the New Testament, and its absence from other letters (except Jas 2:23; 4:4), underlines 3 John's closeness to contemporary secular convention.

Third John thus closes with the ambiguity that has characterized it throughout. Read in isolation it could find a place among many other personal letters from antiquity. Although enigmatic it is no less so than many others:

> Harpocration to Bellenus Sabinus his brother greeting. I wrote to you yesterday too by your Mardon, wishing you to know that because of having been unreasonably opposed I was unable to come down, and as I have to spend a few days here, if you think it right send the receipt [?] of Isas and let us accept the rest of the oil, if you agree. For Teuphilos the Jew came saying, "I have been impressed as a farmer and I want to go to Sabinus." For when he was taken he did not ask us that he might be released but suddenly he told us today. I shall discover whether he is saying the truth. Farewell. Greet the brother Lycos and. . . .[24]

One can only assume that Bellenus Sabinus understood what was going on, or that the messenger explained the situation, the letter mainly serving to express the writer's own concern and his personal appeal for support. There are, however, distinctive features in 3 John, and these imply some awareness of a developing Christian letter tradition as well as of a Christian ethical and even ecclesial vocabulary; in addition there are elements of a characteristic Johannine vocabulary, although these do not always demand a thoroughly Johannine meaning. But what most makes 3 John differ from Harpocration's letter is ultimately its preservation and its no less enigmatic relationship with 2 John, which in turn clearly belongs in some sense with 1 John.[25]

The elder's letter survived, perhaps as much because of who he was as of what he said—particularly if it was believed that "he was the disciple who testifies concerning these things" (John 21:24; see above). Even so, it is difficult to imagine that it would have been preserved unless it was physically attached to 2 John, perhaps written on the same roll, probably not when sent according to the proposal here, but highly likely when archived.[26] Third John serves as a fragmentary record of one of the many controversies that troubled the nascent church, arguably one in which the elder won the day; just how momentous that was for the future will remain unknown, although that will not inhibit the imagination of scholars or of preachers.

---

24. *Select Papyri*, 1:301–2, no. 110 (= P.Fay. 123).
25. Harpocration's letter survives by luck and the curiosity of archaeologists.
26. Many letters survive in archive rolls, either copied or gummed together.

An imaginative construction might suggest that 3 John was preserved as one of the foundation documents of the Johannine group. In it we hear the elder's own voice, in tune unselfconsciously with the distinctive language of the emerging Christian movement but equally unselfconsciously using some of the vocabulary of a particular articulation of the proclamation. The reasons for the hostility from Diotrephes are unclear, but the elder's overtures have been rebuffed; perhaps he takes his own authoritative status for granted just as Diotrephes does his. The ensuing tensions may generate other conflicts, such as that addressed by 1 John. There Christology has emerged as decisive, but there is no cause to assume that the enemy is still Diotrephes. In due course the Fourth Gospel will be claimed as the true legacy of the elder, identified with the Beloved Disciple of John 21, whether literally believed to belong to the generation of Jesus' disciples or seen as the authentic embodiment of such; there may even be a subtle dismissal of what Diotrephes represented in the person of Peter. But the Gospel also wrestles with other actual or feared divisions (6:60, 66; 8:30–33; 10:16). Second John guards against any weakening in loyalty, whether its author is still the elder or a later writer claiming his mantle and adapting his letter style; its authority is reinforced by attaching to it the original elder's letter, recognized by all as true. In the long run the anonymity of 1 John and of the Gospel will serve them better, and they did in any case have more to offer.

# INDEX OF ANCIENT SOURCES

**BIBLE**

**Genesis**

| | |
|---|---|
| 1:1–5 | 51 |
| 3:6 | 95 |
| 3:15 | 137–39 |
| 13:15 | 137 |
| 17–18 | 185 |
| 17:8 | 137 |
| 4:1–16 | 63, 79, 134, 144 |
| 4:9–10 | 156 |
| 4:13–16 | 156 |
| 4:25 | 138–39 |
| 18:22–23 | 228 |
| 22:1–16 | 182 |
| 27:21–22 | 40 |

**Exodus**

| | |
|---|---|
| 19:10 | 125 |
| 19:14–15 | 125 |
| 29:7 | 103 |
| 30:25–32 | 103 |
| 32 | 228 |
| 33:11 | 44 |
| 34:5–9 | 185 |
| 34:6–7 | 16, 58, 64, 179 |
| 34:29–35 | 125 |

**Leviticus**

| | |
|---|---|
| 4–5 | 226 |
| 7:19–27 | 226 |
| 16:15–19 | 56 |
| 16:30 | 56 |
| 17:11 | 56 |
| 19:14 | 81 |
| 19:17–18 | 76, 143, 199 |
| 25:9 | 64 |

**Numbers**

| | |
|---|---|
| 11:26–30 | 160 |

| | |
|---|---|
| 14:18–19 | 58 |
| 24:14 | 98 |

**Deuteronomy**

| | |
|---|---|
| 5:10 | 198 |
| 6:4–5 | 143, 179 |
| 6:5 | 198, 199 |
| 6:6 | 73 |
| 7:7–8 | 178, 183 |
| 7:9 | 58, 178–79 |
| 10:14–15 | 178 |
| 15 | 151 |
| 20 | 90 |
| 27:26 | 258 |
| 29:17–20 | 235 |
| 30:6–8 | 202 |
| 30:10–11 | 202 |
| 30:19–20 | 198 |
| 32:4 | 58 |
| 32:15 | 188 |

**Judges**

| | |
|---|---|
| 11:34 | 182 |

**1 Samuel**

| | |
|---|---|
| 1:12–17 | 223 |
| 16:13–23 | 160 |

**1 Kings**

| | |
|---|---|
| 8:39 | 154 |
| 18:12 | 160 |
| 19:11–13 | 185 |
| 22 | 164 |

**1 Chronicles**

| | |
|---|---|
| 21:1 | 133 |
| 28:9 | 154 |

**Nehemiah**

| | |
|---|---|
| 9:17 | 58, 64 |

**Esther**

| | |
|---|---|
| 4:17 | 107 |

**Job**

| | |
|---|---|
| 1–2 | 89 |
| 2:1 | 133 |
| 16:2 | 62 |
| 29:3 | 53 |

**Psalms** (MT numbering)

| | |
|---|---|
| 1:1 | 53 |
| 9:7 | 73 |
| 27:1 | 50 |
| 51:2 | 56 |
| 71 | 43 |
| 83 | 90 |
| 86:1–7 | 223 |
| 86:15 | 58 |
| 98 | 90 |
| 102:1–2 | 223 |
| 102:12 | 73 |
| 102:26–27 | 73 |
| 103:8 | 58 |
| 106:14 | 94 |
| 115 | 40 |
| 115:3–8 | 235 |
| 115:7 | 237 |
| 118:26 | 255 |
| 119 | 81 |
| 130:4 | 64 |
| 136 | 178 |
| 139 | 44, 154 |
| 145:8 | 58 |

**Proverbs**

| | |
|---|---|
| 8:22–31 | 42 |
| 24:12 | 154 |

**Isaiah**

| | |
|---|---|
| 1:2–4 | 121 |

**Isaiah** (*continued*)
2:1–4                              171
2:2                                 98
6                                  185
6:10                     16, 17, 82
9:2                                 53
10:1–4                            151
26:4                               42
29:18                              83
30:18                              73
40:1–2                             62
40:6–8                             73
42:1                              160
42:7                               83
43:8–13                           218
43:13                             237
43:20                             246
44:8                               43
44:9–20                           235
45:4                              246
45:7                               51
49:10                              62
52:13–53:12          64, 129–30
53:10                             150
54:1–6                            244
54:13                             113
55:3                               42
55:11                              41
56:6                              198
57:12                              43
59:9–10                       40, 53
60:19–20                          50
61:1                              103
62:4                              244
65:17                              78
66:13                              62
66:22                              78

**Jeremiah**
3:14                              121
7:16                              228
10:1–16                           235
11:14                             228
23:28–29                          164
31:31                              78
31:31–34          69, 74, 102, 232
31:34                             113

**Ezekiel**
11:19–20                          74
16                                244

36:25                             211
36:26–27                    74, 255

**Daniel**
7:13                         115, 255
9:9                                64
11:40–12:13                       98
12:2                               42

**Hosea**
2:20                               69
11:1                        121, 178

**Joel**
2:13                               58
2:28–29                          160

**Jonah**
4:2                                58

**Micah**
2:1–2                            151
3:8                                43

**Nahum**
1:3                                58

**Habakkuk**
2:11                               63

**Zechariah**
1:13                               62
14                                 90

**Malachi**
1:2                               178
3:1–2                            115
4:1, 5                           115

**Tobit**
3:5                                64

**Wisdom**
2:10–14                           63
4:12                               94
5:1                               115
7:27                               73
11:24                            179

**Sirach**
2:1                                61
2:11                               58
3:1                                61
3:17                               61
6:4–6                              58
15:14–20                         134

24:8–12                            73
44:20                             169

**Baruch**
4:10–16                           244

**Epistle of Jeremiah**         235

**2 Maccabees**
2:1–3                            235
7:37–38                           63
8:36                              107

**2 Esdras**
2:27, 32                         179

**4 Maccabees**
15:3                               42
17:21–22                          63
18:11                            144

**Matthew**
1:2–16                           120
3:11                             255
4:1–11                           136
5:8–9                            125
5:9                              123
5:39                              89
5:44                              93
5:47                             272
6:7                              272
6:8                              223
7:7                              157
7:7–11                           223
7:21                              96
7:22                             158
10:9–12                          274
10:11–14                         260
10:15                            194
10:22                        88, 147
10:33                       105, 115
10:40                             275
11:22–24                         194
12:31–32                         226
12:32                             92
12:34–35                          89
12:36                            194
13:13–15                          82
13:19                             89
16:17–20                         277
16:23                             81
18:15–22                         277
18:17                            272

| | |
|---|---|
| 18:19 | 157 |
| 19:27–29 | 277 |
| 21:22 | 157 |
| 23:35 | 63, 144 |
| 24:4–5 | 253 |
| 24:9 | 22, 147 |
| 24:11 | 112, 165, 253 |
| 24:24 | 112, 165, 253 |
| 26:64 | 115 |

**Mark**

| | |
|---|---|
| 1:7 | 135 |
| 1:8 | 210 |
| 1:11 | 182, 210 |
| 3:4 | 279 |
| 3:28–30 | 226 |
| 4:3–20 | 138 |
| 4:11–12 | 82 |
| 4:15 | 89 |
| 7:5 | 251 |
| 8:37–38 | 115 |
| 9:7 | 182 |
| 9:41 | 256 |
| 10:30 | 92 |
| 10:45 | 150 |
| 11:23–24 | 223 |
| 12:6 | 182 |
| 12:29–31 | 199 |
| 12:31 | 143 |
| 12:33 | 143 |
| 13 | 98 |
| 13:5–6 | 99, 112 |
| 13:9 | 255 |
| 13:21–22 | 99, 165 |
| 13:22 | 165 |
| 13:22–27 | 171 |
| 14:66–72 | 105 |

**Luke**

| | |
|---|---|
| 1:47 | 188 |
| 4:18 | 103 |
| 5:10 | 43 |
| 5:37–9 | 78 |
| 7:12 | 182 |
| 8:12 | 89 |
| 8:42 | 182 |
| 9:25 | 256 |
| 9:26 | 115 |
| 9:38 | 182 |
| 10:25 | 42 |
| 10:27 | 199 |
| 10:29–37 | 143 |
| 12:8–9 | 115 |
| 12:10 | 226 |
| 12:41–48 | 277 |
| 16:8 | 50 |
| 16:15 | 154 |
| 18:8 | 207 |
| 20:36 | 125 |
| 22:20 | 78, 212 |
| 22:37 | 186 |

**John**

| | |
|---|---|
| 1:1 | 17, 38, 42, 46 |
| 1:1–18 | 17, 36 |
| 1:2 | 46 |
| 1:4 | 46 |
| 1:4–9 | 50 |
| 1:9 | 168 |
| 1:10 | 66, 124 |
| 1:12 | 120, 158, 271 |
| 1:12–13 | 121–22 |
| 1:13–14 | 182 |
| 1:14 | 11, 39, 46, 168, 182, 247, 254 |
| 1:16–17 | 247 |
| 1:18 | 182, 185, 198, 233, 279 |
| 1:26 | 210 |
| 1:27 | 255 |
| 1:29 | 129–30, 212 |
| 1:31 | 129, 210 |
| 1:32–34 | 212, 217 |
| 1:33 | 210 |
| 1:34 | 187, 214 |
| 1:36 | 129–30, 212 |
| 1:41 | 105, 107 |
| 1:46 | 279 |
| 1:52 | 246 |
| 2:4 | 99 |
| 2:19 | 135 |
| 3:1–3 | 163 |
| 3:3–8 | 121 |
| 3:5 | 206 |
| 3:6–8 | 168 |
| 3:11 | 39, 46, 187, 224 |
| 3:15 | 42, 158 |
| 3:16 | 66, 218 |
| 3:16–17 | 180–82, 189 |
| 3:18 | 158, 182 |
| 3:19 | 18, 144, 262, 279 |
| 3:26 | 217 |
| 3:29 | 48, 263 |
| 3:31 | 95 |
| 3:35 | 181 |
| 3:36 | 218 |
| 4:10–15 | 211 |
| 4:11 | 244 |
| 4:23–24 | 214 |
| 4:25 | 43 |
| 4:29 | 107 |
| 4:34 | 224 |
| 4:39–42 | 188 |
| 4:42 | 66, 92, 189 |
| 5:18 | 108 |
| 5:24 | 17, 147 |
| 5:26 | 119 |
| 5:29 | 279 |
| 5:30 | 224 |
| 5:31–32 | 281 |
| 5:31–40 | 217 |
| 5:32 | 214 |
| 5:32–33 | 217 |
| 5:36 | 183, 188 |
| 5:37 | 279 |
| 5:38 | 91, 107, 183 |
| 5:40 | 42 |
| 5:43 | 272 |
| 6:14 | 254–55 |
| 6:29 | 183 |
| 6:32 | 233 |
| 6:37 | 181, 204 |
| 6:37–39 | 102 |
| 6:38–40 | 96 |
| 6:39 | 204, 256 |
| 6:39–44 | 99 |
| 6:45 | 113 |
| 6:46 | 247, 279 |
| 6:51 | 66 |
| 6:51–56 | 168 |
| 6:53–56 | 11 |
| 6:56 | 160 |
| 6:57 | 183, 188 |
| 6:60 | 29, 284 |
| 6:66 | 29, 102, 284 |
| 6:69 | 104, 191 |
| 6:70–71 | 102 |
| 7:7 | 18, 144, 262, 279 |
| 7:8 | 48 |
| 7:12 | 279 |
| 7:13 | 156 |

**John** (*continued*)
| | |
|---|---|
| 7:16–17 | 113, 258 |
| 7:17 | 96 |
| 7:26–31 | 107 |
| 7:29 | 183, 247 |
| 7:30 | 99 |
| 7:38 | 211 |
| 7:41–42 | 107 |
| 8:12 | 50, 66, 82, 92, 107 |
| 8:13–18 | 281 |
| 8:14 | 214 |
| 8:17–18 | 217 |
| 8:23 | 95 |
| 8:29 | 113 |
| 8:30–33 | 284 |
| 8:31 | 91, 158, 258 |
| 8:32 | 246 |
| 8:41 | 135 |
| 8:41–47 | 127 |
| 8:42 | 101 |
| 8:44 | 18, 119, 134, 148, 247 |
| 8:46 | 130 |
| 8:47 | 66, 279 |
| 8:51 | 91 |
| 8:55 | 69 |
| 9:22 | 105, 107, 276 |
| 9:32 | 120 |
| 9:34 | 276 |
| 9:35 | 218 |
| 9:39 | 168 |
| 9:39–41 | 40 |
| 10:11 | 150, 268 |
| 10:15 | 150, 268 |
| 10:16 | 284 |
| 10:17 | 150, 181, 268 |
| 10:18 | 249 |
| 10:30 | 11, 17 |
| 10:35 | 91, 135 |
| 10:36 | 126, 188, 190 |
| 11:9 | 31, 92 |
| 11:9–10 | 82, 101 |
| 11:22 | 224 |
| 11:25 | 233 |
| 11:27 | 190, 191, 255 |
| 11:42 | 224 |
| 11:52 | 120, 246 |
| 11:55 | 125 |
| 12:13 | 255 |

| | |
|---|---|
| 12:23 | 99 |
| 12:25 | 268 |
| 12:31 | 99, 136 |
| 12:35 | 82 |
| 12:35–36 | 50 |
| 12:38 | 48 |
| 12:39–40 | 82 |
| 12:40 | 18, 83 |
| 12:42 | 105 |
| 12:46 | 82, 255 |
| 12:48 | 91, 99 |
| 13:1 | 92, 99 |
| 13:2 | 136 |
| 13:14 | 150 |
| 13:14–15 | 74 |
| 13:23 | 9 |
| 13:30–31 | 101 |
| 13:33 | 61 |
| 13:33–35 | 78 |
| 13:34 | 22, 74, 78, 160, 249–50 |
| 13:34–35 | 142 |
| 13:35 | 107 |
| 13:37–38 | 150, 268 |
| 14–17 | 8 |
| 14:2 | 115 |
| 14:6 | 233 |
| 14:7 | 69, 206 |
| 14:9 | 119 |
| 14:13 | 272 |
| 14:13–14 | 157, 226 |
| 14:13–15 | 224 |
| 14:15 | 202 |
| 14:16 | 62 |
| 14:16–17 | 160 |
| 14:17 | 112, 174, 214 |
| 14:20 | 160 |
| 14:21 | 181 |
| 14:23 | 115, 181 |
| 14:24 | 91 |
| 14:26 | 62, 113 |
| 14:26–27 | 13 |
| 15–16 | 8 |
| 15:1 | 233 |
| 15:4–7 | 160 |
| 15:7 | 91, 157, 226 |
| 15:9 | 181 |
| 15:10 | 74 |
| 15:11 | 47 |
| 15:12 | 22, 74, 78, 142, |

| | |
|---|---|
| | 143, 159, 249 |
| 15:12–17 | 150 |
| 15:13 | 150, 268 |
| 15:14–15 | 112, 282 |
| 15:16 | 157, 224, 226 |
| 15:17 | 78, 142 |
| 15:18–19 | 66, 147 |
| 15:21 | 88, 271 |
| 15:26 | 62, 160, 174, 214 |
| 15:26–27 | 213, 277 |
| 16:7 | 62, 160 |
| 16:8–11 | 62 |
| 16:12–14 | 13 |
| 16:13 | 174 |
| 16:13–15 | 43, 160, 187 |
| 16:16 | 119, 125 |
| 16:20–22 | 48 |
| 16:23–24 | 157 |
| 16:23–26 | 224 |
| 16:24 | 47, 263 |
| 16:25 | 43 |
| 16:26 | 157 |
| 16:28 | 168, 255 |
| 16:33 | 89, 94, 107, 207 |
| 17 | 8 |
| 17:2 | 204 |
| 17:2–3 | 42 |
| 17:3 | 69, 107, 119, 183, 232, 233 |
| 17:6 | 272 |
| 17:7–8 | 247 |
| 17:9 | 226 |
| 17:11 | 104, 272 |
| 17:11–13 | 94 |
| 17:12 | 101, 256 |
| 17:13 | 47, 263 |
| 17:13–16 | 66 |
| 17:13–18 | 172 |
| 17:14 | 91, 95, 147 |
| 17:15 | 89, 226, 279 |
| 17:17 | 91 |
| 17:17–19 | 126 |
| 17:23 | 160, 181 |
| 17:23–26 | 181 |
| 17:25 | 124 |
| 17:26 | 272 |
| 18:8–9 | 150 |
| 18:9 | 48, 256 |
| 18:20 | 156 |
| 18:23 | 279 |

| | |
|---|---|
| 18:36 | 189 |
| 18:37 | 154, 168, 214, 255 |
| 19:15 | 189 |
| 19:25–27 | 244, 245 |
| 19:26 | 9 |
| 19:30 | 212 |
| 19:34 | 212 |
| 19:35 | 46, 187, 212, 214, 217, 224, 281 |
| 19:36–37 | 214 |
| 20 | 244 |
| 20:17 | 90 |
| 20:18 | 40, 187 |
| 20:19 | 282 |
| 20:21 | 282 |
| 20:22 | 112 |
| 20:25 | 40 |
| 20:25–29 | 40 |
| 20:26 | 282 |
| 20:28 | 233 |
| 20:29 | 40 |
| 20:30–31 | 17 |
| 20:31 | 107, 159, 190, 271 |
| 21:1–25 | 17 |
| 21:5 | 61, 90 |
| 21:17 | 156 |
| 21:23 | 269 |
| 21:24 | 3, 28, 214, 224, 281, 283 |

**Acts**

| | |
|---|---|
| 1:4 | 111 |
| 1:8 | 190 |
| 1:11 | 254 |
| 1:24 | 154 |
| 2:17 | 98 |
| 2:33 | 111 |
| 2:38 | 272 |
| 2:42–47 | 44, 211 |
| 3:14 | 63 |
| 3:16 | 158 |
| 4:13, 20 | 156 |
| 4:30 | 158, 171 |
| 4:31 | 91 |
| 4:32–35 | 44 |
| 5:4 | 154 |
| 5:41 | 158, 271 |
| 6:2 | 91 |
| 6:3 | 279 |

| | |
|---|---|
| 6:6 | 41 |
| 7:52 | 63 |
| 9:16 | 271 |
| 9:27 | 158 |
| 10:22 | 279 |
| 10:38 | 103 |
| 10:48 | 272 |
| 13:5 | 91 |
| 13:6 | 165 |
| 13:23 | 111 |
| 13:33 | 121 |
| 14:23 | 242 |
| 15:3 | 269, 272 |
| 15:8 | 154 |
| 15:23 | 267 |
| 16:11–15, 40 | 244 |
| 16:18 | 158 |
| 17:7 | 275 |
| 18:27 | 275 |
| 20:17, 28 | 242 |
| 20:28 | 212 |
| 20:29–30 | 253 |
| 21:13 | 271 |
| 22:15 | 190 |
| 23:11 | 190 |
| 23:26 | 267 |
| 28:14, 15 | 269 |
| 28:25–28 | 82 |

**Romans**

| | |
|---|---|
| 1:8 | 269 |
| 1:10 | 224 |
| 1:17 | 63 |
| 2:28 | 169 |
| 3:25 | 212 |
| 3:29 | 56 |
| 4:5 | 158 |
| 5:9 | 56, 212 |
| 6:4 | 53 |
| 7:6 | 78 |
| 8:4 | 53 |
| 8:15 | 120 |
| 8:16 | 120 |
| 8:21, 23 | 120 |
| 8:32 | 183 |
| 8:33 | 246 |
| 9:5 | 234 |
| 9:8 | 120 |
| 9:26 | 123 |
| 9:31 | 158 |

| | |
|---|---|
| 12:1–2 | 96, 157, 163, 224 |
| 12:12 | 43 |
| 12:13 | 261 |
| 12:19 | 266 |
| 13:8–9 | 143 |
| 15:7 | 74, 75 |
| 15:24 | 272 |
| 15:26–27 | 4 |
| 16:1 | 280 |
| 16:2 | 274, 275 |
| 16:3 | 273–74 |
| 16:5 | 260 |
| 16:17 | 258 |
| 16:20 | 282 |
| 16:23 | 266 |

**1 Corinthians**

| | |
|---|---|
| 1:3 | 35, 45, 247 |
| 1:4 | 269 |
| 1:10 | 146 |
| 1:14 | 266 |
| 1:16 | 260 |
| 1:18 | 41 |
| 1:20–21 | 92 |
| 1:22–23 | 124 |
| 1:23 | 81 |
| 1:27–28 | 92 |
| 2:1 | 146 |
| 2:12 | 92 |
| 3:1–3 | 124 |
| 3:8 | 256 |
| 3:9 | 273 |
| 3:14 | 256 |
| 3:18–19 | 92 |
| 4:6 | 31 |
| 4:16 | 278 |
| 5:9–13 | 262 |
| 5:10 | 92 |
| 6:5–6 | 31, 269 |
| 6:8 | 31 |
| 7:7 | 53 |
| 7:33–34 | 93 |
| 8 | 235 |
| 8:4 | 235 |
| 8:11 | 31 |
| 10 | 235 |
| 10:19–20 | 235 |
| 11:1 | 278 |
| 11:25 | 78, 212 |
| 12:1–3 | 163 |

**1 Corinthians** (*continued*)

| | |
|---|---|
| 12:2 | 235 |
| 12:10 | 163 |
| 13:12 | 125 |
| 14:13–16 | 163 |
| 14:36 | 41, 91 |
| 15:1–11 | 109 |
| 15:3 | 129 |
| 15:23 | 115 |
| 15:58 | 109 |
| 16:6 | 272 |
| 16:11, 12 | 269, 272 |
| 16:15, 19 | 260 |

**2 Corinthians**

| | |
|---|---|
| 1:23–2:3 | 276 |
| 3:1 | 280 |
| 3:6 | 78 |
| 3:18 | 125 |
| 4:4 | 83 |
| 5:9 | 157 |
| 5:12 | 280 |
| 5:17 | 78 |
| 5:21 | 130 |
| 6:8 | 253 |
| 7:1 | 76 |
| 7:13–16 | 273 |
| 7:15 | 274, 275 |
| 8:8–15 | 152 |
| 9:3–5 | 273 |
| 11:4–6 | 102 |
| 12:14 | 282 |
| 12:20–13:4 | 282 |
| 13:1–4 | 276 |
| 13:5 | 163 |
| 13:13 | 43 |

**Galatians**

| | |
|---|---|
| 1:2 | 80 |
| 1:3 | 247 |
| 1:6–9 | 102 |
| 3:16, 19 | 137 |
| 4:14 | 274 |
| 4:19 | 13, 270 |
| 5:14 | 143 |
| 5:16 | 94 |
| 5:22–25 | 160 |
| 6:8 | 42 |

**Ephesians**

| | |
|---|---|
| 1:7 | 212 |
| 2:2 | 92 |

| | |
|---|---|
| 2:3 | 94 |
| 2:11 | 169 |
| 2:13 | 212 |
| 3:12 | 157 |
| 5:1 | 76 |
| 5:8 | 50 |
| 5:10 | 163 |
| 5:20 | 158 |
| 5:25–6:9 | 86 |
| 5:26–27 | 56 |
| 5:29–32 | 244 |
| 6:11–17 | 134 |
| 6:23 | 282 |

**Philippians**

| | |
|---|---|
| 1:5 | 43 |
| 1:10 | 163 |
| 2:1 | 43 |
| 2:1–11 | 152 |
| 2:10–11 | 171 |
| 2:25 | 274 |
| 3:12 | 194 |
| 3:20–21 | 125 |
| 4:3 | 274 |
| 4:15 | 43 |

**Colossians**

| | |
|---|---|
| 1:20 | 212 |
| 3:12 | 246 |
| 3:13 | 74, 75 |
| 3:18–4:1 | 86 |
| 3:21 | 87 |
| 4:5 | 53 |
| 4:11 | 274 |

**1 Thessalonians**

| | |
|---|---|
| 1:6 | 278 |
| 1:9 | 232, 235 |
| 2:12 | 272, 274 |
| 2:19 | 115 |
| 3:2 | 274 |
| 3:13 | 115 |
| 4:1 | 5, 249 |
| 4:3 | 224 |
| 4:9 | 143 |
| 4:12 | 249 |
| 5:1 | 98 |
| 5:5 | 50 |
| 5:21 | 165 |
| 5:28 | 282 |

**2 Thessalonians**

| | |
|---|---|
| 2:1–12 | 99 |

| | |
|---|---|
| 2:3 | 102 |
| 2:3–8 | 128 |
| 2:4 | 99 |
| 2:8–9 | 115 |
| 2:11–12 | 171, 173 |
| 3:6 | 249, 251 |
| 3:7, 9 | 278 |
| 3:11 | 249 |

**1 Timothy**

| | |
|---|---|
| 1:1 | 188 |
| 1:2 | 247, 270 |
| 1:2, 18 | 13 |
| 1:3 | 109 |
| 1:10 | 113 |
| 1:15 | 109 |
| 1:18 | 13 |
| 3:1 | 109 |
| 3:14 | 263 |
| 3:16 | 168–69 |
| 4:1–4 | 165 |
| 4:6 | 109, 113 |
| 4:13, 16 | 113 |
| 5:1–2 | 86 |
| 5:8 | 110 |
| 5:10 | 279 |
| 5:17 | 86 |
| 5:22 | 262 |

**2 Timothy**

| | |
|---|---|
| 1:2 | 247 |
| 1:10 | 188 |
| 1:11–14 | 109 |
| 2:10 | 246 |
| 2:14–19 | 109 |
| 2:18 | 109 |
| 3:1 | 98 |
| 3:1–5 | 165 |
| 3:6 | 253 |
| 3:8 | 109 |
| 3:13 | 258 |
| 3:14 | 110, 258 |

**Titus**

| | |
|---|---|
| 1:4 | 188 |
| 1:13 | 268 |
| 2:3 | 133 |
| 2:13 | 188 |
| 3:6 | 188 |

**Hebrews**

| | |
|---|---|
| 1:2 | 98 |
| 1:5 | 121 |

| | | | | | |
|---|---|---|---|---|---|
| 4:15 | 130 | 5:1 | 242 | 1:8–9 | 1, 15, 57–59 |
| 4:16 | 116, 157 | 5:1–5 | 86 | 1:8–2:2 | 228 |
| 5:11–14 | 124 | 5:13 | 245 | 1:9 | 63, 104, 119, |
| 6:4–8 | 226 | 5:14 | 282 | | 122, 130, 227 |
| 6:12 | 278 | | | 1:9–10 | 20 |
| 8:8 | 78 | **2 Peter** | | 1:9–2:2 | 225 |
| 9:12 | 212 | 1:1 | 2, 188 | 1:10 | 41, 54, 59–60, |
| 9:12–14 | 55 | 1:2 | 247 | | 70, 90, 104, 127, |
| 9:15 | 78 | 1:10 | 146 | | 131, 218, 227 |
| 9:22 | 56 | 1:11 | 188 | 2:1 | 2, 5, 6, 17, 20, |
| 10:19 | 157, 212 | 1:17 | 182 | | 35, 39, 45, 47, |
| 10:35 | 157 | 2 | 102 | | 87, 90, 98, 104, |
| 10:36 | 224 | 2:1 | 253 | | 106, 119, 122, |
| 11 | 207 | 2:1–3 | 165 | | 136, 167, 208, |
| 11:4 | 144 | 2:4 | 194 | | 220, 246 |
| 13:1–3 | 151 | 2:10 | 94 | 2:1–2 | 55, 60–67, 131 |
| 13:2 | 261 | 2:20 | 188 | 2:2 | 49, 65–6, 92, 124, |
| 13:21 | 157 | 3:3 | 98 | | 167, 172, 183, 189, |
| 13:22–25 | 5 | 3:7 | 194 | | 211, 231 |
| | | 3:12 | 115 | 2:3 | 11, 15, 24, 32, 68–70, |
| **James** | | | | | 120, 140, 149, 154, |
| 1:1 | 267 | **1 John** | | | 165, 192, 202 |
| 1:2 | 146 | 1:1 | 15, 37–41, 94, | 2:3–4 | 89, 177, 201, 232 |
| 1:5 | 223 | | 109, 142, 218, 237 | 2:3–5 | 25 |
| 1:17 | 51 | 1:1–2 | 95 | 2:3–6 | 68–75, 159 |
| 2:1–7 | 151 | 1:1–3 | 16, 37–46, 111, | 2:3–11 | 67–84 |
| 2:8 | 143 | | 132, 136, 187, 256 | 2:4 | 15, 16, 21, 60, 79, |
| 2:15 | 80, 269 | 1:1–4 | 35–48 | | 104, 132, 149, 152, |
| 2:23 | 283 | 1:2 | 6, 41–43, 46, 148, | | 184, 186, 192, 193–94, |
| 4:2–3 | 223 | | 180, 219, 233 | | 197, 213, 215, 247 |
| 4:4 | 283 | 1:3 | 6, 7, 15, 42–45, | 2:4–5 | 70–72, 131 |
| 4:8 | 126 | | 57, 90, 106, 116, | 2:4–6 | 32, 77 |
| 5:7, 8 | 115 | | 158, 167, 173, 193, | 2:5 | 71, 90, 93, 123, |
| | | | 208, 262 | | 180, 198, 202 |
| **1 Peter** | | 1:4 | 46–48, 263 | 2:5–6 | 79, 110 |
| 1:1 | 7, 246 | 1:5 | 6, 14, 15, 24, | 2:6 | 2, 40, 50, 72–75, |
| 1:2 | 45, 247 | | 49–52, 111, 142, | | 107, 114, 126, 129, |
| 1:3 | 120 | | 145, 174, 177, | | 132, 133, 143, 148, |
| 1:22 | 143 | | 202, 213, 219 | | 149, 186, 194, 208, |
| 1:23 | 120, 138 | 1:5–7 | 30 | | 215, 258 |
| 2:4 | 246 | 1:5–2:2 | 48–67 | 2:7 | 6, 15, 16, 23, 41, |
| 2:9 | 246 | 1:6 | 11, 39, 42–43, | | 61, 76–78, 88, 109, |
| 2:12 | 279 | | 70, 107, 152 | | 135, 142, 162, 176, |
| 2:14–15 | 279 | 1:6–7 | 52–57, 78, 79, | | 207, 232, 250 |
| 2:21–25 | 64 | | 249, 262 | 2:7–8 | 17, 35, 39, 47, |
| 2:22 | 130 | 1:6–10 | 52–60, 197 | | 157, 201, 249 |
| 3:6 | 279 | 1:7 | 25, 42–43, 61, | 2:7–11 | 71, 75–84 |
| 3:18 | 129 | | 158, 211 | 2:8 | 22, 53, 78–79, |
| 4:5 | 194 | 1:7–2:2 | 128 | | 96, 98, 148 |
| 4:12 | 76 | 1:8 | 61, 70, 104, 112, | 2:9 | 11, 15, 60, 148, 199 |
| 4:15 | 279 | | 127, 131, 152, 173, | 2:9–10 | 79–81, 142 |
| 4:19 | 279 | | 213, 227, 247 | | |

**1 John** (*continued*)
2:9–11        32, 141, 147,
              197–98
2:10          15, 22, 31, 258
2:11          15, 16, 17, 31, 39,
              52, 53, 65, 81–84,
              148, 218
2:12–14       5, 16, 32, 35,
              47, 85–91, 243
2:12–13       87–90
2:12–17       84–97
2:12          158, 180, 271
2:13          16, 69, 109, 135,
              149, 171, 262
2:13–14       11, 15, 38, 71,
              132, 144, 192, 206,
              231, 279
2:14          41, 45, 61, 90–91,
              93, 107, 110, 135,
              149, 160, 232, 258
2:15          71, 91–94, 123,
              148, 152, 177, 198,
              203, 225, 253
2:15–16       90
2:15–17       22, 65, 91–97,
              123, 146, 151, 165,
              180, 231
2:16          19, 94–95, 99,
              134, 167, 237
2:17          19, 22, 96, 98, 224
2:18          6, 10, 12, 14, 61,
              75, 77, 85, 90,
              98–100, 109, 112,
              114, 120, 149, 164,
              194, 196, 222,
              227, 255
2:18–19       25, 29, 161,
              165, 167, 171–72,
              252, 276
2:18–21       22
2:18–22       162
2:18–23       97–108
2:18–28       97–116
2:19          7, 11, 15, 19, 42,
              100–102, 114, 133,
              202, 274
2:20          23, 36, 77, 99, 112,
              113, 138, 202, 232
2:20–21       6, 19, 102–4,
              224, 277

2:21          5, 7, 15, 35, 47,
              54, 57, 142, 154,
              164, 197, 220, 221
2:21–22       218
2:22          10, 54, 75, 90, 99,
              161, 166, 197, 200
2:22–23       45, 69, 105–8,
              116, 136, 158,
              190, 208
2:23          19, 12, 21, 57,
              69, 201, 207, 215,
              219, 259
2:23–24       90
2:24          6, 38, 39, 73, 77,
              88, 107, 108–10,
              135, 138, 142, 148,
              159–60, 252, 258
2:24–28       108–18
2:25          15, 41, 49, 50,
              110–11, 148,
              202, 251
2:26          5, 35, 47, 111–12,
              133, 173, 220, 221,
              253, 277
2:27          15, 23, 36, 54, 73,
              74, 77, 99, 103,
              112–14, 138, 143,
              160, 202, 232,
              258, 277
2:27–28       21, 73
2:28          17, 19, 42, 60,
              114–16, 119, 124,
              125, 128, 132, 154,
              156, 180, 194, 196,
              215, 223, 234,
              237, 254
2:29          16, 59, 104, 117,
              119–23, 133, 144,
              148, 168, 177–78,
              182, 278, 279
2:29–3:3      118–26, 201
2:29–3:10a    16
2:29–3:12     116–45,
              199–200, 229
3:1           45, 69, 106, 123–24,
              146, 177–78, 189, 200
3:1–2         60, 141
3:2           16, 19, 22, 23, 42,
              61, 74, 76, 115,
              119, 128, 129, 147,

              176, 180, 185, 187,
              194, 224, 246, 252, 254
3:2–3         124–26
3:3           75, 117–18, 129,
              133, 143, 149, 183,
              194, 208, 258
3:4           128–29, 148
3:4–6         126
3:4–7         118
3:4–9         131
3:4–10        11, 49, 61, 126–41,
              225, 278
3:5           16, 22, 42, 64, 65,
              75, 129–31, 133, 149,
              167, 180, 183, 208, 212
3:6           73, 117, 131–32,
              149, 177–78, 185,
              192, 194, 198, 228,
              230, 258, 279
3:7           60, 74, 75, 104, 112,
              114, 120, 122, 123,
              132–133, 143–44,
              173, 234, 253, 279
3:7–8         59, 117
3:7–10        122
3:8           16, 20, 22, 42, 60,
              106, 129, 133–36,
              149, 152, 167, 180,
              208, 211, 230, 232
3:8–10        82, 118, 128
3:9           19, 20, 23, 119,
              120, 136–40, 160,
              177, 203, 230
3:9–10        25, 117, 201
3:10          60, 68, 122, 123,
              140–41, 148, 154,
              166, 199, 228,
              232, 279
3:10–12       118, 141–45
3:11          6, 14, 16, 22, 38,
              39, 69, 71, 76, 78,
              88, 108, 111, 145,
              147, 157, 160, 176,
              185, 199, 250, 252
3:12          16, 18, 31, 63, 74,
              79–80, 89, 135, 143–45,
              146, 152, 199, 230, 262,
              275, 279
3:13          82, 92, 146–47,
              180, 189–90, 203

3:13–14                        269
3:13–24                      145–61
3:14            16, 17, 19, 20,
                  31, 119, 147–48,
                  149, 151, 177, 180,
                  194, 219, 224, 228
3:15            16, 73, 119, 135,
                  148–49, 152, 219,
                  224, 228
3:16            31, 75, 149–50,
                  177, 180, 194,
                  208, 273
3:17      71, 94, 110, 151–52,
                  154, 180, 197, 225
3:17–18                          44
3:18      60, 92, 152–53, 246
3:19              15, 57, 68
3:19–20                    154–56
3:19–22                        196
3:19–24                    153–61
3:20                            171
3:21            16, 61, 62, 107,
                  115, 116, 176, 223
3:21–22                    156–57
3:22–24                        201
3:22                      159, 225
3:23        44, 50, 69, 74, 76,
                  88, 106, 110, 114, 136,
                  157–59, 163, 167, 176,
                  190, 191, 199, 207–8,
                  215, 218, 221, 249, 250
3:23–24                  213, 251
3:23–4:6                  106, 215
3:24            73, 103, 138,
                  159–61, 162, 163,
                  166, 168, 174,
                  185–86
3:24–4:1                  185, 187
4:1            12, 54, 61, 76,
                  138, 162–65, 168,
                  176, 191, 204, 274
4:1–3      22, 158, 160, 172,
                  186, 205, 252–55
4:1–5                          124
4:1–6          103, 161–75
4:2            10, 14, 21, 57, 94,
                  194, 208, 210,
                  213, 221
4:2–3              165–70, 190
4:3                12, 77, 112,

4:3–5                    147, 189
4:4            89, 94, 114, 119,
                  170–71, 203, 206
4:4–5          92, 95, 173, 180
4:4–6              12, 15, 171
4:5                12, 22, 65,
                  171–73, 232
4:5–6                            77
4:6            23, 66, 69, 112,
                  165, 173–75, 186,
                  187, 213, 253, 279
4:6–8                            69
4:7            61, 76, 120, 142,
                  182, 192, 196, 200,
                  201, 205, 213
4:7–8          176–80, 199, 232
4:7–10        16, 175, 176–84
4:7–12                          93
4:7–5:4          16, 175–204
4:8                1, 71, 192
4:8–16                          50
4:9            42, 66, 71, 92,
                  129, 167, 172, 222
4:9–10          106, 180–84,
                  188, 191
4:10            55, 64, 189,
                  197–98, 207, 212
4:11            61, 75, 76, 142,
                  150, 180, 273
4:11–12                    184–86
4:11–16          175, 184–92
4:12            10, 69, 71, 73,
                  110, 142, 186, 187,
                  192, 193, 222, 279
4:12–13                  160, 190
4:12–15                        131
4:13            73, 103, 138,
                  165, 186–87
                                213
4:13–15                        213
4:14          9, 15, 39, 43,
                  45–46, 65, 90, 92,
                  106, 124, 172, 180,
                  187–90, 192, 201,
                  207, 213, 231
4:14–16                        167
4:15          73, 106, 110, 166,
                  188, 190–91, 201,
                  205, 207
4:16              1, 9, 73,
                  191–92, 276

4:17            17, 19, 62, 69,
                  74, 75, 92, 94, 115,
                  116, 156, 223
4:17–18                    193–96
4:17–19          175, 193–96
4:18                        65, 71
4:19                            196
4:20            15, 19, 32, 75,
                  143, 152, 185,
                  202, 279
4:20–21                    197–99
4:20–5:1                          93
4:20–5:4              175, 183,
                  196–205
4:21      50, 143, 202, 250
5:1        16, 95, 120, 142,
                  178, 190, 205, 207,
                  230, 254
5:1–2          123, 199–202
5:2        11, 60, 141, 165
5:2–3                          157
5:3        69, 180, 202, 250
5:4        15, 78, 202–4, 221
5:4–5          89, 171, 206–8
5:4–8                      205–15
5:4–13                    205–22
5:5                21, 106, 159,
                  166, 190, 221
5:6              167, 208–14,
                  217, 221
5:6–11                          43
5:7–8          206, 214–15
5:8                            209
5:9          215, 221, 269
5:9–10                    216–19
5:9–11                            9
5:9–12        106, 207, 215,
                  216–20
5:10      54, 107, 158, 221
5:11            46, 49, 111,
                  202, 221
5:11–12    219–20, 221, 233
5:12                            228
5:12–13          21, 107, 220
5:13        2, 5, 14, 35, 36,
                  41, 42, 46, 47, 86,
                  88, 158, 176, 207,
                  218, 220–22, 271
5:14      116, 156, 196, 202
5:14–15                    223–25

**1 John** (*continued*)
5:14–16     157
5:14–17     222–29
5:14–21     222–38
5:16     6, 80
5:16–17     20, 129, 140, 225–29
5:16–18     11, 127, 132
5:16–19     49
5:18     20, 119, 131, 138, 182, 200, 203, 228, 229–31
5:18–19     89, 262, 279
5:18–20     16, 224
5:18–21     229–38
5:19     7, 65–66, 92, 189, 231–32
5:20     21, 42, 46, 60, 69, 72, 119, 158, 207, 215, 216, 232–34
5:21     40, 114, 234–38

**2 John**
1     18, 241–46, 267
1–3     240–48
2–3     246–48
3     18, 246
4     31, 241, 246, 248–49, 270
4–8     248–56
5     78, 244
5–6     18, 249–52
7     10, 18, 23, 112, 211, 239, 252–55, 270, 274
8     22, 241, 244, 255–56
9     31, 107, 248, 249, 257–59, 273, 276
9–11     12, 239, 263
9–13     257–64
10     244, 259–61
10–11     10, 276, 277
11     215, 244, 261–62, 275, 279
12     47, 241, 244, 262–63
13     6, 241, 241–42, 244, 245, 263–64

**3 John**
1     266–68
1–4     266–70

2     268
3     31, 214, 241, 280
3–4     47, 246, 249, 268–70
4     13
5     31
5–6     13
5–7     271–73
5–12     270–81
6     280
7     23, 102
8     14, 241, 273–74
9     241, 257, 274–75
9–10     12, 14, 273
10     10, 241, 275–78, 279, 282
12     3, 9, 214, 217, 279–81
13–14     282
13–15     281–84
15     6, 282–84

**Jude**
1     2
2     247
3     207
11     144

**Revelation**
1:1     3
1:2     190
1:5     212
1:9     3, 190
2–3     241
2:3     88
2:7     90
2:11     90
2:13     190
2:23     154
3:12     78
5:9     212
11:18     256
12     244
12:9     112, 253
12:11     90, 212
13     101
13:11–18     100
16:13     165
19:10     269
19:13     91
19:20     165, 253

20:10     165
21     244
21:1     96
22:3–4     125
22:12     256

**OTHER ANCIENT SOURCES**

**Aeschines**
*Against Timarchus* 90     279

**Alexander of Alexandria**
*Letter* 2.6     28

**Ambrosiaster**
*Comm. on Rom.*
169C     28

**Apocalypse of Adam**
(NHV.5)     139

**Apollonius of Tyana**
*Epistle* 51     274

**Augustine**
*Commentary on 1 John*
10:3     200
*Confessions*
10:27     198
*On Baptism*     28
*On the Trinity*
8     179–80

**Ps. Augustine**
*Speculum*     26

**Barnabas**
5:6, 10     169, 255
6:7, 9, 14     169, 255
12:10     169, 255
18–20     54
18:1–2     54

**Bede**
*On 1, 2, 3 John*     28

**Cheltenham List**     28

**Clement of Alexandria**
*Hypotyposeis*     26, 214, 245, 254

**1 Clement**
21:6    86
44:3    279

**2 Clement**
17:1    236

**Ps. Clement**
*Homilies*
9.35.4    260

**Damascus Document** (CD)
VIII, 14–17    179

**DEAD SEA SCROLLS**

**1QH (*Hymn Scroll*)**
V, 24    179
XIV, 8    56, 58
XIX, 5–9    179
XIX, 28    69

**1 QM (*War Scroll*)**
I, 1    89
XIII, 10–12    174

**1QS (*Community Rule*)**
I, 9–10    81
II, 11, 16–17    235–36
III, 13–IV, 7    24, 161
III, 15–21    51, 53
III, 17–19    174
III, 20–24    134
IV, 5    235–36
IV, 9–11    83
V, 1–5    44
VI, 17–23    40

4Q246    21, 135
4Q548    20
4Q (*Songs of the Sabbath Sacrifice*)    23

**11Q13 (*Melchizedek*)**    63

**Didache**
1–5    54
3:4    236
4:8    44
5:1    236
11:1–2    260, 273, 277
15:1–2    261

**Dionysius of Alexandria.**
See Eusebius, *Ecclesiastical History* 7.25.7–27

**1 Enoch**
6    134
8:2–10:12    63

**Epictetus**
*Dissertations*
2.8.17    107
2.18    94
2.19.27    44
3.22.10    274

**Eusebius**
*Ecclesiastical History*
2.23.25    6
3.24.17–25.7    27
3.39.3–4    242
3.39.5    243
3.39.17    2, 14
5.1.45    245
5.18.5    5
5.20.4–8    243
5.24.14    243
6.14.1    26
6.25.9–10    2, 27, 266
7.25.7–27    27–8
7.25.16    243

**Faustinus**
*On the Trinity*
2:10–13    200

**Gospel of Truth** (NH I.3)
22, 14–18    70

**Hermas**
*Shepherd: Mand.*
4.1.1–2    226
9.4    236
11.12    277
*Sim.*
7–8    226
*Vis.*
1.1–2.4    244

**Ignatius**
*Ephesians*
7:2    168
*Philadelphians*
7:2    277
11:1    279, 280

**Trallians**
Prescript    246, 267
2–3    12
9–10    10, 169, 209–10
*Smyrnans*
1–2    210
1:2    168
2    169
3:1    168, 254
4:1    261
7:1    261
8    261
12:1    278
12:2–13:2    282

**Inscriptiones Graecae**
II. 3273    188

**Irenaeus**
*Against Heresies*
1.6.1–2    139
1.16.3    2
1.26.1    10, 169
2.22.5    242
3.3.4    10, 169
3.11.1    169
3.16.8    2
4.27.1–28.1    242
4.30.1–31.1    242
5.5.1    242
5.21.1    137
5.30.1    242
5.33.3    242

**Jerome**
*On Illustrious Men*
9, 18    27, 243

**Joseph and Aseneth**
8:5    103
11:10    68
15:5    103
16:16    103

**Josephus**
*Antiquities*
1.52–9    139
1.222    182
*Jewish War*
2.122    44
3.459    188
7.344    44

**Justin Martyr**

*Dialogue with Trypho*
136:2                          63

**Lucian**

*Peregrinus*
13                             261

*MAMA*
8.410                          280
8.414                          280

**Muratorian Canon**    26–27

**Optatus**

*Against the Donatists*        28

**Origen**

*Against Celsus*
3.55                           260
*See also* Eusebius,
*Ecclesiastical History*
6.25.9–10

**Papias.** *See* Eusebius,
*Ecclesiastical History*
3.39.17

**Philo**

*Embassy*
22                             188

*Hypothetica*
11.10–13                        44

*Life of Moses*
2.209–10                       122

*On Cherubim*
15                             148

*On Dreams*
1.75                            51

*On Flight*
235                             51

*On Rewards*
163                             57
165–7                           62

*On the Creation of the World*
103                             87

*On the Posterity of Cain*
172–4                          139

*On the Unchangeableness
of God*
58                              51

*Who Is the Heir?*
61–70                          122

**Plutarch**

*Solon*
95B                            275

**Polycarp**

*Philippians*
1:1                            272
7:1              2, 14, 26, 166
14                             280

*Psalms of Solomon*
8:33                           188
9:6                             56
9:7                             57
10:1                            56

*Select Papyri* I
no. 106                        280
no. 110                        283
no. 111                        265
no. 113           267, 268, 282

**Tertullian**

*On the Incarnation*
24                             254

*On Resurrection*               3

*To the Martyrs*
1                              245

**TESTAMENTS OF THE TWELVE
PATRIARCHS**       24–25, 31

*Testament of Asher*
1:3–5                           53

*Testament of Benjamin*
3:3, 4                         199
6:4                             74

*Testament of Dan*
5:1                        74, 107
5:6                            199

*Testament of Gad*
2:1                             57
3:1–4:1                      83–84
6:1             79, 143, 152
6:3                             57

*Testament of Issachar*
5:2                            199
7:1                            227

*Testament of Judah*
19:4                            83
20:1                           174
25:3                           174

*Testament of Reuben*
2:1                            174
3:2                            174
4:6                            236

*Testament of Simeon*
2:7                            174
4:7                             79

**Thucydides**

*Histories*
6.13                            94

# INDEX OF SUBJECTS

Abel, 31, 63, 79, 134, 144
abiding. *See* indwelling
Abraham, 137, 182–83
Adam and Eve, 134, 139
anointing, 23, 73, 99, 102–4, 112–14
antichrist, 12, 16, 22–23, 99–100, 102–4, 106,
  108, 112, 115–16, 161, 165, 170–71, 195,
  236, 252, 274, 278
antitheses, 16, 79, 104, 117–19, 257–58, 278,
apocalyptic, 22–23, 92, 171
Asia Minor, 14, 59, 65
atonement, 56, 149
  day of, 56, 64
  *See also* forgiveness
audience, 4, 15–16, 29–30, 32, 35–36, 48,
  101, 173, 244, 265–67
authors, authorship, 2–4, 6–9, 32, 35–36,
  47–48, 241–44

baptism, 103, 209–14, 218
begetting, 115–20, 182, 199, 200, 203
  *See also* birth
beginning, from the, 15, 37–38, 76–77, 88–89,
  111, 134–36, 157, 237, 250, 252
begotten (of the Son), 180–83, 200–201,
  230–31
belief, 76, 110, 181, 190, 201–2, 207
believe, 157–59, 178, 204, 218, 220–21
  *See also* confession
Beloved Disciple, 8–9, 26
birth from God, 20–21, 95, 116–29, 134,
  136–40, 145, 177–78, 199–200, 203–4,
  228, 230–32
bishop, 12, 277
blindness, 65, 81–84
blood, 11, 55–56, 60, 209–15, 217
boldness, 62, 114–16, 156–57, 194–96, 223

brothers, 12, 79–81, 146, 200, 225, 228, 269,
  271–73, 275–77, 282
  translating, 31–32, 75–76, 80, 269

Cain, 16, 23, 31, 63, 79–80, 129, 134, 138–39,
  144–48, 149, 152, 156, 262, 275
canon, 8, 25–28, 30
Carthage, Council of, 26
Cassiodorus, 26
catholic letters, 3, 5–7, 26, 27–28
Cerinthus, 10, 169, 210
"Children," 13, 60–61, 76, 86–88, 90, 114, 152,
  200, 234, 241, 244, 246, 248–49, 270
  of God, 60, 82, 90, 116–27, 136–42, 105,
  170, 178, 186, 193, 201
  of the devil, 60, 82, 127, 140–42, 148
Christology, 9, 10–11, 12, 14, 21, 160,
  209–10, 230, 284
church, 244, 269, 273, 274–77
  structure, 12–13, 29, 87, 96, 242, 261
Comma Iohanneum, 215
commandments, 41, 69, 73, 76–78, 142,
  157–59, 176, 199, 201–3, 249–52
  obedience to, 12, 19, 69–72, 157, 185, 196
completeness, 48, 71–72, 194, 263
confession (= acknowledge), 12, 21, 105–6,
  161, 163–71, 187, 190–91, 200–201, 205,
  213, 253–55
  of sin, 57, 65–6, 225–27
confidence, 16, 36, 67, 96, 100–102, 104,
  119–20, 147, 154–57, 170–71, 206–7,
  221, 229–34
covenant, 78
Cyprian, 26

darkness, 4, 30–31, 51–52, 53–60, 75, 78,
  80–85, 148, 177

Dead Sea Scrolls, 21, 23, 24, 63, 69, 81, 236
   See also Index of Ancient Sources
death, 147–49, 154, 219, 227
   of Jesus, 55–57, 129–30, 149–50, 152, 180,
      209–15, 218, 226
deceit, deceive (= lead astray), 75, 106,
      111–12, 132–33, 165, 173–74, 253, 259
   See also error
Demetrius, 10, 270, 279–81
denial, 105–8, 115
desire, 94–95
determinism, 19–20, 24, 82, 117–18, 122,
      136–37, 140
Deuteronomy, 17, 178–80, 183, 198, 202
devil, 20, 23, 38, 89, 133–34, 145, 148
   See also evil one; Satan
Dionysius of Alexandria, 27–28, 243
Diotrephes, 9–10, 12–14, 270, 274–79, 281,
      284,
Docetism, 10–11, 23, 169–70, 209–10
dualism, 18–20, 22, 30, 51–52, 80, 82–83, 94,
      117–18, 127–33, 141, 145, 147, 164,
      173–74, 189, 198, 203, 278–79

elder, 1, 6, 7, 9, 12–13, 241–44, 262–63,
      266–67, 271–81
elders, 2, 86, 242–43
elect lady, 6, 244–46, 249, 251, 263
Ephesus, 14, 59
error, 112, 173–74, 253
   See also deceit
eschatology, 8, 12, 17, 19, 96, 98–101,
      114–16, 125–26, 128, 165, 171, 173–74,
      195–96, 253, 255–56, 258–59
eucharist, 211–12, 214
evil one, 89, 94, 144, 171, 230–32, 259–60,
      274–76
expulsion, 9, 10, 12, 105, 276–78
eyewitness, 9, 36, 40–41, 187

false prophets, 54, 99, 112, 162, 164–65,
      172–73, 231, 252–53, 274
   See also lie, liar
Father (God), 21, 42, 45, 73, 90, 93, 95–96,
      106, 110–11, 136, 190, 247–48, 249, 259
fellowship, 15, 43–45, 47–48, 49, 52–55, 96,
      107, 262
flesh, 11, 21, 23, 94–95, 166–69, 253–55
forgiveness, 55–57, 61–66, 88, 183, 189–90,
      210–11, 214, 226–28, 231

friends, 13, 150, 282–83

Gaius, 6, 9, 13, 14, 266–81 passim
gender, 31–32, 86–87
   See also brothers: translating
Gentiles, 23, 25, 272
glory, 8
Gnosticism, 11, 23–24, 69–70
God, understanding of, 20–21, 32, 50–51,
      54–55, 57–60, 67, 83, 116, 122, 125–26,
      154, 177–80, 185–86, 192, 196, 204,
      216–20, 223–25
   See also Father (God)

hatred, 79–81, 147, 149, 154, 198
hearing, 36, 39–41, 48, 77, 110, 142
heresy, 13–14, 28, 263,
holy, 103–4
   and just, 59
hospitality, 28, 259–61, 272–75
household, 244, 259–60, 266, 277
   codes, 86–87

idols, 17, 234–38
Ignatius, 14, 23, 168, 261, 277, 280
   See also Index of Ancient Sources
individual, 19, 75, 80, 110, 132, 153, 160–61,
      180, 184, 202–3
indwelling, 19, 72–74, 79, 110, 131–32, 138,
      148, 159–60, 167–68, 185–87, 190–93,
      247, 258
Irenaeus, 2, 18, 26, 242–43
   See also Index of Ancient Sources
Isaiah, 17, 39–40

James, 27
Jesus, as the Christ, 21, 45, 103, 105–8,
      158–59, 165–67, 190–91, 201, 208, 233,
      253–55, 258
   human experience of, 11, 21, 50, 61,
      74–75, 126, 149–50, 159, 187,
      195, 213
   present significance, 61–63, 65, 194–95
   See also death; Son; Son of God
"Jewishness," 9, 23–25, 49–52, 73–74, 105–6,
      125, 178, 234–36
Jews, 105
Johannine community/school, 24, 28–29, 87,
      256, 269
Johannine corpus, 1, 3, 25–28, 30

literary relationships, 16–18, 22, 38, 42, 82, 99, 120–21, 127–28, 150, 160, 168, 180–82, 189, 212–14, 249, 254–55, 277–78, 281, 283–84
Johannine tradition, 4, 16, 17–18, 28, 30, 36, 62, 150, 217, 269
John, the apostle, 2, 3, 8, 26, 276
John, the elder, 3, 27, 242–43
joy, 47–48, 263, 268
Judas, 101–2
Jude, 26–27, 102
judgment, 154–56, 174, 177, 193–96
just, 58–9, 63, 119, 126
justice, 58–59, 117–19, 122, 128, 132–33, 136–39, 142, 279

knowledge, 13, 102–3, 122, 148–49, 224, 229, 231–34
of God, 12, 19, 24, 68–70, 76, 88–90, 149, 173–74

lamb of God, 129–30, 212
law, 74, 128
letters, 4–5, 239–40, 265, 283
conventions, 248, 262–63, 265–68, 280, 281, 283–84
greetings, 35, 45, 47, 246–47, 267
*See also* Pauline letters
lie, liar, 54, 59, 164, 173, 197, 200, 218
life, 95, 147, 154, 180, 211, 222, 228, 231
eternal, 36, 41–42, 73, 148, 152, 219, 220–21, 233
light, 4, 31, 49–52, 53–60, 66–67, 75, 78–79, 80–82, 84, 145
love, 14, 22, 79, 93, 142, 147–49, 155–56, 175, 246, 251, 267
of fellow believer, 19, 22, 76
of God, 11, 19, 71, 74, 93, 123, 143, 152, 175–204
one another, 142–43, 145, 147, 157, 159, 176–99, 250–52
one's brother, 78–82, 141, 143, 147, 199–201

Melchizedek, 63
message, 49–50, 142
Messiah, 10, 99, 105, 107, 135, 166–67
*See also* Jesus, as the Christ
mission, missionaries, 23, 172–73, 272–73
moral guidelines, 10, 48–49, 96, 151, 283

Moses, 125, 185
murder, murderer, 144, 148–50, 152
mysticism, 23, 125–26, 160, 198

name, 88, 158, 163, 271–72
newness, 39, 77–78, 250

"of," 95, 100, 121–22, 134, 141, 154, 166, 173, 177
opponents, 10–12, 19, 80, 97–102, 104–8, 149, 162–70, 205

Papias, 2–3, 14, 26, 27, 242–43
*See also* Index of Ancient Sources
paraclete, 62–63, 65, 213
parousia, 114–15, 194, 254
"Parthians, to the," 26, 245
Paul, 3, 43–44, 84, 92, 109, 160, 163, 273–74, 276
Pauline letters, 1, 4–5, 30, 35, 45, 240, 247, 281
Peregrinus, 261
persecution, 11, 98, 236–37
Polycarp. *See Index of Ancient Sources*
poverty, 151
prayer, 153–54, 167, 223–28
proclaim, 43
*See also* message
purification, 56–58, 125–26, 133

reassurance, 108, 112, 116, 155
recommendation, 281
resurrection, 21, 40
revelation, reveal, 19, 20, 22, 42, 114, 124–25, 129, 135, 180
rhetoric, 14–16, 19, 36, 172–73

sacrifice, 55–56, 64, 150
Satan, 89
savior, 65–66, 167, 188–90
schism, 22, 25, 29, 100–102
*See also* opponents
scripture, 16, 23–24, 39–40, 48, 65, 76, 82–3, 139, 178–79
seed, 24, 137–40
seeing, 36, 39–40, 185–88, 198–99, 214, 279
sending, 22, 175, 180–83, 188–91, 204, 208
Seth, 139
sin, 10, 11, 19–20, 22, 55–60, 61–66, 70, 117–18, 127–41, 160, 225–30
death-bound, 20, 140, 225–27, 230

sisters. *See* brothers: translating
Son, 42, 73, 107, 121, 181–83, 188–89, 200,
    208, 247
Son of God, 11, 15, 20–21, 45, 63, 106,
    136–37, 144, 149, 152, 158, 166–67, 175,
    190–91, 201, 205–22, 229–34, 237–38
    *See also* begotten (of the Son)
sources, 16, 18, 45–46, 55, 117–18, 176
spirit, 8, 13, 62, 94, 103, 113, 138, 160,
    162–75, 186–87, 190, 212–15
spirits, 64, 112, 161–75, 187, 205
structure, 14–15, 17, 84–5, 96–98, 145,
    220–22
suffering servant, 64, 129–30
Synoptic Gospels, 142, 199

teachers, 12, 240
    traveling, 12, 13, 259–61, 270–74
teaching, 10, 103, 109, 113, 138, 258–60, 277
*Testaments of the Twelve Patriarchs*, 24–25
    *See also Index of Ancient Sources*
testimony, 9, 43, 187–88, 212–21, 279–81

Trinity, 200, 215, 230
truth, 4, 54, 70, 104, 152, 154–56, 162,
    213–14, 232–34, 246–49, 269–70, 273,
    278–79

victory, 22, 89, 171, 203–4, 206–7, 221,
    231–32

walk, 30–31, 53, 75, 81, 249, 251, 270
water, 209–15, 217
"we," 2, 6, 14, 40–42, 100–101, 116, 119–20,
    150, 153, 161–62, 176, 180–82, 191–92,
    197, 221, 229, 249, 256, 275, 281
    and "you," 15, 35–36, 37–39, 52–53, 111,
    170–73, 187–88, 252, 256
wisdom, 42
women, 80, 244, 259–60
word, 41–42, 59, 71, 77, 90–91
world, 12, 18, 65–66, 85, 92–96, 119, 123–24,
    147, 150, 164–65, 167, 171–72, 180,
    188–89, 194–95, 203, 207, 231–32, 237,
    255